California
Preschool
Curriculum
Framework

Volume 1

Social-Emotional Development
Language and Literacy
English-Language Development
Mathematics

Publishing Information

The *California Preschool Curriculum Framework, Volume 1*, was developed by the Child Development Division, California Department of Education. It was designed and prepared for printing by the staff of CDE Press and was published by the Department, 1430 N Street, Sacramento, CA 95814-5901. It was distributed under the provisions of the Library Distribution Act and *Government Code* Section 11096.

This publication was edited by Faye Ong, working in cooperation with Desiree Soto, Consultant, Child Development Division. It was designed and prepared for printing by the staff of CDE Press, with the cover and interior design created by Cheryl McDonald. It was published by the Department of Education, 1430 N Street, Sacramento, CA 95814-5901. It was distributed under the provisions of the Library Distribution Act and *Government Code* Section 11096.

ISBN 978-8011-1682-7

Ordering Information

Copies of this publication are available for sale from the California Department of Education. For prices and ordering information, please visit the Department Web site at http://www.cde.ca.gov/re/pn or call the CDE Press Sales Office at (800) 995-4099.

Notice

The guidance in the *California Preschool Curriculum Framework, Volume 1*, is not binding on local educational agencies or other entities. Except for the statutes, regulations, and court decisions that are referenced herein, the documents is exemplary, and compliance with it is not mandatory. (See *Education Code* Section 33308.5.)

Contents

A Message from the State Superintendent of Public Instruction

I am pleased to present the *California Preschool Curriculum Framework, Volume 1*, a publication I believe will be a major step in working to close the school-readiness gap for young children in our state. Created as a companion to the *California Preschool Learning Foundations, Volume 1*, this framework presents strategies and information to enrich learning and development opportunities for all of California's preschool children.

Like the first volume of the preschool learning foundations, this curriculum framework focuses on four learning domains: social-emotional development, language and literacy, English-language development, and mathematics. Topics include guiding principles, in particular, the vital role of the family in early learning and development; the diversity of young children in California; and the ongoing cycle of observing, documenting, assessing, planning, and implementing curriculum. The preschool curriculum framework takes an integrated approach to early learning and describes how curriculum planning considers the connections between different domains as children engage in teacher-guided learning activities. A description of California's Early Learning and Development System, which places the learning foundations at the center, explains the alignment of the components to the foundations.

The remaining chapters focus on the learning domains. Each chapter provides an overview of a domain, the foundations for that domain, principles in planning curriculum, and curriculum strategies illustrated by vignettes. The strategies pertain to both the learning environment and teachers' interactions with children. These chapters offer key principles and a rich variety of ideas for early childhood educators to support the learning and development of preschool children. There are specific principles and strategies for teaching children who are English learners.

Two themes are interwoven throughout this volume: young children learn through play, and their families are their first teachers. As young children play, they use language to create meaning, explore social roles, and solve mathematical problems. Through studying their play, early educators discover ways to build on young children's lively engagement with learning. Another strategy for expanding young children's learning is to collaborate with their families. Together, early educators and family members can create meaningful learning experiences for young children in preschool and at home.

The preschool curriculum framework speaks to new early childhood educators as well as experienced ones. It recognizes the best practices already used by preschool programs and provides new ideas that bring the preschool learning foundations to life for everyone responsible for the care and education of young children.

Jack O'Connell

JACK O'CONNELL
State Superintendent of Public Instruction

Acknowledgments

The development of the preschool curriculum framework involved many people. The following groups contributed: (1) project leaders; (2) principal writers; (3) community college faculty advisers; (4) universal design advisers; (5) project staff and advisers from the WestEd Center for Child and Family Studies; (6) staff from the California Department of Education; (7) early childhood education stakeholder organizations; (8) participants in the formative and review focus groups; (9) participants in the Web posting process; and (10) participants in the public hearing process.

Project Leaders

The following staff members are gratefully acknowledged for their contributions: **Peter Mangione, Katie Monahan,** and **Cathy Tsao,** WestEd.

Principal Writers

Special thanks are extended to the principal writers for their expertise and contributions.

Chapter 1: Introduction

Peter Mangione, WestEd
Mary Jane Maguire-Fong, American River College

Contributors

Katie Monahan, WestEd
Charlotte Tilson, WestEd
Cathy Tsao, WestEd

Chapter 2: The California Early Learning and Development System

Peter Mangione, WestEd
Melinda Brookshire, WestEd
Jenna Bilmes, WestEd
Jan Davis, WestEd

Chapter 3: Social-Emotional Development

Janet Thompson, University of California, Davis
Ross Thompson, University of California, Davis
Kelly Twibell, University of California, Davis

Chapter 4: Language and Literacy

Language
Roberta Golinkoff, University of Delaware
Kathryn Hirsh-Pasek, Temple University
Literacy
Judith Schickedanz, Boston University

Chapter 5: English-Language Development

Linda Espinosa, University of Missouri
Marlene Zepeda, California State University, Los Angeles

Chapter 6: Mathematics

Osnat Zur, WestEd

Appendix B. Reflections on Research: Phonological Awareness

Appendix C: Reflections on Research: Alphabetics and Word/Print Recognition

Judith Schickedanz, Boston University

Community College Faculty Advisers

Special thanks are extended to the faculty advisers for their expertise and contributions.

Caroline Carney, Monterey Peninsula College
Ofelia Garcia, Cabrillo College
Marie Jones, American River College
Margie Perez-Sesser, Cuesta College

Universal Design Advisers

The following universal design experts are gratefully acknowledged for their contributions:

Maurine Ballard-Rosa, California State University, Sacramento

Meryl Berk, Vision Consultant, HOPE Infant Family Support Program, San Diego County Office of Education

Linda Brault, WestEd

WestEd Center for Child and Family Studies—Project Staff and Advisers

Linda Brault
Melinda Brookshire
Caroline Pietrangelo Owens
Teresa Ragsdale
Amy Schustz-Alvarez
Charlotte Tilson
Rebeca Valdivia
Ann-Marie Wiese
Osnat Zur

California Department of Education

Thanks are also extended to the following staff members: **Gavin Payne**, Chief Deputy Superintendent; **Rick Miller**, Deputy Superintendent, P-16 Policy and Information Branch; **Camille Maben**, Director, Child Development Division; **Cecelia Fisher-Dahms**, Administrator, Quality Improvement Office; and **Desiree Soto**, Consultant, Child Development Division, for ongoing revisions and recommendations. During the lengthy development process, many staff members of the Child Development Division were involved at various levels: **Anthony Monreal,* Michael Jett,* Gwen Stephens,* Gail Brodie, Sy Dang Nguyen, Mary Smith-berger, Maria Trejo,** and **Charles Vail.**

---

*During the development of the framework, these individuals worked for the California Department of Education.

Meredith Cathcart, Consultant, Special Education Division, contributed her expertise.

Early Childhood Education Stakeholder Organizations

Representatives from many statewide organizations provided perspectives affecting various aspects of the curriculum framework.

Action Alliance for Children
Alliance for a Better Community
Asian Pacific Islander Community Action Network
Association of California School Administrators
Baccalaureate Pathways in Early Childhood Education (BPECE)
Black Child Development Institute (BCDI), Sacramento Affiliate
California Alliance Concerned with School-Age Parenting and Pregnancy Prevention (CACSAP/Cal-SAFE)
California Association for Bilingual Education (CABE)
California Association for the Education of Young Children (CAEYC)
California Association of Family Child Care (CAFCC)
California Association of Latino Superintendents and Administrators (CALSA)
California Child Care Coordinators Association
California Child Care Resource and Referral Network (CCCRRN)
California Child Development Administrators Association (CCDAA)
California Child Development Corps
California Commission for Teacher Credentialing
California Community College Early Childhood Educators (CCCECE)
California Community Colleges Chancellor's Office (CCCCO)
California County Superintendents Educational Services Association (CCSESA)

California Early Reading First Network
California Federation of Teachers (CFT)
California Head Start Association (CHSA)
California Kindergarten Association
California National Even Start Association
California Preschool Instructional Network
California Professors of Early Childhood
Special Education (CAPECSE)
California School Boards Association
California State Parent-Teacher
Association
California State University Office of the
Chancellor
California Teachers Association
California Tomorrow
Californians Together
Campaign for High Quality Early Learning
Standards in California
Child Development Policy Institute
Children Now
The Children's Collabrium
Council for Exceptional Children/The
California Division for Early Childhood
(Cal DEC)
Council of CSU Campus Childcare
(CCSUCC)
Curriculum Alignment Project
Curriculum & Instruction Steering
Committee
English Language Learners Preschool
Coalition (ELLPC)
Fight Crime, Invest in Kids California
First 5 Association of California
First 5 California Children & Families
Commission
Infant Development Association of
California (IDA)
Learning Disabilities Association of
California
Los Angeles Universal Preschool (LAUP)
Mexican American Legal Defense and
Education Fund (MALDEF)
Migrant Education Even Start (MEES)
Migrant Head Start
National Council of La Raza (NCLR)
Packard Foundation Children, Families,
and Communities Program

Preschool California
Professional Association for Childhood
Education (PACE)
Special Education Local Plan Area (SELPA)
Organization
University of California Child Care
Directors
University of California Office of the
President (UCOP)
Voices for African-American Students, Inc.
(VAAS)
Zero to Three

Public Input

Ten focus groups consisting of 147 members gave valuable feedback, and others offered suggestions during a public review of the draft that was posted online.

Photographs

Many photographers contributed to a large pool of photographs taken over the years and collected by WestEd. Special thanks are extended to WestEd and the photographers. The following child care agencies deserve thanks for allowing photographs to be taken of the staff, children, and families:

Chandler Tripp Head Start and Chandler
Tripp Preschool for the Visually
Impaired, Santa Clara County Office
of Education, San Jose
Child Development Center, American River
College, Los Rios Community College
District, Sacramento
El Jardín de los Niños, University Preparation School, at California State University, Channel Islands
Friends of Saint Francis Childcare Center,
San Francisco
Hoopa Child Development Program, Hoopa
Supporting Future Growth Child Development Center, Oakland

CHAPTER 1

Introduction to the Framework

Young children enter preschool with a sense of wonder and a love of learning. They have an insatiable appetite for knowledge when they have learning experiences that are engaging and enjoyable. Positive experiences in which children can make choices and explore help them feel competent and confident. How can we offer them engaging and enjoyable learning experiences that fuel their intellectual engines and build their confidence? How can we connect children's fascination with learning in every domain and make the most of their time in preschool? With these questions in mind, the California Department of Education (CDE) developed this curriculum framework for preschool programs, which include any early childhood setting where three- to five-year-old children receive education and care.

This curriculum framework provides an overall approach for **teachers**[a] to support children's learning through environments and experiences that are:

- developmentally appropriate,
- reflective of thoughtful observation and intentional planning,
- individually and culturally meaningful, and
- inclusive of children with disabilities or other special needs.

The framework presents ways of setting up environments, encouraging and building upon children's self-initiated play, selecting appropriate materials, and planning and implementing teacher-guided learning activities.

As much as possible, the writers of this document have used everyday language to describe curriculum concepts and strategies. However, technical terminology does appear in the text. The use of technical terms reflects the need for precision of language and offers the reader the opportunity to connect practice to theory and abstract ideas. To aid the reader, technical words that are highlighted in **boldface** are defined in the Glossary.

What children learn during the preschool years is presented in the *California Preschool Learning Foundations, Volume 1*.[1] As preschool teachers plan learning environments and experiences, the foundations provide the background information to:

- understand children's developing knowledge and skills and
- consider appropriate ways to support children's learning and development.

In essence, curriculum planning should offer children learning opportunities that are attuned to their developing abilities and connected with their experiences at home and in their communities.

In the National Association for the Education of Young Children's accreditation criteria, it is stated that a curriculum includes the goals for the knowledge and skills to be acquired by children and the plans for learning experiences through which such knowledge and skills will be acquired.[2] A preschool curriculum

[a]In this document, a teacher is considered an adult with education and care responsibilities in an early childhood setting. Teachers include adults who interact directly with young children in preschool programs and family child care home settings, as well as those who provide special education services. In family child care, teachers may be referred to as caregivers.

typically defines a sequence of integrated experiences, interactions, and activities to help young children reach specific learning goals. A curriculum framework provides general guidance on planning learning environments and experiences for young children. Thus, as a curriculum framework, this document provides:

- principles for supporting young children's learning;
- an overview of key components of curriculum planning for young children, including observation, documentation, and reflection;
- descriptions of routines, environments, and materials that engage children in learning; and
- sample strategies for building on children's knowledge, skills, and interests.

Four domains are the focus of Volume 1 of the CDE's preschool learning foundations: social-emotional development, language and literacy, English-language development, and mathematics.

California's Preschool Children

A fundamental consideration in planning curriculum for individual children is being responsive to the competencies, experiences, interests, and needs each child brings to the preschool classroom. The state's preschool population includes children who are culturally diverse, speak a language other than English, possess different abilities, and come from diverse socioeconomic backgrounds. When teachers and other program staff partner with families, they make curriculum individually and culturally relevant.

An increasingly prominent factor in the diversity of California's children is their early experiences with language. Language and literacy development contributes to young children's learning and long-range success in many different ways. Children who enter preschool with competence in a language other than English rely on their home language as they learn English. Building competence in English, while continuing to build competence in their home language, allows children to draw on all their knowledge and skills as they engage in learning in every domain. In response to the need to support children with diverse early language and literacy experiences, the CDE has developed *Preschool English Learners: Principles and Practices to Promote Language, Literacy, and Learning*[3] (hereafter referred to as the PEL Resource Guide) and preschool English-language development foundations. This curriculum framework offers strategies aligned to those foundations and the content of the PEL Resource Guide.

Socioeconomic diversity is another trend that merits attention. The percentage of children living in low-income homes is high; almost 20 percent live below the poverty level.[4] At the same time, the benefits of appropriate or high-quality

preschool are more pronounced for children from low-income backgrounds than for other population subgroups. Children from diverse socioeconomic backgrounds are more likely to benefit from preschool when the curriculum is attuned to their learning strengths and needs.

Children with disabilities or other special needs are another part of California's preschool population. Children with disabilities or other special needs benefit from learning in inclusive environments with typically developing children. Studies have shown that children in inclusive environments, with appropriate support and assistance, achieve more than children in segregated environments.[5] Inclusive environments benefit not only children with disabilities or other special needs, but also typically developing children.

As the following information suggests, the diversity of young children means that every preschool program needs a flexible approach to curriculum in order to be responsive to all children who enter its doors.

Demographics

Compared with most other states, California has an extraordinarily diverse population of children, particularly those under the age of five. Of the over six million children enrolled in California's K–12 schools in 2006-07, 48.1 percent were

Latino, 29.4 percent were white, 8.1 percent were Asian, 7.6 percent were African American, and 2.6 percent were Filipino.[6] Similarly, among the 2.7 million children from birth to age five living in California during 2006-07, 50 percent were Latino, 24 percent were white, 8 percent were Asian American, and 5 percent were African American.[7] This trend is anticipated to continue over the next several decades.

English learners

In the 2008 California Report Card, Children Now estimates that 42 percent of five-year-old children in California are English learners, a 3 percent increase from the previous year.[8] Children Now also reports:

> The majority of California's children living in immigrant households, between the ages of 5-17, speak a language other than English at home. Nearly 30 percent of these children live in linguistically isolated homes where the adults living in the home do not speak English well.[9]

In an earlier report, Children Now and Preschool California indicated that ". . . young children living in linguistically isolated homes are less likely to be enrolled in preschool programs."[10]

The broad range of languages spoken by children in the state is clearly a significant factor in developing curriculum for preschool children who are English learners. During the 2006-07 school year, 85.3 percent of California children in kindergarten through twelfth grade who were English learners spoke Spanish, followed by Vietnamese (2.2 percent), Filipino (1.4 percent), Cantonese (1.4 percent), Hmong (1.3 percent), and Korean (1.1 percent).[11] Many families may come from similar geographic regions outside the United States but may not necessarily speak the same language.[12] Preschool offers an important opportunity for children whose families speak a different language at home to learn English while continuing to learn their home language. Competence in two languages will allow children to become adults who can contribute to both the global economy and their local communities. Preschool programs can best support young children by planning curriculum that fosters English-language development and keeps the children connected to the language of their families.

Socioeconomic status

Approximately 20 percent of children in California under the age of five live in families whose income is below the poverty level.[13] Compared with other states, California ranks 20th in the nation in the number of children under age eighteen living in poverty.[14] According to the National Center for Children in Poverty, younger children (birth to six years) are more likely to live in a low-income household.[15] Young children of immigrant parents are 20 percent more likely to live in a low-income family compared with children with native-born English-speaking parents. Young African American, Latino, and Native American children in California are also more likely to live in very low-income families compared with white children.[16]

Children with disabilities or other special needs

There are approximately 45,000 children with identified disabilities in the CDE preschool system. This number does not include children at risk of a disability or developmental challenges. Children with disabilities represent the diversity of California's entire preschool population and necessitate unique educational considerations in the preschool setting. Three-, four-, and five-year-old children with identified disabilities have

individualized education programs (IEPs) that reflect the CDE's preschool learning foundations. Under the Individuals with Disabilities Education Act (2004), all children must have access to the general curriculum and have their progress measured accordingly.[17] In California, the CDE's preschool learning foundations serve as a guide for curriculum planning. Together, the foundations and curriculum framework offer a comprehensive approach to planning access to inclusive learning opportunities for all children.

Overarching Principles

Eight principles have guided the development of this curriculum framework. Grounded in early childhood research and practice, the following eight principles emphasize offering young children individually, culturally, and linguistically responsive learning experiences and environments:

- Relationships are central.
- Play is a primary context for learning.
- Learning is integrated.
- Intentional teaching enhances children's learning experiences.
- Family and community partnerships create meaningful connections.
- Individualization of learning includes all children.
- Responsiveness to culture and language supports children's learning.
- Time for reflection and planning enhances teaching.

The rationales for these principles follow.

Relationships are central

Relationships with others are at the center of young children's lives. Caring relationships with close family members provide the base for young children to engage with others, to explore with confidence, to seek support when needed, and to view interactions with others as likely to be positive and interesting. Recognizing the power of early relationships, preschool teachers and programs build strong relationships with children and families. Just as important, preschool teachers nurture the social-emotional development of young children through those relationships. Research shows that healthy social-emotional development helps young children learn, for example, to sustain attention more easily, to make and maintain friendships, and to communicate needs and ideas. Under the guiding eye of teachers in close partnership with families, young children build their ability to engage in relationships with adults and other children. Preschool offers children a variety of opportunities for social interactions (with familiar adults, peers), group participation, and for cooperation and responsibility. A climate of caring and respect that promotes nurturing relationships between children and within the community of families supports children's learning in all domains.

Play is a primary context for learning

Play is at the heart of young children's explorations and their engagement in learning experiences.[18] During play, children maximize their attention span as they focus on self-selected activities that they regulate themselves. When children make their own choices, engage other children in interaction, and spend time amusing themselves on their own, they learn much about themselves, their own capabilities, and the world around them. At the preschool level, play and learning should be seamless. Children need to

be *engaged* to learn. As Zigler observes, children bring more than their brains to school.[19] When children's hearts and minds are engaged, adults can help them learn almost anything they are ready to learn. In a program where play is valued, children's interests, engagement, creativity, and self-expression are supported through a balance of child-initiated and teacher-guided activities. The environment reflects an appreciation for the value of pretend play, imaginary play, and dramatic play. Play not only provides the context for thinking, building knowledge, being attentive, solving problems, and increasing social skills, it also helps children to integrate their emotional experiences and internalize guidance from their teachers. For some children, it may be necessary to make special adaptations to create access to learning through self-initiated activities and play.

Learning is integrated

Learning engages young children in every possible way. Young children continually use all their senses and competencies to relate new experiences to prior experiences and try to understand things and create meaning. Their learning is integrated while often having a specific focus. For example, during book reading, children use their knowledge and thinking abilities, emotional responses, understanding of language, and the full range of experiences at home and in the community to make new connections and understand. Children come to preschool as experts about many things—among them, their families, their home language(s), and their belongings. When learning builds on what children know and allows them to expand their skills playfully, they are happy to participate in any learning experience or activity, to recite any rhyme, and to count any set. That is why offering children experiences that are personally meaningful and connected is so important. In addition, since children learn using all of their sensory modalities in an integrated way, it is essential to strengthen the modalities with which individual children need special help and build upon their areas of strength. Integrated learning is further described in the section titled Curriculum Planning.

Intentional teaching enhances children's learning experiences

Effective curriculum planning occurs when teachers are mindful of children's learning and are intentional or purposeful in their efforts to support it. In the National Association for the Education of Young Children (NAEYC) publication titled *The Intentional Teacher*, Ann Epstein offers the following description:[20]

> . . . the intentional teacher . . . acts with knowledge and purpose to ensure that young children acquire the knowledge and skills (content) they need to succeed in school and in life. Intentional teachers use their knowledge, judgment, and expertise to organize learning experiences for children; when an unexpected situation arises . . . they can recognize a teaching opportunity and are able to take advantage of it, too.

With an understanding of early learning and development, the teacher works to help young children reach the learn-

ing destinations identified by California's preschool learning foundations. The intentional teacher is flexible in order to accommodate differences in children's learning strengths and needs. Intentional teaching strategies span from planning learning environments, experiences, and routines to spontaneous responses suggested by the moment-to-moment focus of the children.

Family and community partnerships create meaningful connections

Strong connections with families grow from respecting and valuing diverse views, expectations, goals, and understandings families have for their children. Programs demonstrate respect for families by partnering with them to exchange information about their children's learning and development and to share ideas about how to support learning at home and at school. Partnerships with families extend to the community where the families live, come together, and support one another. Building connections to the surrounding community allows a program to become known and make use of community resources. Getting to know the community also gives teachers insights into the learning experiences and competencies that children bring to the preschool setting and informs efforts to make preschool meaningful and connected for children.

Individualization of learning includes all children

Each child is unique. Preschool teachers use their understanding of each child's blend of **temperament,** family and cultural experiences, language experiences, personal strengths, interests, abilities, and dispositions to support the child's learning and development.

Through recognizing and adapting to each child's individual development, teachers are able to offer learning experiences that are meaningful, connected, and developmentally attuned to each child. Creating a classroom environment in which all children feel welcome is important. When children with disabilities or other special needs are included, the partnership with families is especially important. The family is the primary bridge between the preschool staff and special services the child may be receiving. The family, teacher, and other program staff can team together and include other specialists in the preschool setting. Adapting to an individual child may mean modifying the learning environment to ". . . increase a child's access, potential and availability for learning through thoughtful organization of materials and space."[21] Specifically designed professional support and development opportunities, as well as specialized instructional strategies, can help teachers deliver individualized education and care to meet the needs of all the children in a program.

Responsiveness to culture and language supports children's learning

Responsive preschool programs create a climate of respect for each child's culture and language when teachers and other program staff partner and regularly communicate with family members. They work to get to know the cultural strengths each child brings to preschool. An essential part of being culturally and linguistically responsive is to value and support each child's use of home language, for "continued use and development of the child's home language will benefit the child as he or she acquires English."[22] Equally important are nurturing interactions with children and their families in which ". . . teachers

attempt, as much as possible, to learn about the history, beliefs, and practices of the children & families they serve. . . ."[23] In addition to being responsive to the cultural history, beliefs, values, ways of communicating, and practices of children and families, teachers create learning environments that include resources such as pictures, displays, and books that are culturally rich and supportive of a diverse population, particularly the cultures and languages of the children and families in their preschool setting.[24, 25] Community members add to the cultural richness of a preschool setting by sharing their art, music, dance, traditions, and stories.

Time for reflection and planning enhances teaching

Preschool teachers are professionals who serve an important role in society. In nurturing the development of young children, teachers engage in an ongoing process of observation, documentation and **assessment,** reflection and planning, and implementation of strategies in order to provide individualized learning experiences. As increasing numbers of children with diverse backgrounds, including disabilities, participate in preschool programs, it becomes essential to have collaboration, teaming, and communication to extend the benefits of preschool to all children. Curriculum planning requires time for teachers to reflect on children's learning and plan strategies that foster children's progress in building knowledge and mastering skills. Preschool programs that support intentional teaching allocate time in teachers' schedules to allow them to reflect and plan both individually and as a team. With appropriate support, teachers are able to grow professionally through a continuous process of learning together and exploring ways to be responsive to young children's learning interests and needs.

Organization of the Framework

This preschool curriculum framework builds on the *California Preschool Learning Foundations, Volume 1,* which describes the knowledge and skills that preschool children typically demonstrate with appropriate support in the following four domains:

- Social-emotional development
- Language and literacy
- English-language development
- Mathematics

In this introduction, curriculum planning for these domains is presented in an integrated manner (see pages 14 and 15). Within this integrated approach to planning learning activities and environments, each specific domain is the focus of a chapter. Each chapter provides a look at integrated curriculum through the lens of the particular domain addressed by that chapter. For example, Chapter 6, "Mathematics," highlights how vocabulary development relates to children's math learning. Information on strategies to support children's learning may appear in more than one domain chapter because the same strategy or similar strategies apply to multiple areas of growth and development. In essence, this curriculum framework is designed to allow the reader to examine the breadth and depth of each domain in the context of integrated learning.

The domain chapters begin with an overview of principles and strategies for supporting preschool children's learning. Each domain is divided into strands that define the scope of the domain. In each chapter, the strands are introduced, along with information about environments and materials that promote learning, a "Bring-ing It All Together" vignette, "Engaging Families" to support home–school connections, and "Questions for Reflection" to encourage teacher reflection.

Each strand is further divided into substrands. Each substrand section includes:

- A brief overview of the substrand;
- Sample interactions and strategies (e.g., conversations, activities, experiences, routines) for helping children make progress in the specific area of learning identified by the substrand; and
- Vignettes that illustrate the strategies in action. (It is important to note that the interactions illustrated by the vignettes might take place in any language; individual children would appropriately engage in such communication using their home language.)

The sample strategies that are presented range from spontaneous to planned. Some sample strategies focus on how teachers build on children's interests during interaction and instruction. Some rely on planning and teacher initiation, and some reflect a combination of teacher planning and spontaneous responses to children's learning. Taken together, they offer a range of ways in which early childhood professionals can support children's learning and development. The sample strategies are intended to include a broad range of teaching approaches as well as to reflect a variety of ways to address the individual needs of a diverse group of children. However, the sample strategies are neither exhaustive nor meant to be used as recipes to follow. Rather, they are starting points, or springboards, for teachers as they plan and implement their own strategies.

It is noteworthy that some strategies for one domain can just as easily be used to support learning in another domain.

The fact that many strategies overlap across domains reflects the integrated nature of young children's learning. For example, the language and literacy chapter recommends on page 103 the general strategy of providing opportunities in the daily schedule for adult–child and child–child interactions. Of course, adult–child and child–child interactions foster social-emotional learning and English-language development as well as learning in all other domains addressed by the preschool learning foundations. Specific strategies in this section include "Create a block area" and "Create an art area." Creating a block area may sound more like a strategy for the mathematics domain, and an art area may sound more like one for the visual and performing arts domain. However, a preschool environment with those areas will surely promote learning in all domains.

Each domain chapter includes "Teachable Moments" to address the balance between planning for children's learning and being spontaneous and responsive when a child or a small group of children may be absorbed with solving a problem or excited about a new idea or may show emerging understanding of a concept. Planning creates the context for teachable moments. In various places, this framework offers information on "Planning Learning Opportunities." Intentional teaching includes planning interactions, activities, environments, and adaptations. Teachers plan such learning opportunities based on their observations and assessments of children and what they learn from the children's families. When teachers plan learning opportunities, they have in mind how the children might respond. But the plan needs to be flexible to allow the teacher to be responsive to how the children actually engage in learning. The teacher observes the children and listens for the teachable moments made possible by the plan.

English-Language Development and Learning in All Domains

The English-language development foundations and recommended curriculum strategies address the need to give additional focused support to preschool children whose home language is not English. As Chapter 5 states: "Children who are learning English as a second language form a substantial and growing segment of the preschool population served by California state child development programs." The English-language development foundations are distinct from the foundations in other domains because they describe the process of learning important language and literacy concepts as preschool children acquire a second language (as dual-language learners). Children's progress with learning English varies greatly from child to child. Some children enter preschool with practically no prior experience with English. Other children have some experience with English but still do not possess the basic competency necessary to demonstrate knowledge and skills outlined in other domains when the curriculum is provided mainly in English. And there are other children who are learning English as a second language who may be fairly advanced in their understanding and use of English.

Given the great variation among children who are learning English as a second language in preschool, their knowledge and skills in the English-language development domain are described at the *beginning*, *middle*, and *later* levels.

In other words, the English-language development foundations reflect a continuum of second-language (English) learning regardless of an individual child's age. This continuum shows that children who are learning English while they are also developing their home language abilities use their knowledge and skills in their first language to continue to make progress in all other domains. Children who are English learners also vary greatly in the level of proficiency in their first language, which, in turn, influences their progress in English-language development.

In an integrated curriculum, the key to supporting all children is to plan learning activities and environments based on an ongoing understanding of each child's interests, needs, and family and cultural experiences. For young children who are learning English, this approach means focused attention to each individual child's experiences in acquiring a second language and an understanding of how to use a child's first language to help them understand a second language. In applying an integrated approach, teachers take advantage of every moment to provide children with opportunities to communicate with greater understanding and skill while engaged in play or in adult-guided learning activities.

The curriculum framework for English-language development is based on a number of key considerations for supporting children learning English in preschool settings. Chief among these considerations are:

1. Children who are learning English as a second language possess a home language upon which effective teaching strategies can be based.
2. Children who are learning English as a second language may demonstrate language and literacy knowledge and skills in their home language before they demonstrate the same knowledge and skills in English.
3. Children who are learning English as a second language may need additional support and time to make progress in all areas that require English knowledge and skills; therefore, the English-language development curriculum framework presents strategies to support English learners in particular ways so that teachers can both scaffold children's learning experiences and utilize multiple modes of communication (e.g., nonverbal cues).
4. The English-language development foundations and curriculum recommendations focus mainly on language and literacy learning, because it is, by nature, language-specific; it is also recognized that English learners will demonstrate competence in other domains in their home language.
5. An intentional focus on the process of learning English as a second language is necessary at all times in an integrated approach to curriculum in early care and education settings.

The level of additional support and time English learners need to demonstrate the knowledge and skills described by the foundations in domains such as social-emotional development, language and literacy, and mathematics will be influenced by the children's development in both their first language and English. The language the child uses for communication at home as well as the amount of rich experience the child has in the home language will likely affect the amount and type of support the child needs. For example, if a child's home language does not use the alphabet for writing, that child may need different support than a child whose home language uses the alphabet. Regardless of home language, individual children may make progress with some foundations earlier than with other foundations. For example, children may need additional time to make progress in the language and literacy foundations, which are specific to English, such as language conventions, vocabulary, and grammar.

The California Department of Education's DVD titled *A World Full of Language: Supporting Preschool English Learners* highlights the importance of a climate of acceptance and belonging as the starting point for giving children who are learning English as a second language additional support. In effective programs, intentional efforts:

- focus on the children's sense of belonging and need to communicate;
- allow children to participate voluntarily; and
- create opportunities for interaction and play with peers.

Children need to feel comfortable with everyone in the preschool setting and with use of their home language to express themselves nonverbally while learning and trying to use English.

As Chapter 5 states: "Language is a tool of communication used in all developmental domains. Children who are English learners need to be supported not only in activities focused on language

and literacy, but across the entire curriculum." All children, particularly children at the *beginning* and *middle* levels of English language acquisition, may show knowledge and skills in other domains, such as mathematics, using their home language. The preschool Desired Results Developmental Profile (DRDP) recognizes this possibility by considering children's demonstrations of knowledge and skills in their home language as evidence of developmental progress.[b]

Because first- and second-language development varies among English learners, the English-language development foundations and the language and literacy foundations are to be used in tandem with the curriculum framework. It is recommended that, when planning curriculum for all areas of learning, teachers begin by reading and considering the English-language development foundations and the curriculum framework guidance as they gauge each child's current comprehension and use of English. Teachers then develop a plan for how to integrate and use the suggested activities or strategies to support areas of learning that take into consideration the

---

[b] It is important to use the appropriate Desired Results instrument. For children who are typically developing, the Desired Results Developmental Profile (DRDP) is the appropriate instrument. (http://www.wested.org/desiredresults). For children with disabilities receiving preschool special education services, the appropriate instrument is determined by the Individualized Education Program (IEP) team, which includes the family and the child's preschool teacher. All three-, four-, and five-year-old children with an IEP who receive preschool services, regardless of instructional setting, must be assessed using either the Desired Results Developmental Profile (DRDP) or the Desired Results Developmental Profile *access* (DRDP *access*). The DRDP *access* is an alternative version of the DRDP with measures that have an expanded range for assessing preschool-age children with disabilities (http://draccess.org).

diversity of English learners. Intentional teaching requires an ongoing awareness of the home-language development of each child as described in the English-language development foundations as well as the English learner's ability to use English in activities suggested in the other chapters.

Universal Design for Learning

The guidance in this preschool curriculum framework applies to all young children in California, including children with disabilities or other special needs. In some cases, preschool children with disabilities or other special needs demonstrate their developmental progress in diverse ways. Recognizing that children follow different pathways to learning, this framework incorporates a concept known as *universal design* for learning.

Universal design provides for multiple means of representation, multiple means of engagement, and multiple means of expression.[24] *Multiple means of representation* refers to providing information in a variety of ways so the learning needs of all children are met. For example, it is important to speak clearly to children with auditory disabilities while also presenting information visually such as with objects and pictures. *Multiple means of expression* refers to allowing children to use alternative ways to communicate or demonstrate what they know or what they are feeling. For example, when a teacher seeks a verbal response, a child may respond in any language, including American Sign Language. A child with special needs who cannot speak may also respond by pointing, by gazing, by gesturing, by using a picture system of communication, or by any other form of

alternative or augmented communication system. *Multiple means of engagement* refers to providing choices in the setting or program that facilitate learning by building on children's interests. The information in this curriculum framework has been worded to incorporate multiple means of representation, expression, and engagement.

Although this curriculum framework presents some ways of adapting or modifying an activity or approach, it cannot offer all possible variations to ensure that a curriculum meets the needs of a particular child. Of course, the first and best source of information about any child is the family. Additionally, there are several resources available to support inclusive practice for young children with disabilities or other special needs. The resources, Web sites, and books listed in Appendix D are recommended for teachers' use.

Curriculum Planning

Curriculum planning to support children as active meaning makers

Preschool children possess an amazing capacity to organize vast amounts of information. When we watch a preschooler alone in play, in play with friends, or engaged in a conversation, we see an active mind making meaning.

Preschool children experience the world and build knowledge in an integrated manner, during simple moments of play and interaction with objects and with other people. They constantly gather information and strive to make sense of it. Their minds take in words, numbers, feelings, and the actions and reactions of people, creatures, and objects and integrate new information into an increasingly complex system of knowledge. Effective curriculum for young children engages their active minds and nurtures their enthusiastic search for meaning and understanding.

Integrated curriculum

The principle that preschool children actively make meaning in an integrated way offers an important starting point for preschool curriculum. Of most value to young children engaged in inquiry are experiences that support their inclination to explore math, language, literacy, art, and science within meaningful moments of play and interaction. In guiding children's integrated approach to learning, teachers may use a variety of strategies (e.g., interactions, **scaffolding**, explicit instruction, modeling, demonstration, changes in the environment and materials, and adaptations, which are especially important for children with disabilities).[25] By adapting the physical environment, materials, and the curriculum, teachers gain a better sense of individual children's strengths and abilities and how best to support their play and engagement in making meaning. For example, for a child who relies on a wheelchair for mobility, pathways in the classroom are arranged to allow the child's passage to all interest areas, and tables and shelving are set up to allow the child to see, reach, explore, and manipulate the learning materials and thereby make meaning.

Integrated curriculum often has a specific focus yet engages children in multiple ways. The following vignette from a class of mostly three-year-old children illustrates how the children's interests, exploration, and meaning making unfold when their teachers introduce a new learning opportunity.

After observing the children's interest in snails outside, the teachers brought in snails for the children to examine on trays in the science area. Many children went over to see them. Some simply watched, while others held a snail. Whether watching or holding a snail, each child bubbled with curiosity.

Observing the children's curiosity, the teachers decided that the snails might serve as a common interest for children to explore over time, with many possibilities for learning language, math, science, social skills, art, and literacy. Exploring snails offered potential for tapping into many of the children's emerging skills and concepts with increasing complexity over time. The teachers thought of the snails as a ready science investigation. The children would come to know one of the creatures that live in their play yard. The teachers also envisioned possibilities for children's social learning while exploring the snails. Most of the three-year-olds were new to the program and were adjusting to the many new and different faces, languages, and expectations for behavior. The teachers thought that exploring snails would offer experiences supportive of children's progress in various developmental areas. There would be possibil-

ities for discussing how to treat living creatures in respectful ways, conversations with the children about how to care for snails, and being gentle with creatures and also with each other. Caring for the snails might spark much discussion in small groups, a perfect context for children to build new vocabulary and language skills, notice cause-and-effect connections, solve problems, engage in counting and comparing, draw shapes, and use print to capture ideas. The teachers also wondered about how children might weave pretend play and stories into their exploration of snails. Later the teachers reviewed their notes to determine if the children's observed progress in these areas could be measured by the DRDP—cooperative relationships, sharing, developing friendships, conflict negotiation, awareness of diversity, empathy, and self-regulation.

The environment: Interest areas to support children's play and child-initiated learning

Preschool curriculum includes ways in which teachers plan the indoor and outdoor physical environments to support children's play and learning. Intentionally designed play spaces for children are like a studio for an artist or a laboratory for a scientist. When the physical environment is planned with children's self-initiated learning in mind, children encounter places where they can freely explore what things are like and how things work. In such an environment, children investigate, invent, and experiment. To support children's self-initiated play and integrated learning, teachers create environments with a network of **interest areas.** Each area has a distinct focus and a predictable inventory of materials.

Teachers use interest areas to extend children's active search for knowledge. Interest areas are designed to offer a basic inventory of materials with which children can apply emerging skills and develop concepts while they play.

As teachers plan curriculum, they consider ways to augment or add new interests to the basic inventory of materials in an area. Such curriculum plans, which are focused on the play environment, extend or add complexity to the children's play. For children with disabilities, teachers can consider what adaptations should be made to provide greater access. For all children to take full advantage of interest areas that a well-planned curriculum provides, they need long blocks of uninterrupted time for self-initiated play. Interest areas in a preschool environment include the following examples:

Dramatic play area
Block area
Art area
Book area
Writing area
Math area
Science area
Family display area

The example of the snail exploration shows how the teachers made use of the different interest areas in their classroom.

After observing and reflecting on the children's engagement on encountering the snails, the teachers began to add snails to several of the interest areas in the environment. There were possibilities for children to explore both real snails and pretend snails in play.

In the science area, one of the teachers arranged four trays on the table. On each tray, the teacher placed snails, cut grass, leaves, a small jar lid filled with water, and an eyedropper. As the children played, many of them came to explore the snails, some just looking and listening to comments, others touching and holding the snails. Arranging the snails and the materials to make snail "habitats" was the children's primary interest. Teachers were close by to keep the snails safe but did not direct the children's play. That morning, teachers had also added several books on snails (in English, Spanish, and Russian, the home languages of children in the group) as well as a snail puppet in the book/story interest area; a few laminated photos of snails in the art area; and a basket with small plastic snails in the math manipulatives area.

This part of the vignette illustrates how an interest the children first encountered outside was integrated into various interest areas in the indoor environment. Just as the outdoor environment can be brought indoors, so can the indoor environment be brought outdoors. Indeed, the outdoors offers extended opportunities for children's play and exploration. Planning the outdoor environment should include materials and possibilities available in the interest areas indoors.

The Daily Schedule

A well-rounded program has a variety of activities indoors and outdoors in small groups and large groups, supervised by teachers.

Child-initiated play

Children should have ample time during the preschool day to initiate learning through play. When free to make their own choices, children gravitate to different areas of the indoor and outdoor environments and explore materials and ideas playfully and creatively. They choose to cluster in **small groups** to play together, for example, in the block area or in the dramatic play area. Teachers use this time to observe and note ways to build on children's ideas and further engage the children in learning.

Teacher-guided activities

Planning curriculum for preschool children also means planning activities that teachers, rather than children, initiate and guide. Some teacher-guided activities are best done in small groups of four to eight children, in quiet spaces away from distractions of the entire group; others take place in a large group and include all children in the class.

Teacher-guided activities in small groups

Small groups provide a manageable context for children to discuss and explore ideas and experiences. The teacher acts as a guide, listener, and "problem-poser." In small groups away from the distractions of a large group, teachers can easily observe, listen, and converse with children. Teachers can focus on how the children think, express ideas, and use their emerging skills. Teachers' conversations with children can enrich learning in all domains, particularly the children's language learning and vocabulary development. In addition, in order to intentionally guide the development of certain skills, teachers can plan small-group activities (e.g., songs, games, shared reading) that playfully engage children for short periods of time. In programs with English-language learners, small groups can be a time to foster learning among children. The PEL

Resource Guide provides several suggestions for promoting peer learning.[26] Small groups offer excellent times for monitoring a child's developmental progress, for meeting his or her needs, and for providing scaffolds that help a child engage in new and more complex thinking. The chance for teachers to observe, listen, and document children's developmental progress is an important advantage that small groups have over **large groups.** The snail exploration example illustrates how the teachers included documentation in a small-group activity.

During one of their discussions about their observations of the children's interest in the snails, the teachers reviewed the measures on the DRDP that might relate to the children's small-group experiences with snails. They decided to do focused exploration of snails, with small groups of four to six children. In a small group, children would have an easier time building relationships with each other and with the teacher, a learning goal for the whole class. With each small group, the teacher helped the children create a snail habitat in the science interest area. The children could return to the interest area throughout the day for exploration. The teacher and small group worked together over days to transform a glass ter-

rarium into a habitat for snails, with dirt, plants, and enough space for other small creatures. That morning, the parent of a child whose home language was Russian had helped a teacher write out in Russian the words snail, eyes, *and* shell *on each of three folded index cards, with the corresponding words in English on the opposite side of each card. These cards were placed next to the snail habitat in the science area. A parallel set of Spanish and English cards were also next to the habitat.*

During one small-group discussion, the teacher introduced an illustration of a snail labeled with the words eye, tentacle, *and* shell. *Pepe, whose home language was Spanish and who was not yet speaking English, had spent much time playing with the snail habitats in the science area the past week. With a look of excitement, Pepe walked to the illustration of the snail, caught the teacher's eyes, and then pointed to his own eyes. The teacher responded, "Eyes! Yes, those are the snail's eyes, Pepe. How do you say eyes in Spanish?" The teacher waited for Pepe to respond and then commented, "You're making the tentacles, too, I see!"*

Teacher-guided activities in large groups

Large groups work well for singing, playing games, engaging in discussions, sharing stories, building a sense of community, and organizing the whole group's schedule and activities. When children gather as a whole class, they can share experiences with one another and engage in large-group activities such as singing and acting out a song or listening to a story. Storytelling allows teachers, as well as storytellers from the community, to connect with children's knowledge and experiences in meaningful ways. Teachers can also use large-group time to share what new experiences will be available in the interest areas or what will happen in small groups. Large-group gatherings at the end of class time provide opportunities to review noteworthy happenings that day and to anticipate what will be available the next day. While doing the snail exploration, the teachers used the large-group context to support the children's learning in several ways. For example:

*To generate interest in snails, the teachers announced to the children during large-group circle time that the snail trays would be available for exploration. The teachers also used the large-group circle to read books and tell stories about snails. One teacher invented a simple clapping chant to play with the /s/ sound in the new and now popular words—*snails *and* slugs—*"slippery* snails *and* slugs *slowly slithering make slimy stripes." She knew how much the children enjoyed chants, songs, and finger plays. She also knew the value in helping children to hear and make distinct sounds of oral language.*

In the large group, the teachers pointed out that a new kind of helper had been added to the helper chart. Now, two of the children would be "snail helpers." From then on, each day during large-group time, children checked to see whose name cards had been placed next to the snail photo on the helper chart. In the large group, children reported on some of the things they had been doing in their small-group explorations of snails.

Daily routines as curriculum

Curriculum plans include ideas for involving children in daily routines and making routines an important context for learning, in general, and for social-emotional development, in particular. Daily routines provide natural opportunities for children to apply emerging skills, take on responsibilities, and cooperate. Teachers integrate engaging learning opportunities into the everyday routines of arrivals, departures, mealtimes, naptimes, hand washing, setup, and clean-up, both indoors and outdoors. Children enthusiastically apply emerging skills to daily routines: when they are helpers who ring the bell for coming inside; when they count how many are ready for lunch; when they move a card with their photo and name from the "home" column to the "preschool" column of a chart near the room entry; when they put their name on a waiting list to paint at the easel; or when they help set the table for a meal, making sure that each place has a plate, utensils, and a cup. Such routines offer opportunities for children to build language skills, to learn the rituals of sharing time with others, and to relate one action in a sequence to another. Over the course of the snail exploration, the teachers planned ways to extend children's learning within the daily routine.

With "snail helpers" added to the helper chart, teachers involved children in setting up the snail trays in the science interest area. The designated snail helpers counted out four trays as well as the specific number of snails for each tray. Children learned how to check and replace the frozen water bottle. The surface provided snails with moisture and water from condensation. The children also counted out paper towels to use for cleaning the glass walls of the habitat.

The Curriculum-Planning Process

Planning preschool curriculum begins with teachers discovering, through careful listening and observation, each child's development. Observation is an essential skill for a teacher. When teachers mindfully observe, they discover how individual children make meaning in everyday moments of play and interactions and how to deepen their relationships with children.[27] Observing for the purpose of assessing individual children's learning means carefully watching and listening, with thought and reflection. In doing so, teachers find evidence of individual children's meaning making. It may be evidence that pertains to individual children's emotional, social, cognitive, or physical development. If the evidence is clear and significant, teachers hold it in memory with, for example, a note, a photo, or a sample of a child's work. The evidence will often relate to the descriptive levels of the DRDP, which provide a full range of measures of children's developmental progress. Teachers working on the snail exploration found various ways in which the children's engagement in learning about snails related to the developmental profiles of different children. For example:

As the children's interest in the snails continued, the teachers looked for ways to expand learning opportunities and integrate them into the multifaceted experience. The teachers also reviewed individual children's developmental profiles to be mindful

of children's developmental progress in different areas. In addition to the many counting opportunities in the environment, the teachers decided to integrate counting into the children's exploration of snails. Younger children who were making progress with learning to count objects between five and ten were invited to set up a specific number (less than ten) of trays and snails.

Before the children started, the teachers reminded them of an earlier conversation about how to care for snails. In response, one of the children asked to show the others how to handle the snails gently. (Learning about counting was happening at the same time as learning about controlling the impulse to handle other creatures roughly instead of being gentle with them.) Teachers suggested to other children who were continuing to make progress with counting to count out a quantity of sticks, bark, or leaves greater than ten. Other children were asked to divide the snails evenly between the trays. The children kept saying to themselves, "Be gentle," and handled the snails with great care.

As teachers observed each group, they helped children develop mathematical thinking by prompting them and asking questions. For example, at one table, a teacher noticed that children were counting some sticks twice. She said, "I wonder what would happen if we put each stick on the other side of the tray after counting it." The children tried out this idea. Teachers noted children's efforts and placed the notes, with the date recorded, into the children's individual portfolios to be used as evidence for later refer-

ence when considering developmental progress on the DRDP measures of number sense and impulse control.

As teachers observe children's play and interactions, they discover ways to support children's learning. Ideas for the next steps in curriculum planning emerge as teachers reflect on how they might extend or expand children's thinking, language, and interactions. Observation, reflection, and documentation in the moment simultaneously launch an ongoing assessment of each child's progress in learning as well as the curriculum-planning cycle.

Observe, reflect, record

Observation means being present with children and attentive as they play and interact with others and the environment. This mindful kind of presence is different from participating in children's play or directing their play. Whether for one minute or five, an attentive, mindful presence means waiting to see what unfolds in order to gain a complete picture of children's play. A teacher who observes children as a first step in supporting

learning discovers small scientists at work—experimenting, comparing, making assumptions, evaluating assumptions through their actions, and, over time, building mastery of a wide range of concepts and skills. The vignette about the snail exploration illustrates the role of the teacher as observer.

During small-group time with the snails, the teacher noticed a child who had been reluctant to hold a snail. This child had a visual impairment. As the teacher gently placed a snail on this child's hand, two children watched and listened as the teacher commented, "He's sticking his head out now, and he's turned toward your fingers. Can you feel him crawling toward your fingers?" The other children who had been watching intently began to repeat the teacher's encouraging words, saying, "He's sticking his head out. He's going toward your fingers!"

The teacher wrote down her observations and added an interpretive note that the children's behavior may be a

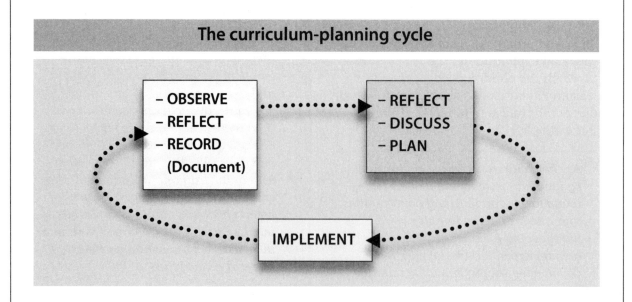

The curriculum-planning cycle

- OBSERVE
- REFLECT
- RECORD
(Document)

- REFLECT
- DISCUSS
- PLAN

IMPLEMENT

growing sign of empathy as measured by the DRDP, and the other child's willingness to hold the snail, a growing sign of curiosity and initiative, also a DRDP measure.

Document

Documenting means gathering and holding evidence of children's play and interests for future use. A common form of documentation in early childhood settings is a written note, often referred to as an observation anecdote. Anecdotal notes, along with other forms of documentation, in particular photos, video recordings, and work samples, serve a dual purpose. First, they hold memories of a teacher's observations of children's expressions of feelings, their thinking, and their learning that are guides to the next steps in day-to-day curriculum planning. And second, anecdotal notes and other evidence can be used to support a teacher's periodic assessment of a child's progress in competencies measured by the DRDP. An episode during the snail exploration highlights the dual purpose of documentation.

During their initial encounters with the snails, the children asked questions and made comments about the snail shells, the way the snails moved across the tray, and what the snails ate. Although several children were reluctant to pick up the snails, others were challenged by having to wait. The teachers recorded children's distinct responses, writing down significant elements of what children said or did. For example, for a child with identified special needs related to self-regulation, a teacher noted: "Jasmine pushed aside Yuri in order to pick up the snail crawling off the tray. Yuri stumbled, fell, and began to cry. Jasmine continued to focus on the snail, saying nothing to Yuri." For the teacher, Jasmine's behavior was significant. This anecdotal note provided some evidence of Jasmine's struggles with impulse control. It added to the growing evidence that Jasmine was still developing impulse control and empathy. Later, as the teacher shared her observation with her co-teacher and with Jasmine's father in a conference, they discussed how the small-group work around keeping the snails safe might support Jasmine as well as other children in reading cues of others and in thinking before acting in order to keep people safe.

Reflect, discuss, plan

As teachers reflect on children's play, they discover possibilities for designing curriculum to sustain, extend, and help children's play to be more complex and, consequently, support the children's continuing learning. Teachers review ideas for possible next steps in the curriculum. Possible steps might include adding materials to interest areas, books to read with large or small groups, activities to do in small groups, or a topic to investigate over time with the children. With clear ideas or objectives in mind, teachers plan curriculum that includes strategies to enhance the learning of all children in a group, as well as strategies to support the learning of individual children. How reflection, discussion, and planning worked in the snail exploration is what will be examined next.

While the children were exploring snails, teachers met each week to reflect and plan for the next steps in the children's explorations. They decided to schedule time for small groups of children to explore the snails in a more focused way, hoping to extend the children's learning and add complexity. The teachers planned a series of walks that would allow all the children to find snails in natural habitats.

Implement

Once a plan is written, teachers implement it. While implementing a plan, teachers observe, reflect, and document. The curriculum-planning cycle begins again (or continues) as teachers watch to discover how children respond to the planned curriculum and how children show evidence of their development during the planned learning encounters. Teachers often approach this step with a sense of wonder, for they may be surprised and amazed by the children's responses. To hold the responses in memory, teachers may record notes, take a photo, or label, date, and keep a work sample, all of which they can later review to assess the impact of the curriculum plans. The evidence collected will help teachers to come up with ideas for supporting and assessing the children's learning. Teachers might ponder the following questions:

- Are children responding as predicted, or were there surprises?
- What do the children's responses tell us? How might we name the children's interest(s) or intention(s)? What concepts and ideas are the children forming within their play?
- How might children who are English learners and children who speak English collaborate in small groups to learn from one another?
- Are children showing evidence of progress on any of the measures of the DRDP?

Here is what happened when the teachers implemented their idea of going on walks with the children to find snails in natural habitats:

Before going on their snail hunt, a small group of children gathered on a blanket with the teacher. Each child was provided with a clipboard with paper for taking "notes" while the teacher explained how the walk would be a way to find snails that lived outside their classroom. Some children pretended to write while the teacher talked, while others drew pictures of snails. In this group, teachers included two children who were fluent in Spanish and learning English. The teachers anticipated much conversation among children during the search for the snails and wanted to give these children a chance to converse in their home language as well as to share experiences with peers who spoke only English.

Before heading off on the hunt, the teacher suggested, "Let's estimate. How many snails do you think we will find? Each of you can guess." On a large sheet of paper that the children could easily see, she wrote each child's name, saying each letter as she did so, and next to each name, the number guessed by that child.

Armed with magnifying glasses, the children went off to collect snails. There were many discoveries along the walk, not just snails. As children found snails, they carried them to a large examination tray set up on a table. Some children took a break from their snail search to examine, touch, and draw the snails already collected. At the end of the hunt, the children lined up the snails on a small log and counted them. The teacher suggested they compare the number they counted with their estimates.

Before returning to their classroom, the children put the snails back into their natural habitats. The children were excited about sharing their experiences with other teachers and peers when they returned.

The teachers examined and reflected on what they saw in the children's writings and drawings on the clipboards. They decided that some of the work samples were significant in showing how individual children were developing an idea, concept, or skill. They filed those samples in the children's portfolios as evidence of developmental progress.

Partnering with families in curriculum planning

As the snail-exploration vignette illustrates in several places, teachers also include the children's families in supporting children's learning. Teachers find it particularly helpful to share documentation of children's learning with children's family members. When families and teachers reflect together on documentation of children's play and learning, family members offer insights into the children's behavior and ideas, as well as share expectations of their children at home or in the community. Teachers also provide

resources to families in order to bridge children's experiences in preschool with experiences at home and in the community. For example, the teachers used the children's interest in the snails to support family members' participation in creating learning opportunities in the following way.

During the snail exploration, teachers posted near the entry a note with a photo of children exploring snails at the science table. They suggested to families to consider doing a snail hunt on the way to school, in a park, or in a yard. A stack of copies of the snail diagram with the words eyes, tentacles, *and* shell *written in Spanish, English, and Russian was available for family members to take with them.*

Connections: Fertile ground for making meaning

The snail vignette illustrates how teachers can help children make connections and thereby make meaning. This exploration allowed children to investigate and learn about creatures from the outdoor environment in the classroom. In doing so, the children were able to make meaning about snails' natural habitats while encountering opportunities to engage in integrated learning in every domain.

Young children's experiences at home and in their communities are a powerful source of connections. Teachers nurture children's appetites for learning and making meaning by building upon the knowledge children bring to the preschool setting. For example, children may come to preschool with knowledge of many family stories. Their teachers may have observed that the children used the stories in the dramatic play area. However, the children did not seem to be aware that their stories could be written down and then read by someone else. In such a case, teachers can partner with families to create a story dictation study. In planning the snail exploration, the teachers and family members may ask:

- Would the children be interested in seeing their family stories written down, and would such experiences help them increase their awareness of print in the world around them?
- What strategies or adaptations might help a child who is nonverbal to become engaged in family storytelling?
- Would children in the group who are English learners make the connection to print more easily if they can dictate their stories in their home language to family members or community volunteers?
- What topics may be interesting and engaging for children to dictate? What kinds of questions would help individual children, English learners, or children with diverse cultural experiences to get started with dictation?
- How might the activity be adapted to accommodate children with disabilities or other special needs?
- Would asking children about how their family helps them get ready for preschool encourage them to dictate a meaningful experience?
- Would a child who likes to draw pictures have an easy time dictating a story about a drawing?

Teachers can explore these questions and see where the exploration leads. When teachers embed children's learning into their lives, into contexts that they have experienced, teachers make everything more comprehensible for them. Teachers also engage children's emotions, making the experience both cognitive and pleasurable. The key is to find out which connections are meaningful for each individual child. When teachers discover what may be personally meaningful for a child, there is a good chance of fully engaging that child in making meaning and learning.

Implementation of the Framework

The concepts and strategies require thoughtful planning and implementation. They are grounded in evidence-based practices that have evolved in the field of early childhood education over decades. The ability to apply a broad understanding of early learning and development in the preschool setting takes time and experience. For teachers to gain the knowledge and skills necessary to approach curriculum as this framework envisions, opportunities for professional development are essential. The CDE's preschool learning foundations and the preschool curriculum framework offer well-researched documents informed by practice that can be used for both preservice and in-service professional development. Those two documents are part of California's Preschool Learning System, along with program guidelines, the PEL Resource Guide, professional development activities, and the Desired Results assessment system. With appropriate professional development, preschool administrators and teachers can use this curriculum framework to guide their planning and implementation of environments and experiences that allow all young children to prosper during the preschool years.

Bibliography

California Child Care Resource and Referral Network (CCCRRN). *2007 California Child Care Portfolio.* Oakland, CA: Author, 2007.

California Department of Education. *Assessing Children with Disabilities Who Are English Learners: Guidance for the DRDP Access and the PS DRDP-R for Children with IEPs.* http://www.draccess.org/assessors/ELGuidance.html#eld (accessed July 17, 2008).

California Department of Education. Statewide English Learners by Language and Grade, 2006-07. http://dq.cde.ca.gov/dataquest/LEPbyLang1.asp?cChoice=LepbyLang1&cYear=200506&cLevel=State&cTopic=LC&myTimeFrame=S&submit1=Submit (accessed July 14, 2008).

California Department of Education. *Statewide Enrollment by Ethnicity, 2005-06.* http://dq.cde.ca.gov/data-quest/EnrollEthState.asp?Level=State&TheYear=2005-06&cChoice=EnrollEth1&p=2 (accessed July 14, 2008).

California Department of Education. *Statewide Number of English Learners, 1995–2007.* http://dq.cde.ca.gov.dataquest/lc/NumberElState.asp?Level=State&TheYear=2006-07 (accessed July 14, 2008).

California Department of Education. *Special Education Enrollment by Age and Major Ethnic Group: Statewide report.* http://dq.cde.ca.gov/dataquest/SpecEd/EnrAgeEth1.asp?cChoice=SpEdEth1&cLevel=State&cYear=2007-08&ReptCycle=December (accessed July 18, 2008).

California Department of Education. *Students by Ethnicity, State of California, 2006-07.* http://ed-data.k12.ca.us/profile.asp?Tab=1&level=04&report (accessed May 28, 2008).

Children Now. *California Report Card 2006–2007: The State of the State's Children.* 2007. http://publications.childrennow.org/publications/invest/reportcard_2007.cfm (Accessed July 14, 2008).

Children Now. *California Report Card 2007–2008: The State of the State's Children.* http://publications.childrennow.org/publications/invest/reportcard_2008.cfm (accessed July 14, 2008).

Children Now. *Children in Immigrant Families: A California Data Brief.* Oakland, CA: Author, 2007.

Children Now and Preschool California. *Kids Can't Wait to Learn: Achieving Voluntary Preschool for All in California.* Oakland, CA: Author, 2004.

Epstein, A. S. *The Intentional Teacher: Choosing the Best Strategies for Young Children's Learning.* Washington, DC: National Association for the Education of Young Children (NAEYC), 2007.

Garcia, O., J. A. Kleifgen, and L. Falchi. "From English Learners to Emergent Bilinguals." In *Equity Matters: Research Review,* No. 1. New York: The Campaign for Educational Equity, 2008.

Guralnick, M. J. *Early Childhood Inclusion: Focus on Change.* Baltimore, MD: Paul H. Brookes Publishing Company, 2001.

Karoly, L. A., and others. *Prepared to Learn: The Nature and Quality of Early Care and Education for Preschool-Age Children in California.* Pittsburgh, PA: Rand, 2008.

McWilliam, R. A., M. Wolery, and S. L. Odom. "Instructional Perspectives in Inclusive Preschool Classrooms." In *Early Childhood Inclusion: Focus on Change.* Edited by M. J. Guralnick. Baltimore, MD: Paul H. Brookes Publishing Company, 2001.

National Association for the Education of Young Children. *NAEYC early childhood program standards.* 2008. http://www.naeyc.org/academy/standards/ (accessed November 30, 2008).

National Center for Education Statistics. *English Language Learner Students in U.S. Public Schools: 1994 and 2000* (issue brief). 2004. http://nces.ed.gov/pubsearch/pubsinfo.asp?pubid=2004035.

National Center for Education Statistics. *The Condition of Education.* 2006. http://nces.ed.gov/programs/coe/2006/ (accessed June 9, 2008).

Pew Hispanic Center. *Statistical Portrait of Hispanics in the United States, 2006.* Washington, DC: Pew Research, 2008.

Pew Hispanic Center. *U.S. Population Projections: 2005–2050.* Washington, DC: Pew Research, 2008. http://pewhispanic.org/reports/report.php?ReportID=85 (accessed July 14, 2008).

Play: It's the Way Young Children Learn. Oakland: Bay Area Early Childhood Funders (pamphlet). http://www.4children.org/images/pdf/Play_pamphlet_eng.pdf (accessed June 29, 2009).

Prekindergarten Learning and Development Guidelines. Sacramento: California Department of Education, 2000.

Preschool English Learners: Principles and Practices to Promote Language, Literacy, and Learning, 2nd ed. Sacramento: California Department of Education, 2009.

University of California Linguistic Minority Research Institute (UCLMRI). *The Growth of the Linguistic Minority Population in the U.S. and California, 1980–2005.* http://www.lmri.uscb.edu/ (accessed June 9, 2008).

U.S. Census Bureau. *2006 American Community Survey: Selected Economic Characteristics: 2006.* http://www.factfinder.census.gov/servlet/ (accessed June 9, 2008).

U.S. Census Bureau. *2006 American Community Survey: United States and States— R1701. Percent of children below poverty level,* 2006. http://www.factfinder.census.gov/servlet/ (accessed June 9, 2008).

A World Full of Language: Supporting Preschool English Learners. Sacramento: California Department of Education, 2007. DVD.

Zigler, E. F. 2007. "Giving Intervention a Head Start: A Conversation with Edward Zigler," *Educational Leadership* 65 (2007): 8–14.

Endnotes

1. *Preschool Learning Foundations, Volume I.* (Sacramento: California Department of Education, 2008).

2. National Association for the Education of Young Children, *NAEYC Early Childhood Program Standards* (Washington, DC: Author, 2008). http://www.naeyc.org/academy/standards/ (accessed November 30, 2008).

3. *Preschool English Learners: Principles and Practices to Promote Language, Literacy, and Learning, 2nd ed.* (Sacramento: California Department of Education, 2007).

4. U.S. Census Bureau, *2006 American Community Survey: United States and States- R1701. Percent of Children Below Poverty Level.* http://factfinder.census.gov/servlet/ (accessed June 9, 2008).

5. M. J. Guralnick, *Early Childhood Inclusion: Focus on Change* (Baltimore, MD: Paul H. Brookes Publishing Company, 2001).

6. *Students by Ethnicity State of California, 2006-07* (Sacramento: California Department of Education, 2007). http://ed-data.k12.ca.us/profile. asp?Tab=1&level=04&report (accessed May 28, 2008).

7. Children Now, *California Report Card 2006–2007: The State of the State's Children.* http://publications. childrennow.org/publications/ invest/reportcard_2007.cfm (accessed July 14, 2008).

8. Children Now, *California Report Card 2007–2008: The State of the State's Children.* http://publications. childrennow.org/publications/ invest/reportcard_2008.cfm (accessed July 14, 2008).

9. *Children in Immigrant Families: A California Data Brief* (Oakland, CA: Children Now. 2007).

10. *Kids Can't Wait to Learn: Achieving Voluntary Preschool for All in California* (Oakland, CA: Children Now and Preschool California, 2004).

11. *Statewide Number of English Learners, 1995–2007* (Sacramento: California Department of Education, 2007). http://dq.cde.ca.gov.dataquest/lc/ NumberElState.asp?Level=State&TheYear =2006-07 (accessed July 14, 2008).

12. *Preschool English Learners: Principles and Practices to Promote Language, Literacy, and Learning,* 2nd ed. (Sacramento: California Department of Education, 2009).

13. U.S. Census Bureau, *2006 American Community Survey: Selected Economic Characteristics: 2006.* http://factfinder. census.gov/servlet/ (accessed June 9, 2008).

14. U.S. Census Bureau. *2006 American Community Survey: United States and States- R1701. Percent of Children Below Poverty Level.* http://factfinder.census. gov/servlet/ (accessed June 9, 2008).

15. A. Douglas-Hall and M. Chau, *Basic Facts About Low-Income Children: Birth to Age 6* (New York: National Center for Children in Poverty, 2007).

16. Children Now, *California Report Card 2006–2007: The State of the State's Children.* http://publications. childrennow.org/publications/invest/ reportcard_2007.cfm (accessed July 14, 2008).

17. Public Law 108-446; 118 Stat. 2647 (H.R. 1350). Individuals with Disabilities Education Act of 2004.

18. J. Van Hoorn and others, *Play at the Center of the Curriculum,* 4th ed. (Upper Saddle Creek, NJ: Pearson Education, Inc., 2007).

19. Deborah Perkins-Gough, "Giving Intervention a Head Start: A Conversation with Edward Zigler," *Educational Leadership* 65, no. 2 (2007): 8–14.

20. A. S. Epstein, *The Intentional Teacher: Choosing the Best Strategies for Young Children's Learning* (Washington, DC: National Association for the Education of Young Children, 2007).

21. *Prekindergarten Learning and Development Guidelines* (Sacramento: California Department of Education, 2000).

22. *Preschool English Learners: Principles and Practices to Promote Language, Literacy, and Learning*, 2nd ed. (Sacramento: California Department of Education, 2009), 43.

23. *Prekindergarten Learning and Development Guidelines* (Sacramento: California Department of Education, 2000), 45.

24. Center for Applied Special Technology (CAST). Universal design for learning. 2007. http://www.cast.org/udl (accessed June 8, 2007).

25. R. A. McWilliam, M. Wolery, and S. L. Odom, "Instructional Perspectives in Inclusive Preschool Classrooms," in *Early Childhood Inclusion: Focus on Change.* Edited by M. J. Guralnick (Baltimore, MD: Paul H. Brookes Publishing Company, 2001).

26. *Preschool English Learners: Principles and Practices to Promote Language, Literacy, and Learning*, 2nd ed. (Sacramento: California Department of Education, 2009).

27. J. R. Jablon, A. L. Dombro, and M. Dichtelmiller. *The Power of Observation*, 2nd ed. (Washington, DC: National Association for the Education of Young Children, 2007).

CHAPTER 2

The California Early Learning and Development System

Chapter 1 highlights how all preschool children enthusiastically engage in learning. Their active minds continually explore ideas and seek to make meaning as they play. To make the most out of their lively engagement with the social and physical worlds, young children need teachers who share and guide their learning experiences. Research on the benefits of high-quality preschool confirms the essential role of the teacher. It is important for teachers to be knowledgeable about young children's learning and skillful at helping individual children and small groups of children build their knowledge and skills.

To support early childhood teachers, the California Early Learning and Development System (see Appendix A) provides an integrated set of resources based on state-of-the-art information on early learning and development and best practices in early education. Each component area in the system provides resources that focus on a different aspect of supporting preschool teachers and links to the resources provided in every other component of the system. This chapter provides an overview of these different component areas and a highlight of some of the resources. One of the system's resources, the Desired Results Development Profile (DRDP), is described in greater detail than the others. This resource allows teachers to assess children's progress in key areas of learning, which is integral to curriculum planning. A description of each component area follows.

Preschool Learning Foundations

At the center of the California Early Learning and Development System are the California preschool learning foundations. The foundations describe competencies—knowledge and skills—that all young children typically learn with appropriate support. Three volumes of foundations are being developed that, taken together, cover nine developmental domains. Already published, Volume 1 includes foundations in the domains of social-emotional development, language and literacy, English-language development, and mathematics. Volume 2 will cover the domains of visual and performing arts, physical development, and health. Finally, Volume 3 will focus on the domains of history-social science and science. Together, the foundations present a comprehensive view of what preschool children learn through child-initiated play and teacher-guided experiences and environments, offering rich background information for teachers to consider as they plan for children. The foundations describe major areas of learning in which intentional teaching can support young children's progress in preschool.

The foundations identify key areas of potential learning. While moving in the direction identified by each foundation, each child will progress along a unique path that reflects both the child's individuality and cultural and linguistic experiences. In essence, the foundations help teachers to understand children's learning and focus on intentional teaching. Other resources for supporting intentional teaching are organized around the foundations. As explained in Chapter 1, strategies for fostering children's learning in each area are organized by the domains, strands, and substrands specified in the three volumes of the foundations. In addition, the DRDP is currently undergoing alignment with the foundations. The final alignment will occur after the third (final) volume of the foundations is completed. The alignment of the DRDP with the foundations will promote a more integrated profile of each child. Instead of a developmental profile of a large number of indicators, the fully aligned DRDP will provide a profile of individual children's progress in each domain. With DRDP information focused on the domain areas, teachers will be able to use the curriculum framework to support each child's learning in various domains in an integrated way.

The foundations are also central to the other components of the California Early Learning and Development System: namely, program guidelines and other resources and professional development. The program guidelines and other resources cover a broad range of policies and practices that influence program quality, including the design of indoor and outdoor learning environments, partnerships with families, cultural diversity, inclusion of children with special needs, and professional ethics. In implementing recommended policies and practices, program directors and teachers set the stage for intentional curriculum planning aligned to the preschool learning foundations. As for professional development, the California Department of Education

has initiated a multifaceted strategy of providing training and technical assistance, which is aligned with the preschool learning foundations to support the use of all resources in the early learning system.

Preschool Curriculum Framework

Ongoing classroom planning is an integral part of intentional teaching. The *California Preschool Curriculum Framework, Volumes 1, 2,* and *3* will be the resources in the early learning system that pertain to planning for children's learning. Each volume of the curriculum framework addresses domains in the corresponding volume of foundations. Volume 1 has chapters on each of the domains addressed in the *California Preschool Learning Foundations, Volume 1:* social-emotional development, language and literacy, English-language development, and mathematics. The curriculum framework presents an integrated approach to the planning of environments, interactions, and strategies to support young children's learning in those domains.

Each chapter offers an in-depth look at ways to help children acquire knowledge and skills in a specific area, always in the context of an integrated approach to support learning. In other words, each domain chapter puts the spotlight on a particular domain, for example, social-emotional development, and the strategies presented in the chapter foster learning in other domains.

The alignment between the curriculum framework and the foundations is easy to see. In a nutshell, the content of each domain chapter in the curriculum framework is organized into the strands and substrands of the corresponding domain in the foundations document.

In the early learning system, the curriculum framework is the resource that supports teachers' ongoing planning. The curriculum framework includes principles, concepts, and practices that reflect a developmentally appropriate approach to plan learning environments, interactions, experiences, and daily routines for young children. In contrast to the approach of some preschool curricula, the curriculum framework does not prescribe activities that teachers are expected to follow. It is flexible and designed to foster respect for the diversity of preschool children, teachers, communities, and programs in California. The curriculum framework encourages teachers to adapt to individual and cultural and linguistic diversity while supporting children's ongoing process of making meaning.

Desired Results Assessment System

Desired Results Developmental Profile

Teachers gain general knowledge of young children's learning from the foundations and ideas for supporting learning from the curriculum framework, but neither of these resources inform teachers about individual children's learning and developmental progress. The resources in the early learning system that assist teachers with documenting individual children's progress are the Desired Results Developmental Profile (DRDP) preschool instrument and the Desired Results Developmental Profile *access* (DRDP *access*),[a] both components

of the CDE's Desired Results assessment system. The DRDP is an observational assessment instrument that is being aligned to the foundations. It provides teachers with a developmental profile of each child's progress. In addition, teachers can look at the individual profiles for an entire classroom to see the extent to which all children in a group are making progress and benefiting from the teachers' ongoing classroom planning.

Information gained from the DRDP helps teachers plan for both individual children and for small groups of children. As illustrated in the snail example in Chapter 1, teachers review individual children's developmental profiles for any emerging knowledge and skills that might be supported in a small-group learning experience. In the example, based on the review of younger children's progress with learning to count objects between five and ten, the teachers invited the

---

[a] The DRDP *access* is an alternative assessment instrument that can be used for children three to five years of age who have a disability. This observation-based assessment instrument is based on a continuum that reflects a broader range of developmental abilities. Each child's Individualized Education Program (IEP) team determines which assessment instrument will be used. Most children's progress will be documented by the DRDP. In the remainder of this chapter, unless "preschool instrument" is specifically indicated, the term DRDP refers to both the DRDP preschool instrument and the DRDP *access*.

children to set up a specific number (less than ten) of trays and snails. (The entire snail vignette appears on pages 14–23 of Chapter 1.) Teachers suggested to other children who were continuing to make progress with counting to count out a quantity of sticks, bark, or leaves greater than ten. Other children were asked to divide the snails evenly among the trays. Teachers noted children's efforts and placed the notes, with the date recorded, into the children's individual portfolios to be used as evidence of developmental progress on the DRDP measures of number sense. This example illustrates how teachers observe and document learning as children engage in play.

Documenting an individual child's learning is key in teachers' efforts to deepen their understanding of how to support each child's learning and development. As teachers observe and document what engages children in learning, especially during child-initiated play, they simultaneously reflect on what they observe, document significant aspects through notetaking or a photo, and begin to appreciate each child's creation of meaning. Ongoing observation, reflection, and documentation occur throughout each day. Teachers continually gain insights and find new ways to connect with the children's developing competencies, expand children's thinking, and encourage further exploration of an emerging idea or ability. The day-to-day documentation of children's learning experiences becomes the source for periodic assessment of children's developmental progress.

Teachers use the documentation they have gathered over time to complete a DRDP for each child. These assessment instruments produce developmental profiles for each child across the major domains of learning and development, such as social-emotional development,

language and literacy, English-language development, and mathematics.

To facilitate curriculum planning, the DRDP preschool instrument summarizes children's progress along a continuum of four levels:

- Exploring: Child shows awareness of the new knowledge or skill and tries it out.
- Developing: Child gains some control of the new knowledge or skill, demonstrating basic competency.
- Building: Child refines and expands new knowledge or skill.
- Integrating: Child connects and combines the new knowledge or skill with other knowledge or skills.

The resulting developmental profile for each child shows the domains in which the child has made progress and whether there are any domains in which he or she needs additional support. As the vignette about investigating snails in Chapter 1 illustrates, teachers use information gained from the DRDP to provide each child with an appropriate level of challenge in specific knowledge and skill areas as children engage in an integrated learning experience.

At all times, young children's learning is integrated. Every experience offers them an opportunity to develop a wide range of knowledge and skills. Likewise, every experience typically engages more than a single competency as children learn. One of the most important competencies that preschool children possess is language. As described in Chapter 1, children who are learning English as well as their home language use both languages as they learn in all domains. Because English learners may show their knowledge of, for example, mathematics, or the arts using their home language, teachers often document and assess demonstration of knowledge and skills in a child's home language. The DRDP user's guide[b] and training information provide guidance to teachers on how to document and assess competencies that English learners demonstrate using their home language.

Families play an essential role in their preschool children's learning. They know their children better than anyone else and are able to provide insights and ideas that add to teachers' understanding of children. Reflection on documentation and a child's individual profile of developmental progress in partnership with family members strengthens the entire curriculum-planning process. Partnering with families in this process honors their role in their children's learning and communicates respect. Together, teachers and families can generate ideas and activities to foster children's development of emerging knowledge and skills at both school and home.

The DRDP is part of the Desired Results assessment system, which, in turn, is part of the larger California Early Learning and Development System. In addition to the DRDP, the Desired Results system includes the Desired Results Parent Survey and the Environment Rating Scale (ERS). Information collected through the system of Desired Results assessment instruments allows early educators to review, evaluate, and reflect on:

- the strengths of their program (for example, a program may already provide a rich collection of literacy materials);
- ways to increase the quality of their programs (for example, a program may discover a need to increase the variety of activities and interactions it offers to support children's mathematics

learning both in the preschool classroom and at home by partnering with the children's families); and
- the effectiveness of their curriculum (for example, information on the children's current progress in engaging in cooperative play would help teachers focus their curriculum planning on the area of social-emotional development).

Desired Results Parent Survey

The Desired Results Parent Survey is used (1) to assess parent satisfaction with the early childhood program, and (2) to gain an understanding of families' strengths and needs in supporting their children's learning and development and in achieving their goals. Programs conduct this survey annually as part of the program's self-review.

Teachers reflect on information from the survey to understand additional information about the children and the program, to identify program strengths, and to determine ways to facilitate family participation in the program and help family members build their capacities to support their children's learning and development.

Environment Rating Scale

The Environment Rating Scale (ERS) assesses the quality of the learning environment (see Harms, Clifford, and Cryer 2005, p. 92). Specifically, teachers use the ERS to assess the quality of the interactions, the space, the schedule, and materials they provide to their group of children. The ERS is completed, summarized, analyzed, and then considered in program improvement plans once a year. Teachers combine information gained from the ERS with other sources to engage in long-term planning and continual program improvement.

---

[b] The DRDP user's guide is available at http://www.wested.org/desiredresults/training/forms.htm.

Program Guidelines and Other Resources

Prekindergarten Learning & Development Guidelines

The CDE offers several resources:

The *Prekindergarten Learning & Development Guidelines* recommends policies and practices that enhance the quality of preschool programs. In addition to giving an overview of preschool children's learning and development and curriculum planning, the publication covers a broad range of topics that contribute to program quality:

- Planning the Preschool Environment
- Addressing Cultural Diversity
- Planning for Assessment
- Including Children with Disabilities or Other Special Needs
- Involving Parents and Families
- Organizing Staff Preparation and Development Programs

As stated earlier in this chapter, the recommendations set forth in the prekindergarten guidelines set the stage for intentional teaching and curriculum planning centered on the preschool learning foundations.

Preschool English Learners Resource Guide

The CDE publication *Preschool English Learners: Principles and Practices to Promote Language, Literacy, and Learning* (PEL Resource Guide) provides guidance on how to support preschool children who are learning English as a second language. This resource guide highlights the role of families in language and literacy development as well as the importance of connecting preschool and the home language. It is organized around ten principles and accompanying practices. For example, Principle 2 states: "Children benefit when their teachers understand cultural differences in language use and incorporate them into the daily routine." It goes on to state: "Culturally responsive teaching practices in the preschool classroom create a positive learning environment. They incorporate the linguistic and cultural resources that children bring with them and thereby promote their learning and overall growth."

The PEL Resource Guide works in tandem with the preschool learning foundations. It provides expanded information about the domain of English-language development. It also provides details on strategies to support children's ongoing learning and use of their home language as well as English. Teachers can draw on these strategies as they engage in curriculum planning.

A World Full of Language: Supporting Preschool English Learners

A resource that complements the PEL Resource Guide is *A World Full of Language: Supporting Preschool English Learners*. Available in both English and Spanish from the CDE, this DVD first gives an overview of the discussion of second-language learning in the resource guide. It then presents the following five strategies that support second-language acquisition:

- Honor the Home Language
- Create a Climate of Belonging
- Provide Scaffolds
- Focus on the Children's Interests
- Encourage Peer Support

These strategies are followed by the following five strategies that support preschool children's inclination toward literacy:

- Strengthen Interest in Print

- Build Letter Knowledge
- Draw Attention to Sounds
- Make Books and Stories Come Alive
- Link Literacy to Home and Community

Of course, the above strategies apply to all children. The DVD shows how the strategies contribute to the learning of children who are developing knowledge and skills in two languages—their home language and English. If supported well during the preschool years, children who are on the path to bilingualism have an opportunity to become competent in two languages and cultures and therefore better equipped for an increasingly global society.

Professional Development

Professional development makes the California Early Learning and Development System come alive for teachers and program directors. The CDE is taking a multifaceted approach to promoting the use of the early learning system in professional development. Initiatives include the preparation and ongoing professional development of preschool teachers in two-year and four-year colleges. In addition, a network has been created to support the continuing development of current preschool teachers. To guide efforts to foster professional development, the CDE has partnered with First 5 California to develop Early Childhood Educator Competencies that are aligned with the preschool learning foundations and all other resources in the California Early Learning and Development System. These competencies describe the knowledge, skills, and dispositions of early childhood educators and will become the CDE's cornerstone for professional development, training, and technical assistance.

In-Depth Understanding and Planning for Children's Integrated Learning

The different resources and activities that make up the California Early Learning and Development System offer preschool program directors and teachers opportunities to explore a wide variety of topics in depth. Likewise, this curriculum framework reflects a dual emphasis on breadth and depth. Teachers can use this framework to consider the details of curriculum planning in different domains. At the same time, rather than being isolated from learning in other domains, the strategies presented for one domain are connected with learning in other domains. In deepening understanding of each domain, one can see new possibilities for integrating curriculum planning and connecting children's learning experiences. The chapters that follow in this curriculum framework explore in depth the domains of social-emotional development, language and literacy, English-language development, and mathematics. As the snail vignette in Chapter 1 illustrates, teachers draw on their in-depth understanding of children's learning in different domains. As teachers observe, reflect upon, and document each child's engagement in making meaning, their knowledge of strategies that support learning in various domains helps them use an integrated approach when planning curriculum. With in-depth knowledge of how to support knowledge and skill development in every domain, teachers can more easily focus on a specific area of learning while being responsive to each child's entire learning experience.

CHAPTER 3

Social-Emotional Development

Social-emotional development indicates how preschool children acquire the social skills, self-awareness, and personal qualities that are interconnected with learning in a classroom. This developmental domain is divided into three interrelated strands.

- The first, Self, covers the qualities of self-awareness, self-confidence, and personality that enable young children to be competent learners.[1, 2, 3] Included in this strand are the development of self-awareness and self-confidence; self-regulation (of attention, feelings, impulses, and thinking); social and emotional understanding; the growth of empathy and caring for others; and preschool children's initiative as enthusiastic, active learners.
- The second, Social Interaction, includes the skills for interacting competently with adults and peers in formal and informal learning contexts.[4] Included in this strand are the growth of social skills for interaction with familiar adults and with peers, understanding of the roles and responsibilities of group participation, and acquisition of the capacity for responsible behavior and cooperation with adult instructions.
- The third, Relationships, focuses on how close relationships influence young children's learning in direct and indirect ways.[5, 6] Included in this strand, for example,

are preschool children's attachments to parents and the bridges between home and the preschool program that support children's learning, close relationships with special teachers and caregivers, and friendships with other children.

Why is social-emotional development important to early learning? One reason is that many social-emotional qualities—such as curiosity; self-confidence as a learner; self-control of attention, thinking, and impulses; and initiative in developing new ideas—are essential to learning at any age. Learning, problem solving, and creativity rely on these social-emotional and motivational qualities as well as basic cognitive skills. Another reason is that when learning occurs in groups, such as in preschool classrooms or family child care programs, the social environment significantly influences how learning occurs. When young children enjoy interacting with adults and other children, they are more enthusiastic about activities and participate more.[7, 8] Furthermore, the interest and enthusiasm of others fuels the child's own excitement about learning, and children are also motivated by others' acknowledgment of the child's accomplishments.

Interviews with preschool and kindergarten teachers indicate that children who have the greatest difficulties in learning are hindered by the lack of these social-emotional qualities more than by the inability to identify letters or numbers.[9, 10] Children who are delayed or impaired in developing these social-emotional and motivational qualities:

- may have difficulty controlling their emotions or behavior,
- may not readily work independently or in a group,
- often appear to lack curiosity or be uninterested in learning, and
- may have difficulties getting along with others, which may undermine the learning environment for all children.

Finally, the importance of social-emotional development to early learning is consistent with the research on brain science.[11] The developing brain is not neatly divided into separate areas governing learning, thinking, and emotions. Instead, it is a highly interconnected organ with different regions influencing, and being affected by, the others. This means, for example, that young children who experience emotional challenges (perhaps because of stress) are less ready for learning because brain regions related to memory are being affected by other regions governing emotion. This conclusion from brain research is, of course, consistent with the everyday experience of teachers of children whose stressful lives often lead to emotional, behavioral, and learning difficulties.

Early learning is thus supported by attention to social-emotional development. Indeed, rather than taking time away from activities promoting learning and thinking, attention to the development of self, social interactions, and relationships is an essential component of an early childhood curriculum designed to promote learning in all young children.

Guiding Principles

▶ Support social-emotional development with intentionality

Attention to the domain of social-emotional development is important. Most children learn in this domain somewhat differently from the way that they acquire language, number concepts, or other academic skills. Growth in social and emotional competencies is not primarily the outcome of specific content taught in a program of organized lessons, but early childhood educators must be as deliberate and intentional in promoting social-emotional development as they are in designing curricula to encourage literacy or number skills. Indeed, they must be even more thoughtful in doing so because supporting learning in this domain is implicit in the design of the classroom environment, in the formal and informal moment-by-moment interactions they share with children, and in many other planned and spontaneous activities. In addition, some children need intentional teaching of specific skills and content to acquire social skills.

Children also need ample opportunities to practice the skills in order to internalize them.[12] Social-emotional development is supported in an early childhood classroom only when adults are mindful of the many ways they influence preschool children's self-awareness, social skills, emotional understanding, personality, and other qualities.[13]

▶ Attend to the impact of overall program design on social-emotional development

Creating an early childhood program that supports social-emotional development depends on how the overall program is designed, the child's role in the learning environment, and the kinds of social interactions that occur there. Group activities specifically planned to focus on caring, cooperation, or friendship skills can play an essential role in the curriculum. That role, however, is to reinforce and extend broader lessons that are learned through (a) the ways that teachers interact with children throughout the day, and (b) teachers' intentional modeling and coaching in many formal and informal social contexts.

▶ **Utilize curriculum practices that support healthy social-emotional development**
Research indicates that there are practices that support healthy social-emotional development in children.[14] These include an overall program curriculum that provides guidance for designing the indoor and outdoor environment, routines and activities, and teacher–child interactions. To successfully support social-emotional development, the curriculum must be designed to:

- allow many opportunities for practicing social interaction and relationship skills;
- provide support for the growth of age- and developmentally appropriate self-regulation abilities;
- encourage curiosity and initiative; and
- provide each child a network of nurturing, dependable adults who will actively support and scaffold his or her learning in a group setting.

Children and Stress

Adults hope to protect young children from trauma and adversity, but for many children, experiences of overwhelming stress are part of everyday life. Living at home with a depressed parent, experiencing physical or sexual abuse, witnessing domestic violence, coping at home with a parent who has an alcohol or other substance abuse problem, chronic poverty, and similar experiences can be crushing for young children. Such experiences are called "toxic stress" and can lead to physical and mental health problems (National Scientific Council on the Developing Child 2005). Those experiences exceed young children's capacity for coping, especially when children lack the support of a warm, competent adult to help them manage the stress. There is growing evidence that the experience of chronic, unpredictable, and overwhelming stress in the early years can lead to the development of neurobiological stress systems in the brain that are sensitive to threat and lead young children to overreact to ordinary stressful events (National Scientific Council on the Developing Child 2005).

Stress is a part of everyday experience, of course, and this is as true for young children as it is for adults. In most cases, children encounter stresses that are manageable for them, whether they involve getting an immunization, tolerating a sibling's teasing, or recovering from a frightening fall. Moreover, young children can usually rely on the assistance of trusted adults to help them cope with everyday stresses. Research has shown that toddlers in secure relationships with their mothers are better able to manage frightening events, both emotionally and physiologically, compared with toddlers in insecure parent–child relationships (Nachmias et al. 1996). Because young children ordinarily rely on the support of trusted adults in coping with stress in their lives, experiences in which their caregivers are threatening or unavailable can be especially difficult for them.

Teachers in an early childhood education program are often the first persons outside the family to become aware that a young child may be experiencing overwhelming stress. They may notice a child who reacts

▶ Encourage play-based active learning

A play-based, active learning approach is most effective in accomplishing these goals.[15] Children must be allowed to freely choose and pursue interests and activities, both alone and with others. They must be allowed to translate their own thoughts, ideas, and preferences into new activities and experiments.[16] They must also have access to these opportunities for activity and exploration, in a thoughtfully planned environment, for a substantial portion of each preschool day. Children with significant disabilities or difficulties in choosing or pursuing activities deserve support and strategies to enable them to participate in active learning. In this context, play is essential and is enhanced if materials are available to encourage creativity and teachers are attentive to the social interactions that surround play. Active learning is essential and is enhanced (1) if materials are readily accessible to children and (2) if teachers are sensitive to the growth that they can foster through children's chosen activities.[17]

This approach of promoting children's active engagement with activities, materials, and other people requires

---

with uncharacteristic aggression to a peer's comment that would not bother another child, or they may notice that a child has become unusually quiet and withdrawn lately. Young children convey their stress in individualized ways: some are emotionally overreactive, while others are emotionally overcontrolled; some become clingy, others withdrawn; some become provocative and defiant. A common characteristic is that young children under stress exhibit a marked change from their ordinary behavior. They often lose their capacity for competence and self-control that they previously had. When teachers observe these changes in a child, it can be helpful to consult with parents to discover whether recent events have created challenges that children are having difficulty managing. Often these challenges arise from within the family.

How can teachers assist young children under stress? One of the most important things they can do is provide the child with a predictable, safe haven where children can feel secure. Teachers can create a comfortable and comforting everyday routine that is child-centered, individualized, responsive, and helpfully structured to give young children a sense of control and predictability that may be lacking in other aspects of the child's life. Central to these efforts is providing children with supportive adult relationships that are reliable and helpful. This may be more difficult than one would expect because young children under stress often test these relationships to see whether teachers and other adults will remain responsive to them even when children act defiantly or negatively.

In some circumstances, it can be helpful for teachers to obtain the advice of an early childhood mental health consultant who can observe the child in the classroom, talk with the teacher about the child's behavior, and suggest strategies for providing supportive assistance. Early childhood mental health consultants can be valuable resources to an early childhood education program. They can help teachers provide much-needed support to young children who may not have other such sources of support elsewhere in their lives.

teachers' own active engagement and planning. The following strategies are key to ensuring social-emotional development:

- Create a program environment and daily routines that offer children opportunities for responsible and cooperative roles in the classroom or family child care community.
- Model desirable behavior and attitudes in interactions with children and other adults.
- Use the family culture to create bridges between the program and the home, supporting children's pride in their family experience, and understand individual differences in background and viewpoint.
- Enlist adults as active co-explorers in children's chosen activities.
- Encourage children's ideas, initiative, and contributions to shared activities.
- Observe children attentively, as they play, to understand each child's needs and interests, strengths, and areas of growth in social-emotional development.
- Establish developmentally and culturally appropriate expectations for children's behavior, especially expectations for self-control and self-regulation.
- Narrate for children what they are observed doing and expressing, providing language to describe their thoughts and feelings and to clarify others' feelings.
- Provide specific feedback to children about their efforts, reinforcing their choices that support learning and linking their actions to outcomes.
- Coach and guide children's behavior by using positive, respectful phrasing and tone to prompt problem solving and to give brief instructions and reminders.

- Use the experiences and emotions of characters in children's books and stories to illustrate social problem solving, cooperative behavior, and other concepts.
- Provide intentional teaching of social skills, friendship skills, and emotion regulation.

Environments and Materials

The physical environment provides young children with expectations for behavior.[18] When educators are mindful of the **aesthetics,** organization, and function of each area in the space, challenging behavior is likely to decrease while constructive, cooperative behavior increases.[19] A program's vision for learning and philosophy of care dictate how an environment is designed.[20] For example, if the curriculum is based on the view that children are competent directors of their own learning, educators develop a physical setting and activities that reflect children's emerging interests and provide easy access to meaningful play materials. Shelves for manipulatives and other materials are near the floor where children can easily reach them. Special areas in the room are designed for individual, small-group, and larger-group interactions. Play materials and other materials are carefully selected to reflect children's emerging interests, as observed in the context of play and conversation. In this environment, adult–child interactions can expand children's questions and comments. This broader vision for children's learning and care thus helps to promote synchrony between the environment, routines, and teacher–child interactions.

High-quality learning environments set the stage for social-emotional exploration and growth.[21] When children are presented with a warm, inviting, and culturally familiar environment, they feel comfortable and secure.[22] The attractive spaces adults prepare for children communicate expectations of responsibility and cooperative care (we all play in and care for this beautiful place together). Preparing a variety of learning areas with open-ended materials encourages each child to participate in meaningful play experiences that match their individual temperaments and abilities. Incorporating elements from the home creates an atmosphere of community while simultaneously acknowledging the presence of individuals.

A physical environment that supports social-emotional learning has the following characteristics:

▶ **Challenging and developmentally appropriate materials**

It provides children with challenging, developmentally appropriate materials that encourage both creative, flexible use (e.g., open-ended materials such as blocks and art supplies) and practice in problem solving (e.g., closed-ended materials such as puzzles and matching games).

▶ **Ample supply of materials**

It offers plenty of materials to avoid conflict between children or long waiting for a turn. Materials are labeled in the languages of the children in the group (e.g., using pictures, words, and symbols) to offer children a menu of opportunities for play.

▶ **Organized learning areas**

The space is organized with designated learning areas for large-group activities (e.g., circle time), small-group explorations (e.g., a work table or science project), and individual activities from which children can choose, ensuring

that all children physically have access to all areas.

▶ **Appropriately sized small-group activities**

It limits the size of small-group activities to promote peer interaction and struggles over turn-taking and use of materials.

▶ **A variety of small-group activities**

Activities are planned so that a range of adult supervision exists: from activities that children can do with minimal adult supervision (e.g., dramatic play, familiar books, and puzzles) to ones that require close adult supervision (e.g., messy art activities, preparing food, learning to use new toys, materials, or games).

▶ **Aesthetically appealing**

The aesthetics (e.g., colors, textures, furnishings, other physical elements of the environment) are designed so that children are comfortable and their energy and attention are focused on the activities. An overstimulating environment is avoided.

▶ **Public and private spaces**

There are both public spaces that encourage peer interaction and private spaces where children can take a break from sociability (areas with materials such as storybooks, pillows, blankets, or stuffed toys).

▶ **Furnishings and materials accessible to children**
Low shelving and child-sized furniture enable children to feel comfortable and confident as they take initiative in choosing activities (collaborative or individual pursuits) without requiring adult assistance.

▶ **Display of children's work**
Children's artwork and other accomplishments are displayed at the child's eye level.

▶ **Space for children's belongings**
There is a space for children's personal belongings, including treasured items from home.

▶ **Reflective of diversity**
The books, photographs, artwork, music, and other materials reflect the diversity of the families of the children in the group. Relationships, cultures, ethnicities, and people of different ages and abilities are portrayed in the environment.

▶ **Space for arrivals and departures**
The physical space, as well as classroom routines, supports arrival and departure experiences with family members.

▶ **Supportive of children's active engagement**
Physical and verbal support are provided to assist the active engagement of children of all developmental abilities in the early learning environment and daily routines.

▶ **Outdoor areas supportive of social-emotional development**
The "outdoor classroom" and natural play spaces are considered an extension of the indoor explorations and are part of the social-emotional curriculum.

Just as the physical environment helps young children successfully meet the social-emotional demands of the curriculum, so too does the design of the daily schedule. Young children are better able to manage themselves and their relationships when daily routines and activities are predictable, transitions are signaled and supported, and there is a balance between relatively active and relatively quiet play and between group and individual activities. In the sections that follow, strategies to support social-emotional development are described in detail.

Summary of Strands and Substrands

The domain of social-emotional development encompasses three strands: self, social interaction, and relationships. The strands and their substrands are as follows:

Self
1.0 Self-Awareness
2.0 Self-Regulation
3.0 Social and Emotional Understanding
4.0 Empathy and Caring
5.0 Initiative in Learning

Social Interaction
1.0 Interactions with Familiar Adults
2.0 Interactions with Peers
3.0 Group Participation
4.0 Cooperation and Responsibility

Relationships
1.0 Attachments to Parents
2.0 Close Relationships with Teachers and Caregivers
3.0 Friendships

Please refer to the map of the social-emotional development foundations on page 88 for a visual explanation of the terminology used in the preschool learning foundations.

Self

Early learning deeply engages the self. Most preschool children approach learning opportunities with enthusiasm and self-confidence, excited by the prospect of new discovery.[23] Their successes (and occasional failures) shape their sense of what they can do and sometimes drive their efforts to acquire new skills. Their achievements and occasional disappointments also provoke the responses of others—adults and peers—that further influence children's self-concept and self-confidence. Young children value learning for themselves because it is valued by the people who matter to them.

In a preschool program, learning is a social activity. Therefore, preschool children's success in learning depends on their capacity to understand and participate constructively in the social environment. Early childhood is a period of rapid growth in social and emotional understanding in which the children's capacity for empathy and caring is also developing.[24] This is also a period of growth in self-regulation as young children are acquiring skills for sustaining their attention, focusing their thinking and problem solving, managing their behavioral impulses, and controlling their emotions.[25] Even so, lapses in self-regulation are as apparent as are young children's successes, and developmentally appropriate expectations for children's self-control are essential.

Therefore, a thoughtfully designed preschool curriculum that supports social-emotional development devotes considerable attention to the direct and indirect ways that children's classroom experiences shape the self. In this section, specific strategies are discussed that support development in each of the following substrands:

1.0 Self-Awareness
2.0 Self-Regulation
3.0 Social and Emotional Understanding
4.0 Empathy and Caring
5.0 Initiative in Learning

1.0   Self-Awareness

Preschool children enjoy interacting with adults they know and are becoming more skilled in sharing their thoughts or feelings, cooperating in play or problem solving, following instructions, asking for assistance, and taking the initiative in social interaction.[26, 27] Adults contribute to these skills when they respond positively and enthusiastically to children's initiatives, model respectful communication and social interaction skills, coach children in their interactions with other adults, and encourage children to confidently share their ideas and experiences with them.[28, 29]

VIGNETTE

Four children work in the block area, racing small cars down two large wooden ramps and arguing over whose turn it is to use each ramp. Later, as they communicate about their morning's activities in a small group, the teacher observes, "Everyone wanted to use the block ramps for their own cars, but there were only two ramps, so you figured out how to make the plain boards into ramps by propping them up with the small blocks. That made enough ramps for all of you!"

TEACHABLE MOMENT

▶ The teacher observes attentively as the children work in the block area, waiting to see whether they will need her help to guide them in solving their dispute. Later, during a group discussion, she tells them what she has observed. She describes specifically the solution they worked out to their problem of needing enough ramps for everyone, and her means of communication, including words and tone of voice, convey how impressed she is with their cooperation and successful problem solving.

VIGNETTE

A child in a wheelchair enters the housekeeping area where three children are pretending to be a family. They have dishes on the table and dolls in the doll bed. The child in the wheelchair moves closer to the table and tries to join the play but cannot get close enough. After a few minutes, one of the children takes some dishes and puts them on the wheelchair tray. The two children play together. Mr. Luke comments, "I like your idea to use Andy's tray as a table."

TEACHABLE MOMENT

▶ The teacher observes attentively as the child using a wheelchair enters the housekeeping area and watches to see how the children will include him in play. When a child uses the wheelchair tray as a table, the teacher comments about the solution using positive words.

The following interactions and strategies can help children grow in self-awareness:

Designate learning areas to help children select preferred sites for exploration. Place active play zones away from quiet areas to better support children in their choices for play. Children seek appropriately stimulating spaces as they learn to monitor their own internal needs.

Observe individual children attentively during a variety of activities to find out about each child's characteristics and preferences (e.g., active, quiet, dramatic, persistent), communication skills, interests, and challenges.

Incorporate artwork and play materials that reflect children's home cultures to help children and families feel comfortable and welcome in the preschool program.

Describe aloud for children observations of what they do and express as they play, explore, and participate in group activities. Use language that labels thoughts and feelings: "You're standing back to admire your block tower, Felipe. You look very pleased about how tall you built it." Or "David, you laughed and thought it was funny when Emma mixed up your puzzle pieces, but Leo looks upset when you do that to his puzzle pieces."

Compare aloud children's past and present abilities as you observe them: "When you first came to preschool, Kim, you couldn't turn on the water by yourself, and now you can turn it on and off." Or "Marco, you used to want to keep all the cars just for yourself, and now you're sharing them with Ben and Jorge. You figured out how you could all play with the cars together."

Give specific feedback to children about their efforts. This shows that adults notice and appreciate their hard work, cooperation, and successful problem solving. Describing specific observations also helps children remember the positive roles they played in an event and will help them repeat similar actions in the future: "You noticed that I was having trouble understanding what Lucia needed at the art table, so you asked her about it in Spanish and then told me that she needed more yellow paint. Thank you— you helped both Lucia and me."

Use planned activities and children's own observations to draw attention to people's similarities and differences, including preferences and feelings. Play circle games that ask children to do actions based on things that distinguish them from each other (e.g., "If you like rainy days, . . . have curly hair, or wear glasses . . . point to yourself or stand up and jump!"). Follow up on a child's comment that "grandmas don't live with you—they just visit," with a group discussion about where various children's grandparents live, including those in the child's household. Use children's observations about each other's characteristics to begin conversations about the many ways that people are the same *and* different.

Set up opportunities to practice problem solving with children who have not yet developed those skills. When serving a snack, ask the children what to do since there is only one apple for four children. As children struggle over the cash register in the dramatic play area, help them think through what the options are that would allow everyone to play—setting a timer, having an extra cash box for a second register, making one person the manager who can help when there is a problem at the cash register, and so on.

2.0   Self-Regulation

Preschool children work hard to manage their attention, feelings, impulses, and thoughts. They seek to cooperate with others, manage their upset feelings, and participate in classroom routines and transitions, but they need ongoing adult support for their efforts.[30, 31] Preschool children differ significantly in their abilities to pay attention in a group, finish a task, cooperate with adults and peers, and express their strong feelings in ways that do not hurt others. Even young children who are sometimes able to do these things will probably not manage them independently all the time, but they will be more capable of self-regulation given adult guidance and support.

VIGNETTE

Ms. Caitlin stumbles in the play yard while carrying a tray of bowls containing acorns, leaf pods, pinecones, and leaves. The items spill across the ground. She describes the accident: "Oh, no! I just sorted all of these, and now it looks like I'll have to do it all over again! It's so frustrating when things like this happen." She sighs and takes a deep breath. "Well, I guess I'll start with the acorns. It shouldn't take too long." Several children nearby offer to help and begin to pick up and sort the items. Teachers and children all work together for a few minutes, picking through the grass and sharing with each other about how many of each item they have found. When all the natural play materials have been sorted back into their bowls, Ms. Caitlin thanks the children and comments on how fast the job went with so many people helping.

TEACHABLE MOMENT

 In this situation the teacher models self-talk to turn an upsetting situation into a teachable moment about constructive emotional coping strategies. She describes the accident and expresses her feelings about it. She continues by modeling a constructive course of action to remedy the situation. The children nearby respond by starting to help pick up the various items (displaying empathy and caring). At the end of the job, she concludes the impromptu lesson by thanking her helpers and commenting on how much faster a job goes when so many people work together (generalizing from action to principle).

The following interactions and strategies can support children's growth in self-regulation skills:

Use appropriately stimulating aesthetic elements such as soothing colors, natural woods and fibers, and soft textures. When children feel calm and comfortable, they constructively interact with adults, peers, and learning materials. Neutral walls and furniture should fade into the background so that children can focus on their "work." Visual clutter should be avoided as much as possible.

Eliminate or reduce background noise to help children with learning disabilities, speech and language impairments, and hearing impairments attend to auditory input. Reducing background noise helps all children, including English learners, focus more readily on oral language as conversations take place near them while they are playing. For more information about strategies to support children who are English learners, see Chapter 5.

Observe individual children closely, especially as they interact with peers, encounter frustration, and are asked to cooperate with adult requests and group routines. Observing each child individually will help identify where that child needs the most adult support for learning (e.g., can the child maintain attention during group activities, show understanding of classroom routines, use language to express emotions, play cooperatively and negotiate disagreements with peers, ask for help when necessary?).

Model behavior and attitudes toward others as an effective way of teaching self-regulatory skills. Because young children closely observe and imitate the behavior of adults they care about,

Research Highlight

Self-regulation is important to school readiness and early school success. One of the most important indicators of self-regulation is a young child's ability to pay attention in the classroom. In one recent study, researchers combined the results of several large-scale, long-term studies of children beginning from the preschool years and continuing well into school. They were interested in the qualities of preschoolers that best predicted how well they would do on school-age math and reading tests. The researchers found that early skill in math and reading was important to later success in these areas, of course. Beyond this, however, they also found that differences in self-regulation, particularly in attention, were important in later school success. Children who concentrated and listened attentively to the teacher as preschoolers and who were less impulsive and distractible achieved higher scores on math and reading tests after entering school.[32]

teachers can intentionally model desired behavior for them. Adults model appropriate concern for others' well-being by communicating with children in a respectful way and treating them the way they would like children to treat each other. They can model enthusiasm for persisting at a task until finishing it by sharing their thoughts while working alongside children (e.g., "It's taking a long time to finish this puzzle, but when we figure out how to fit in the last five pieces, we'll get to see the whole picture"). Finally, adults can model emotional self-control by expressing their own feelings constructively when encountering a problem.

Maintain developmentally appropriate expectations for preschool children's behavior. Make allowance for children's relatively limited capacity to sit and maintain focused attention by planning brief large-group activities and longer periods of self-initiated activity. Help children to manage complex tasks (e.g., getting ready to go outside in the rain) by breaking them down into simpler steps. Ensure that expectations for emotional self-control and behavioral control are appropriate for the child's age or developmental level. Supplying plenty of play materials decreases excessive frustration and increases on-task exploration.

Guide and coach children's behavior by using positive, respectful phrasing and tone to prompt problem solving and to give brief instructions and reminders: "Can you start by telling Jonah why you're so angry? Then we can work together on solving the problem," or "Since lunch will come soon, it's almost time to clean up our room and wash our hands so we'll be ready to eat."

Reinforce children's good choices and link their actions to positive outcomes. Express pleasure and acknowledge children's efforts when children handle situations in mature ways. Draw attention to specific ways a child's behavior made an experience successful: "I know you really wanted to share your story right away, but you waited patiently during Angela's turn. She was so happy to get to tell us about her papa."

Provide a consistent but flexible daily routine. A consistent daily routine facilitates children's trust and focus on the learning environment. This consistency helps English learners predict the day and navigate through it. When children can anticipate what comes now, next, and later, they are better able to regulate their expectations, energy, and activity. Be flexible enough to follow children's emerging interests and allow them to finish projects when possible. Adults can prepare children ahead of time for occasional major changes in the daily routine in order to prevent unease and off-task behavior (e.g., "Today we are walking to the fire station before we eat snack. Usually we go outside after snack, but today we are doing something different"). Many children appreciate having the schedule in picture format, so they can independently check the schedule themselves. Taking pictures of the children themselves engaged in the various activities can be a fun way of making the schedule. Then, when there is a change, a new picture, such as one of a fire truck, can be put in place as a reminder of the change.

Alternate between active and quiet activities. Guiding children through appropriately varied levels of stimulation encourages self-regulation. It leads to more positive behavior and increases children's ability to fully engage with their learning environment, peers, and teachers.

Time group experiences to match children's developing attention spans, social skills, and self-control. Attending to a group experience can be difficult for young children. Group experiences should be brief—between 10 and 15 minutes and, in some instances, up to 20 minutes—depending on children's ages, understanding of the English language, past experiences, and levels of functioning. Ignoring a group's need for a transition can lead to more disruptive behavior and a general lack of cooperation (e.g., a teacher's insistence on finishing a book during a large-group story time despite children's restlessness may cause more problem behavior and work against learning goals). For more information about strategies to support children who are English learners, see Chapter 5.

Introduce children to relaxation exercises. Stretching and relaxation exercises assist children in self-reflection and build self-regulation skills. Teachers can use calming activities informally as well as during group experiences and program transitions. An adult can soothe a frustrated child by drawing attention to the body's response to stress: "You look really upset! Your face is red and tense. Can you feel how fast your heart is beating?" Then guide the child through a deep-breathing exercise and comment on its effects. Initiate a brief group stretching and relaxation exercise between active and quiet routines to help prepare children for more focused exploration.

Prepare "private" spaces for children. The sounds of active learning can be loud and, at times, overstimulating. In these and other situations, many children need "private" spaces where they can find a retreat from group participation. Teachers can make private spaces inviting by including comfortable pillows, blankets, stuffed toys, and a small table for the child who would like to engage in an activity on his own.

Plan developmentally appropriate transitions. Transitions can cause a typically positive classroom climate to unravel as activity and intensity levels increase. Teachers can plan transitional activities to maximize focus and encourage constructive participation. Songs, visual prompts, and key phrases in children's home languages remind children of what is currently occurring, what the child's responsibility is during the changeover, and what a child can do to help self-regulate through the transition. For example, an adult may lead a group of children in singing a "clean-up song" throughout the time they spend picking up and reshelving toys and materials together. Transitions should be kept to a minimum.

Play games with rules periodically to help children learn to focus their attention and regulate their impulses in order to achieve a goal. Small, organized groups are easiest for preschool children to manage. Simple bingo games, matching games, or active games in the play yard such as Red Light, Green Light or Simon Says encourage children to pay close attention and to practice pausing first instead of acting impulsively. Turn-taking in pairs or small groups encourages cooperation. Providing visual cues (e.g., pointing to a picture of a traffic signal or using gestures in coordination with Simon Says), in addition to auditory prompts, helps all children participate in games with success.

3.0   Social and Emotional Understanding

Preschool children are beginning to understand how people are similar to and different from one another, not only in the ways they can observe directly, such as appearance and skills, but also in ways that they cannot observe directly, such as thoughts and personality. They are learning that people vary in their ideas, feelings, and perspectives and that differences in personality and culture are important.[33, 34] Young children are curious about these differences, and teachers help them learn and accept how people's feelings, thoughts, and behavior are related. Teachers share and discuss everyday events. Teachers can also help preschool children better understand their own feelings, personality, and other social and emotional characteristics.[35, 36]

VIGNETTE	*Myesha watches Linh being comforted by her caregiver. She goes over to Mr. Kyle sitting at a table, puts a hand on his shoulder, and suggests, "Linh was crying because she thought her mommy wasn't coming." Mr. Kyle nods his head gently and replies, "I noticed that, too. Do you remember when preschool was over and you were the last one waiting for your mom? You cried because you were worried that she wouldn't come to pick you up. I think Linh was feeling the same way."*

TEACHABLE MOMENT

In this situation, the adult facilitates social and emotional understanding by using the child's observations of a peer's emotional experience to explore the causes of feelings, to explore similarities in emotional response, and to introduce complex emotion vocabulary.

VIGNETTE

Tien watched carefully as Romo interacted with Ms. West, his teacher. After Romo walked away, Tien said "How do you know how to talk to Romo? He talks funny." Ms. West explained, "Romo talks differently than you do because he hears differently. When Romo talks to me, I watch carefully and sometimes he points to things to make it more clear. When you don't understand him, maybe you could ask him to show you. He is playing with the farm animals now. Would you like to join him?"

TEACHABLE MOMENT

The teacher responded to a question from a child who noticed a difference in Romo's mode of communication by explaining how Romo communicated and inviting the child to use the information. By providing information and inviting the child to pursue interaction, the teacher was supporting social understanding while responding to an underlying emotional concern.

The following interactions and strategies can help children grow in their social and emotional understanding:

Observe the levels of social and emotional understanding that children already have when they begin preschool. For teachers, the most helpful observations of children's understandings are made in the course of typical daily activities. Teachers will want to note whether a child is able to label, in any language, a range of emotions expressed by self and others; notices and indicates curiosity about physical differences between people; is able to describe some personality characteristics of others (e.g., friendly, timid, grumpy); and can sometimes accurately describe the reasons behind someone's emotion-driven behavior (e.g., crying when missing a parent). See the Research Highlight, below.

Label the emotions people express and communicate with children about what may be provoking those feelings. Discuss causes and consequences (e.g., what often makes people sad, angry, or excited). Acknowledge with older pre-school children that people can mask their feelings and that the emotion shown may be different from the one a person really feels (e.g., "I know you are afraid of big dogs, but when Peter's dad brought his dog to visit today you acted very calm and brave. That must have been hard"). Introduce more complex emotion vocabulary in their conversations with children (e.g., anxious, delighted, cautious, embarrassed).

Research Highlight

Early social and emotional understanding helps children get along better with other children and teachers in school, but how important is it for school success? This question was explored in a study of young children who were tested on a simple measure of their emotion knowledge (e.g., understanding when someone is surprised or angry) at age five, and then measures of their social behavior and academic achievement were obtained at age nine. The measure of emotion knowledge asked five-year-olds to match emotion labels to facial expressions of emotions. The researchers found that children's performance on this task was significantly associated with their social skills and academic achievement at age nine. Children who had greater emotion knowledge had more positive social skills, showed fewer behavior problems, and had higher academic achievement—perhaps because of how their emotion skills (e.g., ability to deal with frustration) enabled children to get along better with others in ways that encouraged academic as well as social success.[37]

Generalize from specific examples to broader realities, when appropriate, to help children understand psychological complexities and emotional processes they cannot observe directly. "David gets upset whenever you come near his block buildings because you used to try to knock them down. When you have been unkind to someone over and over, it takes a long time for him to trust that you will be kind now," or "Aya does cry every morning when her papa leaves. She has never been to school before, and she doesn't know us very well yet. Sometimes it takes people a long time to feel comfortable in a new place."

Discuss characteristics openly while expressing interest in, and appreciation for, differences. Answer children's questions about physical characteristics, abilities, and different cultural practices with information or find out the answer together. Listen to children and counteract stereotypes expressed by using concrete examples whenever possible. For example: "Yes, all the firefighters in that truck were men, but my neighbor, Sarah, is a firefighter, too. She drives a fire engine and fights fires just like they do." "Mrs. K in the office uses a white cane to find her way around our school. It helps her to know where she is and keeps her from bumping into things." Seek books, tell stories, and display pictures that represent a wide variety of people engaging in activities familiar to the children.

Make use of the experiences and emotions of characters in stories to provide additional examples of ideas and feelings that lead to actions, as well as the fact that people can see things from different perspectives. Read interactively, asking children questions and wondering together about how a character will feel. Near the end of the picture book *We're Going on a Bear Hunt,* by Helen Oxenbury, the family tiptoes into a cave, not knowing what they will find. The readers can identify the waiting bear about to be encountered. "We know there's a bear because the picture shows us," the adult reader can say to a group of listening children. "Does the family know yet? How do you think they will feel when they discover him?"

4.0   Empathy and Caring

Preschool children respond with concern when a child or adult is distressed. Children may be confused about why another child is upset, how he or she will be affected, and what can be done.[38, 39] Teachers can help them understand why another person is upset and what the child can do to help. Teachers can also encourage children to respond helpfully to the needs of other children.

VIGNETTE

Chloe cries in Ms. Julia's arms. Ms. Julia pats her back softly and communicates in a soothing manner. "It sounds like that hurt. You can tell Paz you don't like that. Say, 'I don't like that, Paz.'" Chloe tucks her injured arm in toward Ms. Julia's body, shakes her head slowly side to side, and looks out warily at Paz. Paz stands close with her head lowered. "Chloe is upset because you pinched her arm. It hurt her quite a bit. Is there something you think we could do to help her feel better, Paz?" asks Ms. Julia.

Paz responds softly, "Sorry, Chloe," and reaches forward to give Chloe a hug.

Chloe whimpers and clings more closely to Ms. Julia. "When a friend is hurt, giving a hug often helps. I guess Chloe isn't ready for a hug right now. Thank you for trying, Paz. Maybe we can ask her again later."

TEACHABLE MOMENT

 The adult in this scenario models empathy as she provides nurturing care to the injured child. She labels emotions and prompts a helpful action. Despite the injured child's lack of interest in a hug, the adult expresses appreciation for the thoughtful attempt.

The following interactions and strategies encourage and focus children's empathic responses:

Model behavior and attitudes that are warm, respectful, and caring. Give your full attention to a child who is communicating with you and show your interest in the child's perspective. Show your concern when the child is distressed and respond in helpful ways. Suggest that another child help, if appropriate (e.g., bringing a cup of water for a coughing friend). Show children consideration of their needs when planning activities (e.g., "You all seem tired on this hot day. Let's take time for water and then a story so you can relax before we go on with our plans").

Label children's feelings of upset, sadness, and other emotions that convey distress. Children often still need adults to describe a situation, including the incident or action that prompted distress, and to emphasize the link between causes and consequences (e.g., "You told her that she couldn't play with you, and she is upset about that").

Prompt and guide desired behavior. Adults can help younger children learn appropriate responses by suggesting specific, caring actions that may help another child in distress (e.g., "She seems very frustrated that she can't move her wheelchair through the hallway because of the backpacks that are on the floor. Could you move them for her?"). Adults can also suggest specific, caring actions to help children engage with and include English learners in their play.

Acknowledge and express appreciation for children's empathic responses by drawing their attention to specific ways their actions helped and providing them with a general principle that they can remember in future, similar situations (e.g., "When a friend is sad, giving a hug often helps," or "When someone gets hurt, it's important to find an adult to help right away").

Participate in and elaborate on children's pretend-play scripts that include rescue and caring themes. "Oh, no! It looks like one diver is injured. Should I call 911? What else can we do to help her while we're waiting for the rescue boat?"

Read and tell stories that include characters in distress as well as the caring responses of others. While reading *The Runaway Bunny*, by Margaret Wise Brown, for example, draw children's attention to the many ways the mother bunny shows her care and concern for her child. Encourage children to tell about how people in their own families show their care for each other.

Encourage empathy and caring for the natural world, including plants and animals. Program activities that involve nurturing plants and taking care of pets and outdoor life provide opportunities for the expression of empathy and care.

5.0 Initiative in Learning

Preschool children are active, enthusiastic learners who take pleasure in the ability to discover new things. They have confidence in their capacity to learn more and acquire new skills.[40] Teachers support young children's learning initiative when they invite children to share their own ideas, ask questions, or take the lead in investigating a new discovery and when they respond positively to children's eagerness. Teachers are also helpful in encouraging young children to persist rather than give up when they encounter challenges.[41, 42]

VIGNETTE

Mr. Manuel watches Taiga build a structure with blocks. He smiles as he manages to finish an elaborate wall. As Taiga moves to add a piece to the tall tower, he knocks down the foundation. He drops to his knees and slumps his shoulders. Mr. Manuel moves closer to Taiga and responds with an enthusiastic smile. "Wow, Taiga! This is a big tower! (gesturing with his arms). When you stacked the pieces that way (points to the broken section), they seemed a little shaky (moves his hand, palm face down, side to side). Is there something more stable you could find to use this time (points to flatter blocks)?"

TEACHABLE MOMENT

Adults who observe children's interests and needs individualize their support to build confidence and encourage persistence. The teacher in this example notices a child's exploration and sees an opportunity to promote problem solving. His obvious enthusiasm communicates respect and interest in the child's activity of choice and can do much to encourage persistence. By including physical gestures along with words, adults give English learners a deeper understanding of language as children participate in and observe this teacher-child interaction. For more information about strategies to support children who are English learners, see Chapter 5.

The following interactions and strategies can encourage children's initiative in learning:

Provide ample space, use child-sized shelves and furnishings, and adapt materials to make all learning areas and activities accessible. Children's sense of efficacy is enhanced when they are able to seat themselves in a chair or sit at the table in a wheelchair, reach a sink to wash hands without assistance, or collect materials for play. Children are better able to engage in small-muscle activities when their feet can reach the floor or are flat on a surface while seated. Accommodations must be made to ensure all children's successful movement and autonomous exploration of the early learning environment, particularly children with special needs. Create wide pathways and remove obstructions so that all children have access to all play spaces (e.g., for a child who has limited arm movement, toys of interest can be placed on lower shelves).

Make use of adaptive tools and play materials to help the autonomous exploration of children with special needs. Include tactile activities for children with visual impairments. Modify classroom tools by adding handles or grips for children with orthopedic impairments. Specially made "communication books" in the languages of the children in the classroom make possible plans for play for children with autism spectrum disorders.

Observe individual children while they pursue their own activities to determine the child's general level of engagement with classroom activities and materials; the amount of curiosity and enthusiasm a child usually displays; the child's level of self-confidence in abilities; and the amount of persistence the child shows when trying something difficult.

Model curiosity and enthusiasm when you learn new things. Attitudes are contagious, and children will be drawn to imitate an adult's spirit of exploration and pleasure in making discoveries. This is especially important to model for children who may not previously have been given the message that individual experimentation is a valuable means of learning.

Encourage children to choose activities based on their own interests. Asking children periodically about their plans reinforces the idea that they have the power to make their own choices and can help them to refocus on pursuing

something intentionally if they have lost interest in an initial activity. Ensure that classroom materials are attractively labeled and accessible, and furnishings are child-sized. In this way, children can make choices without requiring adult assistance.

Engage in play and exploration with children instead of simply supervising their activities. Adults who are at the child's eye level and engaged with children can help give language to shared discoveries (e.g., "The cars seem to be zooming down these two ramps at different speeds. I wonder why"), question together how something works, and build on each other's ideas. A teacher's active presence models a spirit of inquisitiveness.

Provide ample time for free exploration, scheduling play and exploration periods of at least one uninterrupted hour at a time. A child's initiative as a learner is encouraged when teachers provide sufficient time for in-depth experimentation and exploration. Additional time for open-ended play should be included throughout the day, in both indoor and outdoor learning environments.

Help children generate ideas for solving problems they encounter as they use materials (e.g., balancing blocks, dressing dolls, fastening together collage materials). Express enthusiasm for children's ideas and encourage them to try solutions rather than tell them that an idea will not work.

Model persistence during challenging tasks such as writing a sign, building a marble track, or stringing small beads. Express to children that their unsuccessful attempts to do something are not failures, but simply steps toward learning what will work (e.g., "When you balanced the pieces that way, they seemed a little unsteady. Is there something more stable you can use as the foundation this time?").

Document and display children's work. Pictures of unique explorations, original projects, and dictated stories posted at children's eye level positively influence a child's sense of self as she sees herself and her creations reflected in the environment. These displays also remind children of previous investigations and inspire them to take part in new explorations.

Periodically reassess the preschool environment to ensure that the materials and activity choices support the abilities and reflect the interests of all children in the group. A curriculum and environment that reflect children's emerging interests will maintain their engagement and eagerness to learn.

Bringing It All Together

Yoon Seo ran around the block area swinging one arm wildly up and down and making loud crashing sounds with his voice. All around him, small groups of children were noisily at play. His teacher, Ms. Gloria, watched Yoon Seo carefully to see if his behavior would decrease on its own or increase in intensity. When it was clear that Yoon Seo was becoming more and more agitated in his surroundings, Ms. Gloria walked over slowly and put a gentle hand on his back. "Yoon Seo, you look really excited. It's pretty busy over here." He continued to move around haphazardly and did not seem to notice Ms. Gloria's comment. "I know it's sometimes hard to play in our busy classroom. Let's go take a rest together in the book area where we can look at books, and you can snuggle with your special blanket."

Ms. Gloria and Yoon Seo spent several minutes in the book area looking at books while Yoon Seo held his special blanket up to his cheek. When Yoon Seo appeared relaxed and focused, Ms. Gloria said, "Sometimes we all need a little rest to feel better. When the room gets too noisy for me, I go to the play dough table. It looks like play dough and your blanket help you feel better."

The strategies described above had been planned for Yoon Seo, but similar techniques can help many preschool children. In this situation, Ms. Gloria recognizes that Yoon Seo is overstimulated by his environment and works to help him attend to his personal cues and preferences. Her interaction style is warm and reassuring and helps maintain a positive sense of self for Yoon Seo. She also lets him know what seems to help him "feel better" as a point of reference for the next time he begins to feel overstimulated.

Engaging Families

The following ideas may be suggested by teachers, published in classroom newsletters, or mentioned in parent–teacher conversations, as ways families can enhance their children's social and emotional understanding and self-regulation abilities at home.

✔ Share stories with their children about what they were like as babies and converse together about the ways they have changed and grown.

✔ Respond to children's observations of other people's characteristics by sharing ideas about the many ways people can be the same *and* different.

✔ In circumstances that evoke frustration or sadness (e.g., accidentally spilling something in the kitchen, missing an absent family member), model for children constructive coping strategies. Letting children know that frustrating and sad things happen to everyone sometimes allows family members to share ideas about how to handle strong feelings.

✔ While sharing a storybook with children, wonder together about how the story's characters might be feeling and why. This is one way families can help children identify emotions and learn words that describe them (e.g., *excited, surprised,* and *frustrated*).

✔ Think about the range of activities their children engage in most days and help them balance vigorous activity with calm and focused times.

Questions for Reflection

1. What aspects of your program are most likely to present self-regulation challenges to children? What could you modify to help children with these challenges?

2. What elements of your program's physical environment have you changed or could you change to help children regulate their own behavior more successfully?

3. How do you communicate information about behavior to children's families in ways that help all of you work together to support children's self-regulation?

Social Interaction

Group learning always involves social interaction. The ease and skill with which children interact with adults and peers (in a preschool classroom or family child care program) and the competence with which they assume their roles and responsibilities as group members significantly influence how they learn. The development of these skills in the preschool years is a foundation for children's capacity to be socially skilled and competent classroom members in the primary grades.[43, 44] For some children, unfortunately, difficulties in social interaction—because children are timid and inhibited, are aggressive or disruptive, struggle with being cooperative, or have physical or behavioral characteristics that often result in them being excluded—can pose significant obstacles to benefiting from social interactions with adults and peers. For them and for all children, attention to social interaction skills can be a significant contribution to preschool children's learning in early childhood classrooms.

A thoughtfully designed preschool curriculum that supports social-emotional development devotes considerable attention, therefore, to the direct and indirect ways that classroom experiences shape the growth of children's social interaction skills. In this section, specific strategies are discussed that support development in each of the following substrands:

1.0 Interactions with Familiar Adults
2.0 Interactions with Peers
3.0 Group Participation
4.0 Cooperation and Responsibility

1.0 Interactions with Familiar Adults

Preschool children enjoy interacting with adults they know and are becoming more skilled in sharing their thoughts or feelings, cooperating in play or problem solving, following instructions, asking for assistance, and taking the initiative in social interaction.[45, 46] Adults contribute to these skills when they respond positively and enthusiastically to children's initiatives, model respectful communication and social interaction skills, coach children in their interactions with other adults, and encourage children to confidently share their ideas and experiences with adults.

VIGNETTE

Ju-Hye paints her palms and fingers with a rainbow of colors. With focused concentration, she slowly pushes her palm onto a piece of paper where she has already painted a "stem." She lifts up her hand quickly. Ju-Hye smiles widely and then picks up her paper to show Ms. Betty, who is playing on the floor with two babies. Ms. Betty looks up and responds with a grin: "You finished your flower. You worked hard at mixing colors to make the color of green you wanted for your stem."

Abigail moved to the raised sand table in her wheelchair. Using her left hand to stabilize her right hand, she filled cups with wet sand and carefully dumped them. When her teacher approached, Abigail said, "Look at my cupcakes." The teacher responded, "I watched how hard you worked to make those cupcakes. They look yummy."

TEACHABLE MOMENT

 Children want to share their work with adults who are important to them. In this situation, the caregiver matches the child's positive expression to convey shared excitement about the completed activity. She provides additional descriptive feedback as an affirmation of the child's important work.

The following teacher interactions and strategies can support children's participation in comfortable and positive interactions with familiar adults:

Get to know each child by observing the child's interests, personality characteristics, and preferred interaction style. Interact warmly with the child's family members at arrival and departure times. Match interaction approaches to the child's social cues (e.g., eager to engage, slower to warm up). For more information about strategies to support children who are English learners, see Chapter 5.

Be at the child's level as much as possible by sitting in a low chair or on the floor near where she is engaged in activity. This sends the message that the teacher is interested in what the child is doing and is available to participate or help. This is also important to do when outside. Finding comfortable places to perch while interacting with children outside can enhance the children's social interactions with adults.

Initiate conversations with children about their activities and experiences at home and in the classroom. Respond with interest or information to children's comments and questions. Taking opportunities to engage in conversation about what children are thinking, planning, and doing builds their confidence in initiating similar conversations in the future.

Communicate observations, verbally or through other means, and offer comments or questions about children's explorations. Provide words to clarify, elaborate on, or explain a child's behavior and allow the child to respond with affirmation, correction, or clarification.

Provide specific feedback to children about their efforts instead of general words of praise (e.g., "Good job"). Adults' reactions are important affirmations of support for children's hard work, cooperation, and problem solving. Acknowl-

edging a specific effort allows a teacher to avoid making broad statements that imply judgment of the child's worth based on a product or behavior (e.g., Try "You worked hard at blending colors to make exactly the shade of green you wanted for your painting," rather than "You painted such a pretty picture").

Show respect for cultural differences in your expectations of adult–child communication. Teachers and caregivers must become knowledgeable about the families in their program and find out about their expectations and goals. If a child's culture emphasizes maintaining a respectful distance between teachers and children, teachers can modify their behavior to remain approachable and friendly but not inappropriately casual or familiar. Alternatively, if the child's family is exceptionally affectionate and physical with one another, the teacher can be warm yet maintain a comfortable boundary with the child while acknowledging the difference (e.g., "I know you and your Uma grandma like to give each other lots of kisses. I like to get just one kiss from you").

Encourage children to see familiar adults as resources and become comfortable in asking regular volunteers and assistants for help and support when needed. Teachers may coach and accompany more hesitant children as they practice approaching other adult helpers and guests (e.g., "It looks like you have a question for our guest reader. Would you like me to come with you to ask it?").

2.0   Interactions with Peers

Preschoolers enjoy interacting with other children and are rapidly developing the skills to socialize cooperatively, negotiate conflict, and respect the feelings of another child. Their interactions become longer and more complex, with greater sharing and mutual communication.[47, 48] This development can be seen especially in pretend play. These abilities are limited, however, especially when children are in conflict; thus adult guidance is necessary to support constructive social interactions and help children find ways of managing disagreements. Adults also encourage the development of peer interaction skills by helping children understand the feelings of other children, suggesting and modeling interaction skills, such as turn-taking, encouraging the use of words when disagreements arise, and reinforcing cooperative efforts.

VIGNETTE

Myrna and Emma sort through dresses in a trunk in the dramatic play area. They dig deep into the pile, tossing aside unwanted costumes. Then, their eyes open wide as they both reach for the pale blue "princess" dress.

"I want to wear it. I'm the princess," shouts Myrna with furrowed brows.

Emma tugs back and says, "No! I want it. It's mine!" The tugging and shouting continues to increase in intensity when Mr. Charlie notices the struggle and walks over to mediate. Mr. Charlie gets down and kneels between the two girls.

"Myrna, you look upset. And Emma, you look mad too! What's happening?"

"I want to wear the princess dress. I'm the princ—" exclaims Myrna.

"I'm the princess!" interrupts Emma.

"It sounds like you both want to wear that dress. You both want to be the princess. We have a problem. I can hold the dress while we think of what to do." The two girls slowly let go of the dress and lower their heads.

"I know. I can have a turn and then Myrna can have it," says Emma, popping her head up with bright eyes.

"I want to be first," Myrna responds with a small scowl.

"You both want to go first. Hmm . . . let's see if we can think of another idea," wonders Mr. Charlie.

"She can wear this one," says Myrna, holding up a purple dress.

Emma looks at the dress and shakes her head. "I'll wear the blue dress, and you can have it in five minutes," offers Emma, holding up five fingers.

"What do you think, Myrna? Emma says she would like to wear the dress for five minutes, and then you may have a turn."

Myrna folds her arms in front of her chest, sighs, and then nods her head slowly. "Five minutes," she says firmly.

TEACHABLE MOMENT

▶ Children with positive experiences in conflict resolution approach such situations with attention and persistence. With practice they are quite capable of offering and agreeing upon solutions. In this situation, Mr. Charlie sees an opportunity to guide children through effective problem-solving techniques. He provides calm support and patience as both children assert their ideas for a reasonable solution. The above example describes children who readily verbalize their emotions. Some children will communicate their strong emotional reactions in other ways. Teachers should be alert to different cues expressed by different children in order to support skill development in this area.

The following teacher interactions and strategies can support children as they learn and refine their skills in interacting with peers:

Observe the level of social interaction skills that each child brings to the group. Social skills will vary across the preschool age range, depending partially on the amount and type of experience with peers that children have encountered prior to preschool. Note especially

whether a child can initiate or enter into play with another child; work with others to accomplish a simple, shared goal (e.g., putting together a puzzle, dividing play dough so that each person has some); communicate with others in acting out a complex pretend-play script (e.g., going on a trip with a family, including assigning and playing family roles); negotiate with another child to resolve a conflict about play materials or behaviors; and ask for and respond to adult coaching in resolving peer disputes and practicing new social skills with peers. Young children with developmental differences or younger children in a mixed-age setting may need additional support and teaching to develop these initial skills with other children.

Model effective and respectful interaction by joining pairs or groups of children as they play and work together. Follow the children's cues about your participation. Teachers can thoughtfully partner English learners with English-speaking peers to help scaffold social interactions and English-language development. Be an interested observer or play supporting roles in pretend-play sequences or constructive play projects (e.g., "You are discussing the animals that will live in the zoo you're building. How are you deciding which ones to choose?" or, "Yes, I could be your new next-door-neighbor. Shall I ask if your family needs any help moving in?"). For a child who is still learning this skill, the teacher can provide more explicit cues and guided interactions (e.g., "You are looking at the truck Pedro is holding and reaching for it. Why don't you ask Pedro 'Can I play with that truck?'" Colby reaches for the truck saying, "My play wif truck?" Pedro hands the truck to Colby and gets a different truck from the shelf for himself. "Pedro, Colby really looks happy that you gave him the truck. That is great sharing"). For more information about strategies to support children who are English learners, see Chapter 5.

Verbalize observations. Provide language to describe children's actions, feelings, and responses observed during play. Be especially sensitive to doing this for children who may find it hard to speak for themselves in a group situation (e.g., "It looks like you are all slithering around like crocodiles. I notice Marcos is standing here watching you. Marcos, would you like to be a crocodile, too?").

Incorporate play materials that promote and encourage peer play. It is a good idea to include indoor and outdoor materials, such as large wooden blocks or heavy loose parts (e.g., tree cookies, small logs) that require the effort and cooperation of a pair of children. Purposefully planning a "birthday party" in the dramatic play area brings about

discussion of friendship and inclusion. Think of encouraging peer play while outside as well. A child who is less able to move quickly or ride the wheeled toys can be the person who takes the toll payment at the bridge or pumps gas at the pit stops.

Suggest extensions for children's cooperative play to add complexity to their interactions and negotiations. Teachers can stay nearby to support them as they practice more complex problem solving together.

Coach young children, step by step, as they learn conflict resolution skills. Model a predictable, effective sequence of steps children can eventually use on their own: acknowledge feelings, gather information about the conflict, restate the problem, ask children to suggest possible solutions, help them choose one to try, and then check back with them soon after as they implement their solution. As they mature and practice, gradually step back and take a less central role in solving problems, prompting children if they "get stuck" on the path to resolution. After they do resolve a conflict, briefly summarize the ways children solved the problem successfully. This reinforces children's skills for the next time a problem arises. See Sample Developmental Sequence: Conflict Negotiation, below.

Generalize from actions to principles to increase children's understanding of the things that helped their interactions

Sample Developmental Sequence
Conflict Negotiation

As children mature, they are able to better understand the perspectives of other people and can negotiate more constructively with peers to resolve conflicts.

Beginning level: Children can express to each other (using words, actions, or facial expressions) their own desires, but adults need to provide ideas for resolving disputes.

Next level: Children begin to use appropriate words and actions to express their perspectives and desires to each other and seek adults for help during disputes.

Next level: Children not only express their own needs and desires to each other during a conflict but can suggest simple solutions based on their own perspectives.

Mature or proficient level: Children can consider each other's perspectives when there is a disagreement and can suggest and agree on some mutually acceptable solutions.

with each other to be successful. "You two both wanted the big blue tricycle, so you told each other that and worked out a plan to take turns for three minutes each. Sharing ideas with each other about problems helps us solve those problems."

Use books, puppet stories, and group discussions to reinforce children's social interaction skills. Select materials and topics that relate to what children in the group are encountering frequently in their interactive play or skills they are struggling to master.

Plan for project work, based on children's emerging interests, in pairs and small groups. During projects, children can explore materials together, collaborate to solve problems they encounter, and communicate with each other as they work. Adults can facilitate the interactions, using language and techniques that match the needs and abilities of the children.

3.0 Group Participation

Preschool children enjoy being part of the classroom and are learning the roles and responsibilities of group participation. These include taking turns, sharing, participating in group activities, taking other children's interests into consideration, knowing what to do during group routines (e.g., circle time) or games (such as Follow the Leader), helping to prepare for and clean up after activities, and understanding and applying rules for classroom behavior.[49] These skills require considerable self-regulation, which is why preschool children benefit when adults provide guidance and coaching, offer reminders about expected behavior, explain why things are done the way they are, reinforce constructive conduct, and use prompts, such as songs or games, to support effective group participation.

VIGNETTE

Ms. Luisa gathers a small group of children outside for an activity. "Okay, everybody. To make a really large bubble that covers Claire, we all have to work together to lift the hula hoop up around her. Do you we think can do it?" The children respond with excitement, "Yeah!" Ms. Luisa smiles and continues, "Well, how will we all know when to lift? Does anybody have an idea? It's really important that we all start at the same time."

Noah asserts, "I know. We can count like a rocket ship."

"You mean a countdown? We could say, 'ten, nine, eight, seven, six, five, four, three, two, one and then lift?" clarifies Ms. Luisa.

"Yeah! Like a rocket ship!" agrees Erika.

"Do you all want to try Noah's idea?" asks Ms. Luisa. The children eagerly agree, and Ms. Luisa leads them in a countdown. On cue, they lift together to surround Claire in a large bubble. Claire smiles excitedly.

Shayna exclaims, "It's working!"

Meera adds, "We did it!"

Ms. Luisa applauds the group. "It did work. Noah, your idea helped everybody make a giant bubble around Claire. We all make a really good team!"

TEACHABLE MOMENT

 In this situation, the adult plans a group-learning experience intended to build cooperation and practice group problem solving. Through this playful activity, the teacher intentionally highlights individual and group strengths.

The following teacher interactions and strategies can support children as they learn the challenging skills required of them for participation in preschool groupings:

Model cooperative behavior and attitudes. Engage in authentic conversation with a small group of children. Use appropriate eye contact and touch with each child. Acknowledge a child who wants to respond to a book or song. Actively listen and respond to a child's idea. Participate in the group interaction with enthusiasm, animation, and full attention.

Plan large-group gatherings with flexibility. Get to know each group of children well enough to learn what they can participate in successfully. Plan for a group dialogue rather than a teacher monologue while reading a story, singing a song, or introducing a concept. Allow for children's active participation and be flexible in changing the lesson plan to follow the group's interest or activity level (e.g., when counting together the ladybugs on a book's page, try to respond to, and possibly extend, a child's comment about the ladybugs the class found on the playground yesterday. If children are restless, briefly flying around the circle like ladybugs may also be a helpful activity extension). Provide an alternative to group participation (e.g., "cool-down

area") where a child can self-regulate away from the group. If the group experiences are meaningful and reflective of children's interests, the children will return to the group activity as their bodies and minds are ready to participate effectively.

Guide and coach children's behavior. Use positive, respectful phrasing and tone to give brief instructions and reminders (e.g., "Jonah, it's easier for all our friends to see the book when you sit down," or "Remember, if you have an idea to share during circle time, please raise your hand first to let us know you want a turn to share your idea"). Quietly suggest an alternative activity to a child who is not able to stay with the group successfully.

Comment on children's actions: "You are all jumping just like frogs!" or "I see that Maddie is trying to find a spot on the rug where she can jump without being pushed. Jorge, thank you for making space for her." Be especially sensitive to doing this for children who may be less inclined to speak up for themselves in a group setting, including children who are English learners and children with physical disabilities.

Rehearse and prompt desired responses. Move to a new activity by reminding the group about how to transition into it successfully (e.g., "We still have time to sing, 'Everybody Do This'. Let's stay on our carpet squares so we each have enough space to move"). Sing call-and-response songs, such as Ella Jenkins's collections of traditional African American and Caribbean songs, to practice listening and responding in unison to a leader.

Acknowledge positive choices. When children participate in positive ways during a small- or large-group activity, comment on what they did that made the activity successful and draw their attention to how it helped (e.g., "When we were exploring the tub of sand at small-group time today, you decided to take turns using the big scoop. That way, everyone got a chance to feel how heavy a big scoop of sand would be").

Generalize from action to principle. After commenting on children's helpful actions, state the general group goal that their actions help to accomplish. Children can understand that they make positive contributions to building a classroom community (e.g., "During circle time, you moved over so the children behind you could see the pictures. In our class, we take good care of each other").

Build a sense of community through planned group experiences. Large-group experiences that are age- and developmentally appropriate make an ideal setting in which to establish community and build shared knowledge. Children learn turn-taking skills and active listening techniques as they participate in cooperative conversation. Build a repertoire of songs and games, some of which incorporate children's names. Activity props (e.g., parachute, large ball) that require teamwork are useful. Dramatize familiar stories (e.g., *Caps for Sale, Ten in a Bed)* that have roles for everyone and do not require advanced English-language skills or

specific physical movements. Teachers can help children to lead group inquiries based on their experiences and ideas (e.g., "When Luis and Kim were weeding our garden, they noticed big holes in some of the lettuce leaves. Here's one they brought in to show us. What do you think could have made these holes?").

Arrange large-group meeting spaces to enhance planned activities. Choose a large, open-area meeting space away from attractive play materials. Sit together in a circle so each individual has a clear view of teachers and peers, enabling members to attend and respond to verbal and nonverbal communication, as well as visual prompts. Carpet squares help young children maintain ample personal space and encourage self- and attentional control. Children with physical disabilities or who use special equipment for mobility can maintain the same (or similar) spacing parameters.[a]

Structure small-group activity areas to maximize focus. Choose a space that is comfortable for work, such as tables or enclosed carpeted spaces. For younger preschoolers, a consistent meeting space builds their knowledge of routines, enabling them to recall and apply group rules and expectations. Older preschoolers demonstrate familiarity and flexibility

[a] When the group includes a child who uses a wheelchair, consideration should be given for finding a way for children to be at the same level, perhaps through small chairs or stools for all the children. Sometimes, assigned seating can help children be in the spaces that will promote their greatest participation. For example, a child who needs gentle physical touch from an adult to remain focused can be placed next to the teacher. A child who is hard of hearing and needs to see the teacher's face can reliably sit directly across from her. Additionally, attention should be given to seating for children who are visually impaired or blind so that they can participate in large-group activities (e.g., Claire is very sensitive to glare because of albinism, so she must sit with the window behind her. Tomas is blind and sits next to the teacher during circle time, so he can touch the things she uses during the activity).

with routines. After meeting in their designated space, older preschoolers are able to engage wherever the selected materials are located.

Think through group size and composition. Choose to plan large-group activities (e.g., musical games) with smaller groups of children. Smaller, large-group activities may be more manageable for younger preschoolers who are new to teacher-initiated experiences that require children's knowledge of routines and higher levels of self-control. To form well-balanced groups, use your knowledge of individual interests, energy, developmental age, and emerging friendships. For more information about strategies to support children who are English learners, see Chapter 5.

Prepare materials ahead of time. Preparing materials in advance of activities is essential to create high-quality learning experiences. Books, songs, and curriculum materials should be intentionally selected based on observations of children's ongoing explorations in the classroom. High-quality curriculum reflects an awareness of the child's home culture and community. Having ample amounts of materials eliminates waiting and ensures the active involvement of all children.

Incorporate nonverbal prompts. Nonverbal prompts, such as props and picture or symbol cues, remind children of routines and expectations and can facilitate communication, group participation and responsibilities, and event knowledge. Showing a picture of musical notes at large-group time may indicate it is time to sing. A picture of an ear can illustrate that it is time to listen to a story. Visual prompts are especially effective in engaging children who are developing English-language skills and children with delays in language or cognition. Posted guidelines for group participation (including pictures and symbols) increase shared understanding. Gestures may be taught to and used by children to express their ideas or choices (e.g., a child may make a gesture for "more" after hearing a favorite song). Teachers may also use gestures to communicate expectations for behavior (e.g., a teacher makes a gesture for "sit" as she says "We sit at circle time").

Address individual needs through the use of strategies and tools. Some children may require extra individual assistance to successfully participate in group experiences. Many strategies were mentioned earlier. In addition, providing something tangible for a child to hold (e.g., a small squeeze toy such as a stress ball or squishy ball) assists children who need something to manipulate with their hands to self-regulate and maintain self-control. Real objects that represent items in a book or a song will help the child with a visual impairment successfully participate in group experiences. For children who blurt out ideas regularly, teachers can have a message board ready to document the child's ideas for a song to sing or a book to read at another time. This can help the group stay focused and reengage a distracted child's behavioral and attentional control.

4.0   Cooperation and Responsibility

Preschool children seek to cooperate with adult instructions in order to obtain the adult's approval and be viewed as helpful, constructive classroom contributors.[50, 51, 52] As self-control is slowly developing, however, young children often need adult support, especially when they are distressed or frustrated.

Adults provide this support when they ensure that classroom expectations are developmentally, culturally, and linguistically appropriate. Children are reminded of expected conduct and of ways in which they can contribute to a classroom environment where children enjoy cooperating with one another.

VIGNETTE

Mr. Ravi and his group of preschool children enter the play yard on Monday morning. As several children run to the sandbox, Vicente shouts with dismay, "Oh, look! Somebody ruined our fort and messed up all the hiding places we dug for our food! That was mean!" Mr. Ravi comes over quickly to join them. He surveys the logs and boulders strewn around in the sand and notes the children's distress and sense of outrage.

Mr. Ravi responds sympathetically, "You all spent so much time working together to build this last Friday. It does seem unfair that it has been destroyed. Do you have ideas about what to do?"

Vicente suggests, "I know! We can make it over again and then you can write a sign that says, 'Keep Out. This is OUR fort.'" The other children agree.

Mr. Ravi says, "It sounds like you have a plan to rebuild and protect your project. I know that Marcos can write words and likes to make signs. Why don't you ask him if he would be willing to make the sign you need?" The children agree with this idea, and Mr. Ravi accompanies them to talk to Marcos, who sits alone on the stairs. "This is going to take a lot of teamwork," comments Mr. Ravi.

"Yeah, but we're getting really good at teamwork," responds Vicente confidently.

TEACHABLE MOMENT

 In this situation, the teacher affirms the group's sense of outrage and stays involved in guiding them to a positive solution while allowing them to take responsibility for making good decisions. He refers them to another, more socially isolated child who has the writing skills their project requires. The teacher follows through to facilitate his inclusion. He affirms the importance of teamwork and conveys his confidence that they are capable of repairing the damage together. An intentional adult draws attention to instances of cooperation and the positive outcome of shared work.

The following teacher interactions and strategies can strengthen children's ability to demonstrate cooperation and responsibility in the preschool setting:

Develop a warm and secure relationship with each child. The quality of adult–child relationships motivates children toward cooperation and responsibility. Children are motivated to cooperate with adult requests and standards partly because of their emotional attachments to those adults and their desire to maintain positive relationships with them. Preschool children need a strong sense of connection and attachment with the teachers and staff. Try to spend at least a brief, special time with each child regularly to maintain a close bond.

Ensure that adult expectations for children's behavior are developmentally appropriate. Preschool children are active and are usually most successful when involved in self-initiated learning activities that engage their interest. Large-group activities that require long periods of quiet attention often do not match their capabilities. Appropriate learning goals can be accomplished through a well-planned program of activities tailored to children's maturity levels.

Move beyond rules to expectations to emphasize guiding principles or values. State a reason along with a request. Communication such as, "Let's all move back a little to make room in the circle for everyone," informs children of the immediate goal of the request. Adding, "In our class we make sure that everyone is included because we are friendly and kind," broadens that goal and states the general principle/expectation behind it: that of including or taking care of each other.

Enlist children's participation in creating examples of school or classroom expectations. Expectations of classroom behavior, such as "We are safe, we are respectful, we are friendly and kind," can be used across all settings within a school. The children can help come up with examples of how they show safety, respect, and teamwork. Photographs of the children engaged in teamwork, for example, may be posted as a reminder. The expectations can be reviewed regularly, as well as acknowledged when observed by the adults, in order to support the learning of the social guidelines.[53]

Focus on building a sense of classroom community among children and adults. Teachers can model and facilitate friendly, responsible behavior that shows respect for other people and for program materials. Enthusiastically draw attention to instances of cooperation and teamwork among children who accomplished a goal together. Group meetings are held to make decisions (e.g., "What shall we name our new guinea pig?") or to brainstorm solutions to problems

that arise. Encourage brainstorming and problem solving in pairs or small groups to build children's trust in their own social competence and good judgment.

Refer children to each other, instead of to an adult, for assistance to facilitate connections. This practice can also serve to include or emphasize the strengths of children who may be overlooked in other social situations. Encourage children to work together on tasks to help maintain the indoor and outdoor program spaces. In this way, children gain a sense of cooperative ownership and responsibility for the space.

Rehearse and prompt desired actions, especially for transition times. Do with children what you are asking them to do until they understand your expectations. Post the daily classroom routine and refer to a picture/word/symbol chart, as appropriate, so that children can anticipate and prepare psychologically for transitions. A transition song or chant can help children focus on a transition task (e.g., "Come and Make a Circle"; "Clean up, Clean up, Everybody

Everywhere"). Give individual reminders about behavioral expectations ahead of time to children who have more difficulty complying with requests or managing transitions. For English learners, individual reminders will help prepare them for behavioral expectations and provide an opportunity to clarify English words and phrases. Prompt a specific, desired behavior by making a request in the affirmative (e.g., "Please move carefully around people's block towers") instead of a negative prohibition (e.g., "Don't run in the block area"). For more information about strategies to support children who are English learners, see Chapter 5.

Bringing It All Together

Lucas stands close to his caregiver, Ms. Mai, who is sitting in the block area. Ms. Mai observes Lucas watching his peers at play as they build a large train. "This train is getting really big," she comments to Lucas with a soft smile and a gentle hand on his back. Lucas nods his head slowly. "I wonder if Martin needs a helper. He said he is the engineer, but an engineer needs a conductor. Would you like to hand out and collect tickets?" Lucas nods his head again and reaches for Ms. Mai's hand as she gets up to move closer to the train. Ms. Mai provides Lucas her hand and another reassuring smile. "You could let Martin know you want to help. Tell Martin 'I can collect the tickets.'"

Lucas pauses and then mumbles (or signs), "Martin, I can collect tickets."

"You all look like you are having fun over here. Lucas wants to help too. Where are the tickets for Lucas to pass out to your riders?" restates Ms. Mai.

"Oh! Over there," responds Martin, pointing over to the basket of torn pieces of paper.

"Thanks, Martin, for your help. Lucas, let's go get the tickets and hand them to our friends. I think these builders will want to fill the train with passengers," observes Ms. Mai excitedly.

This anecdote illustrates the importance of quality teacher–child relationships as a foundation for interaction with peers and group participation. A warm, caring adult can serve as a model for exploring social skills and as a reassuring presence. Providing prompts, narrating social experiences, and participating as a co-explorer in children's play all support social interactions.

Engaging Families

The following ideas may be suggested to families in newsletters or parent–teacher conversations as ways of helping their children learn and practice skills for constructive interaction and cooperation.

✔ Have conversations with children about things they are thinking, planning, and doing. Offer specific comments or questions about children's activities and ask children to describe in more detail things they bring home.

✔ Encourage children to work out a disagreement with a sibling or friend by suggesting to each other ideas for solving the problem. Remind children to consider each other's needs and feelings as they choose a solution to try. Stay close by to help children as they practice using words to resolve a conflict.

✔ Ask children for help with household chores or projects. Discuss, while working together, some things each person can do to help the family.

✔ Emphasize to children the family's values about such things as cooperation, teamwork, good manners, and kindness toward other people.

Questions for Reflection

1. How do you help a child who has trouble entering a group already at play?

2. What kinds of social skills have you been able to effectively help children learn by modeling for them?

3. What are your most difficult challenges when you try to support children during their dramatic play?

Relationships

Relationships shape young children's learning. From infancy, parent–child and family relationships guide and motivate children's love for discovery and learning and provide a secure foundation for the growth of exploration and self-confidence.[54] In the classroom, special adults and friends make preschool an inviting place for children.[55, 56] The teacher is a bridge for the child, connecting her to relationships at home and in the classroom. Young children's close relationships contribute in concert to the growth of early learning.

A thoughtfully designed preschool curriculum that supports social-emotional development devotes considerable attention, therefore, to the direct and indirect ways that children's relationships at home and in the classroom or family child care program are important to early learning. In this section, specific strategies are discussed that support development in each of the following substrands:

1.0 Attachments to Parents
2.0 Close Relationships with Teachers and Caregivers
3.0 Friendships

1.0   Attachments to Parents

Preschool children bring to their classroom the security they receive from their primary family members.[57, 58] Their attachment can be seen most clearly at the beginning and the end of the day, when children affectionately depart from and later reunite with their family members, excitedly sharing achievements or asking for help. It can also be observed when young children are distressed and seek the special comfort and support that their family members provide. Teachers recognize the importance of family to preschool children when they initiate conversations about events at home or family culture and language. Teachers may encourage children to bring things from home to share with the group while helping new children manage separations. A consultation with family members may be needed when teachers notice that a child in their care is showing unusual behavioral or emotional difficulties.

VIGNETTE

Araceli sits quietly at the writing station. Her family child care provider, Ms. Cindy, notices squiggles and letter-like forms on her paper. "What are you working on, Araceli?" Ms. Cindy asks.

"A letter for Mamá. She is on an airplane," Araceli replies with a sad expression on her face.

"That's right. Mamá had to fly to Los Angeles to take care of Grandma. It sounds like you are thinking about her," Ms. Cindy responds as she sits down and leans close.

"I am telling her I miss her. And kiss kiss. She likes kisses."

Ms. Cindy nods her head and offers, "It's hard when moms and dads go on trips. We miss them very much. Would you like any help writing your letter?"

Araceli looks up and responds, "Write 'come home soon.'"

TEACHABLE MOMENT

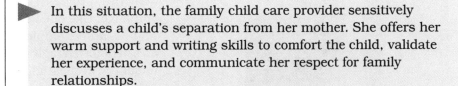

In this situation, the family child care provider sensitively discusses a child's separation from her mother. She offers her warm support and writing skills to comfort the child, validate her experience, and communicate her respect for family relationships.

The following interactions and strategies can help to affirm children's sense of continuity and connection between home and preschool:

Establish a warm and collaborative relationship with each child's family, beginning with the first meeting of the family and continuing through the time of enrollment and beyond. Arrange a "getting-to-know-you" meeting with the child and family or conduct a home visit. Collaborate with the child's family in completing an initial child assessment that includes family goals, expectations, and concerns (e.g., How do the child's family members describe the child? What do they hope will be accomplished at preschool?). A photograph of the child and family may be displayed on a "family board" (at the child's eye level) in the classroom. Invite each family to visit the program and share time, skills, or projects with the group. The child's achievements (e.g., artwork, dictated stories) should be prominently displayed in the classroom for family members to see. Draw parents' attention to the display with appreciative comments.

Talk with children regularly about their families. Listen to and sympathize with children's feelings about separation from their family members. Help children to manage separation by providing consistent, nurturing support during the preschool day. Ask children about their home activities and experiences and encourage them to bring items or share news from home with the group. Communicate positively about each child's family and cultural practices. Find out what language the child speaks at home and incorporate that language in classroom activities. Incorporate family photos and home materials in the classroom environment.

Create predictable arrival and departure routines. Provide a warm and welcome area for children and families at the beginning of the day. Help families design a predictable good-bye routine for their child. Invite them to make use of quiet areas in the classroom to allow slow-to-warm children to make the transition to the space. Offer parents the idea of reading a book or enjoying a simple activity with their child before leaving. Remind parents to avoid sneaking out after their arrival.

Communicate frequently with family members about children's preschool activities, progress, and any concerns you have. Use documentation displays, photos, and examples of children's work as a tool for engaging parents and family members in meaningful conversation. Ask family members to share with you information that could help you to work better with the child. For more information about strategies to support children who are English learners, see Chapter 5.

2.0 Close Relationships with Teachers and Caregivers

Preschool children develop special relationships with teachers and caregivers and rely on these relationships for security and support in the program.[59, 60] This dependence can be observed when young children seek the assistance of a special teacher when distressed or needing help (sometimes refusing the assistance of other adults) or look to a special caregiver to play a game, display a new discovery, or share an experience from home. Teachers recognize the importance of these close relationships to a young child's self-confidence and feelings about preschool when they affirm the child's initiatives, convey enthusiasm for the child's accomplishments, pay attention when the child needs assistance or comfort, and seek to develop a friendly, cooperative relationship with the child's primary family members.

VIGNETTE

Tanya eagerly comes through the front door and greets caregiver Natalya with her news: "Ms. Natalya, we went to the fair last night, and I got to pet goats and sheeps and chickens, except Papa said to stay back from the ducks, because they have bills that can bite you fast!"

Ms. Natalya knelt down, and Tanya reached out to her. "Wow, Tanya! You sound really excited about your night at the fair. Did your whole family go, Grandpa too?" she asked, looking at Tanya's papa, who had accompanied her to the family child care home. Mr. Terebkov smiled and nodded, responding that it had been an enjoyable but late night for all of them. Ms. Natalya prompted Tanya to hug Papa good-bye, and then Tanya reached for Ms. Natalya's hand as they moved together into the play area. Ms. Natalya asked Tanya more about her favorite part of the county fair.

TEACHABLE MOMENT

In this encounter, Tanya's family child care provider demonstrates her warm, responsive relationship with both Tanya and her father at arrival time. She responds with warmth when Tanya reaches out to her and then wants to hold her hand while entering the play area. She expresses interest in the news Tanya shares excitedly and pursues the topic enthusiastically as Tanya makes the transition into her day in Ms. Natalya's program.

The following interactions and strategies can help develop close relationships between teachers or caregivers and children:

Build and maintain a pattern of warm, nurturing interactions with each child in the designated group. Ensure that each child has a primary teacher or caregiver who will greet, support, and consistently respond to the child's needs, especially at times of distress. Engage each child by name frequently. Match the adult's interaction to the child's social cues.

Demonstrate in the child's presence a friendly, cooperative, and respectful relationship with the child's family. Greet, communicate with, and touch the child in ways that are consistent with the values of the child's culture (e.g., whether a child is expected to wait until the teacher speaks or whether he should address the teacher using a formal name rather than a first name).

Encourage child–adult collaboration in learning. Participate as co-explorers in children's projects and explorations. Convey enthusiasm for each child's efforts and interest in their ideas. Engage in extended conversation about topics a child introduces.

Research Highlight

How important is the relationship between young children and their teachers for school success? In one study, researchers measured the quality of child–teacher relationships in preschool, kindergarten, and first grade, and also measured children's social and academic skills in first grade. They found that academic and social skills were each positively associated with measures of child–teacher closeness and negatively associated with child–teacher conflict. Teacher–child relationships at all ages—preschool, kindergarten, and first grade—were important.[61]

3.0 Friendships

Preschool children enjoy the friendships they develop with each other. They typically have one or two particular children whom they identify as friends and with whom they play and share other activities.[62] Teachers recognize the importance of friendships to social and emotional development when they encourage young children to enjoy shared activities with friends. Teachers help children recognize and respond appropriately to their friends' feelings and preferences, assisting in conflict resolution while also encouraging participation in group activities.

VIGNETTE

Adrian enters the classroom with twinkling eyes and a wide smile. He runs to the cubby shelf and quickly stows his backpack. After popping back up, he speeds over to Ms. Caitlin, who is sitting at the art table. "Where's Jorge?"

Ms. Caitlin smiles, kneels down next to Adrian, and says, "Good morning, Adrian! You seem excited to find your friend Jorge. I know how much you enjoy playing with him. Let's see . . . I think I see him building over in the block area." Ms. Caitlin walks with Adrian across the room over to the block area. "I wonder if your plan today is to make a train with Jorge? He looks pretty busy over there."

"I'm gonna help too! Jorge! Jorge!" exclaims Adrian excitedly as he skips over to join Jorge in the block area.

TEACHABLE MOMENT

 In this situation, the child utilizes his close relationship with his teacher to connect with an important friend. The teacher thoughtfully puts language on a developing friendship and helps the child find his preferred playmate in the classroom.

The following teacher interactions and strategies can acknowledge and support the role of friendships within the classroom group:

Plan a program that offers choices of activities and associations with peers. Develop learning areas that reflect the various interests and abilities of members of the class. Provide several areas that comfortably accommodate only two or three children so that friends have opportunities to engage in more complex activities for extended, uninterrupted periods of time. Respect a child's preference for play at times with only one friend or group of friends.

Use ongoing observations to inform your social structuring of experiences. Consider existing friendships when organizing small-group activities or mealtime groups. Stucture small-group activities so that more-hesitant children work on projects with others whose interests and styles seem compatible. Coach and support a child who is more socially isolated to enter into play with another child who shares similar interests and characteristics. Work intensively with children whose social skills are lagging to coach them in social situations. Coach preschool friends through the often intense interactions that may occur between friends with strong emotional attachments to each other.

Use books, puppet plays, and group discussions to identify and reinforce friendship skills (e.g., negotiation and conflict resolution, sensitivity to others' feelings, loyalty). Interactions between the characters in a book, such as the neighborhood children in *Chester's Way,* by Kevin Henkes, can lead to discussions about ways to show loyalty to an old friend while including a new one, and the choices children face when playmates have a variety of personality characteristics.

Communicate with children's families about their preschool friendships and encourage out-of-school contact with school friends, if possible. Reassure family members about age-typical friendship behavior. Concerns about any problematic social behavior observed at preschool should be shared with them, too. Communicate with the families of children who are more socially isolated about strategies used at preschool. Families can reinforce the strategies at home and in the community. Asking families for their ideas about other strategies to try strengthens the home–school connection.

Bringing It All Together

"No, you're not!" shouts Michelle. "Yes, I am! I'm the Mommy!" screams Lily.

"Well, you are a Silly Pilly. You're not my friend anymore" counters Michelle, standing with her hands on her hips and a scowl on her face.

At Michelle's words, Lily's lip begins to quiver. Tears form in her eyes as she yells, "I am your friend! I am!"

Miss Sandra moves over to the confrontation, kneels between the girls, and says with concern, "You both look really upset. Something is wrong. Can you tell me what is happening?"

"She said I am not her friend!" exclaims Lily, trying to overcome her tears.

"She is being a mean-y pants. I don't like her," says Michelle.

"It sounds like both of you have hurt feelings. Being friends with someone means that sometimes we disagree and we get mad or sad. It sounds like that is happening right now. What can we do?"

"I am going to play with David," huffs Michelle as she marches off. Lily leans into Miss Sandra.

Miss Sandra considers what she knows about each child's individual temperament before responding: "It's tricky sometimes with friends. Why don't we take a little break from playing with Michelle? I'll bet she will be ready to play later when you are both feeling better." Miss Sandra helps Lily get involved in a new activity and then makes a mental note to check with each child's parent at departure time.

Children express interests and needs within a peer relationship in a variety of ways. Not all children will be as overt as Michelle and Lily, but the astute teacher can identify these differences and support peers much as Miss Sandra did in the scenario.

As young children explore friendship, they rely on their relationships with adults for support. Teachers and caregivers serve as a resource for understanding individual interests and needs within a peer relationship. Opportunities for independent and guided learning are required for children to build their relationship skills. Sensitive adult support helps children build the flexibility and resiliency needed for the challenges typical in any healthy relationship. Keeping families informed includes them as partners in their child's learning and development at preschool.

Engaging Families

There are ways to both strengthen adult–child relationships and to help children practice relationship skills. The following strategies can be suggested to families for use at home.

✔ Start a special good-bye ritual to use with a preschool child every day (e.g., a hug, kiss, or special words, followed by a wave at the window) when it is time to leave. A predictable routine is reassuring and makes the transition easier.

✔ Find at least a few minutes every day to spend as special time with each child. Family members may choose to read a book together, go on an errand, sing favorite songs, or converse about the day as they do a chore together.

✔ Meet the child's primary preschool teacher or caregiver and greet each other in a friendly way at each arrival and departure. Showing that parents and teachers are working together helps a child see that both value learning and share in teaching.

✔ Make sure that a preschool child has opportunities—at home, in the neighborhood, or with relatives—to play with other children and to practice positive social skills.

Questions for Reflection

1. How did the adult's response in this situation affect the two friends involved? How would you have responded in this situation?

2. What things do you do to help preschool children manage the strong emotions that are often part of their friendships?

3. What kind of information do you share with families about their children's preschool friendships? How do families help inform you about their child's relationships with friends?

Concluding Thoughts

The heart of a curriculum that nurtures children's social-emotional development is play. A play-based, active learning approach allows many opportunities for practicing social interaction and relationship skills. It provides support for the growth of age- and developmentally appropriate self-regulation abilities. It encourages children's own curiosity and initiative. Finally, play in a well-planned early learning program provides each child with a network of nurturing, dependable adults who will actively support and scaffold their learning in a group setting.

To be effective in accomplishing early learning goals, an active, play-based program must allow children to freely choose and pursue interests and activities, both alone and with others. It must encourage them to translate their own thoughts, ideas, and preferences into new activities and experiments. It must give them access to these opportunities for activity and exploration in a thoughtfully planned environment for a substantial portion of each preschool day. And most importantly, it must be planned and led by teachers who actively participate as co-explorers in children's chosen activities. In this context, play is essential and is enhanced if materials are available to encourage creativity and problem solving, and if teachers are attentive to the social interactions that surround children's play. This active, enthusiastic engagement of children and adults together in a learning community can lead to dramatic growth in children's social-emotional understandings and competencies and their readiness for the challenges of school.

Map of the Foundations

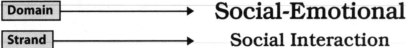

Domain ──────────▶ **Social-Emotional**

Strand ──────────▶ **Social Interaction**

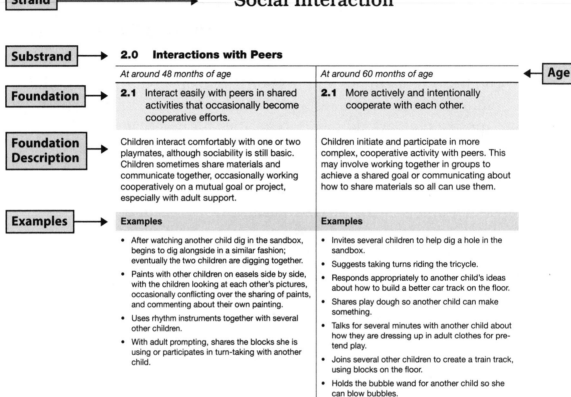

Substrand ──▶ **2.0 Interactions with Peers**

At around 48 months of age	*At around 60 months of age* ◀── **Age**
Foundation ──▶ **2.1** Interact easily with peers in shared activities that occasionally become cooperative efforts.	**2.1** More actively and intentionally cooperate with each other.
Foundation Description ──▶ Children interact comfortably with one or two playmates, although sociability is still basic. Children sometimes share materials and communicate together, occasionally working cooperatively on a mutual goal or project, especially with adult support.	Children initiate and participate in more complex, cooperative activity with peers. This may involve working together in groups to achieve a shared goal or communicating about how to share materials so all can use them.
Examples ──▶ **Examples**	**Examples**
• After watching another child dig in the sandbox, begins to dig alongside in a similar fashion; eventually the two children are digging together. • Paints with other children on easels side by side, with the children looking at each other's pictures, occasionally conflicting over the sharing of paints, and commenting about their own painting. • Uses rhythm instruments together with several other children. • With adult prompting, shares the blocks she is using or participates in turn-taking with another child.	• Invites several children to help dig a hole in the sandbox. • Suggests taking turns riding the tricycle. • Responds appropriately to another child's ideas about how to build a better car track on the floor. • Shares play dough so another child can make something. • Talks for several minutes with another child about how they are dressing up in adult clothes for pretend play. • Joins several other children to create a train track, using blocks on the floor. • Holds the bubble wand for another child so she can blow bubbles. • Sets the table with another child, communicating about what is needed next.

Includes notes for children with disabilities ──▶ * Children may "play" whether or not they are communicating orally, narrating the play, or motorically engaging in activities. For example, they may ask an adult or peer to assist in the motor aspects of play.

Teacher Resources

Bell, S. H., and others. *Challenging Behaviors in Early Childhood Settings: Creating a Place for All Children.* Baltimore: Brookes Publishing Company, 2004.

Bilmes, J., and T. Welker. *Common Psychological Disorders in Young Children: A Handbook for Early Childhood Professionals.* St. Paul, MN: Redleaf Press, 2006.

Birckmayer, J., J. Cohen, I. Doran Jensen, and D. Altman Variano, comp. "Children's Books About Family Relationships and Experiences." *Beyond the Journal: Young Children on the Web* (May 2005):1–5. http://www.journal.naeyc.org/btj/200505/07Birckmayer.asp

Brault, L. M. J., and T. J. Brault. *Children with Challenging Behavior: Strategies for Reflective Thinking.* Phoenix, AZ: CPG Publishing Company, 2005. http://www.braultbehavior.org/

The Center on the Social and Emotional Foundations for Early Learning (CSEFEL) is focused on promoting the social emotional development and school readiness of young children birth to age 5. http://www.vanderbilt.edu/csefel/

Center on the Social and Emotional Foundations for Early Learning. *Using Books to Support Social Emotional Development, Children's Book List,* 2008. http://www.vanderbilt.edu/csefel/practicalstrategies.html#list

Cooperative Children's Book Center, School of Education. *50 Multicultural Books Every Child Should Know.* Madison: University of Wisconsin-Madison, 2008. http://www.education.wisc.edu/ccbc/books/detailLists.asp?idBookListCat=1

Curtis, D., and M. Carter. *Designs for Living and Learning: Transforming Early Childhood Environments.* St. Paul, MN: Redleaf Press, 2003.

Division for Early Childhood, Young Exceptional Children Monograph Series. *Practical Ideas for Addressing Challenging Behaviors.*

Edited by S. Sandall and M. Ostrosky. Longmont, CO: Sopris West, 1999.

Epstein, A. S. *The Intentional Teacher: Choosing the Best Strategies for Young Children's Learning.* Washington, DC: National Association for the Education of Young Children, 2007.

Feeney, S., and E. Moravcik. "Children's Literature: A Window to Understanding Self and Others," *Young Children* 60 (2005): 20–27.

Fox, L., and R. H. Lentini. "'You Got It!' Teaching Social and Emotional Skills," *Young Children* 61 (2006): 36–42.

Gallagher, K. C., and K. Mayer. "Teacher-Child Relationships at the Forefront of Effective Practice," *Young Children* 61 (2006): 44–49.

Gartrell, D. *The Power of Guidance: Teaching Social-Emotional Skills in Early Childhood.* Washington, DC: National Association for the Education of Young Children and Thomson Delmar Learning, 2004.

Greenman, J. *Caring Spaces, Learning Places: Children's Environments That Work.* Redmond, WA: Exchange Press, 2005.

Hohmann, M., and D. P. Weikart. *Educating Young Children* (Fifth edition). Ypsilianti, MI: High/Scope Press, 2002.

Hutter-Pishgahi, L. "All Children Ready for School: Social-Emotional Development." Early Childhood Center." Early Childhood Briefing Paper Series. Bloomington, Indiana University, 2008. http://www.iidc.indiana.edu/ECC/Content/SRUD-SocialEmotional.pdf

Jablon, J. R., A. L. Dombro, and M. L. Dichtelmiller. *The Power of Observation.* Washington, DC: Teaching Strategies, 2007.

Katz, L. G., and D. E. McClellan. *Fostering Children's Social Competence: The Teacher's Role.* Washington, DC: National Association for the Education of Young Children, 1997.

King, M., and D. Gartrell. "Building an Encouraging Classroom with Boys in Mind," *Young Children* 58 (2003): 33–36.

Lamm, S., and others. "Creating Environments for Peaceful Problem Solving," *Young Children* 61 (2006): 22–28.

McArthur Butterfield, P., C. A. Martin, and A. Pratt Prairie. *Emotional Connections: How Early Relationships Guide Early Learning.* Washington, DC: Zero to Three Press, 2004.

The Miller Early Childhood Initiative of A World of Difference Institute. "How Can You Create a Learning Environment That Respects Diversity?" New York: Anti-Defamation League, 2004. http://www.adl.org/education/miller/respect_diversity_nysaeyc.asp

Ratcliff, N. "Use the Environment to Prevent Discipline Problems and Support Learning," *Young Children* 56, no. 5 (2001): 84–88.

Reading Is Fundamental: 100 of the Decade's Best Multicultural Read-Alouds: Pre-kindergarten through Grade 8. Selected and annotated by J. Freeman. http://www.rif.org/educators/books/100_best_multicultural.mspx

Riley, D., and others. *Social and Emotional Development: Connecting Science and Practice in Early Childhood Settings.* St. Paul, MN: Redleaf Press, 2008.

The Technical Assistance Center on Social Emotional Intervention for Young Children (TACSEI), features research that shows which practices improve the social-emotional outcomes for young children with, or at risk for, delays or disabilities. TACSEI creates products free of charge and resources to help decision makers, caregivers, and service providers apply these best practices in the work they do every day. http://www.challengingbehavior.org/

References

Bell, S. H., and others. 2004. *Challenging behaviors in early childhood settings: Creating a place for all children.* Baltimore, MD: Paul H. Brookes.

Bilmes, J. 2004. *Beyond behavior management: The six life skills children need to thrive in today's world.* St. Paul, MN: Redleaf Press.

Brault, L. M. J., and T. J. Brault. 2005. *Children with challenging behavior: Strategies for reflective thinking.* Phoenix, AZ: CPG Publishing Company.

California Preschool Learning Foundations, Volume 1. 2008. Sacramento: California Department of Education.

Cheatham, G., and R. M. Santos. 2005. A-B-C's of bridging home and school expectations for children and families of diverse backgrounds, *Young Exceptional Children* 8, no. 3: 3–11.

Committee on Developments in the Science of Learning, National Research Council. 2000. *How people learn: Brain, mind, experience, and school.* Edited by J. D. Bransford, A. L. Brown, and R. R. Cocking. Washington, DC: National Academy Press.

Committee on Integrating the Science of Early Childhood Development, National Research Council and Institute of Medicine. 2000. *From neurons to neighborhoods: The science of early childhood development.* Edited by J. P. Shonkoff and D. A. Phillips. Washington, DC: National Academy Press.

Curtis, D., and M. Carter. 1996. *Reflecting children's lives: A handbook for planning child-centered curriculum.* St. Paul, MN: Red Leaf Press.

Denham, S. A. 1998. *Emotional development in young children.* New York: Guilford Press.

Denham, S. A., and R. P. Weissberg. 2004. Social-emotional learning in early childhood: What we know and where to go from here? in *A blueprint for the promotion of prosocial behavior in early childhood.* Edited by E. Chesebrough and others. New York: Kluwer Academic/Plenum Publishers.

Developmentally appropriate practice in early childhood settings. 1986. Edited by S. Bredekamp and C. Copple. Washington, DC: National Association for the Education of Young Children (NAEYC).

Developmentally appropriate practice in early childhood programs. 1997. Rev. ed. Edited by S. Bredekamp and C. Copple. Washington, DC: National Association for the Education of Young Children (NAEYC).

DeVries, R., and others. 2002. What is constructivist education? Definition and principles of teaching. *In Developing constructivist early childhood curriculum.* Edited by R. DeVries and others. New York: Teachers College Press.

Dunn, Judy. 1988. *The beginnings of social understanding.* Cambridge, MA: Harvard University Press.

Dweck, C. S., and E. L. Leggett. 1988. A social-cognitive approach to motivation and personality, *Psychological Review* 95: 256–73.

Edwards, C. 2004. Caregiving through a relationship lens. In *Next steps toward teaching the Reggio way,* 2nd ed. Edited by J. Hendrick. Upper Saddle River, NJ: Pearson.

Edwards, C., L. Gandini, and G. Forman, eds. 1994. *The hundred languages of children: The Reggio Emilia approach to early childhood education.* Norwood, NJ: Ablex Publishing Corporation.

Egger, H. L., and A. Angold. 2006. Common emotional and behavioral disorders in preschool children: Presentation, nosology, and epidemiology, *Journal of Child Psychology and Psychiatry* 47: 313–37.

Epstein, A. 2007. *The intentional teacher: Choosing the best strategies for young children's learning.* Washington, DC: National Association for the Education of Young Children (NAEYC).

Fields, M. V., and D. Fields. 2006. *Constructive guidance and discipline.* 4th ed. Upper Saddle River, NJ: Pearson.

Fox, L. 2003. *Positive behavioral support: An individualized approach for addressing challenging behavior.* Nashville, TN: Center on the Social and Emotional Foundations for Early Learning. www.vanderbilt.edu/csefel/wwb.html. (accessed November 26, 2008).

Fox, L., and others. 2003. The teaching pyramid: A model for supporting social competence and preventing challenging behavior in young children, *Young Children* 58: 48–52.

Gandini, L. 2004. Foundations of the Reggio Emilia approach. In *Next steps toward teaching the Reggio way* 2nd ed. Edited by J. Hendrick. Upper Saddle River, NJ: Pearson.

Grusec, J., and J. Goodnow. 1994. Impact of parental discipline methods on the child's internalization of values: A reconceptualization of current points of view, *Developmental Psychology* 30: 4–19.

Harms, T., R. M. Clifford, and D. Cryer. 2005. *Early childhood environment rating scale.* Rev. ed. New York: Teachers College Press.

Harris, P. 1989. *Children and emotion: The development of psychological understanding.* Oxford: Blackwell.

Harris, P. 2006. *Social cognition.* In *Handbook of child psychology.* 6th ed. Vol. 2 of Cognition, perception, and language. Edited by W. Damon, R. M. Lerner, and N. Eisenberg. New York: Wiley.

Harter, S. 1999. *The construction of the self: A developmental perspective.* New York: Guilford Press.

Helm, J. H., and L. Katz. 2001. *Young investigators: The project approach in the early years.* New York: Teachers College Press.

Hendrick, J. 2004. *Next steps toward teaching the Reggio way: Accepting the challenge to change.* Upper Saddle River, NJ: Pearson.

Hohmann, M., and D. P. Weikart. 2002. *Educating young children.* 2nd ed. Ypsilianti, MI: High/Scope Press.

Jones, B., and others. 1994. *Designing learning and technology for educational reform.* Oakbrook, IL: North Central Regional Educational Laboratory.

Kochanska, G. 2002. Committed compliance, moral self, and internalization: A mediated model, *Developmental Psychology* 38: 339–51.

Ladd, G. W., S. H. Birch, and E. S. Buhs. 1999. Children's social and scholastic lives in kindergarten: Related spheres of influence? *Child Development* 70: 1373–1400.

Lewit, E. M., and L. S. Baker. 1995. School readiness, *The Future of Children* 5: 128–39.

Nachmias, M., M. Gunnar, S. Mangelsdorf, R. H. Parritz, and K. Buss. 1996. Behavioral inhibition and stress reactivity: The moderating role of attachment security, *Child Development* 67: 508–22.

National Research Council, Committee on Early Childhood Pedagogy. 2000. *Eager to learn: Educating our preschoolers.* Edited by B. T. Bowman, M. S. Donovan, and M. S. Burns. Washington, DC: National Academy Press.

National Scientific Council on the Developing Child. 2005. *Excessive stress disrupts the architecture of the developing brain.* Cambridge, MA: Center on the Developing Child, Harvard University (http://www.developingchild.net/pubs/wp-abstracts/wp3.html).

Pianta, R. C., S. L. Nimetz, and E. Bennett. 1997. Mother-child relationships, teacher-child relationships, and school outcomes in preschool and kindergarten, *Early Childhood Research Quarterly* 12: 263–80.

Pianta, R. C., and M. W. Stuhlman. 2004. Conceptualizing risk in relational terms: Associations among the quality of child-adult relationships prior to school entry and children's developmental outcomes in first grade, *Educational and Child Psychology* 21: 32–45.

Ratcliff, N. 2001. Use the environment to prevent discipline problems and support learning, *Young Children* 56: 84–88.

Raver, C. C. 2002. Emotions matter: Making the case for the role of young children's emotional development for early school readiness, *Social Policy Report* 16, no. 3: 3–18.

Raver, C. C., and J. Knitzer. 2002. *Ready to enter: What research tells policymakers about strategies to promote social and emotional school readiness among three- and four-year-old children.* New York: National Center for Children in Poverty.

Renninger, K. A., S. Hidi, and A. Krapp, eds. 1992. *The role of interest in learning and development.* Hillsdale, NJ: Erlbaum.

Riley, D., and others. 2008. *Social and emotional development: Connecting science and practice in early childhood settings.* St. Paul, MN: Redleaf Press.

Rimm-Kaufman, S. E., R. B. Pianta, and M. J. Cox. 2000. Teachers' judgments of problems in the transition to kindergarten, *Early Childhood Research Quarterly* 15: 147–66.

Rogoff, B. 1990. *Apprenticeship in thinking: Cognitive development in social context.* New York: Oxford University Press.

Rogoff, Barbara. 2003. *The cultural nature of human development.* New York: Oxford University Press.

Rubin, K. H., W. M. Bukowski, and J. G. Parker. 2006. Peer interactions, relationships, and groups. In *Handbook of child psychology,* 6th ed. Vol. 3 of *Social, emotional, and personality development.* Edited by W. Damon, R. M. Lerner, and N. Eisenberg. New York: Wiley.

Saarni, C. 1999. *The development of emotional competence.* New York: Guilford.

Saarni, C., and others. 2006. Emotional development: Action, communication, and understanding. In *Handbook of child psychology,* 6th ed. Vol. 3 of *Social, emotional, and personality development.* Edited by W. Damon, R. M. Lerner, and N. Eisenberg. New York: Wiley.

Stipek, D., S. Recchia, and S. McClintic. 1992. Self-evaluation in young children, *Monographs of the Society for Research in Child Development* 57 (Serial no. 226).

Strain, P. S., and G. E. Joseph. 2006. You got to have friends, *Young Exceptional Children Monograph Series* 8: 1–22.

Thompson, R. A. 1990. Emotion and self-regulation. In Vol. 36 of *Socioemotional development: Nebraska symposium on motivation.* Edited by R. A. Thompson. Lincoln: University of Nebraska Press.

Thompson, R. A. 2002. The roots of school readiness in social and emotional development, The *Kauffman Early Education Exchange* 1: 8–29.

Thompson, R. A. 2006. The development of the person: Social understanding, relationships, conscience, self. *In Handbook of child psychology,* 6th ed. Vol. 3 of *Social, emotional, and personality development.* Edited by W. Damon, R. M. Lerner, and N. Eisenberg. New York: Wiley.

Thompson, R. A., R. Goodvin, and S. Meyer. 2006. Social development: Psychological understanding, self understanding, and relationships. In *Handbook of preschool mental health: Development, disorders and treatment.* Edited by J. Luby. New York: Guilford Press.

Thompson, R. A., and K. Lagatutta. 2006. Feeling and understanding: Early emotional development. In *The Blackwell handbook of early childhood development.* Edited by K. McCartney and D. Phillips. Oxford, UK: Blackwell.

Thompson, R. A., S. Meyer, and M. McGinley. 2006. Understanding values in relationship: The development of conscience. In *Handbook of moral development.* Edited by M. Killen and J. Smetana. Mahwah, NJ: Erlbaum.

Thompson, R. A., and H. A. Raikes. 2007. The social and emotional foundations of school readiness. In *Social and emotional health in early childhood: Building bridges between services and systems.* Edited by J. Knitzer, R. Kaufmann, and D. Perry. Baltimore, MD: Paul H. Brookes Publishing Co.

Webster-Stratton, C. 1999. *How to promote children's social and emotional competence.* London: Paul Chapman.

Yoshikawa, H., and J. Knitzer. 1997. *Lessons from the field: Head Start mental health strategies to meet changing needs.* New York: National Center for Children in Poverty.

Endnotes

1. S. Harter, *The Construction of the Self: A Developmental Perspective* (New York: Guilford Press, 1999).

2. S. Harter, "The Self," in *Handbook of Child Psychology*, 6th ed., vol. 3 of *Social, Emotional, and Personality Development*, ed. W. Damon, R. M. Lerner, and N. Eisenberg (New York: Wiley, 2006).

3. R. A. Thompson, "The Development of the Person: Social Understanding, Relationships, Conscience, Self," in *Handbook of Child Psychology*, 6th ed., vol. 3 of *Social, Emotional, and Personality Development*, ed. W. Damon, R. M. Lerner, and N. Eisenberg (New York: Wiley, 2006).

4. See generally K. Durkin, *Developmental Social Psychology: From Infancy to Old Age* (Oxford, UK: Blackwell, 1995).

5. J. Dunn, *Young Children's Close Relationships: Beyond Attachment* (Newbury Park, CA: Sage, 1993).

6. R. A. Thompson, "The Development of the Person: Social Understanding, Relationships, Conscience, Self," in *Handbook of Child Psychology*, 6th ed., vol. 3 of *Social, Emotional, and Personality Development*, ed. W. Damon, R. M. Lerner, and N. Eisenberg (New York: Wiley, 2006).

7. G. W. Ladd, S. H. Birch, and E. S. Buhs, "Children's Social and Scholastic Lives in Kindergarten: Related Spheres of Influence?" *Child Development* 70, no. 6 (1999): 1373–1400.

8. G. W. Ladd, B. J. Kocherderfer, and C. C. Coleman, "Friendship Quality as a Predictor of Young Children's Early School Adjustment," *Child Development* 67 (1996): 1103–18.

9. E. M. Lewit and L. S. Baker, "School Readiness," *The Future of Children* 5 (1995): 128–39.

10. S. E. Rimm-Kaufman, R. B Pianta, and M. J. Cox, 2000, "Teachers' Judgments of Problems in the Transition to Kindergarten," *Early Childhood Research Quarterly* 15 (2000): 147–66.

11. R. A. Thompson. "Connecting Neurons, Concepts, and People: Brain Development and Its Implications," *National Institute for Early Education Research (NIEER) Policy Brief* Issue 17 (December 2008).

12. C. Webster-Stratton, *How to Promote Children's Social and Emotional Competence* (London: Paul Chapman, 1999).

13. National Association for the Education of Young Children, *Developmentally Appropriate Practice in Early Childhood Settings*, ed. S. Bredekamp and C. Copple (Washington, DC: Author, 1997).

14. L. Fox and others, "The Teaching Pyramid: A Model for Supporting Social Competence and Preventing Challenging Behavior in Young Children," *Young Children* 58 (2003): 48–52.

15. T. Harms, R. M. Clifford, and D. Cryer, *Early Childhood Environment Rating Scale*, rev. ed. (New York: Teachers College Press, 2005).

16. J. H. Helm and L. Katz, *Young Investigators: The Project Approach in the Early Year* (New York: Teachers College Press, 2001).

17. B. Jones and others, *Designing Learning and Technology for Educational Reform* (Oakbrook, IL: North Central Regional Educational Laboratory, 1994).

18. M. Hohmann and D. P. Weikar, *Educating Young Children*, 2nd ed. (Ypsilianti, MI: High/Scope Press, 2002).

19. N. Ratcliff, "Use the Environment to Prevent Discipline Problems and Support Learning," *Young Children* 56 (2001): 84–88.

20. A. Epstein, *The Intentional Teacher: Choosing the Best Strategies for Young Children's Learning* (Washington, DC: National Association for the Education of Young Children, 2007).

21. D. Riley and others, *Social and Emotional Development: Connecting Science and Practice in Early Childhood Settings* (St. Paul, MN: Redleaf Press, 2008).

22. M. V. Fields and D. Fields, *Constructive Guidance and Discipline*, 4th ed. (Upper Saddle River, NJ: Pearson, 2006).

23. R. A. Thompson, "The Roots of School Readiness in Social and Emotional Development," *The Kauffman Early Education Exchange* 1 (2002): 8–29.

24. R. A. Thompson, "The Development of the Person: Social Understanding, Relationships, Conscience, Self," in *Handbook of Child Psychology*, 6th ed., vol. 3 of *Social, Emotional, and Personality Development*, ed. W. Damon, R. M. Lerner, and N. Eisenberg (New York: Wiley, 2006).

25. M. B. Bronson, *Self-Regulation in Early Childhood: Nature and Nurture* (New York: Guilford Press, 2000).

26. *California Preschool Learning Foundations*, vol. 1 (Sacramento: California Department of Education, 2008).

27. R. A. Thompson and M. Goodman, "Development of Self, Relationships, and Socioemotional Competence: Foundations for Early School Success," in *Handbook of Developmental Science and Early Education*, ed. O. A. Barbarin and B. Wasik (New York: Guilford Press, in press).

28. D. Stipek, "The Development of Pride and Shame in Toddlers," in *Self-Conscious Emotions*, ed. J. P. Tangney and K. W. Fischer, 237–52 (New York: Guilford Press, 1995).

29. D. Stipek, S. Recchia, and S. McClintic, "Self-Evaluation in Young Children," *Monographs of the Society for Research in Child Development* 57, serial no. 226 (1992).

30. C. Kopp, "Antecedents of Self-Regulation: A Developmental Perspective," *Developmental Psychology* 18, no. 2 (1982): 199–214.

31. M. B. Bronson, *Self-Regulation in Early Childhood: Nature and Nurture* (New York: Guilford Press, 2000).

32. G. J. Duncan and others, "School Readiness and Later Achievement," *Developmental Psychology* 43 (2007): 1428–46.

33. C. Saarni, *The Development of Emotional Competence* (New York: Guilford Press, 1999).

34. J. Dunn, *The Beginnings of Social Understanding* (Cambridge, MA: Harvard University Press, 1988).

35. S. Denham, "The Emotional Basis of Learning and Development in Early Childhood Education," in *Handbook of Research on the Education of Young Children*, 2nd ed., ed. B. B. Spodek and O. N. Saracho (Mahwah, NJ: Erlbaum, 2006), 85–103.

36. S. A. Denham, and R. P. Weissberg, "Social-Emotional Learning in Early Childhood: What We Know and Where to Go from Here?" in *A Blueprint for the Promotion of Prosocial Behavior in Early Childhood*, ed. E. Chesebrough and others (New York: Kluwer/Academic Publishers, 2004), 13–50.

37. C. Izard and others, "Emotion Knowledge as a Predictor of Social Behavior and Academic Competence in Children at Risk," *Psychological Science* 12 (2001): 18–23.

38. N. Eisenberg, T. L. Spinrad, and A. Sadovsky, "Empathy-Related Responding in Children," in *Handbook of Moral Development*, ed. M. Killen and J. G. Smetana (Mahwah, NJ: Erlbaum, 2006), 517–49.

39. R. A. Thompson, "Empathy and Its Origins in Early Development," in *Intersubjective Communication and Emotion in Early Ontogeny*, ed. S. Braten (Cambridge: Cambridge University Press, 1998), 144–57.

40. National Research Council, Committee on Early Childhood Pedagogy, *Eager to Learn: Educating Our Preschoolers*, ed. B. T. Bowman, M. S. Donovan, and M. S. Burns (Washington, DC: National Academy Press, 2000).

41. C. S. Dweck, "The Development of Ability Conceptions," in *Development of Achievement Motivation*, ed. A. Wigfield and J. S. Eccles (San Diego: Academic Press, 2002), 57–88.

42. C. S. Dweck and E. L. Leggett, "A Social-Cognitive Approach to Motivation and Personality," *Psychological Review* 95 (1998): 256–73.

43. G. W. Ladd, S. H. Birch, and E. S. Buhs, "Children's Social and Scholastic Lives in Kindergarten: Related Spheres of Influence?" *Child Development* 70 (1999): 1373–1400.

44. R. A. Thompson and M. Goodman, "Development of Self, Relationships, and Socioemotional Competence: Foundations for Early School Success," in *Handbook of Developmental Science and Early Education,*

ed. O. A. Barbarin and B. Wasik (New York: Guilford Press, in press).

45. *California Preschool Learning Foundations,* vol. 1 (Sacramento: California Department of Education, 2008).

46. R. A. Thompson and M. Goodman, "Development of Self, Relationships, and Socioemotional Competence: Foundations for Early School Success," in *Handbook of Developmental Science and Early Education,* ed. O. A. Barbarin and B. Wasik (New York: Guilford Press, in press).

47. K. H. Rubin, W. M. Bukowski, and J. G. Parker, "Peer Interactions, Relationships, and Groups," in *Handbook of Child Psychology,* 6th ed., ed. W. Damon, R. M. Lerner, and N. Eisenberg, vol. 3 of *Social, Emotional, and Personality Development* (New York: Wiley, 2006).

48. K. H. Rubin and others, "Peer Relationships in Childhood," in *Developmental Science: An Advanced Textbook,* 5th ed., ed. M. H. Bornstein and M. E. Lamb (Mahwah, NJ: Erlbaum, 2005).

49. R. A. Thompson and M. Goodman, "Development of Self, Relationships, and Socioemotional Competence: Foundations for Early School Success," in *Handbook of Developmental Science and Early Education,* ed. O. A. Barbarin and B. Wasik (New York: Guilford Press, in press).

50. G. Kochanska, 1997, "Mutually Responsive Orientation Between Mothers and Their Young Children: Implications for Early Socialization," *Child Development* 68 (1997): 94–112.

51. G. Kochanska, "Committed Compliance, Moral Self, and Internalization: A Mediated Model," *Developmental Psychology* 38 (2002): 339–51.

52. R. A. Thompson, S. Meyer, and M. McGinley, "Understanding Values in Relationship: The Development of Conscience," in *Handbook of Moral Development,* ed. M. Killen and J. Smetana, 267–97 (Mahwah, NJ: Erlbaum, 2006).

53. G. Cheatham and R. M. Santos, "A-B-C's of Bridging Home and School Expectations for Children and Families of Diverse Backgrounds," *Young Exceptional Children* 8, no. 3 (2005): 3–11.

54. J. Dunn, 1993, *Young Children's Close Relationships: Beyond Attachment.* Newbury Park, CA: Sage.

55. G. W. Ladd, S. H. Birch, and E. S. Buhs, "Children's Social and Scholastic Lives in Kindergarten: Related Spheres of Influence?" *Child Development* 70 (1999): 1373–1400.

56. G. W. Ladd, B. J. Kocherderfer, and C. C. Coleman, "Friendship Quality as a Predictor of Young Children's Early School Adjustment," *Child Development* 67 (1996): 1103–18.

57. R. A. Thompson, "The Development of the Person: Social Understanding, Relationships, Self, Conscience," in *Handbook of Child Psychology,* 6th ed., vol. 3 of *Social, Emotional, and Personality Development,* ed. W. Damon, R. M. Lerner, and N. Eisenberg (New York: Wiley, 2006), 24–98.

58. E. Waters and others, "Learning to Love: Mechanisms and Milestones," in vol. 23 of *Self Processes and Development, Minnesota Symposia on Child Psychology,* ed. M. Gunnar and L. Sroufe (Hillsdale, NJ: Erlbaum, 1991).

59. *California Preschool Learning Foundations,* vol. 1 (Sacramento: California Department of Education, 2008).

60. R. A. Thompson and M. Goodman, "Development of Self, Relationships, and Socioemotional Competence: Foundations for Early School Success," in *Handbook of Developmental Science and Early Education,* ed. O. A. Barbarin and B. Wasik (New York: Guilford Press, in press).

61. R. C. Pianta and M. W. Stuhlman, 2004, "Teacher-Child Relationships and Children's Success in the First Years of School," *School Psychology Review* 33 (2004): 444–58.

62. J. G. Parker and J. M. Gottman, "Social and Emotional Development in a Relational Context: Friendship Interaction from Early Childhood to Adolescence," in *Peer Relations in Child Development,* ed. T. J. Berndt and G. W. Ladd (New York: Wiley, 1989), 15–45.

CHAPTER 4

Language and Literacy

Language is one of the most crucial tools that children acquire, one that is essential for cognitive development, reading achievement, and overall school performance, as well as for social relations. It allows people to share a society's achievements and history and the deepest emotions. Language includes conventional sounds, gestures, and visual symbols, such as writing, that are used separately and jointly for purposes of communication. The human brain is **"hard-wired"** to learn language, a process quite similar in all children. Yet children differ a good deal as to when they use their first words, start to combine words into sentences, and use complex sentence forms to communicate meaning. Though children begin to develop language and literacy at birth, with nonverbal cues such as eye gaze and gestures, they arrive at preschool ready to communicate with symbols: words, signs, and pictures.

Children's early language and literacy environments often vary, with the amount and kind of experiences differing across families. Some children experience more conversations and book reading than other children[1, 2] and more than one language. Some children see print primarily in the environment (e.g., street signs, store coupons, labels on containers).[3] Other children engage with print in many contexts, including books read to them regularly. Some children have opportunities to scribble, draw, and write with crayons and markers long before they come to preschool, while others have few of these emergent writing opportunities. Teachers should encourage all preschoolers to join in activities that will expand their language and literacy skills. Each child's family should be invited to participate in this exciting process.

The following components constitute oral language:[a]

- Phonology—the sound system of language, such as noticing that *hat, cat,* and *mat* differ by only a single initial sound;
- Semantics—the *meaning* conveyed by words, phrases, and sentences;
- Syntax or **grammar**—the rules that govern how sentences are put together (e.g., the English language relies on *word order* to convey meaning: *Manuel throws the ball to Bertha* versus *Bertha throws the ball to Manuel);*

---

[a] The term *oral language* is used to indicate the inclusion of a phonological component. The other components of language (semantics, syntax, morphology, vocabulary, and pragmatics) are present in both oral languages, such as English and Spanish, and visual languages, such as American Sign Language (ASL).

- **Morphology**—the units of meaning within a language, also called *morphemes*, such as *ed* for past tense (e.g., walk*ed*) and *s* for plural (e.g., dog*s*);
- Vocabulary—the words in a given language; and
- Pragmatics—the rules of language used in social contexts (e.g., one would talk differently to the president than to one's mother). **Pragmatics** includes gathering information, requesting, and communicating. Good conversations depend on staying on the topic and turn-taking.

These components are used in the **auditory** (i.e., listening, speaking) and visual (i.e., sign, reading, writing) modalities.

Language allows children to express their feelings and needs, acknowledge the feelings and needs of others, and to talk about emotions.[4] It is critical that teachers and caregivers be responsive to young children's attempts at communication

Research Highlight

The principles and curricular suggestions offered in this chapter are based on 40 years of scientific research on language acquisition and literacy development. Here are just a few of the amazing discoveries that form the background of this chapter. The following findings come from this vast body of research:

- Even in infancy, children are active learners who use data from the language they hear to grasp patterns.[5] Children learning language behave as young mathematicians who respond to patterns and calculate, for instance, that in English –*ed* generally comes at the end of verbs to indicate the past tense (e.g., he walked or it dropped).[6]
- When young children hear language around them, they are accumulating the data they need to use their skills and to grasp the features of their native language. In addition, the very practice of reading with children (e.g., starting at the front of a book and moving page by page to the end) teaches the patterns of book structure and handling and the general ways that print works (e.g., English is read from the left to right and top to bottom on a page). When book reading is accompanied by explicit comments (e.g., "This is the title of the book: *Whistle for Willie*") and actions (e.g., underlining the title as it is read), children learn even more about the features of books and how print works.[7]

- Children's storytelling skill and vocabulary development are supported through shared reading experiences. Stories have a predictable structure: setting, characters, a problem, and its resolution. As children hear stories, they learn this basic structure and begin to use this knowledge to shape the stories they create.[8] Children also learn the meaning of new words from listening to multiple readings of good stories,[9] **"friendly explanations of words"** (explanations with wording and examples within the preschool child's grasp rather than a more formal definition from a dictionary) offered by teachers and parents as they read stories to children,[10, 11, 12] and from engagement with adults in discussions during story reading.[13, 14]

and language by focusing on things that are meaningful to the children and their families. No single component of any curriculum will have more impact on a preschooler's development than language.

Preschool is also an exciting time for written language development and for promoting interest in reading. If the social and physical environments in preschool and the home support the development of reading and written language, children will want to hear stories from books and to use books to find out more about things of interest. They will also be inclined to create marks that approximate letters and to learn how to write their own names. They will enjoy playing with the sounds of language, as well. All of these experiences are foundations for the conventional reading and writing that come later.

Guiding Principles

▶ Language and literacy work together

Language and literacy support each other. Children with well-developed oral language are likely to succeed in reading comprehension in later grade levels than children with less well-developed oral language.[15] Children with strong oral vocabularies are likely to make more progress in developing phonological awareness.[16] In addition, language and literacy learning often occur together in the same context. For example, talking with a child about what happened the day before supports both language development and **narrative** skills.[17] Helping children find their names on the helper chart and explaining how the helper chart system works support both literacy and language.

▶ Children say or sign what they hear or see

A rich language environment is key for preschool children's language learning as well as for their development as readers and writers. The more language children hear, the more their language grows.[18, 19, 20] Children say, sign, or use touch screens to express what they hear or see. When teachers use conventional language, they provide a model from which children learn how to use language themselves. The same is true for reading and writing. The more adults read and write with children and show children how they use reading and writing in their own lives, the more children grow in their understanding of what it means to be a reader and writer. Adults also have many opportunities to answer children's questions about how print works.

▶ Children learn everywhere

Adults can act as detectives to find language and literacy opportunities everywhere and then use them as teachable moments. For example, when a child relates a personal experience and leaves out information critical for a listener's understanding, asking a question that prompts the child to provide this information helps develop narrative skills (e.g., "Where were you when the wind blew your hat off?").[21] Caregiving situations can provide strong physical support for word meanings and help children learn new vocabulary (e.g., "Rub the *palms* of your hands together, like this, to work up a *lather*").[22] Teachers may refer to the label on the soup can a child tips into the play pan in the house area to cook soup (e.g., "I see we're having tomato soup for lunch") to support print skills. Finding these everyday moments also enriches children's appreciation for the many uses that language and literacy serve.

▶ **Children learn best from experiences that are interesting, useful, and fun**

The world and preschool are interesting and satisfying places for children when they offer experiences that engage and delight children and satisfy their desire to know.[23, 24] When children learn that language can be fun (e.g., singing silly songs and reciting poems with surprising endings) and also gets things done, they will be motivated to use their language. When children hear the words in songs (e.g., "When You're Happy and You Know It") that indicate movements to make or when language learning is embedded into routines (e.g., "If you have a *pocket* in your *shirt or blouse,* please go to the sink to wash your hands"), they see a reason for attending to language and for using it. When they find out that books are full of interesting characters and information (e.g., an ant is an animal!), they will want to hear more books.

▶ **Celebrate and support the individual**

Children differ in temperament and also in their language and literacy experiences. The child who is timid, the child for whom English is not the home language, or the child who uses sign language or an alternative communication system may be reluctant to communicate. Some children hear more books read aloud than do other children, and some are encouraged to share their thoughts about the story while others are encouraged to just listen or to recite portions of the text.[25] Children's access to pen, pencil, and paper in the early years also varies. Knowing that individual children have different starting points, a teacher accepts and delights in each

child's path to language and literacy and expands each child's experiences. Children with disabilities or communication differences benefit from teachers who understand their differences in language and communication and make allowances for them in the daily routine.

▶ **Connect school and home**

Building connections with the child's family members gives parents an opportunity to get more involved in their children's learning. When parents are provided with certain materials and are helped to learn strategies supporting their children's language and literacy development, children's learning benefits.[26] Reaching out to families also gives teachers opportunities to learn about the strengths that each child brings to school and about important individual differences. For example, teachers should ask family members to provide information regarding a child who uses (or is learning to use) an alternative communication system. It is also important to consult with specialists. This knowledge helps teachers to build on and extend the experiences that children have at home.

▶ Create a culturally sensitive environment

Around the world, children in some cultures are encouraged to speak up while children in other cultures are encouraged to remain silent. Teachers need to be respectful of home expectations for language at the same time that they support children to speak up at school.[27] In a preschool classroom that is too silent, children will not experience enough language to learn to use it or to gain knowledge and skills for literacy. Children must be surrounded by language to acquire the vocabulary and sentence structures they need to read and write and think.[28, 29, 30, 31] This means that preschool teachers must talk and also encourage children to use language for negotiating with other children, asking for what they want, and expressing their emotions.

▶ Encourage children to take a turn

Children learn language and learn about reading and writing through social interaction, especially when there is a lot of "back and forth" in a conversation.[32] Strike a balance between surrounding children with language and letting them talk too.[33]

Research suggests that children "talk" very little in the preschool classroom,[34] even though doing so would promote their language development. Children should be asked open-ended questions that require more than one word to answer (e.g., "What are all the foods you like to eat for breakfast?" rather than "What did you eat this morning?"). Then teachers can follow up with additional questions, for example, asking about what the child's family does in the morning. Questions should not test or quiz but serve as prompts that encourage children to generate language. Children will also learn as teachers model for them how to engage in back-and-forth exchange with other children. When teachers ask for children's opinions and ideas, children's confidence soars. Additionally, when teachers encourage children to make choices, for example, about which of two literacy activities they wish to engage in, children will be more invested in the activity.

▶ Make thoughts more explicit to children by thinking out loud

Teachers may share their thinking in a demonstration of how to write a letter to a child who has asked for help. They describe their actions (e.g., "To write the letter K, you start with a long vertical line like this, and then you draw a short diagonal line like this, and then another short diagonal line from here down to here."). Teachers may also share their thoughts during routine tasks, such as cleaning out the clogged spout of a glue bottle (e.g., "I'm going to open up this paper clip and place it in the bottle's spout. If I can get the dried piece out of the spout, the glue will come out again. See the hole? I'm going to stick the end of the paper clip right in there . . .").

Hearing the teacher describe his or her actions increases children's language and literacy learning.[35, 36] Learning can benefit from explicit thinking out loud in routine contexts, just as in planned instructional contexts.[37]

▶ **Support curiosity and confidence**
Children should not be afraid to ask "Why?" and "How come?" Children ask questions in environments that are cognitively interesting and challenging. They are more confident and learn more in environments that are emotionally supportive.[38, 39, 40] Asking questions, such as "I wonder what would happen if . . ." and using comments, such as "Tell me about. . . .," engage children in wondering and thinking and in sharing their thoughts. These prompts also let children know that adults think children's ideas are important.

▶ **Create literacy-rich environments**
Interesting materials, organized attractively to create specific areas in the indoor and outdoor learning environments, prompt children to talk, explore, build, draw, paint, move, inquire, and enact roles in pretend play. Literacy materials and props, embedded throughout the learning environment, make using language and engaging in reading and writing a routine part of each preschool day.

▶ **Observe children**
By observing children's engagement with language and literacy, teachers find ways to enter their world to support and extend their learning. These observations become a guide for intentional classroom practice. As teachers implement planned activities, their observations of children's responses provide vital information that helps teachers meet children's specific needs.

Environments and Materials

How the learning environment is arranged affects how children learn to talk, read, and write. An environment that fosters language development, two-way communication, and literacy skills provides rich curriculum content. The daily schedule accommodates a variety of groupings (e.g., large group, small group, and individual), and the learning materials fascinate children. Children learn more when adults model language and literacy as well as provide playful, purposeful instruction. Play spaces with literacy props (e.g., signs, lists) allow children to congregate and to make choices that foster rich language and literacy experiences.

▶ **The daily schedule for adult–child and child–child interactions**
Program leaders need to create opportunities within the day for adult–child and child–child interaction. Consistency in the daily schedule, routines, and locations of interest areas helps all children, especially those with cognitive or social behavior challenges or with visual disabilities, because it reduces uncertainty. The most beautiful room is only as good as the interaction that takes place inside it. Conversation with adults and with peers, exposure to print, and writing and drawing materials are key to fostering language and literacy.

▶ **Large-group space**
Sitting together for group songs, games, and discussions and facing a wall with attractive and uncluttered displays allow children a clear view of teachers and peers. They can attend

to and respond to verbal and nonverbal communication, as well as visual prompts.

▶ **Small-group spaces**

During some portions of the preschool day, teachers might gather children in small groups. Small groups allow more individual interaction with adults than do large groups, and they help ensure that each child interacts with a teacher every day.

Most literacy skills interventions with demonstrated effectiveness have been done in small-group settings,[41] no doubt, because these settings allow teachers to adapt both interaction levels and teaching strategies to meet individual needs (e.g., language development for children who are English learners). Small groups also benefit children with disabilities, as adults can demonstrate for all of the children how accommodations increase the child's ability to communicate. For example, having picture symbols available that the child uses to initiate comments or respond to questions illustrates the skills needed for fluent conversations.

▶ **A space to display family-related items**

The link between home and school may be strengthened by display-

ing family photographs, child–parent drawings and projects, or drawings of family members that children create at school. Document school-based family activities with photos and display them. Rich lists of words may accompany illustrations to match the occupations of family members or the favorite foods enjoyed in each child's home.

▶ **Centers or interest areas**

Individual centers or interest areas, each focusing on a unique kind of experience, give children a range of choices. These special places encourage preschool children to work collaboratively and to communicate with one another. They also provide children with opportunities to work alone, if they wish. Areas with quiet activities are separate from those with more exuberant activities. Paths leading to areas are free of barriers for children who use mobility devices, such as walkers, and large enough to allow children to interact around the materials. Relevant books, signs, and other print artifacts may be placed in each of the areas, along with writing supplies to support children in using print props in play (e.g., notepads and telephone directories, menus and order pads, road signs) and in routines (e.g., paper for a turns list, name tags for an activities chart, a helper chart). (See more specific suggestions in "1.0, Concepts About Print," page 129).

– **Create a dramatic play area**

The basic **dramatic play area** is a "house area" filled with dress-up clothes, furniture, toy dishes, empty food containers, and dolls.

Ting dresses up like a mother with high heels and a fancy hat. She serves a bowl of plastic noodles complete with make-believe chop-sticks. David joins, asking if he may serve the toy hamburgers. They talk about the different things their families eat and how they eat. As other children join in to create a banquet of pretend foods, the play and the language exchanges become more involved.

Using basic clothing and other props from home and community environments, rather than commercial outfits, encourages children to create their own play scenarios. Sometimes dramatic play introduces cultural differences in preferred foods, clothing, or eating utensils. The children's pretend stories serve as platforms for high-level language and support understanding of stories they hear in books read to them. Using additional play themes during the year (e.g., grocery store, pet store, post office, repair shop) provides more opportunities to introduce cultural variations. It also supports children's varied interests and extends the contributions of dramatic play to children's understanding of a larger range of stories and other kinds of books.

– **Create a block area**
Block play often enlists small groups who are learning to collaborate and communicate as they build a fire station or the tallest tower. As children work together, they use language and learn words such as *above* and *below*. Adults who comment on children's work by using sentences model good sentence structure and also the complex spatial language that is related to later spatial and mathematical abilities.[42, 43] Adding

related books and writing materials to the block area encourages literacy development and appeals to children's delight in adding details to buildings and streets (e.g., signs) to make them resemble what children observe in the real world.

– **Create an art area**
As children hold pens, paintbrushes, markers, and crayons and manipulate scissors, glue bottles, and clay, they not only create works of art but also build the fine motor skills needed for writing, drawing, and painting. Including materials with a variety of handles (e.g., built up, round) enables the child with a different kind of grasp to participate. As children use art to represent their experiences and feelings or to capture something created by their imagination, they also use and develop skills in the use of symbols that support oral or sign language and the composing of messages and stories that can be written down.

– **Create a writing area**
Although children have opportunities to write in all interest areas, an area devoted specifically to writing materials increases children's interest and engagement in writing. White and colored paper (drawing, manila, and

copier) in several sizes, along with a variety of writing tools (e.g., markers, crayons, pens) are available. To avoid conflict over materials, teachers make writing tools (e.g., markers, crayons) available in small sets suitable for use by one or two children rather than in large tubs.

A large whiteboard or an easel make writing accessible to children with limited fine motor skills and those too "busy" to sit down to write. The classroom includes tilted surfaces and writing tools that are adapted for use by children with physical or motor difficulties. (See strategies in the Writing strand, on page 162, for more suggestions.) Some children may need assistance in emergent writing either through **assistive technology** or through the direct help of an adult. Assistive technology, either low tech or high tech, may be as simple as increasing the width of the marker or pencil so that it is easier to grasp or as sophisticated as using a computer. Another possibility would be for an adult

or peer to "write" for the child, who would then approve or disapprove by indicating yes or no.

- **Create a cozy library or book area**
The classroom has plenty of books reflecting the different languages, cultures, and current skill levels of the children. Books should be displayed cover-forward on shelves. Include narrative and information texts, as well as books of verse. A cozy mat or small couch allows children to curl up and read. Flannel boards and flannel stories, puppets, stuffed animals, soft dolls, and story character props in a nearby area are provided. Only a few of these materials are placed in the library area at one time, and the selections are rotated over time to provide a variety of experiences.

Too many materials at a time can overwhelm children and crowd the physical space needed to use materials comfortably. Teachers may post signs in the library (e.g., Reading Zone, Reading Is Fun, Be a Bookworm). Signs for reading and writing areas can also be placed outdoors. Illustrated books are augmented with texture to accommodate children with visual or cognitive disabilities, and books with large print or **braille** are included for children with visual impairments. Photo albums (e.g., of children engaged in activities at preschool, field trips, celebrations) and class books made by the children help them to connect reading with their lives and also support language development as children discuss the photos and help compose captions for the pages.

Some children may need assistance in holding a book or turning the pages either through assistive tech-

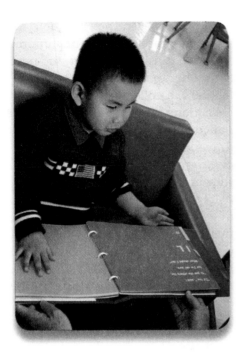

nology or with the help of an adult or peer. For example, a book can be mounted so that a child need not hold it, and sturdy tabs placed on a book's pages make them easier to turn. Another option for children with motor disabilities severe enough to limit book handling is to provide books on CDs.

– **Create a science area**
The science area is full of items that spark curiosity and wonder and prompt children to explore and find out. It has plants and animals under the children's care and many objects to explore (e.g., shells, seeds, rocks, bark, magnets). The outdoor play space is also a science area, with wheels and sloped areas; a variety of interesting substances (e.g., puddles, sand, mud); clouds, wind, and sun; spiders, birds, and leaves; and shadows. **Information books,** placed in the indoor science area as well as outside in suitable tubs or on a cart, extend children's firsthand science experiences. As

children explore science content, they learn rich vocabulary, ask questions, and describe what they see and hear. They also can learn to document investigations with drawings or writing, some of which they dictate to teachers.

– **Create a game area**
When children play language games, they hear and use rich language in the context of the game as well as in their discussion around the game. Negotiating whose turn it is and discussing what happened give children the opportunity to use their language and work with printed materials.

– **Create a math area**
When children play with shapes, find patterns, or play with tangram materials, they are building early mathematical skills, including the language of mathematics (e.g., three sides and three corners; same and different; triangle, square, and hexagon). Board games, such as those with dice and spinners, encourage children to learn number words used in counting as they move ahead three or four spaces. Building knowledge of the quantities represented by number words and the language terms to talk about number relationships helps children learn the foundation of mathematics

(e.g., five is more than three).[44] The teacher's participation in the math activities helps support children in learning math-related vocabulary and prompts children to talk about their actions and discoveries. The activities are important opportunities for children to practice using the math terms the teacher models.

▶ **Prepare materials ahead of time for maximizing language and literacy**
Think ahead about what you want to accomplish with the children and select and prepare materials needed in advance of small- and large-group activities. Books, songs, and other activities are more effective when they relate to children's interests and when the teacher is intentional in their use. Children's experiences will be particularly meaningful if their home culture is tapped. Another way to plan so that classroom time is used effectively is to gather enough materials (e.g., costumes, blocks, books, dolls) to minimize the amount of time that any child spends waiting.

▶ **Arrange learning environments to fascinate children and prompt conversations**
Think ahead about what will fascinate children and make them want to learn.

Perhaps a spot in the classroom may be designated for inspecting interesting things (e.g., shavings from the pencil sharpener, paintbrush bristles, feathers, a collection of seeds, or collections of rocks or shells) with the naked eye or a magnifying glass. Place drawing materials there to prompt children to sketch what they see, if they are interested. The intentional teacher joins children as they explore in learning environments to ask what they are noticing, to help them notice more, and to use new vocabulary (e.g., *shavings, bristles, pebbles, speckled*) in authentic conversations with the children.

▶ **Extend the classroom beyond its walls**
Being on the playground or going on a class trip gives children engaging opportunities to learn important language and literacy content. For example, provide road signs for an outdoor tricycle path and paper and writing tools for making speeding tickets. Child-made flyers advertising lemonade stands and drive-through restaurants can be utilized for outside play. Clipboards support children in writing and drawing outside. Provide a tub of information books outside that relate to natural items children might observe (e.g., insects, worms, flowers, trees). On a field trip—even a walk around the block—read road signs and house numbers, answer children's questions, and point out things the children might not notice at first (e.g., a bird's nest in a tree, workers on a scaffold washing a building's windows). The opportunities are endless.

Summary of Language Foundations

Listening and Speaking consists of three substrands. *Language use and conventions* focuses on how children use their language for a number of purposes, including learning how to participate in short conversations. *Vocabulary* learning is one of the most important accomplishments of early childhood and is related to later reading comprehension. *Grammar* allows children to go beyond mere naming with their vocabularies to express their ideas in sentences. Understanding how words are put together in a sentence (i.e., grammar) is strongly related to reading comprehension—to understanding the meaning in books and stories. Speaking can be accomplished through oral language or **sign language.**

Summary of Literacy Foundations

Reading consists of five substrands. *Concepts about print* involves the understanding that print is meaningful and can be used for a variety of purposes. *Phonological awareness* concerns learning to notice that spoken words have parts. *Alphabetics and word/print recognition* includes identifying alphabet letters and linking letters in printed words to sounds in spoken words. *Comprehension and analysis of age-appropriate text* involves thinking that leads to understanding stories and other kinds of books. *Literacy interest and response* includes children's engagement in and motivation for reading.

Writing focuses on *understanding that print represents ideas* and on *learning to move* from drawing and **scribble writing** to using letters and words. Much exploration with paper and writing tools occurs before children will try to write to convey specific meanings. When children write to convey meaning, they are using their language, their physical ability to hold a crayon or pencil, and the cognitive understanding that the marks they make on the page are symbols that represent a meaning that can be shared.

Summary of the Strands and Substrands

Language

Listening and Speaking

1.0 Language Use and Conventions
2.0 Vocabulary
3.0 Grammar

Literacy

Reading

1.0 Concepts about Print
2.0 Phonological Awareness
3.0 Alphabetics and Word/Print Recognition
4.0 Comprehension and Analysis of Age-Appropriate Text
5.0 Literacy Interest and Response

Writing

1.0 Writing Strategies

Please refer to the map of the language and literacy foundations on page 169 for a visual explanation of the terminology used in the preschool learning foundations.

LANGUAGE

Listening and Speaking

Language takes place all around us—in social interactions between teachers and children, in classroom management, in play between children, and in instructional activities. For example, when children learn mathematics and science, they learn them through language as well as through meaningful, multisensory experiences. Language also enhances or limits children's ability to choose playmates and join in games on the playground. The Listening and Speaking strand has three substrands: language use and conventions, vocabulary, and grammar.

1.0   Language Use and Conventions

How does a child ask for what he needs in a way that is polite and respectful, clear, and easily understood? A four-year-old wants to use the swing that his peer has been on for over ten minutes. A five-year-old wants to share a story about the family celebration of Chinese New Year. Learning to use language effectively is a crucial life skill that develops from describing to predicting, from merely greeting someone to seeking new information about him or her. The very climate of the preschool classroom depends on how well children use language to communicate their needs, ideas, and feelings. Teachers can support young children in the area of language use and conventions by repeating and extending what children say in conversations, by telling stories themselves, and by **modeling** appropriate language usage.

Four skills are described in this substrand, each of which is a foundation. Each of these skill areas calls for a distinct set of practices based on research evidence; therefore, the following curricular suggestions are organized by skills or foundations. This organization offers teachers a structure for creating their own links between foundations that focus on different skills and activities in the classroom.

The four skills are as follows:

- Use language to communicate with others.
- Speak clearly.
- Use accepted language styles.
- Tell a short story or retell something that happened earlier in the day.

Use Language to Communicate with Others

Everyday moments provide special opportunities for children to develop the basics of communication when they *describe* what they found, *comment* on an item of interest, or even *greet* a peer.

VIGNETTE

Armand finds a worm on the playground and gently carries it to show the teacher. A group of excited children follow him, eager to learn more about the worm. Ms. Krim asks, "What did you find there, Armand?" as she signals to others to join the conversation. "Is it alive?" one child asks. The teacher responds, "What do you think? How could we tell?"

TEACHABLE MOMENT

> Building on the child's interest and being "in the moment" with the child, this teacher demonstrates back-and-forth communication and begins a conversation. She engages the children by making it interesting and fun, by encouraging children to take a turn, by taking children's questions seriously, and by letting children contribute to the discovery.

VIGNETTE

As the four-year-olds gather for small-group reading time, Ting sits quietly behind a much taller and more energetic Fernando. A child who speaks Chinese at home, Ting rarely talks in class, never raising her hand amidst the flurry of children who want to be constantly recognized. Her teacher wisely chose a book to read that told a story about Ting's favorite topic: butterflies. For the first time, Ting quietly contributes to the conversation using English, "My grandfather has a butterfly like that."

The teacher, capitalizing on the moment, asks, "Where does your grandfather keep his butterflies?" drawing Ting out further. Other children join in the dialogue and continue to talk as they make paper butterflies in the art area.

PLANNING LEARNING OPPORTUNITIES

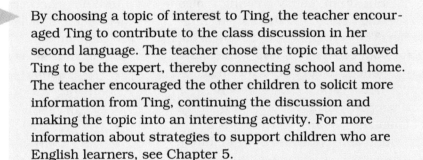

By choosing a topic of interest to Ting, the teacher encouraged Ting to contribute to the class discussion in her second language. The teacher chose the topic that allowed Ting to be the expert, thereby connecting school and home. The teacher encouraged the other children to solicit more information from Ting, continuing the discussion and making the topic into an interesting activity. For more information about strategies to support children who are English learners, see Chapter 5.

In every classroom, there are planned and unplanned opportunities that spark language use and effective communication. The teachers in the vignettes used the following interactions and strategies to support preschool children:

Set the stage for language use. Teachers can make sure that children have a chance to talk by setting aside time for them to discuss and to share their ideas. Teachers know that some of children's time in the classroom must be spent listening, but they also understand that children need to hear their own voices too. Children who communicate with sign language or another system need to have their expressions acknowledged and be included in the conversations and interactions among children.

Acknowledge children's contributions. Treating children with respect helps children become curious and confident. Making eye contact with them at their level when they attempt to communicate, greeting each child by name, and recasting their talk to indicate that they have been heard tells children implicitly, "Your

contribution is valuable." Teachers can also show children that their talk is valued by providing an explanation when children ask questions about what a word means and by building upon what children say.

Play games and make them interesting and fun! Use games that prompt children to talk and ask questions. Hide a toy in a pillowcase and ask children to reach in without looking and describe what they touch. Bring food with a familiar aroma—perhaps the ethnic foods children are acquainted with—and ask children, "What does this smell like? Banana, guava, or chocolate?" Show

children an object they have never seen before—maybe a real kitchen or cleaning tool (e.g., a sieve or a bottle brush). Give each child an opportunity to ask questions to figure out what the item does and what it might be called.

Engage in "getting to know you" conversations. Help children to use language to comment on and learn about others in an engaging way. Have teachers and children teach each other how to say hello and good-bye in other languages. Model the use of conventional greetings when others enter the room, as in "Hello, Ms. Schwartz! How are you?"

Speak Clearly

Communication is effective only when people are understood. When teachers speak clearly, they model good pronunciation, which gently helps children refine their own speech. Sometimes children will be difficult to understand. Most children will improve with time. If teachers see little improvement, they should refer the child to someone who can assess the child and recommend specific strategies that can help the child make progress.

VIGNETTE

Luka announces in circle time that tomorrow is his "birfday." The teacher says with delight, "Your birthday is tomorrow? Yes, your birthday is very soon, and I can see that you are getting excited now that your birthday is almost here."

TEACHABLE MOMENT

Pronouncing *th* as *f* is a common mispronunciation that usually goes away if children are exposed to the conventional pronunciation over time. By consistently using the correct production without embarrassing Luka, the teacher can help children hear the contrast between *f* and *th*. Treating the mispronunciation this way is an example of children saying or signing what they hear or see because most children will eventually say words the way they hear their teachers say them.

The following strategy supports pre-school children:

More games. Teach children a nonsense **rhyme** to music that requires clear enunciation. Model the **syllables** for them with great exaggeration and have them say the rhyme together. For example, "A benny dicky doom bah. A lassa massa mossah. Oh ben away ben awo ben awah." The popular song "Apples and Bananas" also provides opportunities for language play. Exposing children to a variety of such experiences over time keeps their interest high and requires different speech adaptations. Objects or pictures with names that differ by a single sound may be placed in a box. As a child pulls out an object, ask or invite the whole class to say the word and then the contrasting word (e.g., *bat/hat; bow/toe; hand/band*). Children with oral motor involvement who may have difficulty in saying words or syllables as they learn to match, synthesize, or analyze syllables and sounds may demonstrate their knowledge by indicating yes or no in response to an adult's production of sounds or words.

Use Accepted Language Styles

Teachers can help children begin to learn accepted language conventions and styles so that they do not interrupt other children, so that they are polite, and so that they speak in quiet or strong voices where appropriate.

VIGNETTE

Gloria just spent her weekend at the beach collecting seashells. She comes to show Ms. Lutz one of her prize shells. Ms. Lutz asks, "Where did you find these beautiful seashells?"

Tony chimes in before Gloria can answer: "I got new shoes."

Ms. Lutz turns to Tony and says, "I really want to hear about your shoes, and you can tell me later about them. Right now, let's find out more about Gloria's seashells."

TEACHABLE MOMENT

Ms. Lutz illustrates the importance of staying on topic and of respecting others' rights to continue a conversation. By suggesting that Tony wait his turn and listen to Gloria, she reinforces that conversation is a give-and-take. When she asks questions of the children, she encourages them to take a turn.

The following strategy supports preschool children:

Model the use of language conventions and encourage children to do the same. By using complete and clear sentences, the teacher in the vignette showed children how to speak clearly. When teachers use polite and appropriate language, children will follow their lead.

Teachers should also ask questions and encourage children who are hesitant to respond in their "big voice" while encouraging loud children to speak in their "small voice." Teachers can also help children learn when to use their big and small voices (e.g., on the playground—*big* voice, but during naptime—small voice).

Tell a Short Story or Retell Something That Happened Earlier in the Day

Oral narrative, or storytelling, is often considered a bridge between language development and reading. When telling a story about something that happened earlier in the day or inventing a fictional tale, one must take the listener's perspective into account and fill in details that are often not included in a conversation. Telling stories demands not only the use of vocabulary and sentences but also a particular structure: a setting, characters, a problem, and a resolution.

Producing narratives at these ages may vary for children who are communicating with sign language or an alternative communication system. As is true for all children, teachers can support young children's communication knowledge and skills by repeating and extending what children say in conversations. Teachers can also provide opportunities for children to repeat or tell stories as a way of encouraging them to produce narratives.

VIGNETTE

Azadeh and Alberto are dressing up to act out the book the class has read several times. The teacher and the children in the audience remind the actors when they forget to portray crucial moments in the story. Jorge hollers, "Then he saved the frog!" and the actors laugh and depict that scene.

PLANNING LEARNING OPPORTUNITIES

Through guided dramatic play, the children act out a story for the class. The children themselves begin to notice key story elements and remind each other about these moments, all in the spirit of having fun. Silence is not always golden as the children, eager to share their recall of the story, tell the actors what they missed.

VIGNETTE

Adelita is eager to tell the class about the holiday gathering at her house. In her home language, she says, "Vino mi abuelita. Y vino mi tía. Y vino mi tío." (My grandma came. My aunt came. And my uncle came.) The teacher, who knows Spanish, tells the class what Adelita said and then asks her some questions first in Spanish and then in English (e.g., "Did baby Ana come too?"). Adelita's answers delight the class as she tells them about baby Ana's visit.

TEACHABLE MOMENT

The teacher's explanation of what Adelita said enabled everyone to feel included. By making this story engaging for all, the teacher is implicitly valuing Adelita's home language. Follow-up questions to the child's story allow the teacher to not only help Adelita to express herself but also to build narrative skill.

VIGNETTE

It is Lara's turn to share a special story from home. Lara, who is beginning to use an assistive technology communication device, had some key words added to her device that enable her to share. As Mr. Tony holds up the pictures, she pushes the button that labels the picture. Mr. Tony expands the label by saying "Tango. This is your new dog, Tango." Lara beams as the children get excited. "I got a dog like that!" Emilio says, "He is black too." Mr. Tony holds up another picture and asks, "What is Tango doing in this picture, Lara?"

TEACHABLE MOMENT

 Mr. Tony expands on the information because he had the background provided by Lara's father. Mr. Tony makes it possible for Lara to join the others and have a turn at sharing. Children's interactions with Lara may increase because now they have a connection to Lara and her dog.

The following interactions and strategies support preschool children:

Build on preschool children's own experiences. By asking children to recount simple daily experiences such as, "What do you do when you wake up in the morning, before you come to school?" teachers give children a chance to tell a story about a routine they know very well. Children will often take more risks in their home language. A teacher who invites stories from children in their home language conveys respect for the home language. Children also learn English from the teacher's translation. For more information about strategies to support children who are English learners, see Chapter 5.

Use dramatic play and co-construct stories. Encourage children to dress up and pretend. The scripts children create for their play (e.g., baby gets sick and must go to the doctor; Grandma is coming for a visit, and the house must be cleaned) are stories. Creating their own stories in play helps children understand stories that are read to them and is preparation for reading. In circle time, teachers start a story with, "Once upon a time there was a big brown bear who walked quietly up to . . ." and let each child add a piece of the story while moving around the circle.

Give story stems. Sometimes if the teacher just suggests, "The funniest thing that happened to me was . . ." children will fill in the blank with interesting responses. Or ask children in a small-group setting to close their eyes and imagine that they are somewhere else instead of in preschool . . ." Then the teachers asks the children to take turns answering, "Where are you? And who else is there?"

2.0 Vocabulary

The number of words that children learn is strongly related to later school success, because reading comprehension depends on it.[45, 46, 47, 48, 49, 50] So too, is the diversity of the words they know. Children who know many names for things, for example, can be more specific in representing what they mean, in telling people what they want, and in understanding what others say to them and the meaning of language in books. Children who know names for actions and events can use their language fluently to describe the things going on around them, as well as what was and what can be. The language children develop as their vocabulary grows allows them to escape into new imaginary worlds, to solve problems with words (e.g., "How can I get the swing when Jonny is still on it?") and to predict what will happen next in a book or story. When children know literacy-related vocabulary (e.g., *word, vocabulary, pronounce, sounds, meaning, letter, sentence*), they will better understand instructional language they hear in school settings and children can better ask questions about language and literacy contexts (e.g., "What letter is that?" "Whose name is that?" "What does *extinct* mean?").

The vocabulary substrand is organized around three areas:

- Understanding and using words for objects, actions, and attributes
- Understanding and using words for categories of things and actions
- Understanding and using words for simple and complex relations between objects

Understanding and Using Words for Objects, Actions, and Attributes

Preschool children need a vault filled with common words at the start of their journey into language and literacy. That journey begins when they learn the conventional names of familiar objects, actions, and attributes. Some children may speak a dialect of English that uses different words, and others will speak a different language or communicate through sign language or an alternative system. All children need exposure to conventional words.

VIGNETTE

In response to the construction outside their classroom, the room is filled with activity as children use their plastic hammers and wrenches, tool belts, and benches. The planned curriculum includes a Construction Unit. Outside the window, the children can see the cranes move and the workers in hard hats. They hear the sound of hammer against nail. This week the teacher reads to the class stories about construction equipment and information books about how tall buildings are made. The construction outside gives Ms. Vase an opportunity to expose children to the names of common and even not-so-common tools. Ms. Vase sent home a one-page newsletter in the languages of families represented in her classroom, telling parents about the Construction Unit and about vocabulary children are learning. She asked if any parents who are builders or carpenters would like to come to class to share their experiences.

PLANNING LEARNING OPPORTUNITIES

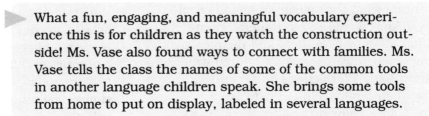

What a fun, engaging, and meaningful vocabulary experience this is for children as they watch the construction outside! Ms. Vase also found ways to connect with families. Ms. Vase tells the class the names of some of the common tools in another language children speak. She brings some tools from home to put on display, labeled in several languages.

The following interactions and strategies support preschool children:

Build on children's interests. Notice where children look and then talk about the things that are the focus of attention and action, using interesting, rich vocabulary. This simple but basic strategy makes people more sensitive listeners and children better learners. "Oh, that is a . . . (e.g., solid, heavy) truck. How are you thinking that you might use it?" Be sure to follow a child's interests. If you see a child examining a door hinge, you might ask, "I think you might be wondering what that is. It is called a *hinge,* and it attaches a door to the wall but also allows the door to move. Do you see where the hinge is attached to the door and to the wall? Yes, it's interesting to open and close the door to see how it works." After a few moments, suggest that the child find other hinges. If possible, bring an unattached hinge for the child to explore the next day. This will increase a child's understanding of how a hinge is designed and what makes it work.

What's my name? Names of things come at different levels. There are types of trucks (e.g., tow truck, dump truck, cement truck), the general **category** "truck," or the larger category, "vehicles," that includes trucks. Young preschool children know the names of categories they encounter frequently—*toys, food, clothes,* or *animals.* Many children may know those words in two languages. As preschoolers develop their understanding of things in the world, their use of categories expands: *reptiles, planets, vehicles, fruits, vegetables,* and *furniture.* As caregivers, teachers, and parents name and describe the things that children notice, children learn more names of things. Yet it is desirable for children not only to know nouns, but also to learn common names of actions (e.g., "Wow, you *run* really fast. Can you *run* even faster?") and properties too (e.g., "It looks like this brush has *stiffer* bristles than that one"). Young preschool children also use words such as *under, in,* and *different.* Older preschool children begin to use words to describe relations between objects such as *next to* and *in front of.*

Language in, language out . . . Narrate!
Narration is another effective way to build children's vocabulary. Preparing for snack time is a teachable moment for the children who are near the teacher as she shares, as if to herself, "Okay, let's put the apple juice on the table and then we'll need to get eight napkins. Even "long" words, such as *herbivore,* can be a part of natural conversation if that word is used many times and across contexts. For example, a teacher may ask a class, "Did you know that the dinosaur called Apatosaurus is an *herbivore?* (said slowly). That's right—herbivores don't eat meat—only plants. Do you know any people who don't eat meat? What do we call people who don't eat meat?"

More word games. Familiar games such as Simon Says can teach language. For example, "Simon Says point to the squirrel. Point to the alligator." Playing the game I Spy as in "I spy . . . a rectangle," is also language-rich. Sing songs in the home language and in English. Words accompanied by melodies are easily learned.

Understanding and Using Words for Categories of Things and Actions

---

Most words name categories rather than single objects; for example, *chair* can be applied to many kinds of chairs, from dining room chairs to beanbag chairs. And *chair* fits into another category called *furniture.* When we learn the names of categories, we are learning where one category begins and another ends. For example, what defines walking versus running?

VIGNETTE

"I'm gonna play the drums, the flute, and the guitar today," said Barney.

"That's great," responded the teacher. "You play a lot of instruments! Does anyone in your family also play an instrument?"

TEACHABLE MOMENT

Here the teacher responded directly to the child and offered a new category word. The teacher also took the opportunity to continue the conversation by connecting home and school. By adding to the conversation, the teacher was even able to use the new word *instrument* twice.

PLANNING LEARNING OPPORTUNITIES

There are many words for many different actions. Teachers can make a list of different actions they see children doing while outdoors. On another day these action words can guide a movement game for children (e.g., "Can you hop on one foot?"). In action songs at circle time, teachers can build in various large- and small-motor actions by adding more verses to those in the original songs.

Many strategies for building better vocabularies work equally well for category learning. Teachers may use categories of actions and attributes. Even though running looks very different when done by an Olympian and a toddler, both examples are called *running*. Similarly, categories for attributes such as colors or shapes contain items that look very different.

The following strategy supports preschool children:

Playing category games. Four- and five-year-olds love sorting games:

"Can you put the circles in the green box and the squares in the red box?"

"Let's put the fruit in the bowl and the vegetables in the box."

"All the children with curly hair, please wash your hands for snack."

One of the best ways to learn categories is by having a stock of books that constitute a category, such as shape books, animal books, and food books.

Understanding and Using Words for Simple and Complex Relations Between Objects

---

Words that describe relationships such as *in front of* and *behind* or *big* and *little* can be difficult for children. These words can also be more difficult because some of these words vary by language. For example, Korean children do not use words such as *in* and *on* but rather describe items as fitting *tightly* (e.g., an interlocking block on another interlocking block or foot in a sock) or *loosely* (e.g., apple in bowl or a book on a table).

VIGNETTE

"Okay. We need to get organized so we can take a picture. You will know your place if you listen closely as we play the Where Do I Go? game. Ying, would you please stand at the front of the line? Vang, would you please stand at the back of the line? Sayed, can you go next to Po? John, please go to the middle of the line. Ivan, please go behind Sarita."

PLANNING LEARNING OPPORTUNITIES

Here the teacher incorporated specific language learning in a transition, making it necessary for children to listen to the words for various spatial relations. Even simple routines, such as going on a neighborhood walk, can be full of language that children need to learn. A language game allows children to learn vocabulary about spatial relations without even realizing it and have fun, too! From the child's perspective, she is getting ready to do something or to go somewhere, even though the teacher also has clear language goals in mind.

As before, vocabulary is best learned in the context of meaningful exchanges and by following children's interests. The interactions and strategies listed for vocabulary on pages 118–120 work well with a few additions:

Detective work. *Same and different:* Show three pictures of bears, two that are exactly the same and one that is different. Can children find the one that is the same? The one that is different? When children seem to understand same and different, make the game a little harder by playing it at a higher category level. An example is the category of animals. A bear and a cat are in the same category, but an airplane is in a different category.

Do the same thing with concepts, such as big and little: Three toy elephants of different heights and weights are placed side by side. "Can you find the big stuffed animal?" Or this strategy may be used with raisins: "Can you find the big (small)

raisin?" Every so often, put all the plastic dishes and flatware used in the dramatic play area in the water table. Add sudsy water and provide dishcloths for children to wash and dry them. To put them back in the dramatic play area, children must notice the difference between big and little plates and type of item (e.g., glasses, knives, forks). The teacher can talk about the difference that children are noticing (e.g., "Oh, you put the big plates on the table today").

Routines: Here we go again! Daily classroom routines represents the many ways for teachers to use language over and over again to name categories and spatial and numerical relations. Simple, repetitive classroom routines, with a little forethought, can be a goldmine for children's language learning. Phrases such as, "Put the chairs *under* the table," "Make sure everyone gets the *same* number of crackers (at snack time)," and, "Who has *more*? Jorge or Chaya?" all use spatial and relational terms that children need to know.

Language opportunities in children's art. Children love to draw. As children express themselves artistically, use spatial language to engage them in telling about their drawings. "What is in the *middle* of the picture?" "Tell me about this part down here near the *bottom*." "This part up here at the top reminds me of an animal or a person. Can you tell me about this part?" By exposing preschool children to spatial terms and category names and by asking them to talk about their drawings, teachers tell children that their drawings have meaning worthy of discussion.

3.0 Grammar

Grammar holds words together to form sentences. Children learn to use grammatical words and elements during the preschool years from parents and teachers. When children say the simple sentence, "The boys want milk," they are using English word order and the grammatical elements *the* and *s* that indicate meaning. The *s* on *boys* tells the listener that there is more than one boy; *the* suggests that this is a specific group of boys. More complex sentences involve describing the item (e.g., *chocolate* milk) or joining two thoughts (e.g., "The boys want chocolate milk, but the girls want juice"). Preschool children move from using simple constructions to complex sentences with two separate thoughts and even complex connectors such as *but* and *before* (e.g., "I want to go play at Juanita's house, but my mother said I need to help her with my baby sister for a little while before I go").

As children learn grammar, they sometimes notice a pattern—such as *ed* on verbs such as *cracked* and *played* to indicate that something took place in the past. Sometimes children extend the use of *ed* more widely than they should, (e.g., *cutted, eated, breaked, and falled*). These charming **overgeneralizations** show that children *pay close attention to the language they hear* and are *thinking*. Children also make errors using pronouns, saying, "Her and I played" when "She and I . . ." is correct. Children also say, "Her did it," and "It's hims." Teachers can help children learn conventional grammatical forms by repeating what children communicate, using the correct forms (e.g., "Oh, I see. Your brother *broke* your pinwheel. I'm sorry. How did it happen?" Or, "Oh, you are telling me that this paint-

ing is *his*, not yours? Thank you. I didn't know *it was his*"). When a teacher's turn in a conversation recasts or expands on what children have said and uses complete sentences rather than just words, it builds on what children already know while helping them learn more. These strategies are particularly helpful to children who are English learners or to children who may have special difficulties in learning language. For children who are deaf or hard of hearing, a teacher of the deaf and hard of hearing should be consulted about the grammar of sign language.

The grammar substrand is organized around two areas:

- First, it focuses on how children understand and use increasingly complex and longer sentences.
- Second, it focuses on how children understand and use age-appropriate grammatical bits such as subject-verb agreement (e.g., *He walks; they walk)*, progressive tense (e.g., walk*ing*), regular and irregular past tense (e.g., *walked, went)*, regular and irregular plurals (e.g., *pails, oxen)*, pronouns (e.g., *him, it)*, and possessives (e.g., *mine*, not *mines)*.

Understanding and Typically Using Age-Appropriate Grammar

Communicating effectively often requires that children knit together two or three ideas into a single sentence. Teachers can encourage children to use increasingly complex and longer sentences by modeling them, especially in conversations with children.

VIGNETTE

"Her hitted me!" an indignant Pedro says loudly as he marches over to tell on Maristella. Ms. Futman is pleased that Pedro did not hit back.

Ms. Futman says to Pedro, "Pedro, did she hit you?" Pedro shakes his head violently. Ms. Futman notices that Maristella is watching and suggests to Pedro, "Please tell Maristella, 'We don't hit people in our classroom.'" Ms. Futman invites Maristella to think of how she can make Pedro feel better.

TEACHABLE MOMENT

Language and communication are involved in all areas in the classroom: from conveying lessons in good behavior to sharing necessary social conventions. By rephrasing what Pedro said and by giving him a rationale to repeat to Maristella for why hitting is not acceptable, Ms. Futman serves as a model of increasingly correct and complex usage.

VIGNETTE

Noticing that some children used their pronouns incorrectly, Mr. Gold invented a game that required children to use pronouns. He gathered some children in a small group and gave one child a small box. He asked the group, "Who has the box?"

They all yelled, "Sadie!"

Then he said, "Whose box is it?"

They said, "Sadie's!"

"Who would have the box if Sadie gave it to the child next to her?"

Again they responded, although much slower this time. "Jorge!"

Mr. Gold said, "Give it to Jorge, Sadie. Is it her box now?"

"No," Susie yelled, "It's his box!" and on and on.

PLANNING LEARNING OPPORTUNITIES

A teacher can plan an enjoyable activity that models correct pronoun usage. The more often children hear correct pronoun usages modeled by their teacher and other children, the more likely they are to correct their own pronoun errors.

The following interactions and strategies support preschool children:

Talk one on one with children. Have conversations with individual children whenever possible. Talk about what children are involved in and eager to discuss. Make responses depend on what they say, repeating children's contribution with more elaborated sentence structures, modeling appropriate grammar when children make an error (e.g., *foots* ➜ *feet*), and adding grammatical elements when they leave things out. When a child says, "I see Sarah coat," the teacher might say, "You are right! That is Sarah*'s* coat" with emphasis on the possessive *s.*

Know your families and individual children. Children whose home language is not English often need special encouragement to talk in their new language. Children with language or cognitive disabilities often need additional clues to help them know when and how to join a conversation. Starting with topics that children know a lot about makes it is easy for them to enter the conversation. Family members, foods, and toys are good choices for topics, as all children have experiences with them. For more information about strategies to support children who are English learners, see Chapter 5. Children with disabilities may also need encouragement or additional cues to join a conversation.

Spin narratives. The teacher, Ms. Shipley, told the children one morning, "What do you think happened yesterday when I went to the grocery store? I saw a man in a clown suit! He had a big red nose and giant floppy feet! Why do you think he was there?" If you tell stories about everyday events, children will be encouraged to do the same. Asking children to predict what will happen next and other questions about a story models language and gets them to talk, too. By having children use language without an immediately relevant context, teachers are preparing them for learning to read. See the "Research Highlight" on page 99.

Bringing It All Together

Small-group reading time was finished, and Ms. Harrington placed the "builder" book that some had been reading face out on the shelf as the children dispersed to choose their own activity. Peter, Mariana, and Julio made a beeline for the block area. "I'm going to be the builder," announced Peter. "Let's build a fire station!"

"Okay, I'll use the hammer," Mariana suggested as she reached for the plastic hammer and pretended to pound each brick into place.

"Let's put all of the big blocks on the bottom," continued Peter.

Their play continued as they arranged and talked about the squares and rectangles, the opening for the doors, and the place for extra trucks. After six minutes, Julio, who was watching from the sidelines, made an abrupt move, grabbing Peter's hammer while insisting in Spanish, "Me toca a mí (It's my turn),"as he pushed Peter to the side knocking down some of the carefully placed blocks.

Ms. Harrington gently intervened, "Julio, ask Peter, "May I use the hammer when you are finished?"

Julio modeled after his teacher, using both English and Spanish: "May I use the martillo (hammer)?" Peter agreed to share "in two minutes" and continued to build with Mariana.

Ms. Harrington then put her arm around Julio, stooped down to his level, smiled, and asked, "Would you like to use another tool until Peter is done? There's a wrench and a screwdriver," as she pointed to the remaining plastic tools. As Julio now joined the others, she asked the three children, "What are you using to build?" They excitedly responded, naming some of the tools they had just learned.

Here the teacher has done a superb job of integrating the reading at small-group time with opportunities during child-initiated play. Understanding that reading and language work hand in hand, she prepared the block area with construction tools and the dramatic play area with dress-up clothes used by builders. Ms. Harrington also knows that when she makes learning language interesting and fun, the children will use the language they learn in new contexts. This strategy helps children cement their understanding of word meanings. They talk about hammers and wrenches, big blocks, rectangles, and what is on the "bottom" of what—all vocabulary terms that were introduced in the book they read about builders. These words are about both objects and relations.

When Julio changes the play context into one of confrontation, the observant teacher gently intervenes while allowing the play to continue. She also reinforces that she understands the child's home language while encouraging the use of English. She models context-appropriate speech for Julio, as children will say what they hear. She wisely offers Julio new options, which makes it easier for him to wait for his turn and also exposes him more to the vocabulary of tools. Stimulating even more talk, she then asks a question at the end that puts the children in charge as they tell her about their creation.

Engaging Families

The following strategies can help families in developing their children's listening and speaking abilities:

✔ **Take the learning home.** To get families talking, send them ideas written in their home language of what to look for on the weekend (e.g., a blackbird). Topics to talk about and stories to tell together can be used to spur conversation, reading, writing, scribbling, and drawing. Teachers can also send home a brief newsletter to give parents information about what is happening at school. For example, if the class went to the zoo, parents might be encouraged to borrow books about animals from the library to read with their children or just to extend conversations about zoo animals by talking about animals at home.

✔ **Communicate with parents**. Teachers and parents are always partners in allowing each child to thrive. Teachers should be comfortable about sharing triumphs with the children's families. Share some of the stories about children's accomplishments with parents, such as when a child who is new to the program asks a question in front of a group of children. If a child has a favorite book or friend, parents would love to know this. If teachers can

share collections of each child's work with parents—including art, writing, and books they have heard—this will encourage parents to keep the conversation going at home.

✔ **Invite parents to come to the classroom and speak with you.** Parents' sharing of their stories, hopes, and concerns with teachers helps teachers understand what is happening in children's lives. A new baby? A divorce or even a visit from Grandma may influence children's behavior in the classroom. When teachers are partners with parents, they can better understand changes they see in children.

✔ **Connect home and school.** Think about doing projects in which children bring something from home. Perhaps a picture of a brother or sister will inspire children to talk to their peers and maybe to draw their own brother or sister.

Questions for Reflection

1. Examine your daily schedule, routines, and your learning environments to make sure that you have time and spaces for child-initiated play, guided play, and teacher-initiated small- and whole-group experiences.

2. How would you go about assembling a group of language-rich materials (e.g., posters, tools, games) to enrich a focus or topic area in which children have shown an interest?

3. How would you respond to Julio?

4. How might you encourage children to use their language in play to exchange information, to negotiate roles in play, and to convey politeness toward a play partner?

5. What are you already doing in your classroom to build connections between reading and language? How can you make this connection even stronger?

6. How do you know whether you are succeeding in building children's language? What indicators do you look for?

7. What are you already doing to connect home and school, and can you think of ways to strengthen this connection?

8. In what ways do you provide opportunities for children to hear and see a variety of languages and means of expression in the learning environment and use these in their interactions at preschool?

LITERACY

Reading

Reading billboards effortlessly on a car ride or making a shopping list involves literacy skills. Literacy includes both reading and writing. Literacy is also involved when people understand language and know enough about the world to comprehend the books they read. Children hear many books read aloud before they can read for themselves, and they can use scribbles to represent the thoughts they compose before they will use conventional print. Literacy does not develop overnight; it comes from being talked to and read to and from being encouraged to look at books, to draw, and to write. Children start on their journey to literacy at birth through visual and auditory observation of their world and through interactions with people and materials, in a variety of daily experiences, both at home and at school.

Reading provides access to meaning represented by print. It requires the translation of print into speech and the interpretation of meaning. Reading depends heavily on oral vocabulary and grammar and also on specific literacy knowledge (e.g., names of alphabet letters) and skills (e.g., detecting sounds in spoken words). Preschool children engage in reading by listening to stories and by retelling familiar books. They also engage in reading when they interpret environmental print by using physical clues (e.g., the stop sign is the red one at the end of their street) or when they reenact through play the literacy-related social behavior of family members (e.g., making a shopping list or pretending to read the cooking directions on a food box).

1.0 Concepts About Print

Concepts about print involve the understanding that print conveys specific meanings and is used for a variety of purposes. Reading grocery lists, messages on street signs, menus, and storybooks are all examples of how people find meaning in the squiggles on a page. Concepts about print also include knowledge about different print units and their names (e.g., *letter, word, sentence,* and *punctuation marks)* and about some basic **print conventions.** For example, in English and in many other languages, conventions include reading print from the left to right and from the top to the bottom of a page, and turning pages of a book, moving through it from front to back. In Chinese, calligraphic characters are arranged in columns read from top to bottom. In Hebrew, print is arranged from right to left, not left to right. Related areas of print awareness, such as learning to recognize and name specific alphabet letters and understanding that letters·

represent sounds in spoken words, are addressed in sections 2.0, "Phonological Awareness," and 3.0, "Alphabetics and Word/Print Recognition" (see pages 133 and 140).

Children with visual impairments can learn letters of the alphabet and about print without being able to see typical print. Access to printed alphabet letters is possible through the use of large print, color contrast, lighting, or braille, which uses a symbol system based on combinations of from one to six raised dots. Teachers should consult a vision instruction specialist to assist young children with vision loss in getting access to print or in learning to read braille symbols.

Preschool foundations for concepts about print are as follows:

- Book-handling behaviors and knowledge of print conventions
- Understanding that print can be read and conveys specific meanings

VIGNETTE

Pairs of children walk hand in hand to return to their classroom after playing outside. Sasha stops walking, points to a sign posted in the hallway, and says to Yasmin, her partner, "That sign says to be quiet because the babies are sleeping." In a soft voice, the teacher says, "Yes, we are walking past the babies' room. We've talked about how they might be sleeping. This sign says, "Remember to Walk." Do you think we need to make another sign for the hallway, one to remind us to talk softly?" The children agree that the second sign is needed, and several offer to help.

TEACHABLE MOMENT

The teacher had often pointed out the signs in the hallway to the children. In previous years, when children with visual impairments were in the class, the teacher made sure to point out large print or braille signs. When Sasha "read" the hallway sign, she knew that print carries meaning, but she did not understand the specific meaning of the hallway sign. Using a natural opportunity to read a posted sign, the teacher demonstrated not only that print can be read but also that it has specific meaning.

VIGNETTE

Later, the teacher asked Sasha if she would like to make the new "talking softly" sign and invited any other children who were interested to help. The teacher gave each of the three children who chose this activity a word printed out individually and kept one herself. The words (e.g., soft, use, voices, please) were those needed to create the new sign, but the teacher did not specify the exact wording for the message, knowing that the same basic message could be worded in different ways (e.g., Use Soft Voices, Please; Please Use Soft Voices). After some back-and-forth discussion, the children decided that the sign should read, Please Use Soft Voices. The teacher then prompted the children to put the word cards down on the table and arranged them in the order of the sentence the children had agreed upon. After all the words were on the table in the right order, the children glued the words onto a piece of poster board to make the sign and then helped the teacher post it in the hallway beside the other sign. Once the new sign was up, the teacher led the children in reading both signs.

PLANNING LEARNING OPPORTUNITIES

Having children discuss the word order drew them into considering the specific meaning of print and how to arrange print from left to right. The teacher's intentional use of the new sign was part of a plan that positioned children to read both the new and old signs and to distinguish between the signs when passing through the hallway on subsequent days. It also inspired them to read the new sign to peers. Had the class included a child with a visual impairment or who was blind, the teacher would have printed the words in much larger print or made the words in two forms, one using alphabet letters, the other using braille. The teacher also planned another sign-making activity for small groups where all children participated. These signs were for a grocery store (e.g., Dairy Products, Fresh Produce, Canned Goods, Store Hours, Open, Closed) set up near the dramatic play area. Children placed their signs in the "store," where they had already grouped empty food boxes and cans and some plastic models of food. The children had observed the same things in a visit to a neighborhood grocery store prior to setting up their play store.

The following interactions and strategies support the development of concepts about print:

Provide print props to support dramatic play. Stock the play kitchen with a range of food containers representing those in children's homes. Include food and toiletry coupons, newspaper flyer ads in multiple languages, simple homemade cookbooks, and telephone directories. Emergency telephone numbers (e.g., poison control, fire department, doctor's office) may be posted on the play refrigerator door. Children also enjoy having some small cardboard books to read to their "babies."

Provide print props for a variety of play themes in the dramatic play and block areas. Replicate the experiences children have in the world with written materials by providing props to support play of other themes, such as the doctor's office (e.g., appointment book, eye chart) or going to a restaurant (e.g., menus, specials signs, food order pads). Support and respect children who communicate in other languages. Use print in other languages on items such as on menus and signs. Paper and markers may be included in the block area for children to make road signs and billboards. Notepads and markers for making shopping lists are in the dramatic play area. Include other print props and raw materials, wherever needed, in response to children's interests.

Use print to designate interest areas. Children pick up the importance of written language incidentally if the classroom contains signs designating various areas. Post signs written in multiple languages in each classroom area (e.g., Block Area, Area de Bloques, 名词; Art Area, Area de Arte, 艺术，美术。). Including a picture or icon, along with the written word, helps to scaffold the meaning of the written text for the child. For more information about strategies to support children who are English learners, see Chapter 5.

Use literacy terminology to help children learn it. Use the terms *letter* and *word* naturally as children engage with print-related materials and in reading and writing situations (e.g., "Oh, you've put many of the *letters* back into the puzzle." Or, "Everyone can help me read the *words* in the *title* of our book (points to the words as each is read) *'Caps . . . for . . . Sale'*)." Label specific punctuation marks when creating these in a writing context. For example, when a child's dictates a story, the child exclaims, "They are yelling for help!" The teacher responds, "You are using a very important *vocabulary* word—yelling—in your story. I can see how excited and worried the people are in your story. I'm going to use a *punctuation mark* called an *exclamation point* to help your mommy know when she reads your story that the people need help right away."

Use print to support classroom routines. Post limits for children in areas where needed. For example, faces may be drawn to designate the limit (and the number word beneath each face). Near sinks, hang a labeled poster showing hand-washing techniques. Other signs remind everyone of important things to do (e.g., Please Turn Lights Off over light switches; Please Use Soft Voices in the book or library area; Remember to Walk, in a hallway leading to the kitchen or the playground). Post a large, printed daily schedule, with each segment illustrated. Create copies of the segments of the posted daily schedule on small cards, and place them on a tray in a puzzle interest area. During choice time, children sometimes enjoy putting the cards in the order of the daily schedule or rearranging the schedule in a playful way.

Read environmental print. On walks, read print on road signs, storefronts, and passing vehicles (e.g., BUS STOP, SCHOOL BUS) to children. Inside the interest area or preschool, help children notice environmental print, such as signs for men's and women's restrooms, exits, and the occupants or uses of rooms (e.g., Director, Staff Room, Caterpillar Classroom), by pointing out and reading the signs. Many such signs include braille symbols, and children are often interested in "why those dots are there" and how Ariel uses her fingers to figure out what they say.

Use print as a tool to get things done and to record information. Write steps on a chart for small-group activities requiring specific directions (e.g., cooking, planting seeds). Pictures of the steps will help connect the print to the directions for each step. Printed titles of songs and poems may be filed in a box. Teachers give children turns to select a poem or song to add to the selections for circle time. Provide Yes and No checklists for children's use in documenting explorations, such as testing objects with a magnet or testing materials' reactions to water.

Use print to support teacher-guided activities. Illustrated charts of poems and nursery rhymes for use at circle time provide meaningful opportunities for using print. Interesting, key words from familiar songs and poems (e.g., "moo-moo," from "Old MacDonald Had a Farm"; "fiddle-ee-fee, fiddle-ee-fee" from "Barnyard Song") may be printed on paper strips and mounted on felt pieces for arranging on a felt board. Children enjoy using these materials as a choice during child-initiated play and sometimes take their dolls to the circle time area and pretend to be the teacher.

Model basic print conventions. When reading book, poem, and nursery rhyme titles, underline the words from left to right. Also underline children's names and the names of helper chart jobs, as these are reviewed each day. Gesture specifically to the print (e.g., point to each word to track the print from left to right).

Write down interesting words as they come up and encourage verbal explanations of word meaning. To create interest in discovering and learning vocabulary and to link spoken words to print, write on a small whiteboard new words that come up throughout the day. Take care not to interrupt a child telling about an event. After the child finishes talking, a teacher might say, "I noticed that you used the word *gigantic* to describe the large crane you saw at the construction site. I am going to write that word down!" Name each letter as it is written down, then read the word back to the child, underlining it from left to right. Later, in a small- or whole-group setting, read each word listed on the whiteboard and provide context information: "This word (underlining it) says *gigantic*. Nathaniel, will you tell everyone what you saw that was *gigantic* and what *gigantic* means?" **Definitional vocabulary skill** (i.e., being able to explain verbally what a word means) is more beneficial to reading comprehension than is simpler identification vocabulary.[51] Expand a child's explanation or prompt the child to do so. For example, if Nathaniel says, "I saw a great big crane," the teacher might say, "Yes, and when you told me about it, you said it was a *gigantic* crane. That was a wonderful word to use, because *gigantic* means . . ." (teacher pauses to let Nathaniel explain).

2.0   Phonological Awareness

Phonological awareness is the ability to notice and manipulate the sounds in spoken language. If children are invited to play with language and to participate in specific, sound-focused activities, they will first detect and manipulate larger chunks of spoken language: words in compound words, **syllables** in words, then smaller chunks, such as **onset** and **rime** portions of words (e.g., /b/ in *bat* is the onset; /at/ in *bat* is the rime) and, eventually individual sounds—**phonemes** (e.g., /c/-/a/-/t/)—in spoken words.

Phonological awareness is not an oral language skill that focuses on meaning. It is the ability to detect or manipulate the sounds in spoken words, without attending to their meaning. Phonological awareness can refer to the detection or manipulation of large and concrete units of sounds, such as words and syllables, or to smaller units, such as onsets (e.g., the /t/ in *tail)*, rimes (e.g., the /ail/ in *tail)*, and phonemes (e.g., the /c/ – /a/ – /t/ in *cat).* Phoneme awareness, one subtype of phonological awareness, is the ability to detect and manipulate the smallest units of sound in words—phonemes. Phonological awareness is not the teaching or learning of letter-sound relationships. Phonological awareness is an important early literacy skill to develop because it makes possible children's later *understanding* that the sound sequences in spoken words are related to the letters in written words. Phonological awareness can be developed in children without any reference to print, even though its eventual useful-

ness to reading comes from linking individual sounds in spoken words to symbols (i.e., letters) used in written words. Without an underlying understanding of sounds in spoken words—without phonological awareness—children will not understand the phonics lessons (i.e., the direct teaching of letter-sound relationships) their first-grade teachers provide. For more information on letter-sound relationships, see the strategies on page 144. A teacher of the deaf should be consulted for strategies that are appropriate for children who are deaf or hard of hearing.

Phonological awareness does not develop naturally over time, but as a consequence of children's engagement in specific experiences. Children will need to reach phoneme-level awareness (e.g., understand *bat* as the series /b/ /a/ /t/) if they are to understand reading instruction later in school. Most children achieve the phoneme segmentation level of awareness in kindergarten, although older preschool children sometimes reach this level. The majority of phonological awareness strategies discussed in this chapter are designed for use with four-year-olds (i.e., children between 48 and 60 months of age), but not three-year-olds (i.e., children between 36 and 48 months of age).

The preschool foundations in phonological awareness are as follows:

- Blend and **delete** words and syllables without picture support.
- Blend onset, rimes, and phonemes and delete onsets with picture or object support of pictures or objects.

VIGNETTE

Ms. Sheck engages children in word play, explaining that she will say two words and put them together to make another: "If I say rain *first and then say* drop *right after it, I make the word* rain-drop. *If I say* fire *and then say the word* fly, *I make the word* fire-fly. *Okay, now you help me: If I say* rain *first and then say* coat *right after it, what word does it make?" A child answers,* rainbow. *Another says,* raincoat. *Ms. Sheck says, "Actually, if I say* rain *first and say* coat *right after it, I make* raincoat. *"If I say* rain *first and then say* bow, *what word do I make? Children answer,* rainbow. *"Yes,* rainbow. *You are learning how this game works. Let's make a few more words. This time we'll start with* sun *and say another word right after it. Okay, here we go: If I say* sun *and then say* shine *right after it, what word do I get?"*

PLANNING LEARNING OPPORTUNITIES

Knowing that children need considerable guidance to learn to blend two words to create new ones, Ms. Sheck models the blending and then asks children to do it. By continuing with different pairs of words to blend, using *sun* as the first word and another relevant word for the second word (e.g., *sun-shine, sun-set, sun-rise*), she provides more opportunities for children to learn how to blend.

TEACHABLE MOMENT

In any planned activity, teachers observe children and use whatever they observe to adapt to children's individual needs. When a child creates a compound word composed of the teacher's first key word but not the second, the teacher again models blending to provide more instruction and then provides two words for the child to blend. She uses words the child had offered earlier, as a mistaken guess. In this first experience for the child, Ms. Sheck knew that a balance between modeling and giving the child a turn to try was required. She used children's responses to judge when to return to modeling and when to give the children another opportunity to blend words.

VIGNETTE

After singing "Down by the Bay" at circle time, Mr. Zhang used an illustrated book to review the song and engage children in playing with some sounds in the words: "Here's the funny bear, combing his hair. Bear, /b/-/ear/; hair, /h/-/air/. The last parts of those words [i.e., the rime portion] sound the same, don't they? They rhyme." Several children agreed enthusiastically. "And who's on this page?"

"The llama," shout several children.

"Eating his /p/ . . . (pause)" Mr. Zhang continued.

"Pajamas!" several children called out.

As he turned the page, several children called out, "The fly with a tie."

"Yes, the fl-y wearing a t-ie. Before I turn the next page, I'll give you a clue about what you'll see next: A /wh/-ale . . ."

"A whale!" the children called out.

"With a polka-dot /t/-ail,"the teacher continued.

"Tail," several children called out.

PLANNING LEARNING OPPORTUNITIES

Mr. Zhang planned this song because he knows that children love songs and poems full of rhyming words. He also knows that mere exposure to rhyming words, whether through songs or poems, does not support phonological awareness at the levels children need. Reviewing the song with a book provided an opportunity for Mr. Zhang to say the words with their onset and rime portions separated, to stress the common rime portions for each rhyming pair, and to use the word *rhyming* to help children understand what it means (i.e., as a vocabulary teaching opportunity). (See Appendix B.)

VIGNETTE

Given the children's high engagement, Mr. Zhang continued for a few more minutes to engage the children in playing with segmenting and blending onset and rime units. "I have an idea of another word that has /air/ as its last part, like b-ear and h-air. I'll give you a clue about the word I am thinking of: /k/. . . ." When no one answered after a brief pause, Mr. Zhang said, C-are.

Several children said, Care!

Mr. Zhang said this was the word he was thinking of and added, "The last part of care is /air/, just like in b-ear and h-air."

Before Mr. Zhang could continue with the onset clue for another example, a child said, "I know one: gare!"

Mr. Zhang said, "Yes, gare, g-are, sounds like b-ear and h-air. Its last part is /air/."

Then another child said, "No, it's not one."

Mr. Zhang replied, "Are you thinking that gare is a made-up word, not a real word?"

"Yes," said the child, "It's not a right word."

Mr. Zhang then explained that silly words were okay to use when we are playing with sounds in words.

TEACHABLE MOMENT

> When no one guessed the word after Mr. Zhang gave the onset clue, he provided both the onset and rime units for the children to blend. Mr. Zhang then isolated the rime units to make explicit how this word was like *bear* and *hair*. In the explanation, the teacher separated the rime portion (e.g., /air/) of the nonsense word from its onset, which helped the children to focus on the relevant unit of sound in this task and to understand that phonological awareness tasks focus on sounds in words, not on their meanings. Mr. Zhang supported children's confidence by acknowledging that *gare* was correct and explaining why it was appropriate to use a nonsense word in this situation.

VIGNETTE

A small group of children and Ms. Fontana look at four pictures on the table. Ms. Fontana explains, "I say a word and ask you to say it without its first sound to make a new word. The new word is the name of one of these pictures. This is a picture of a block of ice. These are some little insects we call ants. What's this picture?" "An ear," the children say. "And this one," the teacher asks, prompting the children to identify the egg. "Okay, let's start. If I say leg and you say leg without the /l/ sound [i.e., the onset], what word is it? Leg without /l/?" The children look at the pictures. Suddenly, one child points to the picture of the egg and says, "That's it!" The other children say egg! "Yes, leg without /l/ is /eg/. Okay, here's the next word: If I say rice without the /r/ sound [i.e., the onset], what word is it?" The children scan the pictures and soon say ice. "You're getting good at guessing the words," Ms. Fontana tells the children. "Let's do another one!"

PLANNING LEARNING OPPORTUNITIES

> Ms. Fontana knows that deleting the onset of a word to create a new word is new for the children. She provides pictures as supports, reviews their names before starting the game, and also repeats the word and the sound to delete when presenting the first few examples. Because the game is new, the children are concentrating not only on understanding their task but also on remembering the word and the sound in it they are asked to delete from its beginning. It helps children to hear more than once the word and the specific sound to delete.

The following interactions and strategies support development of phonological awareness:

Play language games that focus on blending sounds. Select an appropriate level of sound (e.g., larger or smaller chunks) for a focus. Model blending and then ask children to do it (e.g., "If I say *bird* first and then say *seed* right after it, I make the word *birdseed*." Or, "If I say *c-ar*, I make the word *car*"). With smaller chunks, provide information before presenting the individual sounds (e.g., "This word is the name of a vehicle. We have these in our block area: *c-ar*"). Also use objects (e.g., doll, a dish, and a fork from the dramatic play area) or pictures with younger preschool children to provide support. After providing blending experiences with words and with onsets and rimes earlier in the year, begin to present individual phoneme segments (e.g., *b-u-s*), making sure to have pictures or objects available to support children in forming the words.

Play language games that focus on segmenting sounds. Hide an object from the children's view (e.g., in a shoebox with a lid). Model the game first:

"Okay, here's how we play: If I say b-all, *you might guess* ball, *and you'd be right (takes a small ball out of the box to show). What clues did I give? A few children say* b-all. *Others say,* ball. *"This is a ball, the teacher continues. The clues I gave were* b-all. *Okay, I'm going to give clues for something else:* c-up. *Yes,* cup *(takes a small cup out of the box). What clues did I give? Okay, now you get turns to give the clues." When each child comes to sit beside the teacher, the teacher puts a "secret" object in the shoebox. After Jamal peeks at the*

small car inside the box, his teacher prompts him to give the clues. Jamal says, car, *then realizes he has said the whole word, not its parts. Jamal is given another object and is asked to whisper the clues to the teacher before saying them out loud. The teacher asks other children to do the same for their turn.*

Easier forms of the game use word (e.g., *paint-brush, tooth-brush, blue-berry*) or syllable segments (e.g., *ba-na-na, nap-kin, sau-cer*). A more difficult form of the game uses phoneme segments. Pictures or small objects can be used in the box.

Play language games that focus on deletion. After providing children with experiences in blending and segmenting each level of sound segmentation—word, onset and rime, and phoneme—begin to play sound games that involve deletion of words and onsets. Model first and then ask the children to try. Use pictures to support the children's thinking.

Sing songs and say poems each day. All children enjoy the rhyming words and **alliteration** (words used in a phrase or verse that begin with the same sound) found in many songs and poems. Children also enjoy songs that manipulate sounds. "Apples and Bananas" and "Willoughby-Wallaby-Woo" are good examples. Use the framework provided by "Willoughby-Wallaby-Woo" as a model to sing the children's names in a funny way. Singing songs and saying poems help children to notice the sounds in spoken language. Applying the sound play patterns in songs to other words, such as children's names, further heightens children's sound sensitivity and is likely to encourage children to play with the sounds of language.

Play with sounds by adding new verses to a familiar song. Make up new verses for songs, such as "Down by the Bay," and ask children to select the ones that fit the pattern.

"What about 'Did you ever see a cat swinging a bat?' Should we use this verse for our song?" Children think it is a good verse. "Yes, I think that verse would work because /c/-/at/ and /b/-/at/ both have /at/ as their last part." "What about 'Did you ever see a skunk eating a pear?' Would that be a good new verse for our song?" "Some of you are shaking your head no, and you are right. /Sk/-/unk/ has /unk/ as its last part and pear has /ear/ as its last

part- /unk/ and /ear/ aren't the same. Those words don't fit the pattern we need. Okay, let's sing the song and add our new verse this time."

Use phonological awareness activities for transitions. Tell children that you are going to send them to go wash hands by saying each of their names in parts (e.g., "Me-lin-da; Cin-dy; Gi-o-van-na"). Tell children to raise their hand if they think you have said their name, and say their name "the right way," not the funny way you have said it. Also use other phonological awareness activities, such as the onsets and rimes of words for children to blend (e.g., "Rochelle, here are sounds for you to put together:

Research Highlight

Researchers working in the area of phonological awareness generally agree that the process of acquiring the various levels of phonological awareness is not rigid and stage-like, but overlapping. This means that while children are becoming aware of larger chunks of speech such as words and syllables, they are also slowly becoming aware of the smaller units that make up words (e.g., onset and rime, and phoneme).[52]

Children are able to indicate their awareness of a linguistic unit (e.g., words, syllables, onset and rime, or phonemes) in some phonological awareness tasks before they can indicate it in others. This is because different tasks involve different demands. Detection tasks (e.g., "Do the words *boat* and *bear* begin with the same sound or different sounds?") are easier than tasks requiring manipulation (e.g., "Say *boat* without the /b/"). **Blending** (e.g., "What word do you get

when you put /b/ and /at/ together?") is easier than segmenting (e.g., "Say the sound you hear at the beginning of the word *dog).*[53, 54]

Rhyme production is a higher-level instructional task because of all that it requires of children. First, children must search their memories to find words that rhyme with a target, while they hold the target word in mind. Second, when children's expressive vocabularies are fairly small, they have few relevant words to retrieve for a rhyme-production task.[55] Thus, relying too heavily on rhyme-production instruction or embedding too little scaffolding and **explicit instruction** in rhyme-detection and production activities (when they are used) does not provide the level of support many children need to help them develop their onset and rime sensitivity.[56, 57] Please refer to Appendix B for additional information.

/b/-/ig/. Rochelle says, *big)*, or words from which children can delete the first sound (e.g., "Rochelle, what's *chin* without the /ch/ sound?"). Ask children to detect the first sounds in their names: "If your name begins with /s/, you may go wash your hands." If Sarah does not raise her hand, the teacher can say, "Sarah, your name begins with /s/: /S/-*arah.* You may go wash your hands."

Discuss rhyming words and words that begin with the same sound. Rhyming words have identical rime units (e.g., *c-at, b-at).* Words that begin with the same single consonant phoneme have identical onsets (e.g., *c-at, b-at).* Some traditional games play with these two units of sound (e.g., "I'm going to say two words, and you tell me if their last parts sound the same." Or "Can you think of words that rhyme with . . . ?" If such games, in addition to activities that involve blending, segmenting, and deleting onset–rime units are used, make sure to provide some examples and also segment and blend onset–rime units as part of the game. For example, after a child responds

to *tall* and *ball,* you might say, "Yes, *t-all* and *b-all* rhyme. They both have /all/ at the end." Similarly, rather than say, "Yes, you are right," to a few children who correctly detect that *man* and *boy* do not start with the same sound, say, "Right, those words do not begin with the same sound. *Man* begins with /m/, and *boy* begins with /b/." Accept non-English and nonsense words that rhyme or begin with the same sound. A child's phonological awareness develops as well when activities use nonsense words and words from other languages. See the "Research Highlight" on page 138 and Appendix B.

3.0 Alphabetics and Word/Print Recognition

Alphabetics and word/print recognition involve recognizing and naming alphabet letters and learning that letters in printed words stand for sounds in spoken words or signs in sign language. When children have gained this insight about the function of letters, teachers say that children understand the **alphabetic principle.** Preschool is an exciting time for learning the names of many alphabet letters and for beginning to learn that letters "have sounds" and that these sounds are in spoken words. In kindergarten, children will learn more about print and sound links and will consolidate this learning in ways necessary for learning to read. Although few clear differences have been identified for kindergarten-age children compared to preschool-age children on a range of literacy skill interventions, there is still relatively little research at the preschool level about the benefit of linking letters to sounds in spoken words.[58] Preschool teachers must judge what is appropriate for individual children in their classrooms. Please refer to Appendix C, "Reflections on Research: Alphabetics and Word/Print Recognition," for additional information.

Preschool children often recognize words based on clues provided by familiar contexts, such as when they read "stop" on a stop sign.[59] Or, children might use length clues to guess what some words say (e.g., Christopher thinks his name is on the helper chart when it is Josephine's—another long name). When children know the first letter in their own name but have little understanding that it, as well as every other letter, appears in a multitude of words, they might claim any word that starts with "their letter" as "their name." For example, Josephine thinks her name is on the helper chart when the name posted is Jamal.[60, 61] In these instances, children are not yet using the print to actually *decode* words—to link letters and assigned sounds. Older preschool children begin to notice words they know in books and on signs and sometimes play with reading these by touching the word as they say it. Older preschool children might try to read unfamiliar words by applying letter and sound knowledge—by trying to decode the words. Typically, though, preschool children do not succeed in reading unfamiliar words without adult help. Children's success in learning to read later in school depends on them learning how to decode.

The preschool foundations for later success in word recognition are as follows:

- Recognize letters in their own names.
- Recognize their own name and a few common words.
- Name many uppercase and lowercase letters.
- Recognize that letters are assigned specific sounds.

VIGNETTE

The caregiver shares an alphabet book with a few children. "This is the page for the letter B. Here is the big B and here's the little b." She engaged the children to help identify the pictures on the B page: "Blueberries, broccoli, beets, bananas, beans." Then she comments, "B is the first letter in each of these words. This word (pointing to the first letter in blueberry, printed above a picture of a box of blueberries) *starts with the letter* B. *It says,* Blueberry *(underlines the rest of the word, as she reads it).* Blueberry *starts with the /b/ sound. What do you think this word says? (She points to the word above the picture of some bananas.) One child says, "banana;" another says, "platano." The caregiver confirms that banana can be called by either name, one Spanish and the other English. "The words in this book are written in English—/b/ is for* banana *(points to banana). I think we could write some of these words in Spanish and paste them into the book. We could write* brecol *to put here with* broccoli." "When can we do that?" a child asks. "After rest time today, if you'd like. Miguel and Alexandria will still be sleeping. I can help you and Aaliyah spell Spanish words that will work in this alphabet book. We can type them on the computer and then print them out to paste in our book."*

PLANNING LEARNING OPPORTUNITIES

This caregiver brought key features of alphabet books to the children's attention (e.g., a letter on each page; pictures of things whose names begin with that letter). She anticipated that some children would offer food names in Spanish and English, because she had helped them learn the names in both languages during lunch and snack time conversations. The children also sometimes drew pictures of foods and asked for help in writing their names in both languages. Knowing that only some of the foods pictured in the alphabet book had names that begin with the same letter in both languages, she realized that discussing Spanish words to add would be useful in helping children understand links between letters and sounds. (See Appendix C.)

VIGNETTE

Ms. Cone had used the children's name tags in transition activities for quite some time, at first pointing out and naming the first letter in each name as she called children to go wash hands or to get their jackets before going outside. Somewhat later, she held up each of the name tags and pointed to the first letter as she asked the child to name it. Today, she is using the first sounds in names to send a few children at a time from the circle time area to wash hands for lunch: "If your name starts with /k/, you may go wash your hands. Yes, **C***-onnie and* **C***-arolina, you may go to the sink. Both of your names start with the /k/ sound." Cindy sees Connie* *and Carolina stand up, and she stands up too. Ms. Cone explains that Cindy begins with the /s/, not /k/ sound, and that she'll get a turn soon. Cindy says, "I'm a C too!" Ms. Cone says, "Oh, you are right. Your name begins with the **letter** c like Connie and Carolina, but it starts with a different **sound.** We hear /k/ at the beginning of Connie and Carolina—/k/ Connie, /k/ Carolina. We hear /s/ at the beginning of your name—/s/—Cindy. I'm going to say that sound next: 'If your name starts with /s/, you may go wash your hands.'" Sabrina stood up, joined hands with Connie, and they walked to the sink together.*

TEACHABLE MOMENT

Ms. Cone knows that children become increasingly familiar with their own and other children's names and with their first letters and sounds as the year progresses. She also knows that using names frequently in transition activities helps children to notice some interesting things about letter and sound relationships. In English, some letters can stand for more than one sound (e.g., *c* is used for both /s/, as in Cindy, and for /k/, as in Connie and Carolina), and some sounds are represented by different letters (e.g., *g or j* for /j/, as in Giovanna and Jessica). Ms. Cone's acknowledgment of the child's puzzlement, along with her concrete examples, helped the children begin to understand the situation.

The following interactions and strategies support preschool children:

Use children's printed names as labels and to support routines. Place name cards on the tabletop for a mealtime or snack time to designate children's seats or use placemats with children's names on them. Post lists of names near a small group's meeting place. Label cubbies and cots with children's names as well as helper charts and attendance charts. For cubbies and cots, pair a picture with the name to help children "read" it using something other than print clues. Pairing the printed names with the child's picture supports children who are just beginning to notice printed material. In other contexts, such as a helper chart, where children's names are changed daily and a teacher scaffolds children's reading attempts, she may use printed names only. Using *some* printed labels in a few contexts gives children opportunities to move to higher levels of print skill (i.e., use their print and sound knowledge to try to read words). Otherwise, young children will pay scant attention to print and will learn little about how it works.[62, 63, 64] Use braille or larger print, as appropriate, for the children in the classroom who may have vision problems.

Use children's printed names and letters in transition activities. Show children's names, underlining each from left to right while reading it. After a name is read, children then move from the current area to the next activity (e.g., washing hands for lunch or walking to their small-group table). After children are familiar with one another's names, hand out name tags, giving each child another child's name. Ask two or three children at a time to read the name tags they hold, assisting them, as needed, to dismiss children. Later they use a letter focus in transitions. For example, dismiss children by holding up and naming letters that are the first in the children's names (e.g., *"If your name starts with the letter S, you may go outside to play")*. Later teachers hold up each name, point to its first letter, and ask the child whose name it is to call out the letter.

Use children's names in teacher-guided activities. Graphs (e.g., to indicate children's preferences, the number of buttons on clothing) and a telephone directory for dramatic play are ways to use names in teacher-guided activities. To familiarize children with the telephone directory concept and to engage them with the names, ask children to dictate the letters in their names for you to type at the computer. After printing the names, assist children in figuring out what letter their name starts with and help them place it where it will go in the telephone directory (e.g., "Where's the letter E on our alphabet poster? Does it come before the B here in Belinda's name or after it?"). Or, children who are especially interested in making the telephone directory can arrange all of the children's names, with a teacher's help, and then paste them into the directory.

Provide children's names as a resource or reference. Print children's names and bundle these into sets of three or four with a metal ring binder. The sets may be placed in the writing area for children

to use as a reference, if they wish. The child's name is written in the home language on one side of the name tag and in English on the other, if the alphabet system is different. Provide the name in braille for a child with a visual impairment and a "name sign" (in sign language) for a child who is deaf or hard of hearing.

Provide access to alphabet letters in a variety of contexts. Include alphabet books in the library area. Place alphabet puzzles, magnetic letters, letter tiles, and children's name cards in the manipulatives area. Post English and Spanish alphabet posters at eye level as well as posters in other languages represented by the children in the classroom. Post alphabet signs that are used by children who are deaf or hard of hearing. Children need many opportunities to see alphabet letters in a variety of fonts or styles. Children "read" environmental print by using many clues that surround it, with the consequence that children pay little attention to print details, such as the specific letters used in words.[65] Providing alphabet materials increases children's opportunities to engage in alphabet learning.

Focus on first letters and sounds in alphabet books and posters. Experience with alphabet books has been linked to children's knowledge of letter names and phonological awareness skill.[66, 67] Alphabet books provide a context in which adults reading to children might link specific letters to specific sounds, helping children get a beginning idea of what letters "do" in written words—stand for sounds in spoken words. Read a variety of alphabet books—those with connected text (e.g., *Dr. Seuss's ABC, Pignic, The ABC Bunny)* and also those with only a letter and several pictures on each page (e.g., *Eating the Alphabet* and *From Acorn to Zoo).* For alphabet books with connected text, stress the first sound in key words while reading (e.g., "Ben brought beans from Boston"). When sharing alphabet books with only pictures and no text, stress the first sound in the names of items pictured as you identify them with the children (e.g., *"blueberries, broccoli, beets, bananas, beans").* Comment that all of these words start with the letter B and that all also begin with the /b/ sound. Help children make wall posters of items beginning with the same letter and sound. These are similar to the clusters of pictures on pages of alphabet books.[68, 69]

Point to each letter as its name is sung in a song. Many songs have letters in the lyrics. One of these is the "Alphabet Song." Other favorite songs of preschoolers also include letters (e.g., "Bingo," the farmer's dog's name, is spelled repeatedly in the song; "Old MacDonald Had a Farm" has the E-I-E-I-O refrain). Pointing to letters as their names are sung in a song helps children learn letter names. For both "Bingo" and "Old MacDonald Had a Farm," make specific letter props for a flannel board or write the relevant letters on a whiteboard. For the "Alphabet Song," a pointer can be used with a large chart of the alphabet. The alphabet poster should be at eye level on a chart stand or a wall as a choice for center time. Children can sing the "Alphabet Song" and attempt to point to letters on the chart as they sing the song.

Use activities and games to interest children in letter matching and naming. Make lotto-like cards printed with letters and matching letter tiles for each lotto card. Place a somewhat different selection of letters on each card in the lotto card set to expose children to the full set of 26 uppercase letters. Join children, as they play, to provide letter names (e.g., "Yes, that's the matching E"). Otherwise, children will learn only to match items, not to name them. Play letter bingo in small groups. As children's knowledge of letter names increases, give children turns to hold up letters and call them out. Coach individual children in this role, as necessary. The Go Fish game can also be played using alphabet letters. When the game is played in small groups, prompt children to ask others for a letter (e.g., "Do you have an F?") and to tell a friend to "go fish," when no one is holding a letter a child has requested.

Use everyday opportunities to model attending to print details in words. Gesture specifically to the print in book and poem titles (e.g., point to each word and to the first letter in each word) to help children begin to understand how print relates to speech. If a child confuses his name with another child's (e.g., Joshua begins to sit at the lunch table where Jonathan's name card appears), help the child compare letters in the two names by sounding them out).

Provide materials with environmental print in an interest area. Puzzles of vehicles and other items with names printed on their pieces (e.g., taxicab, школьный автобус, Xe ta xi; mail carrier, почтальён, *Nguoi dua thu;* firefighter, пожарник, *Linh chua lua)* are provided in several languages. Point out the print as children use the materials. Make small word cards that match some of the environmental print in picture books (e.g., *Truck,* by Donald Crews) or the interesting words (e.g., *crunch* and *munch, dart* and *dip)* appearing amid the illustrations in some books (e.g., *In the Tall, Tall Grass,* by Denise Fleming; *Dazzling Diggers,* by Tony Mitten and Ant Parker). Word cards may be laminated and secured in sets with a metal ring binder. The book and word card sets may be placed in the library area or an interest area with other literacy materials, such as alphabet tiles.

Provide predictable textbooks in library and listening areas. If children have opportunities to hear **predictable textbooks** numerous times, they memorize the texts. As children "read" these books to themselves, they sometimes search for certain words they know are on the pages. Though not yet reading by **decoding,** preschool children can recognize words by finding known words in a familiar book. Use audiotapes or CDs at a listening area to give children opportunities to listen to predictable textbooks as often as they would like. Some children may need additional materials to support their engagement in a listening area experience. Braille can be added to a copy of predictable textbooks to enable a blind child to find known words in the book while using the listening area. A sign language interpreter's help may be used to prepare videos of signed versions of predictable textbooks for a deaf child in the classroom.

4.0 Comprehension and Analysis of Age-Appropriate Text

When a friend calls and tells a story about someone, people commonly use the skills that children will need in order to understand stories. People want to know who the story is about (i.e., characters), where it took place (i.e., setting), what the problem was, and how it was resolved. Teachers help children comprehend stories by talking with them as stories are shared and by asking questions and responding to the children's comments and questions, such as "Why'd he do that?" or "Why's he crying?" At first, children rely heavily on a storybook's illustrations and interpret these from their own experience, sometimes disregarding or misinterpreting important information in the book.[70] Personal experience and knowledge are required in comprehending stories, but they must be integrated with the information in the book. As teachers help children to bridge their own world with a new one presented in a book, children gradually realize that other people have ways of feeling and interpreting that differ somewhat from their own, and they begin to take these different views into account as they interpret a story. This broadening of perspective develops over a long period of time, with only a few important first steps taken during the preschool years.

Preschool children also learn to comprehend information books—books that tell about, for example, whales or vehicles; explain why it thunders during a storm; or how to make a cake. Some important printed information is not in books. Examples include train tickets, restaurant menus, and even grocery lists. Those types of printed information fascinate children, because they see people use them in their daily lives. Teachers capitalize on this fascination by making these texts available for children's use in play.

The preschool foundations in text comprehension and analysis are as follows:

- Demonstrate knowledge of familiar story details (e.g., characters, settings, events, and event sequences).
- Demonstrate and use knowledge from information texts (e.g., label and describe an animal, take on the role of astronaut, explain what a seed needs to grow).

VIGNETTE

The teacher starts to read Corduroy *for the first time to a small group of children. She rewords some sentences (e.g., "He waited a long time with all the other toy animals for someone to buy him and take him home") and stops, after reading the second page, to review the story so far: "Oh, there are a lot of shoppers in this store—people there buy things" (points to the people pictured in the department store). "Here's a man, right here (points to man). He's looking at something (points to a fire truck) that he's thinking about buying. It looks like one of the trucks in our block area."*

"Fire truck," says a child.

"Yes, it does look like the fire truck. It has ladders (points to ladders). Are any shoppers looking at Corduroy, the little bear in green overalls, over here on the shelf (points to Corduroy)?"

"No," say several children.

The teacher continues: "Right. No one is looking at Corduroy (said sadly). No one seems to want to buy him (said sadly). He's hoping someone will look at him and buy him. He wants to go home with someone. Let's read some more and see what happens to Corduroy."

PLANNING LEARNING OPPORTUNITIES

The teacher had planned ways to support the children in understanding the reading of this story. She kept in mind the children who were learning English and also the fact that all preschool children have difficulty understanding the mental states of story characters. She planned simplifications of some of the book's longer sentences and ways to state information in some places more concretely than the book stated it. She also planned for stops to review the story while using the illustrations explicitly to help children understand the meanings of words and sentences in the book. After reading the first two pages, the teacher focused on the story's setting—the department store with its many shoppers, what a shopper does, the shoppers' relationship to the main character, Corduroy (e.g., not paying attention to him), and on Corduroy's desires and feelings (e.g., he wanted someone to buy him and was sad that no one wanted to). The teacher mostly commented, rather than ask a lot of questions. The goal in this first reading was to help children understand and enjoy the story while the teacher learned to use the illustrations as support.

The following interactions and strategies support preschool children's comprehension and analysis of text:

Read stories daily. Children learn to comprehend and analyze stories as they listen and think about stories in the company of adults who respond to their comments and questions and who ask questions and share their thinking. If teachers read stories daily, children have abundant opportunities to hear and talk about stories. Some children need special support to benefit from story reading. (See the "Research Highlight" on page 99.) A teacher can consult with a special education service provider for the deaf and hard of hearing to learn some signs for the book. For example, a teacher skilled in using sign language would provide both oral language and sign language if a deaf child is in the classroom or would wear a microphone to increase the volume of speech for a child who is hard of hearing. A second teacher assists in holding the book for children to see if a teacher must both speak and sign its reading.

Plan support for story reading. A great deal happens in a good story—settings change, characters interact with one another, and the story problem is gradually resolved through a series of related events. Study the storybooks beforehand, thinking carefully about each one and identifying parts that might be more difficult for children to understand. Plan comments to make, questions to ask, and ways of using the illustrations to aid children's understanding of the story as you read it for the first time.

Read a story several times over a few days. Multiple readings help preschool children understand a story better. During a second reading of a book with a small group of children, teachers can *prompt* children's thinking and verbal engagement by asking some questions. For example, during a second reading of *Corduroy,* a teacher might ask on the first page, "So, where does Corduroy live?" A child might say "in there" or "at a store." The teacher *expands* the child's response (e.g., "Yes, Corduroy lives in the toy department of a big store") and follows by encouraging the child to say, "toy department." On the page where Corduroy comments about his lost button and his plans to find it, the teacher might ask, "What is Corduroy thinking here? What does he plan to do?" A child might say, "The button." The teacher *expands* what the child said: "Yes, you are right. Corduroy says, 'Tonight, I'll go and see if I can find it.'" Then, before turning to the next page, the teacher might ask, "What happens next?" With this approach, a teacher monitors a child's understanding of a story, helps a child understand more of the story's parts, and expands the child's expressive language, all of which help a child learn to retell a story on his or her own.[71]

Help children understand the words and sentences in a story. Children's comprehension of text depends on their understanding the words, sentences, and illustrations in the book. While reading a book, teachers can explain explicitly the meanings of some new words, using friendly explanations. That is, they offer a definition that uses words a young child already knows rather than a more formal definition from a dictionary that is likely to have words not yet in a preschooler's vocabulary.[72] An example of a friendly explanation would be, "Oh, the little bird was *exhausted.* That means she was very, very tired. She worked hard to build her nest and to pull up juicy worms to eat. She's going to rest now, because she's very, very tired—completely *exhausted.*" Support children in learning new words, upon encountering them in the story, by pointing to a relevant part of an illustration on the page. Use your voice to support the meanings of words when this strategy makes sense (e.g., "Over it fell with a *crash!*").[73] See the "Research Highlight" on page 99.

Discuss a story after reading it. A short discussion after the reading of a story can also increase children's understanding. Questions that require only recall of small details (e.g., the teddy bear's name, the color of Corduroy's overalls) rarely lead to back-and-forth discussions and do little to help children engage in the kind of **inferential thinking** that stories require (i.e., piecing information together to determine why a character did something or what a character will likely do next). Instead of asking primarily literal questions, use questions that prompt children to think and to use their language (e.g., "Why do you think Corduroy wanted to find his missing button?" "How do you think Corduroy felt when the night watchman took him back to the shelf in the toy department?"). Be prepared to guide and scaffold children's language and thinking as they respond in any language.[74]

Model deeper levels of reasoning. Suppose that a child says, "Corduroy wanted to find his button because that little girl's mommy said, 'No, we can't buy him.'" A teacher might say, "Yes, you are right. The little girl's mommy said that" and then go further to link this event to Corduroy's wishes and actions. Thinking out loud shares the reasoning and indicates how people use information from the story to reason about it (e.g., "I'm thinking that when Corduroy heard the little girl's mommy say this, he started to worry that no one would ever want to buy him and take him home . . .

unless he found his button. Remember, Corduroy really wanted someone to take him home"). Even though children will not always grasp the whole line of reasoning, they will realize that thinking is something people do when reading books. Starting in the earliest years, teachers can let children know that active, inferential thinking in the story context matters and can help to prevent later reading-comprehension problems. Teachers can give children a feel for thinking in this context by modeling it[75, 76, 77] and by using discussion questions that focus on big ideas rather than on mostly literal details.[78]

Read information books. Find books that support children's current interests and the development of new ones. Read them in conjunction with firsthand experiences (e.g., growing plants, caring for fish or other animals, playing doctor's office), in support of interests that emerge at preschool, or in the context of children's families (e.g., finding a worm outside, seeing new leg braces worn by a peer, birth of a new baby, a grandmother's visit, soccer, or some other sport they like).

Include information books among the materials utilized for science activities and other hands-on experiences. When planting seeds or observing the behavior of a snail or some fish, use information books, including the diagrams. Specific information might be found in many books without reading the book as a whole. The table of contents and index are useful for finding specific information of interest, such as what whales eat or how water comes out of their spouts. The other parts may be read later as children's curiosity expands.

Model authentic uses of book and nonbook forms of information text. Just as anyone would do before tackling a new task, use information texts when setting up a new aquarium, making muffins, or drying flowers. To prepare for a field trip, use information books, brochures about the destination, and simple maps of the path children will travel. Also read to the children any notes and permission forms that are sent home to their parents about field trips. Help children make information books for use in dramatic play (e.g., cookbooks, telephone directories, photo albums of children engaged in activities), and provide nonbook information texts (e.g., newspaper food ads, restaurant takeout menus, children's magazines, food coupons), making sure that the variety represents the range of restaurants and languages that mirrors those used by children's families.

Plan for children to use information gained from an information book. When you read an information book to children to inform them about a process for an upcoming activity (e.g., planting seeds in small pots, making hand shadows on the wall, making paper-plate rhythm shakers, cleaning the fish aquarium), ask the children to describe the process before starting the activity. Support children's recall, as needed, to help children provide the details of the steps they will follow in the activity.

Plan the environment to support independent story retellings. After children have heard a story read aloud several times, place copies in the book area for children to retell, perhaps to an audience of peers or stuffed animals. Children also can retell by stories using flannel pieces or puppets, or they can dramatize stories by using simple costumes and props. Some retellings take place during quiet times, such as when children look at books as they rest. Others can take place as children read to a baby doll in the dramatic-play area, if small cardboard versions of familiar books are placed there. Children also represent story ideas creatively in the art area through drawing, painting, or sculpting.

Place information books in all areas. Information books are resources that increase understanding of many things. Place books about shells near a seashell collection, books about building houses in the block area, and cookbooks in the dramatic play area. Make sure all are easy to reach. Racks can be provided to display some open books throughout the learning environment, both indoors and outside on the playground. This approach exposes a part that might engage children to consult the book while playing in an interest area. Provide information books in braille for children who have a visual impairment and in the languages represented by the children in the class. Set out assorted types of printed information (e.g., newspaper food ads, takeout menus from restaurants, children's magazines, bus and airline tickets, food coupons) for children's use in play. Community newspapers in the different languages of children in the class may be used.

5.0 Literacy Interest and Response

Literacy interest and response involves motivation to engage with books and other print-related activities. When children find themselves in a warm and encouraging classroom that respects their family and culture and their experiences with books and writing are fascinating and delightful, their interest and engagement in literacy activities will take off. Children's motivation for reading and other print-related activities is also supported when adults scaffold their learning in ways that encourage sustained effort in learning new literacy-related understandings and skills. Adults also support children's motivation to engage with books and print when they show interest and delight in books and use print themselves.

The preschool foundations for literacy interest and response are as follows:

- Demonstrate enjoyment of literacy activities (e.g., choose to spend time in the book or writing areas, or choose a literacy-related activity with a friend).
- Engage in routines common in literacy activities (e.g., asking a question about a picture in an information book, borrow a book from the lending library, putting a "letter" inside an envelope, and scribble an address on it before delivering it to a friend).

VIGNETTE

Javon usually knew exactly the book he wanted from the classroom lending library. One day, a book he had hoped to take home had already been checked out. Javon decided to make a list of books and post it on the wall near the lending library to inform his friends that they should return a book on the list as soon as possible. (The classroom rule was that children could keep a book for a week.) Javon got a piece of paper and asked his teacher how to write, "Books to Check Out." With help, he wrote the words at the top of the paper and then drew six or seven lines across it. He taped the list up on the wall near the lending library shelves, to "do later." He turned his attention to searching among the remaining books in the lending library. Before long, he found one he liked. The empty list stayed on the wall for several weeks. One day, Javon took it down and gave it to his teacher. "You can have this," he told him. "You might need it sometime."

TEACHABLE MOMENT

Javon's teacher read stories to children daily and often brought in information books to support children's interests. His teacher also frequently suggested to children that they make signs or lists for use in their play. The teacher sometimes engaged children in composing notes to thank classroom guests. His teacher also suggested to children that they make birthday or get-well cards for peers. Given the teacher's use of books and support for writing, it was not surprising that Javon loved books or that his first thought of solving his problem was to write a list of books to post on the wall. Even though Javon never actually used the form he made, its creation demonstrated how much he loved books and how his teacher's strong support of writing made quite an impression on him.

The following interactions and strategies support preschool children:

Make stories come alive and encourage the children to do the same. There are good reasons why seeing a play or a well-crafted movie is enjoyable. The actors bring a story to life, which engages the audience in feeling the story in ways that sometimes differ from a reading of the same story from a book. When reading stories to preschool children, convey the personalities and emotions of characters and also reveal (through voice, signs, facial expressions, and pacing) the tone or mood of each story event. Read and think carefully about stories before reading them to the children, asking, "How does the character feel right here? Disappointed or frustrated? Excited or surprised? How can I capture that with my voice and pacing?" If adults know the stories and enjoy the characters and plots, they are better able to engage and delight the children when reading to them. When children act out the stories that teachers read, they mimic the teacher's voice, signs, and pacing.

Use voice for expression and with variation. Reading expressively does not mean reading at a constantly loud and high pitch. When a reader's voice does not vary, children do not receive the scaffolding they need to understand the feelings of characters or distinguish between

a calm part of a story and one full of suspense. If adults use appropriate variation in voice and expression when reading to children, children are likely to understand more of the content and attend for longer periods of time.

Make story time not too long, not too short, but just right. Preschool children tire when they are asked to sit and think too long. Although stories are generally interesting to children, a certain book and the conversation that takes place around it might not be of keen interest to every child in the group. Preschoolers can sustain attention and engagement for short periods under these circumstances, but not for a long time. Wise teachers plan the length of story time and other teacher-led literacy activities so that children might still want *more* rather than when they are worn out. There is always a later time to read another story or to do another literacy activity. Children are more likely to look forward to doing literacy-related activities if they know that teachers or caregivers engage them for a reasonable amount of time on each and every occasion.

Make reading and writing meaningful and useful. Bring books that support children's interests, and model how to use books to get information. For classroom topics of investigation, find related books and let children know that you are learning new things, too. If the class gets a new aquarium or a table or anything else that must be assembled, show the directions to the children and let them help, when appropriate. When classroom guests are invited to share a hobby or their occupation with the children, ask the guests to bring books used in their work. In most cases, the books will not be appropriate for reading to children. Guests can explain that these are just manuals, guides, or information books they use in their work.

Seek children's input. Devise a plan for children to request stories, songs, and poems for the teacher to read at circle time or at times during the day when children choose their activities. A system can be as simple as writing "Requests" at the top of a piece of poster board and mounting it on a wall. Children can then dictate requests to teachers to write on paper that is taped to the poster board. Or, children can draw a picture to convey their message, scribble a note, and tell the teacher what it says.

Bringing It All Together

A family dinner, a tradition at Children's Corner Preschool, is three weeks away. Mrs. Nguyen reads a book that features a diverse group of children and the food each brings to a potluck. The characters' names and the food each brings start with the same first sound and letter. After reading the book, Mrs. Nguyen tells the children the exciting news. Very soon, they will have a family dinner at school.

Mrs. Nguyen also reads aloud a note to the children: "You are invited to a special family dinner at Children's Corner on Thursday, May 24, at six o'clock. Please suggest a favorite food dish of your family—a salad, a vegetable, a main dish, or a dessert. Please write down the ingredients needed for the food dish. Our school kitchen staff will make some of the dishes for our special dinner. Family members will visit our classroom to bring the ingredients for their favorite dish and tell about the dish and how it is made. The kitchen staff will then prepare the dinner. If a dish can be made the evening of the dinner, families can bring the ingredients and help prepare the dish then. I will contact each family to discuss a food dish and how it can be prepared at school. We will have coffee, tea, milk, and water to drink, and the school will provide cups and plates and eating utensils. We hope that you will come!"

Nicolas asks, "We're doing a potluck?" Mrs. Nguyen responds that they are having a big dinner like a potluck and explains that theirs will not be just for children, as in the book they read, but for all of the children and their families. She also explains that the food dishes will be prepared at school, not at home. However, the children and their families will help on the night of the dinner. Cesar says, "My note needs Spanish." Katerina adds, "Lianna needs Russian." Mrs. Nguyen reassures the children that she has notes in all of the languages needed by the families. Gabriel asks, "What we bring?" Mrs. Nguyen explains that each family will suggest a favorite dish and that some families will bring ingredients to school before the night of the dinner or on that night.

Before Mrs. Nguyen dismisses the children to interest areas, she shows some new materials—two sets of small pictures of foods. Mrs. Nguyen picks out two—bananas and beets—and holds up one of them. "I think you know what kind of fruit this is," she says. The children say, "bananas." Mrs. Nguyen agrees and then shows the second picture. " I think you also know what kind of vegetable this is." One child says, "radish." Another says, "beet." Mrs. Nguyen agrees that both vegetables have ball-shaped roots. "I brought some books about vegetables that we can use to figure out what some of these pictures are." She and the children determine that the vegetable on the picture card is a beet. Then Mrs. Nguyen says, "There's something the same about the names, banana and beet. Did you notice their first sounds? Banana, beet," Mrs. Nguyen says again.

Several children say, "They start with /b/!" Mrs. Nguyen agrees. "Yes, and that's why bananas and beets are on the same page in this alphabet book (shows the B/b page of Eating the Alphabet). *If you'd like to find other foods on the picture cards in this book, you may use these materials today." Vladimir asks, "Or look at those others?" "Or, look at the other books, of course."*

In the remaining days before the family dinner, Mrs. Nguyen read several stories about children helping their parents prepare foods. She talked with children about their families' ideas for the food dish they would suggest and help to make.

The teacher supported concepts of print by demonstrating that print can be read and has specific meaning. The teacher supported the development of children's **phonological awareness** and **alphabetic and word recognition skills** by reading an alphabet book and discussing the food that each character brought (e.g., the character's name and food dish for the potluck started with the same sound and letter). She pointed out both the character's printed name and the printed name of the food. Mrs. Nguyen also used picture cards of foods to help children who were ready to focus on first sounds that are similar in different food names and to link these first sounds to the letters used to write the sounds. She used another alphabet book in which children could find pictures of the same foods on the book pages. Reading the potluck book and the note to the families and discussing children's questions about the preschool dinner helped them learn to comprehend and analyze age-appropriate texts: the book and the note. Both

provided meaningful contexts in which to use information texts as resources. The children's literacy interests and responses were supported when the teacher continued to read more books that related to the preschool family dinner.

Engaging Families

The following ideas may engage families in developing children's interest in books:

✔ **Send books and other reading-related materials home with children.** Parents often welcome ideas to support their children's learning at home. They also appreciate getting materials for their use from their child's teacher. Occasional meetings and workshops at school are helpful for parents, especially when the teacher demonstrates ways that parents can use materials with their children. Arrange for interpreters, if needed, to be available at meetings.

✔ **Support children and families in sharing books at home.** Provide books in a lending library in the home languages of the children in the group. Encourage parents to use the home language when sharing books with their children. Translators are needed to produce text for books not available in a child's home language. Glue the translated text into the book to create a version that can be read in the home language.

✔ **Share ideas with parents about questions they might ask about books, and provide these in the home language.** Provide a list of the kinds of questions that parents might ask when sharing books with their child. In addition to asking children to

identify items in a book's illustrations, also suggest higher-level questions, such as how a character is feeling or why a character behaved in a certain way. Those more thoughtful questions can be discussed only when children have adequate language, which means that supporting parents in sharing books at home is essential for English learners, especially in the early phases of learning English. Make sure some of the stories read at circle time are available in the lending library. For more information about strategies to support children who are English learners, see Chapter 5.

✓ **Suggest ways that parents can send a response back to the classroom.** The child might draw a picture about a favorite part of a book that was shared with a parent or other family member, or the family member might label the picture using the home language. Send simple packets of crayons and

a few sheets of paper home with books that children check out of a lending library. All families need access to such materials. The teacher's action will support family members in following up a book's reading with an activity that prompts additional talking and thinking.

✓ **Introduce parents to community resources to get books for home.** It is important to help families learn about resources where they can get access to more books. A preschool meeting is a good time to introduce families to a local public library and invite the librarian to come to meet families. It is also important for children to have at least a few books that are their very own. Find resources (see the "Teacher Resources" section on page 170) that might make this possible. Distribute books directly to parents, at a meeting, or when they come to preschool to pick up their children. In this way, the parent can enjoy giving the book to their child.

✓ **Send simple alphabet activities home.** Consider sending home materials that a child and parent can use to create a name card for the child. A strip of poster or tagboard long enough to fit all of the letters of a child's name, paper letter "tiles" needed to write the name, and a small bottle of glue are all that is needed. Send directions in the family's home language about how a family member can help the child assemble the letters to make the child's name and glue the letters onto the strip of heavy paper to make a name card. Some crayons may be included in the materials to encourage the child to decorate the sign.

Questions for Reflection

1. What opportunities have you used to integrate children's literacy learning with other activities throughout the day?

2. How have you used information books in your program?

3. What experiences do children have in the classroom interest areas in which they use information books as resources and see you model this use?

4. How does a focus on a picture card set of beginning letters and sounds support the development of alphabetic skills?

5. What challenges might the children have in using picture cards as an independent activity? What experiences did the teacher provide that might decrease those difficulties? How did the information books provide support?

6. How have you included families in classroom activities and events?

7. What did the children's responses to the note to families reveal about the teacher's respect for families and the children's home languages?

8. How did this integrated set of reading-related experiences support children's vocabulary and concept development?

9. In what ways might the family dinner experience support children's social development?

LITERACY

Writing

Developing as a writer depends on the writer's understanding of how a particular written language looks and on the writer's language and thinking skills. Conventional writing requires knowledge of alphabet letters and an understanding that letters stand for sounds in spoken or signed words. Deciding what to write requires oral or sign language, knowledge, and thinking. Preschool children engage in writing when they use scribble marks and proudly announce their meanings (e.g., "This says ____"). Preschool children frequently use drawing, rather than writing marks, to represent their thoughts, and they often combine scribble or other writing-like marks with their drawings to communicate. Preschool children are happy to serve as their own interpreters, telling people what their early writing and drawing is meant to say. Teachers are careful not to criticize children's early scribble productions. To find out what a child's writing means, teachers may ask a child: "Tell me about these wavy lines down here."

1.0 Writing Strategies

Young preschool children use scribble to make their first pictures and also as their first form of writing (Exploring, DRDP). They arrange their scribble marks differently in the two contexts, placing scribble in lines to indicate, "This is writing, not a picture" (Developing, DRDP). As children see more print and begin to explore individual alphabet letters (e.g., puzzles, magnetic letters, alphabet posters, and books), their scribble marks change to letter-like shapes and real letters (Building, DRDP). The form of the letters children write continues to improve throughout the preschool years and beyond, as fine-motor skills increase and children acquire more detailed letter knowledge. By late in the preschool years, children combine and place lines to create letters that are legible (Integrat-

ing, DRDP). Children also begin during the preschool years to use letters to write their names and other familiar words (Integrating, DRDP).

When young preschool children realize that drawing and writing are used intentionally to represent thoughts, they begin to tell what their marks mean. A bold patch of bright orange and yellow represents, "the sun" or "my umbrella." A few zigzag lines represent, "my name," or mean "I like to go fishing with my brother" (Developing, DRDP).

Some older preschool children can write letters and letter patterns that correspond to the sounds that they "hear" in spoken language. Children have still more to tell than what their drawings and invented spellings alone can convey (e.g., "I got a bike and it's red. It has more

Sample Developmental Sequence
Writing

The Desired Results Developmental Profile–Preschool© (2010) (Measure 21, LLD 10 of 10)[a] provides a basic summary of writing development over the preschool years. The four levels described in the developmental profile may be summarized as follows:

Exploring: The child explores with marking tools on a variety of writing surfaces, creating scribble marks. The child some-

times focuses on making marks without any intention of using these to stand for writing. Sometimes the marks prompt the child to think of something from the child's world that is familiar, and the child attributes meaning to scribbles (e.g., "that's a car" or "that says 'I am going to the zoo'").

Developing: As the child continues to explore with mark making, the child organizes scribble marks into lines when "writing," which indicates the child's observation that marks for writing and marks for pictures are organized differently. Often, the child will point to scribble marks that

[a] The Preschool Desired Results Developmental Profile-Revised 2 (DRDP-PS© 2010) is one edition of the DRDP. In this publication, "DRDP" refers, in general, to all editions of this assessment instrument. "LLD" stands for Language and Literacy domain, and "10 of 10" identifies which measure is referenced.

(continued on next page)

wheels so I don't fall over. When I am big, they come off").

Some children may need assistance in emergent writing. Assistive technology, either low tech or high tech, may be as simple as modifying a writing tool to make it easier to grasp or as sophisticated as using a computer with adaptations such as covers with individual finger openings. Another helpful strategy is for an adult or peer to "write" for the child, who then approves or disapproves by indicating yes or no. Preschoolers will sometimes have much to say and will appreciate an adult's offer to take their **dictation**—to do the physical writing for them.

The preschool writing foundations are as follows:

- Experiment and adjust grasp and body position for the use of writing and drawing tools.

- Use scribbles, letters and letter-like shapes to represent ideas or words.
- Write one's own name.

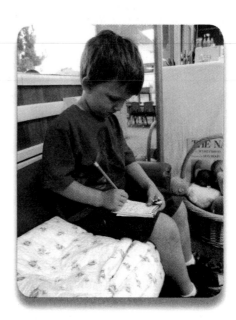

Sample Developmental Sequence of Writing (Continued)

are lined up and say, "This says . . ." In other words, children begin to attribute meaning to their scribble writing.

Building: Children's skill in using marks to create both pictures and writing increases to the point where others can recognize a child's intentions. Although the marks are still not always well formed, adults have a good idea what the child intended to portray and the letters a child intended to write. Children sometimes make up new designs that look remarkably like actual letters. They do not yet know that there are just 26!

Integrating: At this phase, children know most, if not all, of the uppercase alphabet letters, and they combine these to make

words. Some of the words are ones they see frequently, such as their names. Most are quite legible, although not perfectly formed, of course, and a letter might be written with its orientation reversed. In addition to their names, children sometimes write a few simple words, such as love or yes and no. They also might string letters together in sets that look like words and ask adults, "What word is this?" A few older preschoolers might have figured out that letters selected to make words relate to the sounds in the spoken words, and invent spellings, such as KK for cake or CD for candy.

VIGNETTE

Ross enjoys the paper letter tiles organized in tackle-box trays in the writing area. He surveys the letters, picks one, and then dabs his glue stick on his paper. He arranges four to six letters together, in a line (e.g., ONOSR, SOSRS, OSSRO, SRARRO).

He asks, "What are these letters?"

The teacher understands that he wants to know what words he has made and begins to read. They laugh together when a collection of letters is not a word. When the teacher reads SOSRS (saucers), Ross laughs at first, but then he says, "Oh, that's like one in the dramatic play area."

"Right. Saucers is a real word," the teacher confirms. Although only one of five letter strings is a real word when the teacher reads it, Ross announces that he is "going to make more words" and turns back to the tray of letters.

TEACHABLE MOMENT

The teacher is wise to read Ross's "words" rather than ask him to tell her what they say, because children attribute meaning on their own to their pretend words if using them with intention (e.g., "This says, 'Look out. There's alligators all over here' "). When they ask what their words say, they are usually playing with making words. In sounding out the letters in Ross's "words," the teacher demonstrates how the writing system works. With more experience of this kind, combined with other experiences that focus on letter names and sounds in words, Ross will learn that people select letters to stand for sounds when they are spelling words. For now, the teacher enjoys watching Ross's investigations and answers his questions.

VIGNETTE

Jessalyn is delighted with the birthday card picture from a peer and wants to write a thank-you note. She draws a picture and then tells the teacher, "I want real words, too, but I can't make them."

"What would you like the words to say?" the teacher asks. Jessalyn dictates: "I liked the pretty picture of me. It was a pretty birthday card." "Do you want me to write that down or help you?"

"I can do letters," Jessalyn explains, "but I can't make words. Well, just love." The teacher helps Jessalyn spell the word pretty by segmenting some of its sounds and naming the letters needed to write the sounds. After the teacher names the last letter in pretty, Jessalyn remarks, "y? Why not e?" The teacher explains that e is used to write this sound in many words, but, in others, y is used.

Then the teacher asks, "What letter is at the end of your friend Jeremy's name?"

"Oh, y!" Jessalyn realizes. "Do we have anybody with e?" she asks.

"Not this year. But last year, there was a girl named Kaylee, and she used e to write the /e/ sound."

TEACHABLE MOMENT

Rather than simply dictate letters or write words for Jessalyn to copy, her teacher segments some of the sounds in the words and discusses the letters needed to write them. Jessalyn, who is almost five, already has the idea that letters stand for sounds. When she writes, she sometimes uses her letter name knowledge to match a letter to a sound in a word. She would have used the letter E to write the last sound in *pretty,* if working on her own. When the teacher advises the letter Y, anticipating that Jessalyn would ask why, she helps Jessalyn discover some surprises in writing English words. Some sounds can be written with more than one letter, and some letters can stand for more than one sound (e.g., The letter C can stand for /s/ or /k/, as in *city* and *candy;* the letter G can stand for /j/ or /g/, as in giraffe and gate). Jessalyn is learning a lot about writing when her teacher engages her in natural situations, such as when helping her write the thank-you note. The teacher adapts her approach to each child's interests and current levels of understanding.

The following interactions and strategies support writing and its varied uses:

Set up a well-stocked writing area (See "Environments and Materials," page 103.)

Add new materials frequently to the writing area. New materials can support units of study (e.g., envelopes, stationery, card stock cut into postcard sizes, and stickers for use as stamps when children are investigating the post office) or spark children's interest in writing. Be creative and provide gel pens or pens with glitter ink, hole punchers, scissors, little blank books, colored card stock folded like greeting cards, printed photographs of children engaged in classroom activities for note cards or post cards. Consider finding ways that children can write with their fingers in addition to writing with tools. For example, children can write in trays of sand.

Provide writing materials in other interest areas, inside and outside. In the block area, provide materials for children to make signs and masking tape for attaching them to buildings. Place small notepads in the dramatic play area for children to write messages or grocery lists. Children enjoy opportunities to write and draw in mud outside and to mark in damp sand with their fingers or sticks. They also enjoy creating print props for their play—tickets for a wheel toy "toll booth" or a sign for a pretend lemonade stand or roadside restaurant. Placing a variety of writing materials on a rolling cart makes it easy to take those materials outdoors. Provide access to keyboards and computers (e.g., with adaptations such as covers with individual finger "openings"), as appropriate, for children with disabilities. There should be ample opportunities to use different writing utensils for marking, scribbling, and drawing. (See Appendix D.)

Embed writing in everyday transitions and routines. For some transitions, tell children they may go to the next activity when you write on the whiteboard the first letter of their name. After a while, children whose names begin with letters that start with the same stroke (e.g., T, F, E, M, N, L, B, D, R and other letters) might begin to guess their own first letter after you complete the long vertical line. Tell children that you are not yet finished and to keep watching. By attending until the letter is completely formed, children learn that some letters are similar to but also different from other letters. For other transitions, write each of the children's first names, one at a time. This activity is especially informative if some children's names are similar, for example, if there is a Jamal and a Jamie or an Alessandra and an Alexis in the class. After some experience with this transition activity, children learn to watch closely until two, three, or even four letters of their name have been written, because the first two or three letters in their name are also in a classmate's name. Encourage children to write for a purpose as part of a routine, for instance, by signing their artwork, using any level of writing they can, or by signing their name on a turns list when an interest area is already filled to capacity and a child must do something else while waiting for a turn.

Encourage children to write in the art interest area. Preschool children love to finger paint on a tabletop. Add a few drops of water, as needed, to keep the paint slippery as a child explores. Provide pieces of newsprint to use in making prints of children's finger-painted marks. Children can also write on slabs of clay using popsicle sticks or wooden tools. Encourage children to sign their drawings and paintings with whatever marks they can, helping when they ask. When drawings and paintings represent stories, inviting a child to "tell me about it" and then writing down the dictation supports children's budding narrative skill. When a child wants to describe a process (e.g., "I made orange when I mixed yellow and red together"), taking dictation supports a child in learning how to record explorations and discoveries. Children often enjoy the freedom afforded by large pieces of paper on an easel to paint individual letters or even their whole names, which they sometimes decorate elaborately.

Respond sensitively to children's emergent writing. Focus on the meaning that children are trying to convey (e.g., "Tell me about this") rather than on the form of their writing (e.g., "What's that letter?"). In other words, when children first start, let them know that scribbles or letter-like designs are wonderful attempts and that people know children love to experiment with lines and designs. Let them know that you are interested in knowing the thoughts they might have tried to capture in their writing. See "Sample Developmental Sequence of Writing" on page 159.

Respond to children's questions and requests for help. When children ask questions about how to form a letter, describe actions while demonstrating on a separate piece of paper (e.g., "First, we make a long vertical line, like this; then we add a short diagonal line from up here right to the middle of the vertical line . . ."). When children approaching 60 months of age request help in spelling, make the sounds in the words explicit and name letters needed to write the sounds (e.g., "Okay, I hear a /b/ sound first, in *baby*. We write that sound with the letter *b*. I hear /a/ next, in baby, and we use the letter *a* to write /a/. Then, I hear another /b/--*ba-by* . . ."). As children learn more letter names, ask children what letter they think should be used to write /b/ or /t/ or other sounds that are in a letter's name (e.g., "d" has the /d/ sound in its name; *p* has the /p/ sound in its name").

Model writing. If children see a teacher write for particular purposes (e.g., a list of items to bring to preschool for a project, a note to a child's parent) and if a teacher enlists children's help in deciding what to write for class letters, notes, or signs, children will come to understand the value of being able to express thoughts on paper. Plan to write frequently in a whole-group setting for a variety of purposes (e.g., a thank-you note to a guest, a note to the custodian about a broken towel dispenser, a sign for a hallway display of children's drawings). Engage children in helping to compose a message, and write it on a surface that is large enough for all of the children to see the writing (e.g., a whiteboard or a large piece of newsprint paper mounted on an easel). Read the entire message when it is finished.

Display children's writing. A bulletin board to display children's writing and drawing is helpful. Rather than wait for writing or drawing related to specific activities, such as a trip to the children's museum, display items that children create daily (e.g., tickets for bus play in the block area, a list for grocery shopping in the dramatic play area, a colorful painting of letters, a little book or a paper on which a child has written all of the letters of the alphabet at the writing area, just because he wanted to). Post class photos too, and write down children's captions (e.g., "Here's when my sand mold broke all up." "Ricardo and I made this pirate boat in the block area"), or help children to write the captions. A display lets children know that their writing efforts are noticed and valued and can be shared with others.

Bringing It All Together

Nicolas finishes drawing on one side of a crease on a piece of card stock and then adds zigzag scribble marks and a few rudimentary letters on the other side of the crease. He explains that the picture is a bowl of salad with some carrots and tomatoes, and his writing says, "This is where salads are."

Preparations for the family dinner have been underway for almost three weeks. Mrs. Nguyen's preschoolers have written name tags for each member of their family and have made a variety of Welcome signs for the front door of the preschool and for the hallway leading to their classroom. Today, after a discussion about the different kinds of food that families have suggested for the dinner and will be helping to prepare at school, Mrs. Nguyen explains how foods are organized on a buffet table— all the salads are in one place, all the main dishes are in another, and so on. Nicolas and some of his peers chose to make signs for the tables (e.g., salads, vegetables, main dishes, breads, desserts). They are using card stock that Mrs. Nguyen creased in the middle to make them stand on the table when finished.

On the last day before the big event, at small-group time, Mrs. Nguyen provides yeast dough for the children to shape into rolls. When finished, they carry the trays of rolls down to the preschool's kitchen where staff will bake them. A day earlier, the children helped Mrs. Nguyen compose a note to ask kitchen staff members if they would be willing to help. They wrote back, saying they would.

This teacher not only provided an integrated set of reading-related experiences to provide background knowledge about the preschool and family dinner event, but also thought of many meaningful writing experiences in which to engage the children. The children used a variety of writing and drawing tools to write family members' names and to make Welcome signs and signs for the food tables. Some children used scribble and letter-like designs on the name tags and signs. Other children, mostly the older preschoolers, used very well-formed letters to write their own names and the messages for signs and Welcome banners. The children and their parents and teacher could not have been prouder of all their preparations.

Engaging Families

The following strategies can help families develop children's interest in writing:

✔ **Send writing materials home with children.** Send home a few pieces of paper and a few crayons at a time, rather than larger quantities. In an accompanying note, in the family's home language, indicate that the materials are for the child to draw on and then sign his or her name. Suggest ways that the family member might help with the name (e.g., say the letters or characters, show the child how to write the letters or characters, write the name for the child while naming the letters or characters).

✔ **Use displays to help family members understand the developmental nature of writing.** When family members come to pick up their child, children's artwork and writing should be displayed in areas they pass by. A broad range of writing, drawing, or painting efforts on a board communicates to parents that preschoolers are still learning how to write, paint, and draw.

✔ **Provide ideas about where family members can find paper on which their preschooler can write and draw.** In a parent meeting, teachers can show parents how to cut up cereal boxes and other light cardboard food containers, as well as envelopes from mail they receive. These items are blank on the inside. Children also enjoy looking at the flip side (i.e., the side that originally was the outside of the panels) and sometimes are inspired by the writing on it. Children also like to write and draw on newspapers, ignoring the print as they add their own drawing or writing over it.

✔ **Encourage family members to share writing with their child.** Teachers may send ideas home, in the family's home language, for ways that family members can use the writing they do at home to help their child learn about writing. For example, some family members might make shopping lists or write letters to relatives. A teacher may suggest that family members show these to their preschool child and explain what they are. If older siblings in the family do homework, parents can encourage the older sibling to show the younger sibling what she is doing (e.g., "I'm writing a story for my class" or "I worked some math problems").

Questions for Reflection

1. How did the writing experiences engage children in the family dinner activities in ways that the reading activities could not?

2. What do you think Mrs. Nguyen did when a child refused to write the names of family members on name tags, saying, "I can't write." What would you do?

3. How can you help parents understand the early phases of children's writing?

4. Would you feel a need to write the correct and recognizable words (e.g., salads, desserts) on the food table signs that children prepared? Why or why not?

5. How might these meaningful experiences with writing affect children's motivation to write?

6. Do you think that preschool children should have only meaningful writing experiences, such as the ones they used for the preschool family dinner event, or should children be asked to practice writing letters and their names just to practice? Why?

7. If you have ever seen children practice writing on their own—a teacher had not asked them to—what environmental materials, structure, or previous experiences might have influenced and supported their decision to practice some aspect of writing?

Concluding Thoughts

Decades of research have shown that playful learning, intentional teaching, and a rich curriculum help children learn about the world and master language and literacy. The principles and strategies provided in this chapter are based on this research. Teachers must be mindful of what the research has revealed about how children acquire a vast array of knowledge and skills. However, teachers must also assume responsibility for weaving together a program that combines children's play with their own specific plans in ways that secure a bright academic future for each child. By definition, this means that children's interest in and motivation to learn are maintained. The satisfaction and joy of teaching come from knowing that the very best efforts were made and from seeing the results of such efforts in the children's faces every day. The progress documented for each child over the course of a year also brings joy and satisfaction.

Map of the Foundations

Domain ——————→ # Language and Literacy

Strand ——————→ ## Listening and Speaking

Substrand ——→ **1.0   Language Use and Conventions**

Age ←——

At around 48 months of age	At around 60 months of age
Foundation → **1.4** Use language to construct short narratives that are real or fictional.*	**1.4** Use language to construct extended narratives that are real or fictional.*
Examples	**Examples**
Examples → • The child draws attention or points to pictures on the wall of a special class event: "The mama bird built a nest in our toy box. The baby birds flew away." • The child describes an unfolding event at snack time: "I want to put peanut butter on my bread. I'm going to put jelly on, too." • The child relays events from the day's morning: "My daddy's truck broke down. We walked to school. It was a long way."	• The child tells a brief story that unfolds over time: "I went to the park with my mommy, and we played in the sandbox. Then we had a picnic. After that, we went to the store." • The child tells about activities of interest to him or her that day: "First we come to school and sit on the carpet. Then we have our circle time. And then we do the centers. And then it's time for lunch." • The child retells the major events of a favorite story: "The boy wrote to the zoo, and they kept sending him animals. But he doesn't like them. So, then he gets a puppy, and he keeps it. He was happy then."

Includes notes for children with disabilities →

* Producing narratives may vary at these ages for children who are communicating with sign language or alternative communication systems. As is true for all children, teachers can support young children's communication knowledge and skills by repeating and extending what children communicate in conversations. Teachers can also provide opportunities for children to repeat or tell stories as a way to encourage them to produce narratives.

Teacher Resources

The Alliance for Childhood encourages playful learning and play. http://www.allianceforchildhood.org/

Association for Library Service to Children—Great Early Elementary Reads http://www.ala.org/ala/alsc/booklists.

The Born Learning Campaign of the United Way http://www.bornlearning.org/default.aspx?id=33

Cooperative Children's Book Center, School of Education, University of Wisconsin-Madison: Multicultural Books http://www.education.wisc.edu/ccbc/books/detailLists.asp?idBookListCat=1

The Encyclopedia on Early Childhood Development (of the Centre of Excellence for Early Childhood Development of Canada) http://www.child-encyclopedia.com/en-ca/language-development-literacy/according-to-experts.html

The Future of Children is a Web site of Princeton University's Woodrow Wilson School of Public and International Affairs and the Brookings Institution. http://www.futureofchildren.org/

The National Association for the Education of Young Children (NAEYC), *Beyond the Journal.* This online resource provides information and resources that are not included in *Young Children* articles. Authors sometimes provide book lists and professional development suggestions for inclusion in the Beyond the Journal resource. http://www.journal.naeyc.org/btj/about.asp/

The National Center for Children in Poverty of the Mailman School of Public Health at Columbia University http://www.nccp.org/

The National Head Start Family Literacy Center (NHSFLC) is funded by the Office of Head Start, to provide training and technical assistance to Head Start programs to improve the quality and positive outcomes of their family literacy efforts. This center also has resources for early math. http://www.sonoma.edu/cihs/familyliteracy/

The National Institute for Literacy. *A Child Becomes a Reader: Proven Ideas from Research for Parents and Shining Stars: Preschoolers Get Ready to Read* http://www.nifl.gov/ *Developing Early Literacy: Report of the National Early Literacy Panel* http://www.nifl.gov/

The Perpetual Preschool: Early Childhood Language Development Sites http://www.perpetualpreschool.com/language_links.html

The Public Broadcasting System Web site provides a wide variety of resources for teachers, parents, and children, including children of preschool age. http://www.pbs.org/

Reading Is Fundamental provides resources for parents, teachers, and children. http://www.rif.org/about/

Reading Is Fundamental—Favorite Books for Children Ages 3 and 4 http://www.rif.org/educators/books/three_and_four.mspx

Reading Is Fundamental: 100 of the Decade's Best Multicultural Read-Alouds, Pre-kindergarten through Grade 8, selected and annotated by J. Freeman http://www.rif.org/educators/books/100_best_multicultural.mspx

Reading Rockets: Launching Young Readers http://www.readingrockets.org/

U.S. Department of Education: Office of Intergovernmental and Interagency Affairs. *Helping Your Child Become a Reader* (available in English and Spanish). http://www.ed.gov/parents/academic/help/hyc.html

Zero to Three National Center for Infants, Toddlers, and Families http://www.zerotothree.org/site/PageServer?pagename=key_language

References

Bardige, B., and M. Segal. 2005. *Building literacy with love.* New York: Zero to Three.

Developmentally appropriate practice in early childhood programs serving children from birth through age 8. 2009. 3rd ed. Edited by C. Copple and S. Bredekamp. Washington, DC: National Association for the Education of Young Children (NAEYC).

Dowling, J. L., and T. C. Mitchell. 2007. *I belong: Active learning for children with special needs.* Ypsilanti, MI: High/Scope Educational Research Foundation.

Duke, N. K. 2003. Reading to learn from the very beginning: Information books in early childhood. *Young Children* 58, no. 2: 14–20.

Epstein, A. S. 2007. *The intentional teacher: Choosing the best strategies for young children's learning.* Washington, DC: National Association for the Education of Young Children (NAEYC).

Golinkoff, R. M., and K. Hirsh-Pasek. 1999. *How babies talk: The magic and mystery of language in the first three years of life.* New York: Dutton/Penguin [In French, Italian, and Spanish].

Hirsh-Pasek, K., and R. M. Golinkoff. 2007. *Celebrate the scribble: Appreciating children's art.* Easton, PA: Crayola Beginnings Press.

Hirsh-Pasek, K., and R. M. Golinkoff. 2003. *Einstein never used flashcards: How our children really learn and why they need to play more and memorize less.* Emmaus, PA: Rodale Press [In Indonesian, Japanese, and Chinese].

Hirsh-Pasek, K., and others. 2009. *A mandate for playful learning in preschool: Presenting the evidence.* New York: Oxford University Press.

Johnston, P. 2004. *Choice words: How our language affects children's learning.* Portland, ME: Stenhouse Publishers.

Justice, L. M., and C. Vukelich, eds. 2007. *Achieving excellence in preschool literacy instruction.* New York: Guilford Press.

Kalmar, K. 2008. Let's give children something to talk about: Oral language and preschool literacy. *Young Children* 63, no. 1: 88–92.

McNair, J. C. 2007. Say my name, say my name! Using children's names to enhance early literacy development. *Young Children* 62, no. 5: 84–89.

National Center for Family Literacy. 2008. *Developing early literacy: Report of the national early literacy panel.* Jessup, MD: National Institute for Literacy. http://www.famlit.org

Schickedanz, J. A., and R. M. Casbergue. 2009. *Writing in preschool: Learning to orchestrate meaning and marks.* 2nd ed. Newark, DE: International Reading Association.

Strickland, D. S., and J. A. Schickedanz. 2009. *Learning about print in preschool: Working with letters, words, and beginning links with phonemic awareness.* 2nd ed. Newark, DE: International Reading Association.

Wasik, B. A. 2001. Teaching the alphabet to young children. *Young Children* 56, no. 1: 34–40.

Yopp, H. K., and R. H. Yopp. 2009. Phonological awareness is child's play! *Young Children* 64, no. 1: 12–18; 21.

Endnotes

1. B. Hart and T. Risley, *Meaningful Differences in the Everyday Experience of Young American Children* (Baltimore, MD: Brookes Publishing Co., 1995).

2. R. Needlman, P. Klass, and B. Zuckerman, "A Pediatric Approach to Early Literacy," in vol. 2 of *Handbook of Early Literacy Research*, ed. D. K. Dickinson and S. B. Neuman (New York: Guilford Press, 2006), 333–46.

3. V. Purcell-Gates, "Stories, Coupons, and the TV Guide: Relationships Between Home Literacy Experiences and Emergent Literacy Experiences and Emergent Literacy Knowledge," *Reading Research Quarterly* 31, no. 4 (1996): 406–28.

4. E. Izard, "Emotion Knowledge and Emotion Utilization Facilitate School Readiness," *Society for Research in Child Development Social Policy Report* 16 (2002): 7.

5. P. W. Jusczyk, *The Discovery of Spoken Language* (Cambridge, MA: Massachusetts Institute of Technology Press, 1997).

6. G. F. Marcus and others, "Overregularization in Language Acquisition," *Monographs of the Society for Research in Child Development* 57, no. 4 (1992), Serial No. 228.

7. L. M. Justice and H. K. Ezell, "Print Referencing: An Emergent Literacy Enhancement Strategy and Its Clinical Applications," *Language, Speech, and Hearing Services in Schools* 35, no. 2 (2004): 185–93.

8. N. L. Stein, "The Development of Children's Storytelling Skill," in *Child Language: A Reader*, ed. M. Franklin and S. S. Barten (New York: Oxford University Press, 1988), 282–95.

9. W. B. Elley, "Vocabulary Acquisition From Listening to Stories," *Reading Research Quarterly* 24 (1989): 174–87.

10. Ibid.

11. I. L. Beck, M. G. McKeown, and L. Kucan, *Bringing Words to Life: Robust Vocabulary Instruction* (New York: Guilford Press, 2002).

12. S. Q. Cabell and others, "Strategic and Intentional Shared Storybook Reading," in *Achieving Excellence in Preschool Literacy Instruction*, ed. L. M. Justice and C. Vukelich (New York: Guilford Press, 2008), 198–220.

13. G. W. Whitehurst and others, "Accelerating Language Development Through Picture Book Reading," *Developmental Psychology* 24, no. 4 (1988): 552–59.

14. *National Center for Family Literacy, Developing Early Literacy: Report of the National Early Literacy Panel* (Jessup, MD: National Institute for Literacy, 2008).

15. S. A. Storch and G. J. Whitehurst, "Oral Language and Code-Related Precursors to Reading: Evidence from a Longitudinal Structural Model," *Developmental Psychology* 38 (2002): 934–47.

16. C. L. Peterson, B. Jesso, and A. McCabe, "Encouraging Narratives in Preschoolers: An Intervention Study," *Journal of Child Language* 26, no. 1 (1999): 49–97.

17. M. L. Rowe and others, "Does Linguistic Input Play the Same Role in Language Learning for Children With and Without Early Brain Injury?" *Developmental Psychology* 45, no. 1 (2009): 90–102.

18. E. Hoff, "Environmental Supports for Language Acquisition," in vol. 2 of *Handbook of Early Literacy Research*, ed. D. K. Dickinson and S. B. Neuman (New York: Guilford Press, 2006), 163–72.

19. J. Huttenlocher and others, "Language Input and Child Syntax," *Cognitive Psychology* 45, no. 3 (2002): 337–74.

20. C. L. Peterson, B. Jesso, and A. McCabe, "Encouraging Narratives in Preschoolers: An Intervention Study," *Journal of Child Language* 26, no. 1 (1999): 49–67.

21. Z. O. Weizman and C. E. Snow, "Lexical Output as Related to Children's Vocabulary Acquisition: Effects of Sophisticated Exposure and Support for Meaning," *Developmental Psychology* 37, no. 2 (2001): 265–79.

22. D. Stipek and others, "Effects of Different Instructional Approaches on Young Children's Achievement and Motivation," *Child Development* 66 (1995): 209–23.

23. J. C. Turner, "The Influence of Classroom Contexts on Young Children's Motivation for Literacy," *Reading Research Quarterly* 30, no. 3 (1995): 410–41.

24. S. McNaughton, "Considering Culture in Research-Based Interventions to Support Early Literacy," in vol. 2 of *Handbook of Early Literacy Research*, ed. D. K. Dickinson and S. B. Neuman (New York: Guilford Press, 2006), 229–40.

25. *National Center for Family Literacy, Developing Early Literacy: Report of the National Early Literacy Panel* (Jessup, MD: National Institute for Literacy, 2008).

26. S. McNaughton, "Considering Culture in Research-Based Interventions to Support Early Literacy," in vol. 2 of *Handbook of Early Literacy Research*, ed. D. K. Dickinson and S. B. Neuman (New York: Guilford Press, 2006), 229–40.

27. B. Hart and T. Risley, *Meaningful Differences in the Everyday Experience of Young American Children* (Baltimore, MD: Brookes Publishing Co., 1995).

28. J. Huttenlocher and others, "Early Vocabulary Growth: Relation to Language Input and Gender," *Developmental Psychology* 27, no. 2 (1991): 236–48.

29. J. Huttenlocher and others, "Language Input and Child Syntax," *Cognitive Psychology* 45, no. 3 (2002): 337–74.

30. E. Lieven and others, "Early Syntactic Creativity: A Usage-Based Approach," *Journal of Child Language* 30, no. 2 (2003): 333–70.

31. D. K. Dickinson, "Putting the Pieces Together: Impact of Preschool on Children's Language and Literacy Development in Kindergarten," in *Beginning Literacy with Language: Young Children Learning at Home and School*, ed. D. K. Dickinson and P. O. Tabors (Baltimore, MD: Brookes Publishing Co., 2001), 257–87.

32. Ibid.

33. D. K. Dickinson, A. McCabe, and N. Clark-Chiarelli, "Preschool-Based Prevention of Reading Disability: Realities Versus Possibilities," in *Handbook of Language and Literacy: Development and Disorders*, ed. C. A. Stone and others (New York: Guilford Press, 2004), 209–27.

34. Z. O. Weizman and C. E. Snow, "Lexical Output as Related to Children's Vocabulary Acquisition: Effects of Sophisticated Exposure and Support for Meaning," *Developmental Psychology* 37, no. 2 (2001): 265–79.

35. A. Olofsson and I. Lundberg, "Can Phonemic Awareness Be Trained in Kindergarten?" *Scandinavian Journal of Psychology* 24 (1983): 35–44.

36. S. A. Craig, "The Effects of an Adapted Interactive Writing Intervention on Kindergarten Children's Phonological Awareness, Spelling, and Early Reading Development: A Contextualized Approach to Instruction," *Journal of Educational Psychology* 98, no. 4 (2006): 714–31.

37. S. H. Birch and G. W. Ladd, "Children's Interpersonal Behaviors and the Teacher-Child Relationship," *Developmental Psychology* 34, no. 5 (1998): 934–46.

38. B. K. Hamre and R. C. Pianta, "Can Instructional and Emotional Support in the First-Grade Classroom Make a Dif-

ference for Children at Risk of School Failure?" *Child Development* 76, no. 5 (2005): 949–67.

39. C. Howes, "Social-Emotional Classroom Climate in Child Care, Child-Teacher Relationships, and Children's Second Grade Peer Relationships," *Social Development* 9, no. 2 (2000): 191–204.

40. National Center for Family Literacy, *Developing Early Literacy: Report of the National Early Literacy Panel* (Jessup, MD: National Institute for Literacy, 2008).

41. J. Huttenlocher and others, "Language Input and Child Syntax," *Cognitive Psychology* 45, no. 3 (2002): 337–74.

42. R. S. Klibanoff and others, "Preschool Children's Mathematical Knowledge: The Effect of Teacher 'Math Talk'," *Developmental Psychology* 42, no. 1 (2006): 59–69.

43. R. S. Siegler and G. B. Ramani, "Playing Linear Numerical Board Games Promotes Low-Income Children's Numerical Development," *Developmental Science* 11, no. 5 (2008): 655–61.

44. A. Biemiller, "Vocabulary Development and Instruction: A Prerequisite for School Learning," in vol. 2 of *Handbook of Early Literacy Research*, ed. D. K. Dickinson and S. B. Neuman, 41–51 (New York: Guilford Press, 2006).

45. H. W. Catts and others, "Language Basis of Reading and Reading Disabilities: Evidence From a Longitudinal Investigation," *Scientific Studies of Reading* 3, no. 4 (1999): 331–61.

46. A. E. Cunningham and K. E. Stanovich, "Early Reading Acquisition and Its Relation to Reading Experience and Ability 10 Years Later," *Developmental Psychology* 33, no. 6 (1997): 934–45.

47. M. Senechal, G. Ouellette, and D. Rodney, "The Misunderstood Giant: On the Predictive Role of Early Vocabulary to Future Reading," in vol. 2 of *Handbook of Early Literacy Research*, ed. D. K. Dickinson and S. B. Neuman (New York: Guilford Press, 2006), 173–84.

48. E. G. Spira, S. S. Bracken, and J. Fischel, "Predicting Improvement After First-Grade Reading Difficulties: The Effects of Oral Language, Emergent Literacy, and Behavior Skills," *Developmental Psychology* 41, no. 1 (2005): 225–34.

49. S. A. Storch and G. J. Whitehurst, "Oral Language and Code-Related Precursors to Reading: Evidence from a Longitudinal Structural Model," *Developmental Psychology* 38 (2002): 934–47.

50. National Center for Family Literacy, *Developing Early Literacy: Report of the National Early Literacy Panel* (Jessup, MD: National Institute for Literacy, 2008).

51. J. L. Anthony and others, "Phonological Sensitivity: A Quasi-Parallel Progression of Word Structure Units and Cognitive Operations," *Reading Research Quarterly* 38, no. 4 (2003): 470–87.

52. Ibid.

53. H. K. Yopp, "The Validity and Reliability of Phonemic Awareness Tests," *Reading Research Quarterly* 23, no. 2 (1988): 159–77.

54. C. Chaney, "Language Development, Metalinguistic Skills, and Print Awareness in 3-Year-Old Children," *Applied Psycholinguistics* 13, no. 4 (1992): 485–514.

55. B. M. Phillips, J. Clancy-Menchetti, and C. J. Lonigan, "Successful Phonological Awareness Instruction with Preschool Children: Lessons From the Classroom," Topics in *Early Childhood Special Education* 28, no. 1 (2008): 3–17.

56. F. P. Roth and others, "Promoting Awareness of Sounds in Speech: An Initial Report of an Early Intervention Program for Children with Speech and Language Impairments," *Applied Psycholinguistics* 23, no. 4 (2002): 535–65.

57. D. R. Reutzel and others, "Reading Environmental Print: What Is the Role of Concepts About Print in Discriminating Young Readers' Responses?" *Reading Psychology* 24, no. 2 (2003): 123–62.

58. *National Center for Family Literacy, Developing Early Literacy: Report of the National Early Literacy Panel* (Jessup, MD: National Institute for Literacy, 2008).

59. L. C. Ehri and L. S. Wilce, "Movement into Reading: Is the First Stage of Printed Word Learning Visual or Phonetic?" *Reading Research Quarterly* 20, no. 2 (1985): 163–79.

60. L. C. Ehri and L. S. Wilce, "Cipher Versus Cue Reading: An Experiment in Decoding Acquisition," *Journal of Educational Psychology* 79, no. 1 (1987): 3–13.

61. P. E. Masonheimer, P. A. Drum, and L. C. Ehri, "Does Environmental Print Identification Lead Children Into Word Reading?" *Journal of Reading Behavior* 16, no. 4 (1984): 257–71.

62. L. C. Ehri and T. Roberts, "The Roots of Learning to Read and Write: Acquisition of Letters and Phonemic Awareness," in vol. 2 of *Handbook of Early Literacy Research*, ed. D. K. Dickinson and S. B. Neuman (New York: Guilford Press, 2006), 113–31.

63. R. Reutzel and others, "Reading Environmental Print: What Is the Role of Concepts About Print in Discriminating Young Readers' Responses?" *Reading Psychology* 24, no. 2 (2003): 123–62.

64. L. C. Ehri and T. Roberts, "The Roots of Learning to Read and Write: Acquisition of Letters and Phonemic Awareness," in vol. 2 of *Handbook of Early Literacy Research*, ed. D. K. Dickinson and S. B. Neuman (New York: Guilford Press, 2006), 113–31.

65. S. R. Burgess, "The Development of Phonological Sensitivity," in vol. 2 of *Handbook of Early Literacy Research*, ed. D. K. Dickinson and S. B. Neuman (New York: Guilford Press, 2006), 90–100.

66. B. A. Murray, S. A. Stahl, and M. G. Ivey, "Developing Phoneme Awareness Through Alphabet Books," *Reading and Writing* 8, no. 4 (1996): 307–22.

67. B. Byrne and R. Fielding-Barnsley, "Evaluation of a Program to Teach Phoneme Awareness to Young Children: A 1-Year Follow-Up," *Journal of Educational Psychology* 85, no. 1 (1993): 104–11.

68. B. Byrne and R. Fielding-Barnsley, "Evaluation of a Program to Teach Phonemic Awareness to Young Children: A 2- and 3-Year Follow-up and a New Preschool Trial," *Journal of Educational Psychology* 87, no. 3 (1995): 488–503.

69. L. Bradley and P. Bryant, *Rhyme and Reason in Reading and Spelling.* International Academy for Research in Learning Disabilities Monograph Series No. 1 (Ann Arbor, MI: University of Michigan Press, 1985).

70. I. L. Beck and M. G. McKeown, "Text Talk: Capturing the Benefits of Read-Aloud Experiences for Young Children," *The Reading Teacher* 55, no. 1 (2001): 10–20.

71. G. W. Whitehurst and others, "Accelerating Language Development Through Picture-Book Reading," *Developmental Psychology* 24, no. 4 (1988): 552–58.

72. L. Beck, M. G. McKeown, and L. Kucan, *Bringing Words to Life: Robust Vocabulary Instruction* (New York: Guilford Press, 2002).

73. W. B. Elley, "Vocabulary Acquisition From Listening to Stories," *Reading Research Quarterly* 24, no. 2 (1989): 174–87.

74. I. L. Beck, M. G. McKeown, and L. Kucan, *Bringing Words to Life: Robust Vocabulary Instruction* (New York: The Guilford Press, 2002).

75. J. M. DeTemple, "Parents and Children Reading Books Together," in *Beginning Literacy with Language: Young Children Learning at Home and School*, ed. D. K. Dickinson and P. O. Tabors (Baltimore, MD: Brookes Publishing Co., 2001), 31, 51.

76. D. K. Dickinson and M. Smith, "Long-Term Effects of Preschool Teachers' Book Readings on Low-Income

Children's Vocabulary and Story Comprehension," *Reading Research Quarterly* 29, no. 2 (1994): 104–22.

77. P. D. Pearson and M. C. Gallagher, "The Instruction of Reading Comprehension," *Contemporary Educational Psychology* 8, no. 3 (1983): 317–44.

78. W. H. Teale and M. G. Martinez, "Reading Aloud to Young Children: Teachers' Reading Styles and Kindergarteners' Text Comprehension," in *Children's Early Text Construction,* ed. C. Pontecorvo and others (Mahwah, NJ: Lawrence Erlbaum Associates, 1996), 321–44.

CHAPTER 5

English-Language Development

Children who are learning English as a second language form a substantial and growing segment of the preschool population in California served by state child development programs. Approximately 42 percent of California kindergarten children were identified as children who are **English learners** in the 2006-2007 school year. Recent reports estimate that about 39 percent of all children ages three to five are English learners; however, it is difficult to identify accurately the number or proportion since many English learners do not attend state-supported preschool programs where those data are collected. In some counties, the percentage of children who are identified as English learners at kindergarten entry is more than 50 percent (e.g., Los Angeles County).

The *California Preschool Learning Foundations, Volume 1,* defines English learners as those "children whose first language is not English and encompasses children learning English for the first time in the preschool setting as well as children who have developed various levels of English proficiency. For the majority of these children, Spanish is the **home language,** followed by Vietnamese, Cantonese, Hmong, Tagalog, Korean, and other languages."[1]

Children who are English learners bring a wealth of ability and knowledge as well as varied cultural backgrounds to early childhood settings; English learners also require curricular adaptations to make the most of their abilities while they progress toward full English proficiency. The high-quality early childhood

practices described in the other domains will also benefit preschool children who are English learners, but they may not be enough. Current knowledge, based on successful practices and sound research, strongly suggests that specific teaching strategies, individualized interaction approaches, and enhanced environments are critical to the long-term success of young children who are not native speakers of English. The strategies described in the social-emotional

development, language and literacy, and mathematics chapters are applicable and essential for *all* preschool children, including those who are English learners. However, many young children who are English learners will need the adaptations described in this chapter as they are developing their proficiency with the English language.

Because first- and second-language development of children who are English learners varies, the English-language development foundations and the language and literacy foundations are each to be used in tandem with the curriculum framework. It is recommended that, when planning curriculum for all areas of learning, teachers begin by reading and considering the information in the English-language development foundations and the curriculum framework as they gauge each child's current comprehension and use of English. Teachers then develop a plan for how to integrate and utilize suggested activities or strategies to support learning in language and literacy and the other areas of learning that consider the variability of children who are English learners. Intentional teaching requires an ongoing awareness of the home-language development of each child (as described in the English-language development foundations), as well as the English learner's ability to use English in activities suggested in this curriculum framework.

Early childhood educators working with preschool English learners need to be knowledgeable about the role of home language in the process of learning English, the influence of cultural values and norms, as well as the stages of second-language development for preschool English learners. Specific curricular and assessment adaptations are needed to optimize young children's development of a second language.

Research Highlight

The National Literacy Panel on Language Minority Children and Youth conducted a meta-analysis of 15 scientific studies that focused on early literacy instruction for English learners and concluded "... it is evident that we can enhance the literacy development of English language learners with better instruction" and

> English language learners may learn to read best if taught both in their native language and English from early in the process of formal schooling. Rather than confusing children, as some have feared, reading instruction in a *familiar language may serve as a bridge to success in English because decoding, sound blending, and generic comprehension strategies clearly transfer between languages that use phonetic orthographies, such as Spanish, French, and English.*[3]

Guiding Principles

The following overarching principles were developed for the preschool curriculum framework to assist practitioners in their work with children who are English learners. A complementary document was developed by the California Department of Education entitled *Preschool English Learners: Principles and Practices to Promote Language, Literacy, and Learning* (PEL Resource Guide).[2] It discusses core beliefs and principles that inform teaching approaches and strategies. As should be expected, there is overlap between some of the present overarching principles and those outlined in the earlier document. Where commonalities exist, they are referenced in this chapter.

▶ Families matter

The education of children who are English learners is enhanced when preschool programs and families form meaningful relationships. It is through these relationships that teachers will not only learn about home language use but the hopes and aspirations that parents have for their children's overall development (PEL Resource Guide, Principle 1).

▶ Recognize existing language and literacy strengths in the home language

Engaging in multiple literacy practices, such as reading books, singing songs, and reciting poetry, is part of the daily life of many families. It is important to recognize that English learners have a variety of literacy experiences in their home language that range from an emphasis on oral language development to literacy activities involving print (PEL Resource Guide, Principles 2 and 9).

▶ Respect cultural values and behaviors reflected in the child's language and communication

Language and culture are highly integrated, so attention must be paid to cultural values and behaviors, which are embedded in both the language and communication style of the home language and the new language being learned.

Children benefit when their teachers understand cultural differences in language and communication use and incorporate them into their daily routine. Teachers must be understanding of how the child's culture is reflected in his communication styles (e.g., child waits for the adult to initiate the conversation, child looks away from adult) (PEL Resource Guide, Principle 2).

▶ Allow the child use of the home language to have immediate access to the entire curriculum, concept development, and high levels of interaction

Continued use and development of the child's home language will benefit the child as she acquires English. Experimenting with the use, form, and purpose of the first and second languages leads to growth in acquiring a second language. For example, when children are first exposed to *The Napping House,* it should be in their home language. A discussion of the key words and concepts in the home language precedes exposure to the story in English. In this way, children have the basis to build their understanding of the story. The similarities and differences between the sounds of the two languages can also be pointed out during these discussions (PEL Resource Guide, Principle 6).

▶ **Support English-language development across all domains**

Language is a tool of communication used in all developmental domains. Children who are English learners need to be supported not only in activities focused on language and literacy, but across the entire curriculum.

▶ **Use language as a meaningful tool to communicate**

English learners, like all young children, learn through interactions that use language as a meaningful way to communicate. Successful interactions promote extended conversations that include repeated turn-taking and shared experiences to communicate interests, ideas, and emotions (PEL Resource Guide, Principle 3).

▶ **Make children's learning interesting and fun for English learners**

Language development and learning are promoted when preschool teachers and children creatively and interactively use language (PEL Resource Guide, Principle 4).

▶ **Accept code switching as normal**

Code switching (i.e., combining English words with home language words) is a typical part of language development for many bilingual children (PEL Resource Guide, Principle 7).

▶ **Give preschool English learners time**

As preschool children who are English learners adjust to a preschool classroom, it is important to help them feel welcome without putting too much pressure on them to respond to questions or directives in English. In conversations and group activities, teachers should always include preschool children who are English learners by smiling at them, mentioning their names, and making it clear that they are part of the group. During the early stages of English-language development, much of the language used by preschool teachers is probably not understood by preschool English learners. Initially, those children need a safe setting without too many demands on their emerging English-language abilities.

▶ **Allow for children's voluntary participation**

While a child who is learning English is in the early stages of English-language development, he or she may not feel confident enough to respond in this new language. Each child who is learning English is different, and it is important for teachers to allow the child to decide when he is ready to "go public" with the new language.

Environments and Materials

In the early childhood classroom, the physical environment for young children who are English learners needs to be modified to create a learning environment that provides access to the curriculum content through multiple avenues. The learning environment allows English learners to feel welcome, safe, and secure while acquiring a new language and promotes enriched language interactions, both verbal and nonverbal. Teachers need to provide a physical environment that is rich in visual aids such as pictures, photographs, toys, and picture books that encourage hands-on learning and peer interaction. English learners must initially rely on nonverbal information to understand communication in another language. For example, labeling a block area with drawings or pictures of the various types of blocks will help the English learner understand that certain types of blocks are grouped together in a certain area.

The physical environment of the classroom needs to reflect the child's home culture. This can be accomplished by incorporating cultural artifacts from the child's background into the classroom setting, including educational materials in the child's home language, if available (e.g., books on tape or CD in the listening area), and serving meals and snacks that reflect the cultures of the families. Feeling accepted and valued allows diverse learners to be full participants in the activities of the classroom.

The following adaptations are suggested for preschool children who are English learners:

▶ **Provide safe havens where the child does not have to speak to anyone.**
It is important to arrange small spaces with a choice of manipulatives such as play dough, puzzles, or interlocking blocks. In this way, children can be physically engaged in an activity that they intuitively understand and be near peers who speak English without high demands for producing a language they have not yet mastered. It allows for a "break," deferring control to the individual child to talk when ready.

▶ **Establish consistent classroom routines and procedures.**
Consistent and predictable routines help foster a sense of safety and security for all children but are especially important for children who are English learners. Young children learning English can quickly learn the daily routines (if they are predictable) and will be able to focus energy on the learning goals rather than trying to figure out what they are supposed to do.

▶ **Provide space in the classroom environment for children to interact in small groups and one-on-one.**
Many preschool children who are English learners are highly motivated to interact with and form friendships with other children in the classroom. In their quest to join social groups and form friendships, many English learners will spend time in proximity to children who are native speakers of English, watching their actions and closely listening to their conversations. Small group and individual interactions with peers provide preschool English learners with additional time and opportunities to practice their English. "More experienced peers, those with more advanced mastery of the language, can also be effective language models for children who are newcomers to the community."[4]

▶ **Provide space where teachers and other adults can interact individually and in small groups with children who are learning English.**

As preschool children who are English learners increase their comprehension of English, they will need many opportunities for small-group, targeted instruction as well as individualized responsive language interactions in both English and their home language.[a] For example, when soft seating and small tables are placed throughout the classroom, teachers can sit next to English learners and model English language dialogue informally. While the young English learner is stacking blocks or manipulating puzzle pieces, teachers can label the objects and describe the activity without expecting a response in English. In addition, teachers can organize a small group of English learners at a small table and re-read a storybook that was previously read to the whole group with special attention to key vocabulary words.

▶ **Provide linguistically and culturally appropriate materials.**

All areas of the classroom should reflect the family culture, customs, and language. Family artifacts and pictures of special talents (e.g., musical or artistic) should be displayed prominently throughout the classroom. Environmental print that reflects the languages of the children, as well as English, should also be incorporated into classroom activities and routines. High-quality books in both English and the children's home languages should

---

[a] Every effort should be made to recruit speakers fluent in the child's home language, such as volunteers, parents, and community members, so the child will experience language interactions in their home language.

be readily available. The materials should be accessible to all children in the setting, including those with physical or sensory disabilities.

▶ **Make clear signs and explicit picture cues for interest areas.**

As preschool English learners rely more on nonverbal cues to understand the classroom routines and expectations, it will be important to have interest areas and materials clearly labeled. Materials and interest areas labeled with pictures and words in English and the home languages represented in the classroom will promote associations between words and objects in both languages. The daily schedule should also be designed to include both words and pictures at the child's eye level.

▶ **Make use of computers to introduce and reinforce content of activities.**

Teachers can use computers effectively to individualize instruction and provide additional practice and targeted exposure to English for children who are English learners.

Summary of the Strands

The domain of English-language development encompasses listening, speaking, reading, and writing.

The Listening strand contains one substrand with three areas of focus. The first area of focus is on developing beginning words in English. In this focus area, the child begins by attending to words in English to demonstrate an understanding of a larger set of words. In the second focus area, the child begins to understand requests and directions that increase in complexity over time and relies less on contextual cues to understand words in English. The third focus area con-

centrates on understanding basic and advanced concepts underlying particular words in English.

The Speaking strand consists of three substrands with varying focus areas. The primary focus of these substrands is in the oral production of language that employs both the home language and English. With increasing exposure to English, the child will produce more English across all substrands. Social conventions, or the rules of a particular language, are also part of the Speaking strand.

The Reading strand consists of six substrands that emphasize important expectations related to reading and literacy development. Included in this strand is appreciation of reading, an increasing understanding of book reading, an understanding of print conventions and print meaning, letter knowledge and recognition, and phonological awareness. Throughout the Reading strand, children who are English learners rely on their home language as a means of understanding a second language.

The Writing strand contains one substrand focused on the use of markings on paper or other mediums as forms of communication. Children who are English learners may use their home language in their understanding of written language.

Summary of the Strands and Substrands

The strands and substrands of the domain of English-language development are outlined below. The substrands are numbered.

Listening

1.0 Children Listen with Understanding

Speaking

1.0 Children Use Nonverbal and Verbal Strategies to Communicate with Others

2.0 Children Begin to Understand and Use Social Conventions in English

3.0 Children Use Language to Create Oral Narratives About Their Personal Experiences

Reading

1.0 Children Demonstrate Appreciation and Enjoyment of Reading and Literature

2.0 Children Show an Increasing Understanding of Book Reading

3.0 Children Demonstrate an Understanding of Print Conventions

4.0 Children Demonstrate Awareness That Print Carries Meaning

5.0 Children Demonstrate Progress in Their Knowledge of the Alphabet in English

6.0 Children Demonstrate Phonological Awareness

Writing

1.0 Children Use Writing to Communicate Their Ideas

Please refer to the map of the English-language development foundations on page 225 for a visual explanation of the terminology used in the preschool learning foundations.

Cultural Context of Learning

Children have diverse learning and communication styles that are linked to language background and culture. All children have cultural identities learned early in life that influence how they interact with adults, how they approach formal learning tasks, and how they express their emotions. For example, a child may demonstrate little or no eye contact while listening, and others may look away during a language exchange with an adult as a sign of respect. Some children have developed preferences for group learning and are uncomfortable with individual attention. A related issue is that of physical proximity when speaking. In some cultures, social interactions are characterized by close physical contact, while in others it is more acceptable to interact from a distance. Acceptance of different communication styles sends the message that cultural differences are valued.

When the home language and culture are viewed as assets and resources, it becomes the foundation for enhanced learning. Preschool children who are English learners need targeted classroom support, intentional focus on vocabulary development and English language and literacy development, and close collaboration with families. At the same time, the home language and culture are to be respected, honored, and supported. This chapter provides guidance on how to design environments, structure activities, engage in responsive interactions, and plan for assessment of preschool children who are learning to communicate in English as a second language in all domains.

Stages of Second-Language Development

Preschool children who are learning to communicate in a second language go through predictable stages of language development.[5] These stages are as follows:

- First stage. The child uses her home language to try to communicate.
- Second stage. The child figures out that he is not successful using the home language with English speakers, so he passes through a period of observation and listening.
- Third stage. The child attempts to use English in a more abbreviated form through the use of one-word sentences or phrases. The use of these one- or two-word sentences or phrases is sometimes referred to as the telegraphic or formulaic stage.
- Fourth stage. The young child begins to use more elaborated phrases and short sentences to communicate in English.

Learning a Second Language and the California Preschool Learning System

FOUR STAGES	THREE LEVELS
(Preschool English Learners: Principles and Practices to Promote Language, Literacy, and Learning, 2009)	*(California Preschool Learning Foundations [in English Language Development], 2008)*
1 Use of home language in second language setting 2 Observational and listening period	BEGINNING
3 Telegraphic and formulaic communication	MIDDLE
4 Fluid/Productive language use	LATER

Adapted from the California Preschool Instructional Network, "Foundations in English-Language Development Module" developed by WestEd under contract with the California Department of Education, Child Development Division.

In the preschool English-language development foundations, the first and second stages of second-language development mentioned above are combined to represent the beginning level. The third stage is represented in the middle level of the preschool English-language development foundations, and the fourth stage is represented by the later level. It should be noted that young English learners will be at different levels of development depending on their prior experiences with English and skills with their home language. Also, because English learners vary in the amount of time it takes to become fully proficient in English, many will need additional time beyond the preschool years to achieve full English fluency.

Research Highlight

As children move toward fluid language use, the types of English that they use may be characterized as (1) social English and (2) academic English. *Social English* refers to language that is informal and predominantly oral in nature. *Academic English* refers to language that is more formal, requiring complex sentence structures, a rich vocabulary, and the use of English across the Listening, Speaking, Reading, and Writing strands.[6]

Assessment Approaches for Preschool English Learners

Given the complexity of English language development, reliable, comprehensive assessment of preschool English learners is a critical aspect of designing effective instruction; it is also a challenging endeavor for multiple reasons. The first task is to determine which children are English learners. In California, preschool children who are English learners are those children whose first language is not English and includes both those who are learning English for the first time in the preschool setting and those with some English proficiency. Asking the parents or family members a set of simple questions about their child's early language experiences can help make this determination. As recommended in the DRDP, each child's home language abilities should be assessed. Ongoing assessment will include the items in the DRDP addressing the English-language development (ELD) of all preschool children who are English learners. The following strategies are recommended for reliable assessment of preschool children who are English learners:

- Accurate assessment of preschool children who are English learners requires observation over time and in multiple settings (e.g., during small- and large-group times, on the playground, and at the beginning and end of the day).
- Assessment using the DRDP items for English-language development requires a team approach, including someone who is fluent in the child's home language and knowledgeable about the home culture. Family members should be included on the team and consulted about the child's language experiences and usage.
- Focused observations should be guided by curricular goals and expectations; for example, preschool children who are English learners will gradually begin to understand and follow directions in English as they are consistently provided with appropriate learning opportunities. The child's initial responses to simple instructions in

English should be noted and the date recorded. If the child knows very little English, it may be necessary to assess his ability to follow directions in the home language or to ask the parents simple questions about the child's listening skills. If the teacher knows that a child is able to listen with understanding in her home language, then it is easier to design instruction that builds on this skill while promoting English development.

- Early screening and intervention are available for children who may have a hearing loss or a language-processing problem. It is important to make a distinction between the normal process of learning to listen and understand in a new, unfamiliar language and cognitive, or neurological, problems that can interfere with listening in any language.[b]

---

[b] When a child who is learning English appears to have difficulty listening, and a hearing impairment is suspected, procedures described in the *Assessing Children with Disabilities Who Are English Learners: Guidance for the DRDP Access* and the *PS DRDP for Children with IEPs*, should be followed (http://www. draccess.org/assessors/ELGuidance.html).

Listening

Active listening forms the foundation of a child's language development in any language. As young children first learn language, their receptive knowledge of the language exceeds their productive capabilities. This is also the case for children who are English learners as they begin learning a second language. They are often able to understand much more than they can produce. The ability to listen to the features of a language and process the meaning of the new sounds while applying relevant knowledge from the first language is a critical skill for preschool children who are English learners. Through listening, preschool English learners actively process the features of the English language including vocabulary, grammar, phonology, and pragmatics. Preschool English learners become familiar with English by making hypotheses about how the language works and testing them in conversation with others.

During the early stages of learning a second language, children who are English learners will utilize gestures, behaviors, and nonverbal responses to demonstrate their listening skills and indicate understanding of this new language.[7]

Modeling the English language requires deliberate and intentional instructional practices that help the young child to hear the sounds of the second language, such as speaking slowly, clearly, and often. Preschool English learners need time to adjust, feel safe, and be given opportunities to engage with others. When interacting with children who are English learners, teachers should use body language, gestures, and spoken language that is well pronounced and utilizes clear referents (e.g., concrete representations and visual aids as appropriate). It is important to make sure young children who are English learners are included in a variety of activities that promote listening and comprehension, because they may be relatively nonverbal when entering the classroom.

1.0   Children Listen with Understanding

Listening is an essential aspect of oral language development, and understanding what is heard is critical to the development of reading and writing skills. The development of good listening skills should be a goal of all early childhood programs. Young children can learn good listening skills in any language; these skills will facilitate the ability to attend to and comprehend spoken English.

VIGNETTE

Portrait of a Preschool English Learner

Lonia

Lonia is a three-year-old child from a family who recently emigrated from the Republic of Sudan. She is quite thin for her age and appears withdrawn from the other children. Lonia rarely looks at any of the adults or responds in any way when asked to participate. Some trauma may have been associated with the immigration, but the family has not shared any details. Lonia appears somewhat fearful and mostly watches other children at first. However, she seems very interested in snack and lunch. She smiles at the teacher when he asks if she wants crackers and cheese. She always eagerly eats all types of food. She also constantly rubs a plastic bracelet that she wears high on her left arm. The teacher wonders if Lonia knows any English at all or if she is unusually timid and slow to warm up. Lonia is indirectly communicating many aspects of her development and learning needs that teachers will explore in more depth through detailed observations and careful curriculum planning.

When Lonia first entered Ms. Sarah's preschool classroom, she quietly stood next to the door looking uncertain about what to do after her mother kissed her and waved good-bye. Ms. Sarah knew that Lonia's family had just relocated to her community. Ms. Sarah observed that both Lonia and her mother seemed most comfortable speaking in a dialect of Arabic. That first day, Ms. Sarah took Lonia's hand, bent down, smiled directly at her, and said in a soothing voice, "Welcome, Lonia. We are very happy to have you in our classroom. It is circle time now. I will show you where to sit." Ms. Sarah then walked Lonia over to the rug and patted a small area next to the teacher's reading chair and pantomimed sitting down while saying "This is your spot. You can sit here during circle time."

TEACHABLE MOMENT

▶ Ms. Sarah was aware of Lonia's limited ability to comprehend English as well as her apprehension about entering a strange setting in which the language and customs were unfamiliar. Although Lonia may not have been able to understand the exact words, she could perceive a friendly tone and follow the physical cues from Ms. Sarah.

PLANNING LEARNING OPPORTUNITIES

▶ Teachers of young English learners need to be aware of the stages of second-language development so they can anticipate the kind of individual attention preschool English learners may need. By paying attention to the behavior of children who are not fully proficient in English, teachers can help ease the transition into the new learning environment. In this case, Ms. Sarah was not certain how much English Lonia understood, so she used many gestures and nonverbal cues to help Lonia understand what was expected.

The following interactions and strategies support preschool children who are English learners:

Model good listening skills. All children know when adults are really listening to them; to promote good listening skills among preschool children who are English learners, teachers must first demonstrate good listening skills, especially for children who may have difficulty expressing themselves. As preschool English learners acquire the vocabulary to communicate in English, they may be hesitant to talk at all or they may use elements of both languages. During those stages, it is important to listen patiently, make eye contact, be at the eye level of the child, and respond positively, both verbally and nonverbally. If teachers convey the message that they are too preoccupied or uninterested in what the child is saying, preschool children who are English learners may become discouraged in their attempts to communicate in English.

Use the home language for comprehension. By stating common words and phrases in English and the home language (e.g., *papel,* paper; *bola,* ball; *adiós,* good-bye), teachers can help preschool children who are English learners make the connections between the language they know and the language they are learning. When a child who is learning English is in the early stage of comprehending spoken English, it may be necessary for a fluent speaker of the home language to provide interpretation. This support will promote acceptance and valuing of the child's home language, a means for the child to participate in the classroom activities, and opportunities for other children to learn a few words in a new language.

Keep messages and directions short when talking with preschool children who are English learners. Directions should be broken down into short, sequential steps that are supported by pictures, visual cues, and graphic prompts whenever possible. By using simple, grammatically correct directions and by modeling language, teachers increase the chances that preschool English learners will understand what is being asked of them and will successfully adjust to the classroom. For example, the teacher says, "It is time to come to the rug" and then walks over and demonstrates where to sit. Gradually increase the use of complex vocabulary and grammatical structures as the children's comprehension of English increases.

Teach children how to listen, repeat messages, and ask questions. Establish listening cues (e.g., a signal such as "freeze" or a timid puppet who needs a quiet classroom to enter) that communicate to children when they need to pay attention. It is always a good idea to check for understanding by having preschool English learners actively respond to messages ("If you are going to the block area, put your hands on your head") and ask clarification questions. As many researchers have pointed out, all children need to learn how to restate, repeat, summarize, and reflect on classroom activities. Teachers can help preschool children who are English learners listen carefully by asking them

to talk about what has just happened and then listen patiently while accepting their language usage, which may include code switching.

Have a listening library in the home language and in English. In addition to the audiotapes, CDs, and DVDs available in English, have a parent or other fluent speaker of the child's home language record favorite books, stories, songs, and poems. For instance, when reading *The Very Hungry Caterpillar* as part of a planned book reading, make sure there is a home-language version of the book in the listening area along with key vocabulary words in both languages.

Summarize or provide key phrases of a story in a book, finger play, or song in the child's home language before introducing it in English. This step provides the child with the opportunity to use the home language as a basis for transferring concepts and understanding from the home language to English.

Use language and literacy activities that contain repetitive refrains so that the English learner can hear the idea or concept multiple times (e.g., *Brown Bear, Brown Bear, What Do You See?*). By repeating a phrase and linking it to visual cues, teachers can promote the understanding of new English vocabulary.

Use running commentary when the child is engaged in an activity. For example, if the child is climbing up the ladder to the slide, the teacher might say, "You are going up the ladder and then you will go down the slide," touching the object while naming it. Teachers can also emphasize key words such as *up* and *down* as part of the daily learning experiences. By talking about what she is doing while she is doing it (e.g., "I am putting your picture in your cubby"), the teacher is connecting the language with the behavior and providing additional scaffolds for the child who is learning English.

Use multiple methods for scaffolding communication depending on the stage of English-language development of the child. Combine words with some type of gesture, action, or directed gaze (e.g., picture cues, physical gestures, facial expressions, and pantomimes, props, and interpreters, if necessary). For example, in the book *The Three Bears*, it will aid in the child's comprehension if the teacher shows pictures from the book, displays flannel cutouts of the bears and Goldilocks, and acts out the expressions. (See PEL Resource Guide, pages 54–55, for more detail.)

Target both the content and English-language development in every activity. Design activities with a dual purpose: understanding of the concept and the English label associated with it. For example, when working with a shape puzzle, demonstrate how a triangle has three corners and fits into the puzzle and that the word *triangle* is the name of this particular shape.

Observe preschool English learners during group time, storybook reading, and in small groups. Teachers will need to continually observe preschool children who are English learners to determine their progress in English comprehension and adjust expectations accordingly. As teachers engage the children in the focused listening activities described above, they observe preschool English learners' attention to the language used (e.g., are they looking at the speaker, do they respond nonverbally with facial expressions or gestures to speakers, do they follow along with other children when asked, do they respond appropriately to peers and adults when asked to complete a task?). The answers to these types of questions help inform teachers as they plan individualized activities for children.

Flannel Board Activity: An Example of Building Listening Skills

OVERVIEW

DAY 1	Read *The Very Hungry Caterpillar* in the home language and in English during different times of the day. The teacher can read it in the home language, have it taped in the child's home language, or have a parent or family member read it in the home language prior to reading it in English. Point out key vocabulary words in both the home language and then in English.
DAY 2	Review the book in English, emphasize key vocabulary words, and pass out flannel board pieces with images of story narrative. Summarize key events in the story with visual cues from the book. Then ask children to place pictures on the flannel board when the story so indicates.
DAY 3	Leave the flannel board for small groups and for free time when children choose their own activities. Read and retell the story only to Lonia, checking for comprehension. Ask her to place appropriate pictures of key events on the flannel board.

INDIVIDUAL ADAPTATIONS

If Lonia has three plums and looks blank when asked, "Who has the plums?" the teacher could hold up a plum, look at her, and say, "Do you have this?" If she still does not respond, the teacher might ask her to show what she has and nonverbally indicate that she should hold it up, "This is a plum" and then ask her what she calls it. If a fluent speaker of Arabic were available, it would be useful to have the book read in Arabic and for key vocabulary to be translated into Arabic.

OBSERVATION AND DOCUMENTATION

Observation is part of this activity to learn more about Lonia's developmental level. From this interaction, the teacher begins to gather information about Lonia's ability to understand some English vocabulary words, whether she understands simple instructions, and which concepts she understands. The teacher would note her responses on this date and continue to observe her language and listening skills across other contexts, documenting her progress.

Bringing It All Together

After Lonia had been in the classroom for several weeks, Ms. Sarah observed that Lonia was consistently following the routines of the classroom: moving to the rug, cleaning up, and sitting down, when asked. She also sat quietly and attended during circle time. However, Ms. Sarah was not sure if Lonia was merely imitating the behaviors of the other children or if she truly understood the English words. It was also evident that Lonia was forming friendships with two other girls, often playing with Mariela and Sheena in the dramatic play area. Lonia mostly interacted with the girls nonverbally; when she did speak, it was in single words that were softly spoken and not clearly understood.

One day Ms. Sarah sat down with Lonia for an extended conversation. "Lonia, tell me about what you are drawing." Lonia just looked at Ms. Sarah and kept drawing her picture. (The picture had human-like figures that appeared to be in the forest.) "Is this your family?" asked Ms. Sarah, Lonia nodded and muttered, "Um hum." "Do you have a big family?" Lonia nodded enthusiastically and said, "Lots of family." "Do you have any brothers and sisters?" asked Ms. Sarah. Lonia nodded and pointed to three small figures in the drawing. "What are their names?" asked Ms. Sarah. Lonia quickly said their names adding, "She's baby," pointing to the smallest figure.

Ms. Sarah then asked Lonia if she would hold the picture up so the other children could see it, which Lonia did.

Finally, Ms. Sarah asked Lonia if she wanted to take the picture home, and Lonia emphatically said, "Yes." "Be sure to put the picture in your cubby so you will remember to take it home today," said Ms. Sarah. Lonia suddenly ran over to her cubby and carefully put the picture away.

At this point in Lonia's development, Ms. Sarah wanted to probe Lonia's English comprehension in a more individual and specific interaction. Ms. Sarah carefully posed questions about Lonia's picture, starting with simple questions and ending with a request. Through this interaction, Ms. Sarah was able to determine more about Lonia's ability to listen, comprehend, and follow simple directions in English.

Engaging Families

The following ideas may help families with children who are Engish learners to develop listening abilities:

✔ When working with families who have limited English-language proficiency, teachers will need to communicate in the parents' preferred language. Employing a bilingual interpreter may be necessary.

✔ Many of the recommended strategies in this chapter can be translated into a child's home language and provided as a take-home activity for families. For example, parents can be asked to record a native song or story in their home language and make this available both at home and in the classroom.

✔ Families with children who are English learners should be encouraged to continue family traditions (such as storytelling, family celebrations) and household routines in their native language. The ability to hear, understand, and respond to directions, stories, and complex language can be developed in any language and will facilitate the development of those skills in English.

Questions for Reflection

1. What would you do when the preschool English learner seems to follow directions in groups, possibly by imitating the behavior of their peers, but has difficulty with directions given to her individually?

2. How do you know if an English learner comprehends English and to what degree?

   – Does the child attend and follow along with a story read in English or does he tend to look away and appear uninterested?
   – Does the child show interest in and attend to books read in her home language?
   – Does the child actively engage with peers during dramatic play and respond to the English language conversations? Does the child spend more time on the fringes of groups, watching and listening to others?

3. Does the child comply with the mother's directions in her home language when she is dropped off, such as, "Come here and give me a kiss before I leave"?

4. How are you providing focused listening opportunities in the child's home language?

Speaking

The Speaking strand focuses on children's use of both nonverbal and verbal means of communication. Most experts in the field agree that the development of oral English proficiency for children who are English learners is an essential first step for later reading development.[8] In early care and education settings, aspects of a language's phonology (i.e., the sounds of a language) and syntax (i.e., the order in which words occur) are revealed through both formal and informal listening and speaking activities. In addition, young children begin to use oral language as a means of gathering more information about their environments through the use of questions. While young children who are English learners are hearing the sounds of English, familiarizing themselves with words in English, and learning how words go together in phrases and short sentences, they will begin to try out

these new sounds, words, and phrases. For children to practice this new language, they need to be in a comfortable and welcoming environment that allows language experimentation and accepts children's efforts to communicate. Young children's first attempts to speak may be tentative and halting.

1.0 Children Use Nonverbal and Verbal Strategies to Communicate with Others

Young English learners rely heavily on nonverbal cues when trying to understand a second language. Thus, teachers must be conscious of the importance of combining the spoken word with nonverbal signs to assist the child. It is also important for teachers to make an effort to learn key words and phrases in the child's home language as a way to communicate that they are interested in the child and his background.

VIGNETTE

It is the first day of preschool for Lai, a young girl who speaks Vietnamese. She is holding on tightly to the teacher's hand and is looking primarily at the floor. Ms. Linda, her teacher, holds Lai's hand as she tells all the other children to gather for circle time. As the children gather on the rug, Ms. Linda gently walks Lai to the rug and gestures to her to sit next to her. Ms. Linda begins to speak to the children as a group and introduces Lai by name to the children. Ms. Linda and Lai continue to hold hands. Ms. Linda does not expect Lai to say anything or to even to make eye contact with other children. After a few minutes, Lai begins to relax, and she pulls her hand away from the teacher. Lai continues to maintain close physical contact with Ms. Linda throughout the day while Ms. Linda communicates with smiles and gestures.

TEACHABLE MOMENT

▶ Ms. Linda understands that Lai feels nervous and possibly does not understand much of anything that is being said. Ms. Linda uses this opportunity to communicate to Lai that she will help her begin to navigate an environment that she does not understand.

VIGNETTE

Mr. Ralph gathers all the children around for a read-aloud. The book he is going to read is A Hat for Minerva. *It is about a hen searching for warm things in the snow. Because Mr. Ralph has three children in his group whose primary language is Hmong, he did his research to find out how to pronounce some key words in the book such as* garden hose, pot, hen, *and* snow. *While he is reading the book to the group, the Hmong children are interested in looking at the pictures, but when Mr. Ralph gets to the word hen he says to all, "You know, the way you say hen in Hmong is poj qaib. When the Hmong children hear this, their eyes widen and they smile at each other.*

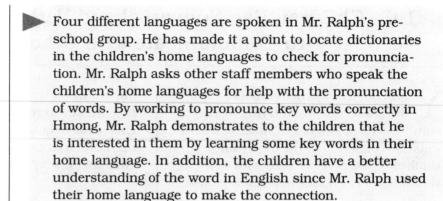

Four different languages are spoken in Mr. Ralph's preschool group. He has made it a point to locate dictionaries in the children's home languages to check for pronunciation. Mr. Ralph asks other staff members who speak the children's home languages for help with the pronunciation of words. By working to pronounce key words correctly in Hmong, Mr. Ralph demonstrates to the children that he is interested in them by learning some key words in their home language. In addition, the children have a better understanding of the word in English since Mr. Ralph used their home language to make the connection.

VIGNETTE

All the children are playing outdoors, and the teachers have set up a board with openings in different shapes (e.g., circle, square, triangle, rectangle). Jasmine, a child who speaks Farsi, is looking toward the board and appears interested. Mr. Li gestures to Jasmine to come closer and picks up a beanbag. He models for Jasmine how to throw the beanbag toward the board at the different openings. While he throws the beanbag with an underhand motion, he simultaneously says, "Look, Jasmine, I swing my arm and throw the beanbag." Mr. Li repeats the physical action several times while simultaneously describing his actions. He then encourages Jasmine to try it. When Jasmine picks up the beanbag, Mr. Li smiles and repeats, "Swing your arm and throw. That's the way to do it, Jasmine!"

**TEACHABLE
MOMENT**

 Mr. Li saw that Jasmine was interested in the activity and used the opportunity to teach her some key vocabulary words in the activity. He combined both gestures and narration to get his points across.

The following interactions and strategies support preschool children who are English learners:

Learn how to pronounce the child's name as accurately as possible. Since a child's name is so closely linked to a sense of self, it is important to use the correct pronunciation. Teachers should ask for help from a native speaker and practice saying it aloud so that a native speaker can help with the pronunciation. Sometimes it may be helpful for the native speaker to record the child's name on audiotape so the teacher can refer to the recording as a resource.

Learn some key words or phrases in the child's home language. Teachers can ask parents, siblings, other teachers or staff members who speak the child's home language to provide a few key words and phrases for *hello, goodbye, thank you, please,* and *sit down.* When the teacher makes an effort to learn the child's language, even a few words and phrases, it conveys the message that the child's home language is important. When reading a story in English, the teacher may translate key words or phrases into the child's home language as a means of validating the importance of the child's home language as well as increasing the child's interest.

Repeat common phrases slowly and clearly to the child so he can begin to make the connection between the phrase and the action, (e.g., circle time or naptime). Modify the rate of speech and pronounce each word clearly so that the child has time to hear good examples of the words and phrases in English. Combine gestures, pictures, and touching of objects.

Allow the child to start slowly. Children who are learning English need to have many opportunities to observe the classroom routine to begin to make sense of how things are done in the early childhood setting. The child needs ample time to watch and become comfortable before utilizing spoken English as a primary means of communication.

Allow for wait time. It is important to wait for children who are English learners to process information in English. Additional wait time benefits children not only for the development of English comprehension but also for verbalizing a response in a language that they are learning.

Scaffold communication by combining English words with some type of body gesture or visual cue such as pointing to an object or showing a picture. Make sure to include body gestures and visual cues to assist children who are English learners in understanding the concept of the word in English. For example, in reciting "Two Little Black Birds," use pictures of black birds or stuffed animals representing black birds to illustrate the concept. When reciting the word *flying,* act out a flapping motion to demonstrate a bird in flight.

Be thoughtful about helping children understand what words mean (e.g., explaining, defining, showing). Children who are learning English will need additional assistance in understanding not only the word or phrase presented in English, but also the concept to which it refers. It is important for adults to be deliberate in their teaching actions by clarifying, describing, or demonstrating what is meant.

Plan for vocabulary development. It is important to identify key vocabulary words and how those key vocabulary words will be used in both formal and informal activities prior to use. Connecting vocabulary words to a visual aid or a gesture helps to make a clearer association for children who are English learners. The intentional use of key vocabulary words throughout the day will assist English learners to make a connection between the word and its meaning.

Expand and extend the child's language. Once a child who is learning English begins to use words or phrases in English, catch them using English and extend and expand upon their language. For example, if the child says "car," the teacher could say, "Oh, you want the red car"; or if the child says "more" at the snack table, the teacher points to the milk and asks, "Do you want more *milk* or more *orange juice?*"

Create small groups for book reading. For children who are learning English, it is important to provide reading opportunities in small groups. Children who are learning English can have closer interactions with the material, and the teacher can slow the pace of reading and use words or phrases in the home language to assist with understanding and scaffold learning.

2.0 Children Begin to Understand and Use Social Conventions in English

Social conventions refer to what children should know about the use of English apart from the language itself in order to use the language in a socially acceptable manner. Social conventions are typically considered as the social rules that govern language use such as eye contact, degree of proximity to the speaker, and when and who may initiate conversation. These social conventions are often learned through observation and trial-and-error learning.

VIGNETTE

Ms. Cathy has always had children call her by her first name. This year Ms. Cathy has Spanish-speaking children in her group. She noticed that some Spanish-speaking parents scold their child when he refers to her by her first name. Ms. Cathy asks her Spanish-speaking assistant, Ms. Maria, about the interaction. Ms. Maria mentions that Spanish-speaking parents view teachers as authority figures, requiring respect and deference. Children are accustomed to addressing the teacher by her last name.

TEACHABLE MOMENT

 Ms. Cathy learned that culture influences how children address adults, especially teachers. This moment is an example of how culture and language intersect in the daily life of children. Ms. Cathy may want to have a conversation with Spanish-speaking parents to discuss how children could address her respectfully in the program. Ms. Cathy needs to acknowledge parental preferences and work with parents to arrive at an acceptable approach.

The following interactions and strategies support preschool children who are English learners:

Ask a family member or knowledgeable community resource to share appropriate social conventions for the child's language and culture. Paraprofessionals and staff members who speak the child's home language can help explain to the teacher important social rules surrounding language. For example, a teacher might ask questions: How are children expected to talk to the teacher? Is it okay to use the teacher's first name? In the home setting, do children initiate conversation with adults? Is there a formal versus an informal form of address in the home language? When the teacher and family members have discussions about specific social conventions, it becomes part of the ongoing dialogue that builds a partnership as the teacher and family work together to support the preschool English learner.

Observe the child during drop-off and pick-up for cues about how the parent or other family members interact with the child and how the child reacts and behaves during those interactions. One way of figuring out social rules used in the home language is to observe parents and their children during these interactions. How do parents respond to the child? What is the physical proximity between the child and the parent? How animated is the parent when she is speaking? What is the child's reaction? Is the child more spontaneous in her speech or does she wait for a cue from the parent that it is time to talk? Although parental behaviors outside the home setting may be different from what may occur in the home, in many cases the behavior may reflect social conventions in the home language.

Through observation, teachers can learn about the ways that children have experienced communication and language interactions in their culture. Using that knowledge, teachers can think about how their communication and language styles are consistent with or different from the children and their families. Teachers may want to modify their communication and language approaches to include styles that may be more familiar to children. For example, if communication usually takes place across a distance and not in proximity, the teacher may want to use this style when speaking with the children. Or if children are expected to speak only when spoken to, the teacher can make sure to ask questions of the individual child and not pose questions to the group, expecting the individual child to respond.

During circle time or small-group time, talk to children about the different ways they greet adults and other children in their families. Ask children how they say hello and good-bye to adults. The explanation can be role-played through the use of finger puppets or figures of a family. Are there differences in the ways children interact with adults versus peers?

3.0 Children Use Language to Create Oral Narratives About Their Personal Experiences

This substrand relates to the development of a child's use of narrative to describe both personal and fictional stories. The oral language that children hear is the basis for the development of their discourse skills. Focusing on stories about themselves and their families is an appropriate first step for teachers encouraging children's narrative development. Talking about one's own personal experience is often easier than talking about imaginary events.

VIGNETTE

Soon-hui, a child who speaks Korean, is looking at a wordless picture book in the library area. James, an English-speaking child, is sitting next to her looking at another picture book. Mr. Luis observes that Soon-hui begins to say a few words in English while pointing to the pictures. Mr. Luis approaches and sits down on the floor next to Soon-hui and James. Soon-hui looks up and smiles at the teacher. Mr. Luis says, "Soon-hui, you are using your English words." Soon-hui smiles and looks at James.

TEACHABLE MOMENT

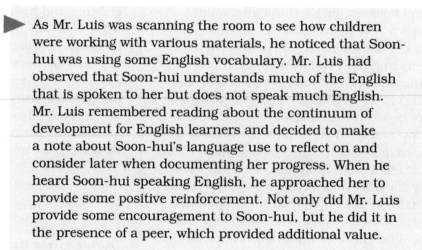

As Mr. Luis was scanning the room to see how children were working with various materials, he noticed that Soon-hui was using some English vocabulary. Mr. Luis had observed that Soon-hui understands much of the English that is spoken to her but does not speak much English. Mr. Luis remembered reading about the continuum of development for English learners and decided to make a note about Soon-hui's language use to reflect on and consider later when documenting her progress. When he heard Soon-hui speaking English, he approached her to provide some positive reinforcement. Not only did Mr. Luis provide some encouragement to Soon-hui, but he did it in the presence of a peer, which provided additional value.

VIGNETTE

Lorena and Fermin, two children who speak Spanish, are playing together in the dramatic play area. The children found the doctor's kit and appeared to be playing doctor. Fermin lay on the bed saying, "Me sick, me sick."

Lorena, with a worried look on her face, bent over Fermin and touched his face, then shook her head, and said, "Muy sick, mucho sick. Let's go al hospital," and "Al hospital."

PLANNING LEARNING OPPORTUNITIES

The dramatic play area had different types of props for the children to use. Lorena and Fermin played with them, incorporating in conversation some of the English words that they were learning. Providing children who are English learners with environments in which they can experiment with language is extremely important.

VIGNETTE

Ms. Amy approaches Jose and Jaime, two children who speak Spanish, who are using only the rectangular blocks to build a tower together. Ms. Amy says to the boys, "That is a great looking tower." She points to a set of triangle-shaped blocks and says, "How can you use those blocks in your tower?" Jaime looks at her and shrugs his shoulders, suggesting that he does not know. Ms. Amy says, "Why don't you try it? She hands Jaime a block and says, "Try it."

Jaime takes the block and puts it on the top of the tower and says, "I try it." Seeing this, Jose grabs one of the triangle blocks and places it on top of the tower, which begins to lean and falls down in a crash.

"What happened?" says Ms. Amy.

Jose responds, "It falled."

"Oh, no," says Jaime.

TEACHABLE MOMENT

 Ms. Amy used some open-ended questions to stimulate conversation using different blocks in the tower construction. Even though Jose and Jaime had limited English for their response, Ms. Amy continued the conversation and provided opportunities for Jose and Jaime to talk about what they were doing.

The following interactions and strategies support preschool children who are English learners:

Listen appreciatively to children's stories. When children begin to provide narrative in English, they may do so in a tentative manner and possibly mix English with their home language. When this occurs, it is important to provide the child with as much undivided attention as possible. During these interactions, it is helpful to provide positive reinforcement about their attempts to relate a story to the teacher.

Ask open-ended questions and sustain the conversation over a number of turns. Provide opportunities for the child to practice English. For example, during circle time, small-group time, or snack time, ask the child what she did over the weekend or during the holiday break. Teachers need to provide time for daily sharing that moves beyond one-word responses.

Help children understand idioms. English, like all languages, has specific idiomatic phrases that need to be pointed out to all children but particularly to second-language learners who may never have heard the idiom before. Phrases such as "it is raining cats and dogs," "two peas in a pod," or "Mommy is going to be late because she's tied up at work" need to be explained to young children. When preparing book-reading presentations, finger plays, or singing songs, make sure to note where idiomatic expressions occur and plan to add an explanation.

Provide materials that help stimulate talking (or oral narratives as used in the *California Preschool Learning Foundations*, page 122). The dramatic play area or an area where puppets, dolls, and miniature figures are easily available will encourage children to express themselves in more spontaneous ways. In those scenarios, the child pretends to be someone or something else, and the burden of language performance is lessened. The use of tape recorders to hear her own speech, the sight of photographs of herself, and the presence of other children in the setting may help elicit oral language development.

Provide wordless picture books. Wordless picture books give the child an opportunity to make up his own stories. Children may begin telling a story in their home language and, as time goes on, begin incorporating words or phrases in English. Wordless picture books also permit parents who do not speak English to interact with their children in their home language.

Bringing It All Together

Enrique and Bernardo are cutting pictures out of catalogs and newspaper circulars. Ms. Jane has asked that they glue the cutout pictures grouped by color, that is the reds with the reds, the yellows with the yellows, and so forth. Ms. Jane tries to pronounce each child's name correctly as she asks, "Enrique, how many colors do you have?" Enrique responds by pointing at the three colors he has been concentrating on: red, blue, and orange, slowly saying the color names in Spanish. "That's right, in Spanish it is rojo, azul, and naranjo. In English it is red, blue, and orange," responds Ms. Jane. "Which color do you like the best?" Enrique points to red. Ms. Jane says, "Why do you like that color?

Enrique says, "I dunno." "I like."

In this vignette, Ms. Jane recognizes the importance of correctly pronouncing the children's names as a means of validating their cultural identity. She also demonstrates that the colors have different labels in Spanish and in English. She also tries to move from closed-ended questions to more open-ended questions even in the face of no verbal responses. Ms. Jane understands that it is important to move conversation from one-word answers to more extended and elaborated speech.

Engaging Families

The following ideas may help families with children who are English learners:

✔ Invite parents and other family members of preschool English learners to share some of their cultural practices. Sharing may include a cooking activity in which a dish characteristic of their nationality can be made, a music or dance activity highlighting particular sounds or movements that are used in their homelands, or a craft activity characteristic of the culture. Take photographs of the presentations, and place them in a photo album. Later, the teacher can ask the child to describe or recount the activity to her or the child's peers.

✔ Encourage parents and other family members to continue to use the home language during family activities while also encouraging early literacy skill development in the primary language. Communicate with parents on an individual basis, during parent meetings, through bulletin boards, or newsletters in their home language regarding the importance of speaking to their children in their home language. Parents may welcome suggestions about how to engage their young children in conversation during everyday activities such as walking in the neighborhood or shopping at the supermarket. Stress the importance of concept formation (e.g., colors, numbers, and shapes) in verbal interactions with their children. After a parent meeting focused on how to read a book with a young child, provide the parents with books written in their home language and suggest that the parent or a family member read to their child.

If books are not available in the home language, send wordless picture books home that can be discussed in the family's language.

Questions for Reflection

1. What activities best encourage open-ended conversations with young children who are learning English?

2. How could Ms. Jane have structured the conversation differently to elicit more verbal responses from the children?

3. Why did Ms. Jane use both Spanish and English in her communication with the children?

4. How can teachers help parents encourage oral language development in their children?

Reading

Early literacy in the preschool classroom is based on strong oral language abilities, knowledge of how print works, phonological awareness, and a personal desire to become a skilled reader. The Reading strand comprises six substrands that have been identified as critical for preschool English learners:

- Appreciation and enjoyment of reading and literature
- An increasing understanding of book reading
- An understanding of print conventions
- An awareness that print carries meaning
- Progress in knowledge of the English alphabet
- Phonological awareness

It is important to remember that children who are English learners may have already learned some of these early literacy skills in their home language. For example, Lonia, the young girl from Sudan described in the Listening section (page 189), may have a keen interest in books that were read to her in Arabic by her mother and have age-appropriate phonological awareness in her home language. To fully understand Lonia's abilities and needs, program staff will need to determine which language and literacy skills Lonia has mastered in her home language by using skilled interpreters who can interview the family and observe Lonia across different contexts, as well as her level of English proficiency.

Phonological awareness, letter knowledge, and discourse skills in the home language appear to provide the necessary background for learning these skills in English. However, the claims for transfer of skills from the home language to a second language are primarily based on research in transfer of Spanish to English and speakers of other European languages. There is little current research on how readily certain literacy skills in Asian languages are transferred to English. Nevertheless, each child's existing knowledge about language, the structure of language, vocabulary levels, and literacy skills should be understood as important prior knowledge that children who are English learners can build upon. Once a teacher knows that a child has already learned age-appropriate skills in a home language, the teacher can expect that this English learner will be able to use these existing skills to develop proficiency in English.

Attention to the bridging of the home language and English, strategic use of the home language, and connecting content to preschool English learners' cultural knowledge will help to foster their motivation to learn the specific literacy skills addressed in the English-language development foundations.

1.0 Children Demonstrate Appreciation and Enjoyment of Reading and Literature

To stay motivated to learn the complex skills required of fluent readers, young children need repeated opportunities to associate reading with pleasure, positive feelings, and interesting learning. Learning to read is promoted by close and nurturing relationships with adults who foster interactions with interesting and engaging print.

VIGNETTE

During a conference with Mrs. Kim, Yeon's mother, Ms. Maria described Yeon's preferred activities in the preschool classroom. Yeon almost always played in the block area and rarely participated in group literacy activities. He seemed to enjoy pushing trucks up and down the block roads, but Ms. Maria could not remember a single time that he picked up a book or joined her when she read to a small group. Maria asked Mrs. Kim if they read books together at home. At this point, Mrs. Kim looked uncomfortable and said, "Not much." She explained that they did not have any books in Korean, and she could not read English books. Ms. Maria then suggested that Mrs. Kim borrow a classroom picture book on transportation and sit with Yeon and make up stories in Korean about the pictures. Ms. Maria encouraged Mrs. Kim to use Korean to tell Yeon stories, sing songs with him, look at magazines together, and point out signs. Mrs. Kim asked, "Won't this confuse Yeon?" Maria reassured Mrs. Kim that the important thing was for her to expose Yeon to lots of experiences with print and books in a playful and engaging way and that speaking to Yeon in Korean would not confuse him.

TEACHABLE MOMENT

 Ms. Maria was uncertain how much exposure to print Yeon received at home. She was able to encourage Yeon's mother to engage in appropriate literacy activities while also promoting continued use of the home language.

The following interactions and strategies support preschool children who are English learners:

Expose children enthusiastically to all types of print (e.g., magazines, billboard signs, books, posters). When teachers and other adults create a warm and positive climate for individual and small-group book reading and storytelling, children respond by increased motivation to learn to read. As adults show enthusiasm for the content of the story in a nurturing setting, preschool English learners learn to value these activities and associate the act of reading with positive feelings. This creates an interest in books and print and the desire to know how the squiggles on a page are connected to the words of the story. For preschool English learners, it is important for them to hear stories repeatedly in their home language, which will help them understand the story narrative once it is read in English. Reading to children in their primary language also provides opportunities to build background knowledge, promote concept development, and expand vocabulary comprehension in the home language. Skilled storybook reading and storytelling in English will help build English skills in language and literacy that are critical to young English learners' future school success.

Connect literacy to the home culture and community. Knowing as much as possible about the children's home life, family activities, personal interests, and familiar settings will help teachers identify books, stories, and strategies that naturally build on the children's background. By inviting storytellers from the community into the classroom and by reading or telling stories in the home language, the program is helping preschool children who are English learners connect literacy activities to family customs and history.

Story packs with quality books translated into the child's home language, CD players, and audio recordings in English and

the home language can be sent home periodically. This practice promotes family literacy time when parents engage in reading, storytelling, and sharing a love of print in their home language.

Build on existing strengths. All children have areas of development where they show strength and perhaps an unusual amount of background knowledge. For example, a young girl from Korea might display well-developed physical agility and interest in the performing arts. For this child who is learning English, opportunities to "move like the wind," "run like a river," or be "silent as a cat" may help her learn new English vocabulary while demonstrating her own unique talents. Many children of recent immigrant families have been shown to have exceptional skills in social relations. If a child who is an English learner shows strengths in forming peer relationships, teachers can systematically arrange small groups so that English learners have opportunities to both learn English and learn through their home language with peers.

Use read-alouds. For preschool children who are English learners, **read-alouds,** or book-reading activities, are best conducted in small groups. Choosing books that are of high interest to preschool English learners and authentically reflect their home culture will help engage their attention. Teachers introduce key concepts and vocabulary words in the children's home language and English before reading the book. Skillful interactive reading of the text will enhance the child's development of new vocabulary. By pointing out key vocabulary words, providing expanded definitions with visual aids, and using the new vocabulary in multiple contexts, teachers will facilitate understanding of the text and English-language development. See the "Research Highlight" on page 186.

2.0 Children Show an Increasing Understanding of Book Reading

As children have many experiences with print of all types, they gradually come to understand that all books share common elements. The knowledge that print in books is organized in specific ways for specific purposes is important for children's development of reading skills. Adults promote this skill development by pointing out the features of books, engaging in skillful storybook reading, and helping children to create books of their own.

VIGNETTE

During morning circle time, Alonzo was quite excited and wanted to share an outing he had taken with his family over the weekend. Alonzo's home language was Spanish, and he kept repeating certain phrases in Spanish at such a rapid pace that Ms. Sheila could not understand him. Ms. Sheila asked her assistant, who was fluent in Spanish and English, to help interpret. Alonzo then described the wedding of his Aunt Lucinda. He went into great detail about who was there, what they had to eat, and the special clothes everyone had to wear. Ms. Sheila then asked the assistant to help Alonzo make a book with pictures of the wedding. During small-group time, she wrote the words in Spanish as Alonzo dictated the events of the wedding. They made a cover page identifying Alonzo as the author, made up a title (Aunt Lucinda's Wedding), *then numbered the pages, and bound them together. The next day Alonzo proudly read the book to the class, very carefully turning each page after showing everyone the pictures and narrating the sequence of events.*

TEACHABLE MOMENT

 Ms. Sheila was able to capitalize on Alonzo's strong feelings about an important family event and direct them to a rich book-making activity. All children get excited about sharing family news and, with some skilled help, can be energized to create narratives in book format. See the "Research Highlight" on page 179.

The following interactions and strategies support preschool children who are English learners:

Connect print material to children's interests. All young children have personal interests, cherished family members, and familiar activities. These interests can be brought into the classroom to help connect what the child knows and is motivated to learn more about to curricular content and skill building. Because the routines and language of the classroom may be unfamiliar to a child who is learning English, the teacher needs to find out the interests of preschool English learners in the classroom, and use this information to build a comfortable and motivating context for learning.

Invite children to discuss and react to story narratives. After reading a book to an English learner in the home language, the teacher can check for comprehension of meaning by asking the child simple questions about the story (e.g., *Who was your favorite character? Has anything like this ever happened to you? What do you think will happen next? Which pig was the smartest? Why would you want Goldilocks to be your friend?*). During the beginning stages of English-language development, it will be important to read and discuss the books in the child's home language. By using the child's home language initially, the teacher will be able to assess the child's understanding of story narrative and ability to make personal connections to events in the story. After this has happened in the home language, the teacher can then read the same book in English to a mixed group of children who are native speakers of English and children who are English learners.

Encourage children to dictate, retell, and create their own books. One of the best ways to help children comprehend story structure is to have them tell personally meaningful stories that are written down by adults. Simple story narration and recording, having children retell stories that have been read to them, or asking children to write or dictate stories from their personal lives can accomplish this.

3.0   Children Demonstrate an Understanding of Print Conventions

During the preschool years, children begin to understand that print may be organized in different ways depending on the purpose of the writing. They also learn that English print follows certain predictable rules (e.g., read from left to right, starts at the top of the page, book pages turn from right to left). These understandings support their ability to track print and learn the English alphabet.

VIGNETTE

Right after sharing and posting the morning message, Ms. Sarah noticed two young girls, Ping Shu and I-Chun, staring at the daily schedule and having an animated conversation in Chinese. She deduced that they were talking about the field trip to the local farmers market planned for later in the day. It also seemed that they were confused about what they were supposed to be doing before going on the field trip. Ms. Sarah moved to the girls and pointed to the morning schedule of times and events, illustrated both in writing and with pictures. Ms. Sarah bent down, carefully pronounced each girl's name, and said, "This message tells us what we will be doing today. Later we will be going to the farmers market." She pointed to the picture of the market. Then she read the message slowly while pointing to each word, linking it to the picture. By pointing to each picture and orally linking it to its corresponding word in the order they were written, left to right, and top to bottom, Ms. Sarah was helping the girls understand print conventions and the meaning of the morning message.

TEACHABLE MOMENT

 Ms. Sarah could see the girls were puzzled over the timing of the day's field trip and used this as an opportunity to reinforce the day's schedule. She carefully used the pictures that accompanied the print to enhance the girls' understanding of the message.

The following interactions and strategies support preschool children who are English learners:

Point out print features during shared reading (shared reading can include all types of print, not just storybooks). While reading a morning message, big books, daily schedules, and other shared reading activities, teachers indicate each word—emphasizing the direction (i.e., from left to right), the way print is organized on pages (i.e., from top to bottom), and how the author is identified.

Point out print features during shared writing. While recording dictated messages, teachers can say things such as, "We start at the top of the page when we write and go across the page, left to right." Teachers can also point out the way a piece of writing begins and ends (e.g., Once upon a time, The End).

Equip all learning areas with books and writing materials. When preschool English learners have the opportunity to explore the properties of books individually and with small groups, they get to practice and share their knowledge in low-demand settings. Books and other forms of print, along with colored chalk and other writing tools, can also be placed in outside areas. Provide adaptations as appropriate, if the child has a disability. (See Appendix D.)

Help children create their own books. Have preschool children who are English learners dictate and illustrate their own "All About Me and My Family" books. The children can collaborate with family members, friends, caregivers, and teachers to create these small books in which the children themselves are the main characters. By talking about, writing about, reading about, and publicly sharing their personal life histories, preschool English learners will develop pride in their cultural identity, create a positive orientation to literacy, and create meaningful and engaging text. Teachers can then have these "All About Me and My Family" books printed, laminated, and shared in the classroom. Children eventually take the books home to share with their families.

4.0 Children Demonstrate Awareness That Print Carries Meaning

An important precursor to fluent reading is the understanding that certain symbols (e.g., signs and print) have deliberate and consistent meanings attached to them. The knowledge that the letters of their name always spell their name even if it is next to a picture of a different child is developed during the preschool years. This knowledge is critical to the development of early literacy skills.

VIGNETTE

Marcela was looking intently at Ting's family pictures on the bulletin board. The Chinese characters in the captions seemed to fascinate Marcela. When Ms. Lucinda came over, Marcela asked her in Spanish, "What are those marks?" Ms. Lucinda replied in Spanish, "These are the names of Ting's family written in Chinese. Chinese is the language Ting's family speaks at home." Ms. Lucinda then pointed to the names written in English and said in English, as she pointed to each name, "This says, Ning Liu, Ting's mother, and this one says, Jun Chan, Ting's father." Ms. Lucinda continued, "This writing tells us the names of the people in the picture. On the first line the names are written in Chinese characters, and on the second line the names are written in the English alphabet."

TEACHABLE MOMENT

 When young children show an interest in print or another child's family or language, this is a good time to point out that different forms of print can carry the same meaning. A child's name can be represented in multiple ways and still mean the same thing.

The following interactions and strategies support preschool children who are English learners:

Point out the meaning of print around the classroom and in the community. Young children often start the process of linking printed letters to sounds of words by learning the printed versions of their own names. An English learner should have a personal storage space (e.g., cubby) labeled with his name in both English and his home language if the alphabet is different. Consistently repeating the names of words used in labeling (e.g., art area, block area, and book area) will also help preschool children who are English learners associate specific printed forms with meaningful words. On neighborhood walks, teachers can point out signs and repeat their meaning; it is especially helpful if the teacher can find signs in multiple languages so the children start to see that different print can represent the same meaning.

Have lots of clear print in multiple languages in the environment. The sight of posters, pictures, and signs with print will allow preschool children to begin learning individual letter names and connecting print with specific meaning. Teachers should ensure that the environmental print displayed in the classroom represents both English and children's home languages; many have found it useful to color-code each language so children and teachers have a way of distinguishing the languages. Teachers will need to find out about the writing systems of their preschool English learners so they can use it in the classroom. Then English learners can understand that print can look and sound a lot of different ways but carry similar meanings about the world.

Engage children in purposeful writing. Young preschool children who are English learners can write notes and letters to important people in their lives for authentic purposes (e.g., a thank-you note to Grandma for a birthday present or a letter to an aunt about a trip to the pumpkin patch). Often they will write letters and words using both the home language and English, which is a normal part of early literacy for preschool English learners. Teachers can point out the sounds and meanings of each word and watch for the child's ability to understand print in the classroom in both English and the home language.

5.0 Children Demonstrate Progress in Their Knowledge of the Alphabet in English

Knowledge of the English alphabet is especially important for young children as they are learning to decode English print. Much research has found a strong relationship between children's ability to recognize letters of the English alphabet and their later reading success. This skill is important to the decoding and recognition of words and seems to be connected to the ability to remember the sounds associated with letters.

VIGNETTE

Yeon Ha rapidly used the alphabet stamp to print letters onto a big piece of construction paper. She seemed to be printing them at random: S, P, B, D, A. Because Yeon Ha had not been in the classroom very long, Ms. Laura was not sure how much English she understood. Ms. Laura gently asked Yeon Ha if she was writing her name. Yeon Ha looked at Ms. Laura but did not respond. Ms. Laura then picked out a piece of paper and started printing out the letters of her own name while saying to Yeon Ha, "I am going to make my own name with these letters." She stamped an L and said, "My name starts with the letter L" and made the /l/ sound. Ms. Laura named each letter of her name and then held up the paper and said to Yeon Ha, "These are the letters in my name: Laura."

Yeon Ha smiled broadly at Ms. Laura and said, "My name is Yeon Ha." Ms. Laura then repeated the name and helped Yeon Ha identify, call out, and stamp the letters of her name.

TEACHABLE MOMENT

 Ms. Laura was able to take Yeon Ha's interest in letters and focus it deliberately toward an activity to identify the letters in her name. Ms. Laura approached the activity indirectly, engaging Yeon Ha first in the letters of her own name (Laura), then helping Yeon Ha stamp the letters of her own name.

The following interactions and strategies support preschool children who are English learners:

Have children identify the letters of their own names in any language. During morning circle time, teachers can hold up name cards for each child and point out the first letter of each name. Teachers should also make sure the name is represented in both English and the home language when the languages have different writing systems.

Provide English alphabet letters in multiple forms (e.g., magnetic letters, wooden letters, paper tracing letters, letter stamps, and alphabet charts) throughout the classroom. While preschool English learners are playing with and manipulating alphabet puzzles, stamps, or magnets, teachers can point out and reinforce the names of the letters in an engaging manner.

Read alphabet books in multiple languages. There are many colorful and culturally appropriate alphabet books available in multiple languages that can be used to emphasize letters in both English and the home language (e.g., *Gathering the Sun,* by Alma Flor Ada). The non-English version can be read one day, and the English version can be read another day. (Additional suggestions are listed in the PEL Resource Guide, pages 77–79.)

6.0 Children Demonstrate Phonological Awareness

Children's ability to hear and understand how the specific sounds in their language are organized is critical to the process of learning to read. Complex interrelated skills include the child's ability to hear and manipulate the individual sound units in the home language. Although phonological awareness can and should be taught through age-appropriate activities, preschool children do not begin to learn some components of phonological awareness, such as syllable segmentation (e.g., "What word do you get when you take the *tur* away from *turkey?*"), until late in the preschool years or in kindergarten. Phonological awareness can be promoted in preschool English learners through singing, chanting, sound and word play, and storybook reading in both their home language and

English. During those activities, teachers should help children who are English learners attend to, discriminate among, and identify the sounds of language. The skills and strategies described in Chapter 4, "Language and Literacy," are also important to the literacy development of preschool English learners. However, the progress of English phonological awareness may look different for children who are English learners because of the following factors: the similarity of their home language to English, the amount of exposure they have to English, the extent of early language and literacy learning in their home language, and the intensity of their English preschool experiences.

VIGNETTE

Mr. Aaron had noticed that the children who spoke Spanish were singing songs and rhymes in Spanish on the playground. Because he did not know these songs, Mr. Aaron asked Lucinda, who was fluent in Spanish, to translate them for him. One of the songs, "Arroz con Leche (Rice Pudding)," was included in the book Pío Peep. *Mr. Aaron ordered a copy of the book, which contains traditional nursery rhymes in Spanish and English, and the CD with accompanying songs in both languages. He then read one song or rhyme each day and played the corresponding music, alternating between Spanish and English.*

TEACHABLE MOMENT

▶ Many books, tapes, and CDs are available in multiple languages. Mr. Aaron recognized preschool English learners' knowledge and interest in rhymes and songs in their home language and was able to use the children's language abilities in their home language to build English-language skills.

The following interactions and strategies support preschool children who are English learners:

Sing silly English songs that can be phonetically manipulated. Songs such as "Apples and Bananas" that allow preschool children who are English learners to hear, repeat, and make up their own sounds help them to learn and manipulate the sounds of English. Since these skills transfer across languages, rhyming songs can also be sung in home languages whenever possible.

Sing songs, recite poems, clap rhythms, and do finger plays that emphasize rhymes daily. Many preschool songs and poems emphasize the sounds of language, which is an important aspect of phonological awareness. By hearing these sounds and participating in the activity, preschool English learners will start to learn the way sounds go together to make up words in this new language. Even though the children may not understand the meaning of the words and may be imitating their English-speaking peers, those activities will help preschool English learners to perceive and eventually produce the unique sounds of English.

Rhyming does appear to be a skill that transfers across languages (e.g., Spanish, French, and other alphabetic languages as well as Chinese), so these activities can be conducted in the home language as well. Some books contain songs, rhymes, and poems in more than one language and can be used to strengthen these skills in both languages. A good example of such a book in Spanish and English is *Pío Peep! Traditional Spanish Nursery*

Rhymes.[10] For preschool English learners, it is appropriate to expect rhyme detection and repetition; however, rhyme production is a complex skill that often requires advanced vocabulary (see pages 133–135 in Chapter 4, "Language and Literacy"). See the "Research Highlight" on page 138.

Identify and practice English sounds that do not exist in the home language. Use common English words with sounds that are not found in the child's home language throughout the day (e.g., emphasize the *sh* sound in *shoes* when helping a child who is Spanish-speaking tie his shoelaces, or point out the "little ladybug" in the insect book to children who speak Japanese).

Use real objects and emphasize syllables and phonemes. As preschool English learners learn the English vocabulary words for common objects and actions, they often find something around the classroom and ask how to say it (e.g., "Teacher, what is this?" while holding up a plastic bowl. This is an opportunity to say *bowl*, emphasizing the /b/ sound).

Play games that emphasize the first sound of common words (e.g., letter bingo, body freeze). Teachers play simple games that ask the child to name words that begin with the same sound as the first sound of her name, such as *Maria, mama, meat.* "What other words start with the same sound?" Games help preschool children who are English learners recognize similar onsets or the first consonant or consonant cluster in a syllable.

Research Highlight

"Building on a child's language abilities in his or her L1 [home language] will not only help the child fully master that language, but provide him or her with the tools to deconstruct the L2 [English]. Early development of language skills, such as semantics, syntax, narrative discourse, and morphology, as well as phonological awareness, will provide the child with a 'meta' understanding of language that he or she can apply to language development and literacy skills in the L2."[9]

Note: L1 refers to home language, and L2 refers to English. "Meta" understanding of language refers to the ability to think and talk about the features of language (e.g., when speaking about something that happened in the past, you must change the verb, "She is here," to "She was here").

Bringing It All Together

Ms. Lucinda's preschool class was studying a unit on families during the first month of the school year. She had carefully selected books about different aspects of family life; she had found bilingual staff and volunteers who read each story to English learners in their home language, pointing out the key vocabulary words before reading the book in English to the whole class. After reading Abuela *in English during story time, Ms. Lucinda asked the children about their grandmothers. All of the children were excited to share something about their grandmothers.*

Ms. Lucinda set out paper with writing and coloring materials on small tables. The children went to different tables during the course of the day. She, or her co-teacher, talked with each child about their grandmother and with the help of the teacher, each child made a book with pictures and print. Ms. Lucinda then laminated each book and had the author invite their grandmother to the class and read the story during circle time. Finally, all the children took their books home to share with their families.

The topic of families has a high level of interest for all children and yields many possibilities for supplementary books, materials, and activities. Family members may be invited to the classroom to share details from their lives and honor the culture and languages of the children. Young children who are English learners are able to learn critical English literacy skills while deepening their pride and knowledge of their own family.

Engaging Families

The following ideas may engage families in helping a child who is an English learner:

✔ Families that are not literate may be reluctant to read to their child in their native language. Parents should always be encouraged to read storybooks in their home language and, if they are not able to read their home language, they can tell stories orally, "read" wordless picture books, and say rhymes and sing songs.

Research Highlight

The conclusions from recent studies suggest that young children may gain important metalinguistic skills from learning more than one language, that they are quite capable of learning early literacy and language skills in two languages, and that many early language and literacy skills learned in the home language (L1) contributed positively to the development of English (L2) language and literacy.[11, 12, 13]

Note: In this research, *metalinguistic* skills refer to the ability to reflect upon and manipulate the structural features of spoken language such as the morphology, sentence structure, and pragmatics of language.

✔ Parents can also be shown how to make an early literacy activity interactive by having their children make predictions, add to stories, or make up their own.

✔ Most communities in California have a public library that can be a wonderful resource for families of children who are learning English. Parents can be helped to locate the public library, apply for a free library card, and introduced to all the books, materials, and learning opportunities that are often available in Spanish and English.

Questions for Reflection

1. How does a child who is an English learner demonstrate early reading skills (e.g., appreciation of literacy activities, print awareness, phonological awareness) in her home language?

2. What strategies are you using that incorporate the home language in classroom routines and materials?

3. How are community volunteers who are fluent in the children's home languages and who can read to the children who are English learners encouraged to come to the preschool?

Writing

The Writing strand for children who are English learners is not substantially different in focus from the language and literacy Writing strand. The primary distinction between the two sets of foundations is that the English learner's home language may be reflected in the development of the child's writing stages. For children who are native speakers of English and children who are English learners, writing is a process of active discovery about a language's symbol system as visually represented. These foundations emphasize writing as a means of communication, the beginning of writing forms, and writing to represent their names.

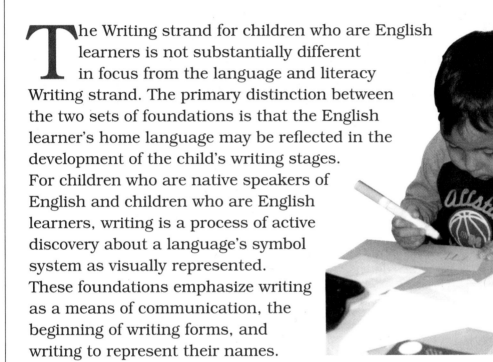

Young children are attempting to gain control over a language's symbol system by figuring out what symbols mean while trying to make marks on paper that approximate those symbols.[14] Environments that encourage writing should first and foremost view children as capable of making these connections regardless of home language.[15, 16] According to Sulzby and Teale,[17] it is important for teachers to engage children as socially competent participants through adult–child and peer–peer interaction around books. When this occurs, opportunities for writing emerge that may provide children with practice in writing. To the extent possible, it is important to provide children with a rich oral language environment in both their home language and English, because emerging writing skills are linked to a child's oral language development.

1.0 Children Use Writing to Communicate Their Ideas

Through exposure to writing as a means of communication, children begin to learn that writing has many purposes, such as the provision of information, entertainment, and describing and remembering an event that has already occurred. When children make the connection between the written symbol and its meaning, cognitive growth ensues. "When children write, they have a fixed representation of oral language. They can explore it, as it doesn't vanish like the spoken word."[18] For children who are English learners, more instructional support is needed in other language areas, such as listening and speaking, to become successful writers. Children who are English learners benefit from opportunities to write in their home language.[19]

VIGNETTE

Jaime and Sarita are playing in the dramatic play area, which has been supplied with food props (e.g., plastic fruits and vegetables) and writing materials. Jaime is carefully looking at the fruits and vegetables when Sarita says, "Por qué no jugamos restaurante?" (Why don't we play restaurant?) as she pulls Jaime's arm to make him sit down in the nearby chair. Jaime goes along with the play and sits down. In the meantime Sarita grabs some paper and markers that are located in the dramatic play area and quickly scribbles some lines on a piece of paper and hands it to Jaime. Sarita says, "¿Qué gustarias?" (What would you like?) "Gustarias un banana, un apple?" Jaime smiles at Sarita and says, "Un apple, por favor."

PLANNING LEARNING OPPORTUNITIES

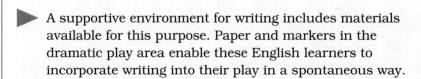 A supportive environment for writing includes materials available for this purpose. Paper and markers in the dramatic play area enable these English learners to incorporate writing into their play in a spontaneous way.

The following interactions and strategies support children who are preschool English learners:

Look for opportunities for adult- and peer-mediated conversation about writing by using the child's home language to initiate this discussion. When children are engaged in writing, it is important for the teacher to ask what they are writing about. For children who are English learners, the teacher needs to know the child's level of second-language development before structuring a question (e.g., in the home language or with key words in the home language). Ask for clarification or elaboration of concepts. For example, if the child is writing about the animals he saw at the zoo over the weekend, the teacher asks questions about the outing. This type of interaction may provide opportunities to reinforce words and phrases in English and build vocabulary. The teacher may also provide opportunities in the classroom where the children can interact with others and discuss what they are writing. In the writing area children have paper, markers, crayons, and letter stamps.

Link writing to listening and speaking so preschool children who are English learners can draw from other language strengths. The classroom environment should be rich with printed materials, including books in the child's home language, and wordless picture books that children can use as a basis of discussion in their home language and then move on to writing activities. For example, teachers may read *The Little Red Hen* and then discuss with the children why the other animals in the story did not want to help the little red hen. For children learning English, it is recommended that the story be read to them in their home language. See the "Research Highlight" on page 216. If this is not possible, it is recommended that program staff or other adults who speak the child's home language read the book in the home language and stress key concepts. Afterwards, when the book is read in English, the child who is an English learner will be better able to understand the story line and words in English that may correspond to words in her home language. In related follow-up activities, teachers provide finger-puppet facsimiles of farm animals in the block area so that English learners have an opportunity to play with the finger puppets and act out the story in their home language. Later, the children draw the red hen or some of the other animals in the story and dictate a story or passage to

accompany the drawing. Teachers should allow code switching in children's dictated stories.

Focus writing activities on literature. It is helpful to connect writing to stories that are being used in the classroom and are available in the book area. This strategy will provide the child with opportunities to revisit the story multiple times to strengthen their understanding of specific words and concepts in both their home language and English.

Supply learning areas with writing materials (e.g., dramatic play, science, and cooking). Children will have the tools to incorporate writing into their dramatic play. They can create such things as menus, personal letters, grocery lists, and charts. For children who are learning English, having access to writing material in interest areas means there is no pressure for them to perform and provides them with opportunities to experiment with their second language both in written form and orally.

Have children dictate their own short stories. Dictated stories are a good way to introduce the child to writing as a means of description. Teachers may encourage the child to share her stories and, if the child uses her home language, adults who understand and can write the home language write down what the child is saying. These adults then read the child's words back to her. Teachers should allow for code switching in children's dictation. If no adult is available who can understand and write the child's home language, a peer might be engaged to interpret the description for the teacher and child.

Bringing It All Together

The recent topic of study has been ocean life, and Mr. Jason has been reading related stories to the children. Throughout the month, the storybooks have been placed in the writing area, and children have been asked to dictate the story to an adult who then writes it down. Children can then draw pictures about their story, and it is placed on the wall near the writing area.

Gustavo, a Spanish speaker, is sitting at a table with a large piece of chart paper with lines for writing text and space for drawing a picture. Ms. Adelaida, a bilingual teacher assistant, sits next to him and asks in English, "What story do you want to write about?" She sees that Gustavo looks at her quizzically, and she then says in Spanish, "¿De cual de los cuentos quieres escribir?" Gustavo replies, "Swimmy" and points to the book on the shelf. Ms. Adelaida picks up a marker and says to Gustavo in Spanish, "Okay, ¿Gustavo, qué gustarias decir sobre el cuento?" (Okay, Gustavo, what would you like to say about the story?) Gustavo begins by saying, "Este es un cuento de un fish, Swimmy. Swimmy swims fast." As Gustavo speaks, Ms. Adelaida repeats exactly what Gustavo says and writes it down on the paper. Gustavo goes on to describe the story using a combination of Spanish and English.

Later in the week, Gustavo points to his story, which is displayed on the wall, as Ms. Adelaida stands nearby. Gustavo begins to recount the story he had previously dictated using both Spanish and English vocabulary. Ms. Adelaida smiles and then repeats his story, pointing to each word as she speaks. Gustavo asks Ms. Adelaida how to say the word negro *(black) in English because Swimmy is a little black fish.*

Mr. Jason and Ms. Adelaida know that children who are beginning to learn vocabulary in English may mix the two languages (i.e., code switch), and that is typical. These teachers know that the primary goal of the writing activity is the connection between the written word and a particular concept or idea. They also know that children who are English learners will use their home language to transfer concepts or ideas to English, as is the case when Gustavo asks how to say the word *negro* in English. See the "Research Highlight" on page 216.

Engaging Families

The following ideas may engage families in helping their child who is an English learner:

✔ Encourage parents to provide opportunities for their children to draw and scribble "stories" at home. If needed, send home writing material. Encourage parents to work with their child to write a story about their family or a special family celebration that they attended. These stories can be in either the home language or English or a combination of the two.

✔ Encourage parents to draw children's attention to print during daily routines.

As parents go about their day, they can point out the print that is in their environments to help children make the connection between the concept or idea and the written word. Print may be in their home language or in English.

✔ Encourage parents to read stories or poems in their home language to strengthen the child's home language. By hearing stories or poems in their home language, children may begin to link print as a representation of either English or their home language.

Questions for Reflection

- Why was it important for the teachers to allow Gustavo to mix languages (i.e., to code switch)?

- What are some other ways to use dictated stories with English learners?

- What is the relationship between listening, speaking, and writing for the English learner?

Concluding Thoughts

Diverse voci fanno dolce note; cosi diversi scanni in nostra vita rendon dolce armonia . . . (Diverse voices make sweet music; as diverse conditions in our life render sweet harmony.)

—Dante, Paradiso IV:124–126

Being exposed to two or more languages at a young age is a gift. It is a gift because children who are able to learn through two or more languages benefit cognitively, socially, and emotionally. Children who develop bilingual competence show greater cognitive flexibility as they deal with the meaning and structure of two different language systems.[20] These children also show a greater concentration of brain growth and development, which appears to confer long-term cognitive and academic benefits. Learning two languages has definite social advantages because it allows children to learn about another culture and way of life, thus expanding their worldview. Speaking two languages provides an opportunity for multiple interpretations of words and meanings, thus widening the learner's universe and often providing a basis for greater tolerance of different ideas, beliefs, and values. Because there is a clear relationship between a child's sense of identity and his first language,[21] valuing the child's first language and including it as an important part of instruction will help a child feel a greater sense of belonging in the educational setting, which, in turn, enhances learning. Exposure to more than one language should be celebrated as a growth opportunity that offers many learning and social advantages. Children who are developing bilingual abilities are developing unique strengths that will add to the cultural and linguistic resources of California.

Map of the Foundations

English-Language Development

Domain ⟶ **English-Language Development**

Substrand ⟶ **3.0 Children demonstrate an understanding of print conventions.**

Focus ⟶ *Focus: Book handling**

Level ⟵

Foundation ⟶

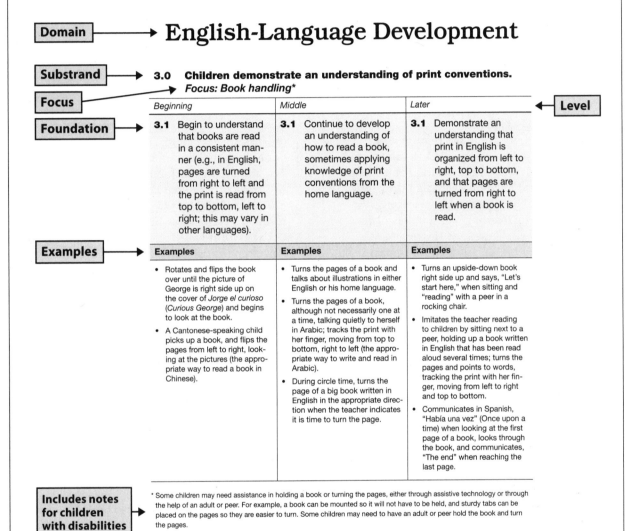

Beginning	Middle	Later
3.1 Begin to understand that books are read in a consistent manner (e.g., in English, pages are turned from right to left and the print is read from top to bottom, left to right; this may vary in other languages).	**3.1** Continue to develop an understanding of how to read a book, sometimes applying knowledge of print conventions from the home language.	**3.1** Demonstrate an understanding that print in English is organized from left to right, top to bottom, and that pages are turned from right to left when a book is read.
Examples	**Examples**	**Examples**
• Rotates and flips the book over until the picture of George is right side up on the cover of *Jorge el curioso* (*Curious George*) and begins to look at the book. • A Cantonese-speaking child picks up a book, and flips the pages from left to right, looking at the pictures (the appropriate way to read a book in Chinese).	• Turns the pages of a book and talks about illustrations in either English or his home language. • Turns the pages of a book, although not necessarily one at a time, talking quietly to herself in Arabic; tracks the print with her finger, moving from top to bottom, right to left (the appropriate way to write and read in Arabic). • During circle time, turns the page of a big book written in English in the appropriate direction when the teacher indicates it is time to turn the page.	• Turns an upside-down book right side up and says, "Let's start here," when sitting and "reading" with a peer in a rocking chair. • Imitates the teacher reading to children by sitting next to a peer, holding up a book written in English that has been read aloud several times; turns the pages and points to words, tracking the print with her finger, moving from left to right and top to bottom. • Communicates in Spanish, "Había una vez" (Once upon a time) when looking at the first page of a book, looks through the book, and communicates, "The end" when reaching the last page.

Examples ⟶

Includes notes for children with disabilities ⟶

* Some children may need assistance in holding a book or turning the pages, either through assistive technology or through the help of an adult or peer. For example, a book can be mounted so it will not have to be held, and sturdy tabs can be placed on the pages so they are easier to turn. Some children may need to have an adult or peer hold the book and turn the pages.

Teacher Resources

Academy for Education Development (AED). 2008. *Making a Difference, A Framework for Supporting First and Second Language Development in Preschool Children of Migrant Farm Workers.* http://www.aed.org/Publications/loader.cfm?url=/commonspot/security/getfile.cfm&pageid=3352

American Speech-Language-Hearing Association (ASHA). Communication Development and Disorders in Multicultural Populations: Reading and Related Materials http://www.asha.org/about/leadership-projects/multicultural/readings/disabilities.htm

American Speech-Language-Hearing Association (ASHA). Learning Two Languages (available in Spanish and as a brochure) http://www.asha.org/public/speech/development/BilingualChildren.htm

California Association for Bilingual Education (CABE). http://www.bilingualeducation.org

California Department of Education. Web site for Teachers of Preschool English Learners http://www.preschoolenglishlearners.org

Colorín Colorado: A Bilingual Site for Families and Educators of English Learners. http://www.colorincolorado.org/

Cooperative Children's Book Center, School of Education, University of Wisconsin-Madison. *50 Multicultural Books Every Child Should Know.* http://www.education.wisc.edu/ccbc/books/detailListBooks.asp?idBookLists=42

The Early Authors' Program, Ryerson University. Toronto, Ontario, Canada. http://www.ryerson.ca/~bernhard/early.html

Espinosa, L. 2008. *Challenging Common Myths About Young English Learners. Foundation for Child Development.* http://www.fcd-us.org/resources/resources-show.htm?doc_id=669789

Genesee, F. 2006. Bilingual Acquisition. Earlychildhood NEWS. http://www.colorincolorado.org/article/12916?theme=print

Journal of the National Association of the Education of Young Children (NAEYC). 2005. *Resources for Embracing Diversity in Early Childhood Settings.* http://www.journal.naeyc.org/btj/200511/DiversityResourcesBTJ1105.asp

National Center for Learning Disabilities. *Get Ready to Read.* http://www.getreadytoread.org/frontpage/Itemid.1/

National Clearinghouse for English Language Acquisition (NCELA). 2006. Washington, D.C. *Resources About Early Childhood Education.* http://www.ncela.gwu.edu/resabout/ecell/index.html

National Institute for Early Education Research (NIEER). 2009. Research Topics, English Language Learners. http://nieer.org/research/topic.php?TopicID=4

National Taskforce on Early Childhood Education for Hispanics. 2007. Expanding and Improving Early Education for Hispanics. http://www.ecehispanic.org

Reading Is Fundamental (RIF). 2008. Additional Parent Tip Sheet: Helping Your Children Become Readers (literacy). http://www.rif.org/parents/articles/default.mspx

Reading Is Fundamental (RIF). 2008. Bilingual Children's Books. http://www.rif.org/educators/books/Bilingual_books.mspx

Reading Is Fundamental (RIF). 2008. Bilingual Versions of Popular Children's Books. http://www.rif.org/educators/books/Bilingualversions.mspx

Reading Is Fundamental (RIF). 2008. Wordless and Almost Wordless Picture Books. http://www.rif.org/educators/books/Picture-Books.mspx

Reading Is Fundamental (RIF). 2008. *100 of the Decade's Best Multicultural Read-Alouds, Pre-Kindergarten through Grade 8.* Selected and annotated by J. Freeman. http://www.rif.org/educators/books/100_best_multicultural.mspx

Reading Rockets: Launching Young Readers http://www.readingrockets.org/

RealeWriter (free, family-friendly picture books). http://www.realebooks.com

Roberts, T. A. 2009. *No Limits to Literacy for Preschool English Learners.* Thousand Oaks, CA: Corwin Press.

This valuable resource helps teachers understand how English learners ages three to five acquire the foundations for literacy. It offers practical, research-based strategies for teaching language and literacy skills. http://www.corwinpress.com/ booksProdDesc.nav?prodId=Book232561

Roseberry-McKibbin, C., and A. Brice. 2005. Acquiring English as a Second Language: What's "Normal," What's Not. American Speech-Language-Hearing Association. http://www.asha.org/public/speech/ development/easl.htm

U.S. Department of Education. 2007. *Teaching Our Youngest: A Guide for Preschool Teachers, Childcare, and Family Providers.* http://www.ed.gov/teachers/how/early/ teachingouryoungest/index.html

References

Au, K. H. 2000. A multicultural perspective on policies for improving literacy achievement: Equity and excellence. In *Handbook of reading research*, vol. 3, ed. M. L. Kamil, P. B. Mosenthal, P. D. Pearson, and R. Barr. Mahwah, NJ: Erlbaum.

August, D., and T. Shanahan. 2006. *Developing literacy in second-language learners: Report of the national literacy panel on language minority children and youth.* Mahwah, NJ: Erlbaum.

Ballantyne, K. G., and others. 2008. *Dual language learners in the early years: Getting ready to succeed in school.* Washington, DC: National Clearinghouse for English Language Acquisition. http://www.ncela. gwu.edu/resabout/ecell/earlyyears.pdf

Barone, D. M., and S. H. Xu. 2008 *Literacy instruction for English language learners: Pre-K–2.* New York: Guilford.

Bernhard, J. K., and others. 2005. The early authors program: Implementing transformative literacy in early childhood education. Paper presented at the annual meeting of the American Educational Researchers Association, Montreal, Quebec, Canada, April.

Bredekamp, S., and T. Rosegrant. 1995. *Reaching potentials: Transforming early childhood curriculum and assessment.* Washington, DC: National Association for the Education of Young Children (NAEYC).

Espinosa, L. 2008. A review of the literature on assessment issues for young English language learners. Paper prepared for the meeting of the NAS Committee on Developmental Outcomes and Assessments for Young Children. Washington, DC, January.

Espinosa, L. 2009. Classroom teaching and instruction: What are 'best practices' for young English language learners? In *Enhancing the knowledge base for serving young English language learners*, ed. E. Garcia and E. Frede. New York: Teachers College Press.

Genishi, C., S. E. Stires, and D. Yung-Chan. 2001. Writing in an integrated curriculum: Prekindergarten English language learners as symbol makers, *The Elementary School Journal* 101: 399–416.

Goldenberg, C. 2008. Teaching English language learners: What the research does—and does not—say, *American Educator* 32, no. 1 (Summer): 8–23, 42–44.

Hoff, E. 2001. *Language development.* 2nd ed. Belmont, CA: Wadsworth.

Lopez, L. M., and D. B. Greenfield. 2004. Cross-language transfer of phonological skills of Hispanic Head Start children, *Bilingual Research Journal* 28, no. 1 (Spring): 1–18.

National Task Force on Early Childhood Education for Hispanics. 2007. *Para nuestros niños: expanding and improving early education for Hispanics.* Tempe, AZ: Arizona State University.

Preschool English learners: Principles and practices to promote language, literacy, and learning. 2009. 2nd ed. Sacramento: California Department of Education.

Rivera, C., and E. Collum. 2006. *State assessment policy and practice for English language learners: A national perspective.* Mahwah, NJ: Lawrence Erlbaum.

Samway, K. 2006. *When English language learners write.* Portsmouth, NH: Heinemann.

Shanahan, T., and I. Beck. 2007. Effective literacy teaching for English-language learners. In *Developing literacy in second-language learners: Report of the national literacy panel on language minority children and youth*, ed. D. August and T. Shanahan. Mahwah, NJ: Erlbaum.

Slavin, R. E., and A. Cheung. 2005. A synthesis of research on language of reading instruction for English language learners, *Review of Education Research* 75, no. 2: 247–81.

Sulzby, E., and W. Teal. 1991. Emergent literacy. In Vol. 2 of *Handbook of Reading Research*, ed. R. Barr and others. New York: Longman.

Tabors, P. O. 2008. *One child, two languages: A guide for early childhood educators of children learning English as a second language*. 2nd ed. Baltimore: Brookes.

Yaden, D. B., and J. M. Tardibuono. 2004. The emergent writing development of urban latino preschoolers: Developmental perspectives and instructional environments for second-language learners, *Reading and Writing Quarterly* 20: 29–61.

Endnotes

1. *California Preschool Learning Foundations,* Vol. 1 (Sacramento: California Department of Education 2008). 103.

2. *Preschool English Learners: Principles and Practices to Promote Language, Literacy, and Learning,* 2nd ed. (Sacramento: California Department of Education, 2009), 71–88.

3. T. Shanahan and I. Beck, "Effective Literacy Teaching for English-Language Learners," in *Developing Literacy in Second-Language Learners: Report of the National Literacy Panel on Language Minority Children and Youth.* Edited by D. August and T. Shanahan (Mahwah, NJ: Erlbaum, 2007).

4. *Preschool English Learners: Principles and Practices to Promote Language, Literacy, and Learning,* 2nd ed. (Sacramento: California Department of Education, 2009), 71–88.

5. P. O. Tabors, *One Child, Two Languages: A Guide for Early Childhood Educators of Children Learning English as a Second Language,* 2nd ed. (Baltimore: Brookes, 2008).

6. *Preschool English Learners: Principles and Practices to Promote Language, Literacy, and Learning,* 2nd ed. (Sacramento: California Department of Education, 2007), 71–88.

7. E. Bialystok, *Bilingualism in Development: Language, Literacy, and Cognition* (Cambridge, UK: Cambridge University Press, 2001).

8. C. Goldenberg, "Teaching English Language Learners: What the Research Does—and Does Not—Say," *American Educator* 32, no. 1 (Summer 2008): 8–23 and 42–44.

9. L. M. Lopez and D. B. Greenfield, "Cross-Language Transfer of Phonological Skills of Hispanic Head Start Children," *Bilingual Research Journal* 28, no.1, (Spring 2004): 13.

10. A. Ada, F. I. Campoy, and A. Schertle, *Pio Peep! Traditional Spanish Nursery Rhymes* (New York: HarperCollins, 2003).

11. W. Thomas and V. Collier, *A National Study of School Effectiveness for Language Minority Students' Long-Term Academic Achievement* (Santa Cruz, CA: Center for Research on Education, Diversity and Excellence, 2002).

http://www.cal.org/resources/digest/ResBrief10.html (accessed November 26, 2008).

12. L. Espinosa, "Classroom Teaching and Instruction: What Are 'Best Practices' for Young English Language Learners?" in *Enhancing the Knowledge Base for Serving Young English Language Learners,* ed. by E. Garcia and E. Frede (New York: Teachers College Press, 2009).

13. R. E. Slavin and A. Cheung, "A Synthesis of Research on Language of Reading Instruction for English Language Learners," *Review of Education Research* 75, no. 2 (2005): 247–81.

14. D. B. Yaden and J. M. Tardibuono, "The Emergent Writing Development of Urban Latino Preschoolers: Developmental Perspectives and Instructional Environments for Second-Language Learners," *Reading and Writing Quarterly* 20 (2004): 29–61.

15. C. Genishi, S. E. Stires, and D. Yung-Chan, "Writing in an Integrated Curriculum: Pre-kindergarten English Language Learners as Symbol Makers," *The Elementary School Journal* 101 (2001): 399–416.

16. Ibid.

17. E. Sulzby and W. Teale, "The Development of the Young Child and the Emergence of Literacy," in *Handbook of Research on Teaching the English Language Arts.* Edited by J. Flood and others (Mahwah, NJ: Erlbaum, 2003), 300–13.

18. D. M. Barone and S. H. Xu, 2008, *Literacy Instruction for English Language Learners: Pre-K–2* (New York: Guilford, 2008), 110.

19. K. Samway, *When English Language Learners Write* (Portsmouth, NH: Heinemann, 2006).

20. E. Bialystok and M. M. Martin, "Attention and Inhabitation in Bilingual Children: Evidence from the Multidimensional Change Card Sort Task," *Developmental Science* 7 (2004): 325–39.

21. *Eager to Learn: Educating Our Preschoolers,* ed. by B. T. Bowman, M. S. Donovan, and M. S. Burns (Washington, DC: National Academy Press, 2000).

CHAPTER 6

Mathematics

Mathematics is a natural part of the preschool environment. Young children actively construct mathematical knowledge through everyday interactions with their environment, whether inside or outside. When building in the block area or sorting blocks by shape, children explore geometry in the real world. When measuring two cups of flour and three spoons of sugar in a cooking activity, they learn principles of measurement. Climbing in and out of cardboard boxes, crawling through a tunnel, or riding a bike helps children develop a sense of spatial relationships (e.g., on, under, over). Mathematics learning grows naturally from children's curiosity and enthusiasm to learn and explore their environment. Teachers should encourage children's natural enthusiasm and interest in doing mathematics and use it as a vehicle for supporting the development of children's mathematical concepts and skills.

Young children seem to have an innate sense of informal mathematics. They develop a substantive body of informal knowledge of mathematics from infancy throughout the preschool years. By the age of three, they have already begun to acquire knowledge of number. They have learned to say their first number words and count small concrete sets of objects. They understand the idea of more and less. If they are given more crackers (or more of a substance such as play dough), they understand they have *more* than they did before, and if some were taken away, they now have *less*. During the preschool years, children continue to show a spontaneous interest in mathematics and further develop their mathematical knowledge and skills related to number, quantity, size, shape, and space.

With the growing evidence about children's math capacities in the early years and the significance of early math experiences, there is a general consensus "that high-quality, challenging and accessible mathematics education for three- to six-year-old children is a vital founda-

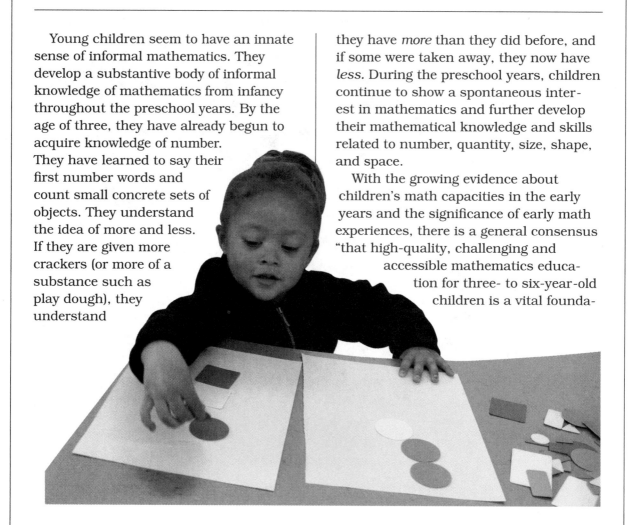

tion for future mathematics learning."[1] High-quality mathematics education in preschool is not about elementary arithmetic being pushed down onto younger children. It is broader than mere practice in counting and arithmetic. It is about children experiencing mathematics as they explore ideas of more and less, count objects, make comparisons, create patterns, sort and measure objects, and explore shapes in space. Mathematics learning happens throughout the day, and it is integrated with learning and developing in other developmental domains such as language and literacy, social-emotional, science, music, and movement.

Teachers have a significant role in facilitating children's construction of mathematical concepts. They may not always realize the extent to which their current everyday classroom practices support children's mathematical development. For example, when singing with children "Five Little Ducks Went Out One Day," incorporating finger play with counting, the teacher develops children's counting skills and understanding of number. Discussing with children how many children came to school today and how many are missing supports children's arithmetic and reasoning with numbers. Playing with children in the sandbox by filling up

different cups with sand and discussing which cup is the *smallest* or the *largest* or how many cups of sand it would take to fill up a bucket introduces children to concepts of comparison and measurement. Preschool teachers nurture children's natural enthusiasm and interest in learning mathematics. They help children build their knowledge and skills of mathematics over time, by providing a mathematically rich environment, by modeling mathematical thinking and reasoning, and by introducing children to the language of math.[2] Teachers guide, support, and challenge children in the journey of exploring and constructing mathematical knowledge. As stated by the National Council of Teachers of Mathematics (NCTM):

> . . . adults can foster children's mathematical development by providing environments rich in language, where thinking is encouraged, uniqueness is valued, and exploration is supported. Play is children's work. Adults support young children's diligence and mathematical development when they direct attention to the mathematics children use in their play, challenge them to solve problems and encourage their persistence.[3]

When teachers join children in becoming keen observers of their environment and in reasoning about numbers, shapes, and patterns, mathematics is enjoyable and exciting for all.

Guiding Principles

The following principles will guide teachers' classroom practices in establishing a high-quality, challenging, and sensitive early mathematics preschool program. These principles are partially based on the ten recommendations in *Early Childhood Mathematics:*

Promoting Good Beginnings set forth by the National Association for the Education of Young Children and NCTM in 2002.

▶ **Build on preschool children's natural interest in mathematics and their intuitive and informal mathematical knowledge**
Young children are mathematically competent, motivated, and naturally interested in exploring mathematical ideas and concepts. Teachers should recognize children's early mathematical competence and build on children's disposition to use mathematics as a way to make sense of their world.

▶ **Encourage inquiry and exploration to foster problem solving and mathematical reasoning**
Mathematical reasoning and problem solving are natural to all children as they explore the world around them. The most powerful mathematics learning for preschool children often results from their own explorations. Teachers should maintain an environment that nurtures children's inquiry and exploration of mathematical ideas and that values problem solving. They should ask children questions to stimulate mathematical conversations and encourage mathematical reasoning through everyday interactions. Teachers' meaningful questions can lead to

clarifications, more advanced challenges, and the development of new understandings.

▶ **Use everyday activities as natural vehicles for developing preschool children's mathematical knowledge**
Children can learn mathematical concepts through play and everyday activities as they interact with materials and investigate problems. Putting toys away, playing with blocks, helping to set the table before snack, or playing with buckets of varying sizes in the sand are all opportunities for children to learn about key mathematical concepts such as sorting, geometry, number, and measurements. Teachers should build upon the naturally occurring mathematics in children's daily activities and capitalize on "teachable moments" during such activities to extend children's mathematical understanding and interest.

▶ **Introduce mathematical concepts through intentionally planned experiences**
In addition to the meaningful mathematics that preschool children acquire spontaneously through play and everyday activities, teachers should provide carefully planned experiences that focus children's attention on particular mathematical concepts, methods, and the language of math. Mathematical experiences planned in advance would allow teachers to present concepts in a logical sequence and forge links between previously encountered mathematical ideas and new applications. Teachers should build on what the child already knows and reasonably challenge the child in acquiring new skills or knowledge. Teachers can foster children's understanding

of mathematical concepts over time through intentional involvement with mathematical ideas in preschool and by helping families extend and develop these ideas.

▶ **Provide a mathematically rich environment**

Arranging a high-quality physical environment is important for children's mathematical development. It should offer children opportunities to experiment and learn about key mathematical concepts naturally throughout the classroom and throughout the day.

▶ **Provide an environment rich in language, and introduce preschool children to the language of mathematics**

Language is a critical element in mathematics. Children should be introduced to mathematical vocabulary as well as to natural language in meaningful contexts. During the preschool years, children learn mathematical language such as the number words, the names for shapes, words to compare quantity (e.g., *bigger, smaller),* and words to describe position and direction in space (e.g., *in, on, above).* Children often have an intuitive understanding of mathematical concepts but lack the vocabulary and the conceptual framework of mathematics. By introducing children to mathematical vocabulary, teachers help "mathematize" what children intuitively grasp. Language allows children to become aware of their mathematical thinking and to express it in words. Children with delays in development, especially in language development, may need more frequent repetition of the words combined with a demonstration of the concept.

▶ **Support English learners in developing mathematical knowledge as they concurrently acquire English**

Teachers should be aware of the challenges faced by children who are English learners and apply specific instructional strategies to help children learning English acquire mathematical concepts and skills. To provide children who are English learners with comprehensible information, they should simplify the terms they use, make extensive use of manipulatives, illustrate the meaning of words by acting and modeling whenever possible, and encourage children to use terms in their home language. Repetition, paraphrasing, and elaboration by the teacher also help preschool children who are English learners understand the content of the conversation. Teachers are encouraged to use mathematical terms as often as possible and in as many different settings as possible. Teachers' attentive and modified talk helps young children learning English to understand mathematical concepts and to develop the language skills they need to communicate mathematical ideas.[4]

▶ **Observe preschool children and listen to them**

Observe children thoughtfully, listen carefully to their ideas, and talk with them. Close observation allows teachers to identify thought-provoking moments through everyday play, where mathematical concepts can be clarified, extended, and reinforced, and children can be prompted to make new discoveries. Observing and listening to children also allows teachers to learn about children's interests and attitudes and to assess children's mathematical knowledge and skills.

Take into account that mathematical knowledge is not always expressed verbally. Children may know a lot about number, size, or shape without having the words to describe what they know.

▶ **Recognize and support the individual**

Provide an environment in which *all* children can learn mathematics, set appropriately high expectations for all children, and support individual growth. Children differ in their strengths, interests, approaches to learning, knowledge, and skills. They may also have special learning needs. Young children, therefore, may construct mathematical understanding in different ways, at varying rates, and with different materials. To be effective, teachers should respond to each child individually. They should find out what young children already know and build on the children's individual strengths and ways of learning. Teachers should provide children with a variety of materials, teaching strategies, and methods to meet children's different learning styles and promote access to and attainment of mathematical concepts by all children. The strategies presented in the next sections for supporting children's development in the mathematics domain apply to all children. Children with disabilities and other special needs, like all children, benefit from multiple opportunities to experience math concepts through playful activities that build on their interests. They particularly benefit from hands-on activities, using a variety of manipulatives, and from teachers' support and verbal descriptions of what they are doing. If children are receiving special education services, teachers should ask for ideas from the specialists and families.

▶ **Establish a partnership with parents and other caregivers in supporting children's learning of mathematics**

Parents and other caregivers should be partners in the process of supporting children's mathematics development. Parents serve as role models for children. When parents become involved in their children's mathematics education, children become more engaged and excited. Teachers should communicate to parents what preschool mathematics is about, age-appropriate expectations for mathematics learning at the preschool level, and how mathematics learning is supported in the preschool environment. They should also convey to parents the importance of mathematics and what they can do at home for supporting children's math development. By talking with parents, teachers could also learn about children's interests, natural knowledge, and home experiences related to math. They may need to remind parents about the numerous opportunities to talk with children about number, shape, size, and quantity during everyday home routines and activities. For example, while walking to school or taking the bus, parents can point out the yield signs, stop signs, and so on and say the name of each shape (triangle, rectangle, square) and can count the number of footsteps to the front door. While cooking, they can count the number of cups of rice or beans. Throughout the year, teachers should also provide parents with information about the child's development and progress in learning math concepts and skills.

Environments and Materials

Young children actively construct mathematical knowledge through everyday interactions with their environment. Setting up a high-quality physical environment is essential for children's mathematical development. The preschool environment sets the stage for children's physical and social exploration and construction of mathematical concepts. It should provide access to objects and materials that encourage children to experiment and learn about key mathematical concepts through everyday play.

▶ **Enrich the environment with objects and materials that promote mathematical growth.**
Provide children with access to developmentally appropriate, challenging, and engaging materials. A high-quality environment offers children opportunities to count objects; to explore and compare objects' size, shape, weight, and other attributes; to measure; to sort and classify; and to discover and create patterns. For example, wooden blocks, geometric foam blocks, cylinders, cones, and boxes would encourage creativity while stimulating concepts of geometry. Collections of small items such as rocks, beads, cubes, buttons, commercial counters, and other items can be used for counting, sorting, and categorizing. Containers of different sizes and measuring cups and spoons can illustrate the concepts of volume and capacity. The environment should also include number-related books; felt pieces or finger puppets to go with the books; and counting games using dice, spinners, and cards. It may also include computer software and other technology materials focused on math. Materials and props will support all children in learning mathematics and are particularly important in teaching preschool children who are English learners. The props and materials give concrete meaning to the words children hear in the context of doing mathematics.

Children with physical disabilities may need assistance in exploring the environment and manipulating objects. Children with motor impairments may explore through observation or may need assistance from an adult or a peer in manipulating objects to do things such as count, sort, compare, order, measure, create patterns, or solve problems. A child might also use adaptive materials (e.g., large manipulatives that are easy to grasp). Alternately, a child might demonstrate knowledge in these areas without directly manipulating objects. For example, a child might direct a peer or teacher to place several objects in order from smallest to largest. Children with visual impairments might be offered materials for counting, sorting, or problem solving that are easily distinguishable by touch. Their engagement is also facilitated by the use of containers, trays, and so forth of materials that clearly define their workspace.

▶ **Integrate math-related materials into all interest areas in the classroom.**
Math naturally takes place throughout the classroom and throughout the day. Children explore objects and learn about shapes and numbers as they go about their daily routine and play in different areas in the classroom. Number symbols, for example, naturally appear throughout the classroom,

from real-life objects such as a tape measure, a telephone, a calculator or a scale to puzzles, stickers, books, and cards with numbers. Some teachers may choose to have a math table or a math area in the classroom for math-related materials, games, books, and manipulatives. In addition, the teacher should integrate math-related materials and props into all activity areas in the classroom. The dramatic play area can include a scale, a calculator, a measuring tape, and other math-related tools. The art area can include shape and number stickers, magazine cutouts of numbers, and shapes for collage making. The same tool can be used in various places throughout the environment. Measuring cups and spoons, for example, can be used for cooking, but also in the science or discovery area, in the dramatic play area, and for playing with sand and water.

▶ **Provide real-life settings in the preschool environment.**
Real-life settings to investigate, such as a grocery store, a restaurant, a woodshop, or a bakery, help children learn naturally about everyday mathematics. They present children with numerous opportunities for mathematical reasoning and problem solving. Such settings demonstrate for children mathematical concepts through props and concrete objects, familiarize children with numbers in their everyday use (e.g., price tags, labels, measurements) and with the function of various tools (e.g., a scale, a register, a measuring tape). A real-life setting such as a grocery store or bakery, for example, can engage children in sorting and classification of items, in measurement experiences (e.g., measuring the weight of produce), and in solving simple addition and subtraction problems. Children enjoy learning mathematics through the acting out of different roles in real-life settings.

▶ **Use materials and objects that are relevant and meaningful to the children in your group.**
Mathematical concepts and skills such as counting, sorting, and measuring can be learned with different materials and in various contexts. It is valuable to introduce math in a context that is familiar and relevant to children's life experiences. Use materials, books, and real-life settings that reflect the culture, ways of life, and languages of the children in the group. When mathematical concepts are embedded in a context that is personally relevant to individual children, experiences are more pleasurable and meaningful.

▶ **Use children's books to explore mathematics with children.**
Include books with mathematical content, and use children's literature to develop mathematical concepts. Children's books provide interesting and powerful ways to explore mathematics. Teachers can use books to introduce and illustrate different

mathematical concepts, to encourage the use of mathematical language, and to develop mathematical thinking. Some books, such as counting books and shape books, directly illustrate mathematical concepts. Other books, such as storybooks, provide context for mathematical reasoning (e.g., *The Very Hungry Caterpillar* or *Goldilocks and the Three Bears).* The following sections include suggestions about how teachers can use literature to present and discuss different mathematical concepts, including counting, addition and subtraction, patterns, shapes, comparison language, and spatial positions. Many stories can be acted out by including concrete objects and manipulatives. While reading aloud books with mathematical content, teachers can pose questions to children, ask them to predict what comes next based on an underlying principle or a repeated pattern in the story, or invite children to re-create stories in their own way. See the "Teacher Resources" on page 297 for a list of children's books with mathematical content and other related resources on the use of literacy in teaching mathematics. For ideas on adapting books for children with physical disabilities, please refer to the Literacy section on pages 106 and 107.

▶ **Be intentional and mindful in setting up and using the physical environment.**
A math-rich environment is very important, but it does not guarantee that children will engage in meaningful mathematical experiences. The teacher should be intentional when planning a math-rich environment and think about how different math-related objects in the classroom can be utilized to promote meaningful mathematical exploration and reasoning. Teachers

should allow children the time to become involved with the materials, help children reflect on what they are doing, and extend their learning and discoveries through questioning and mental challenges. The next sections include more detailed information about how to set up a rich physical environment to promote number sense, classification, measurement, and geometry concepts for all children.

Summary of the Strands and Substrands

The California preschool learning foundations in mathematics identify a set of age-appropriate goals expected for children at around 48 and 60 months of age in five developmental strands.

- **The Number Sense strand** refers to concepts of numbers and their relationships. It includes the development of counting skills, the understanding of quantities, recognizing ordering relations (which has more, fewer, or less), part-whole relationships, and a basic understanding of "adding to" and "taking away" operations.

- **The Algebra and Functions (Classification and Patterning) strand** concerns the development of algebraic thinking and reasoning. Included in this strand is the ability to sort, group, and classify objects by some attribute and to recognize, extend, and create patterns.

- **The Measurement strand** involves comparing, ordering, and measuring things. Included in this strand is the child's ability to compare and order objects by length, height, weight, or capacity; to use comparison vocabulary; and to begin to measure.

- **The Geometry strand** concerns the study of shapes and spatial relationships. Included in this strand is the child's ability to identify, describe and construct different shapes, and to identify and label positions in space.

- **The Mathematical Reasoning strand** is a process in learning and developing mathematical knowledge in all areas of mathematics. Included in this strand is the child's ability to reason and apply mathematical knowledge and skills to solve problems in the everyday environment.

Please refer to the map of the mathematics foundations on page 296 for a visual explanation of the terminology used in the preschool learning foundations.

The following curriculum framework in mathematics provides teachers with strategies to promote preschool children's reasoning and understanding of key mathematical concepts in each of the five strands. The strategies provide teachers with tools for building children's understanding of mathematics over time, through a mathematically rich environment, through interactions and conversations with children during play and everyday routines, and through intentionally planned mathematical experiences. Examples of "Mathematical Reasoning in Action" are interwoven throughout the chapters, illustrating children's reasoning about different mathematical concepts, whether in natural situations or while engaged in planned mathematical activities.

Number Sense

Number sense refers to children's concept of numbers and their relationships. It starts early on with an infant's ability to visually recognize the number of elements in a small set and continues with children's verbal counting, as they further develop the sense of quantity, number relationships (e.g., less than, greater than), and the fundamental understanding of addition and subtraction. Children enter preschool with an intuitive understanding of number and **operations** and with a natural curiosity and eagerness to learn about numbers. All children, whatever their socio-economic or cultural backgrounds, have the tendency to count and reason about numbers in everyday life. Children's intuitive sense of number does not imply, however, that every-thing they need to learn about numbers and operations comes naturally. Teachers have an extremely important role in supporting children's understanding of number and operations, making them aware of number concepts and introducing them to the language of mathematics. All preschool children benefit from opportunities throughout the day to count, compare quantities, and solve problems involving numbers. The following strategies provide suggestions as to how teachers can help children build number sense.

1.0 Understanding Number and Quantity

From a very young age, children can determine the quantity of objects in a small set without counting **(subitizing)** and can label "two" or "three" when looking at small collections of objects. Repeated counting experiences develop a child's counting skills and her understanding of quantity. Children learn that counting determines the quantity of objects in a set (e.g., "One, two, three, four, there are four") and that different numbers represent different quantities. Preschool children also begin to recognize and name written numerals.

Counting

Counting is a fundamental skill in children's early understanding of numbers and quantities. It provides the basis for the development of number and **arithmetic** concepts and skills. Early on, children attempt to count everything around them, the number of steps on the way home, the cookies on their plate, or the number of blocks in a tower they built. This tendency to count everything is of considerable importance for the development of counting, as it provides the child with practice in learning the counting procedure.[5] At first children often omit some numbers when saying the list of number words or skip objects when counting. With repeated counting experiences and adult guidance at home and in preschool, children learn to apply counting skills precisely and use counting to determine the number of objects in a set.[6]

As teachers observe the children throughout the day, they are likely to encounter a great deal of spontaneous counting and reasoning about numbers: "One, two, three, five, seven, eight," the child may recite counting words when swinging outside. "Teacher, I am three," shares a child and counts, "One, two, three," showing three fingers. Preschool children's spontaneous counting and use of number words present teachers with wonderful opportunities to assess what children know and to facilitate their skills.

Sample Developmental Sequence
Counting

✔ Saying number words in sequence. May omit some numbers when reciting the number words. For example, the child's counting list may consist of the following number words: "one, two three, seven, eight, ten."

✔ Counts a small set of objects (five or six) but may have trouble keeping **one-to-one correspondence.** The child may point to more than one object when saying one number word or say a number word without pointing to an object.

✔ May count correctly a larger set of objects (about ten), keeping track of counted and uncounted objects by pointing and moving objects while counting.

✔ Understands that the number name of the last object counted (e.g., the number five when counting five objects) represents the total number of objects in the group (i.e., **cardinality**) and repeats this number when asked, "How many?"

✔ Knows to say the number words one-to-ten in the correct order, but is still learning the number sequence between ten and twenty. May omit some "-teen" words (e.g., 13, 14, 16, 18).

✔ Creates a set with a certain number of objects. For example, when asked to give three beads, the child counts out three beads from a larger pile of beads.

✔ Knows to say the number words up to twenty correctly.

Mathematical Reasoning in Action: Counting Ladybugs

VIGNETTE

Antonio was looking at a counting book, and in Spanish he counted the number of ladybugs in the picture, "Uno, dos, tres, cuatro." Mr. Moises noticed him counting, repeated the Spanish counting words, and then responded in English, "Yes, four ladybugs: one, two, three, four." They moved on to the next page, and the teacher invited Antonio to count the ladybugs with him. The child counted in Spanish and the teacher then counted with him in English.

TEACHABLE MOMENT

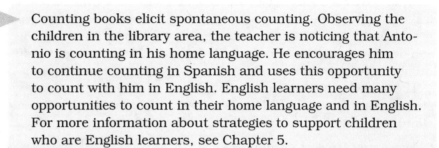

Counting books elicit spontaneous counting. Observing the children in the library area, the teacher is noticing that Antonio is counting in his home language. He encourages him to continue counting in Spanish and uses this opportunity to count with him in English. English learners need many opportunities to count in their home language and in English. For more information about strategies to support children who are English learners, see Chapter 5.

Mathematical Reasoning in Action: Who Has More Cars?

VIGNETTE

Playing with cars on the rug, a child argued, "I have more: one, two, three, seven, nine, ten." His friend replied, "No, I have more: one, two, three, four, five, six, seven." The teacher intervened and asked, "How do you think we can find out who has more cars?" "I count," said one of the children. The teacher suggested, "Let's count together," and she modeled counting together with the children. She put the cars in each set, in a row, and lined up the two sets against each other. The teacher pointed to each car while counting.

TEACHABLE MOMENT

Rather than telling children which one of them has more cars, she asks them for a solution (e.g., "How do you think we can find out who has more?") and lets them come up with a strategy to find out the answer (i.e., counting). She models for the children the use of counting. She also facilitates correct counting by putting the cars in each set in a row and by pointing to each car while counting. These strategies help children keep track of which cars were already counted and which cars are yet to be counted.

As illustrated in the above examples, preschool children's spontaneous counting and use of number presents learning opportunities, or "teachable moments." The teacher uses these spontaneous opportunities to facilitate and reinforce children's counting and mathematical reasoning. The teacher encourages individual attempts to count and reason about numbers and **scaffolds** as necessary, to introduce or reinforce mathematical concepts. The following strategies provide suggestions as to how teachers can develop children's understanding of number and quantity.

The following interactions and strategies promote preschool children's understanding of number and quantity:

Observe and listen to children's counts. Observe children's spontaneous counting and note their developmental level. Do the children tend to use a stable counting list? Can they recite the number words in the correct order? In what language? Up to what number? Can they keep track of the counted and uncounted objects while counting? Do they use counting as a means to quantify a set of objects? Are they comparing two quantities? Do they comprehend or use terms such as *more, less, same*? Observing preschool children's spontaneous counting and reasoning will enable teachers to assess and plan successfully and meet the needs of all children, including those with special needs. See "Sample Developmental Sequence of Counting" on page 242.

Encourage counting during everyday interactions and routines. Learning the sequence of number words in English involves the rote learning of the first 13 number words and later the rules for producing the subsequent "teens" number words and the beyond-twenty number words. This may proceed slowly and requires a lot of practice because learning number names in order takes practice. This does not mean that teachers should drill children to learn numbers. The teacher's modeling and the child's tendency to count and self-correct will facilitate the learning of the conventional sequence of number words. Encourage all children to count together as opportunities come up throughout the day. Children hear, say, and experience counting in the correct order over and over. Everyday interactions and routines offer numerous opportunities for counting and reasoning about number: during clean-up, "Everyone put five pieces away and then we'll be done"; in morning circle time, "How many children are wearing boots today?"; at snack time, "Please make sure every table has six apple slices"; during movement, "Let's jump seven times"; and at music time, counting while clapping with rhythm, "One, two, three, four, five."

Include preschool children's home language in counting activities, whenever possible. Use of the home language will reinforce counting skills and will show value for the child's home language and culture. Children who are English learners usually know how to count in their home language before they demonstrate the ability to count in English. In the beginning, they may not feel comfortable counting in English. Teachers should encourage them to participate and to count in their home language. Preschool English learners may need time to observe other children count in English before they feel comfortable taking an active part counting in English. For more information about strategies to support children who are English learners, see Chapter 5. For children who communicate in sign language, it is helpful to learn the number signs.

Ask questions that encourage purposeful counting. Use counting to determine quantity and answer a child's question within context: "I wonder how many stickers Ana has? One, two, three, four. She has four." To compare two quantities, the teacher might ask, "Which table has more children? How many more?" To create a set with a number of objects,

the teacher could suggest, "Derek needs four sticks." Or to solve addition and subtraction problems, ask "How many blocks do we have altogether? How many are left?" Combine counting with pointing or touching objects to reinforce the concept.

Foster one-to-one correspondence within the context of daily routines. Preschool children practice **one-to-one correspondence** as they gather and distribute materials, such as placing one shovel in each bucket, giving one paper to every child, or as they help to set the table. Lunch helpers, for example, count out and distribute dishes, napkins, or fruit. The following dialogue between the teacher and the child helping to set the table before mealtime serves as an example.

Mathematical Reasoning in Action: More Cups

VIGNETTE

Mr. Raj asks, "Do we have one cup next to every plate?" Amy checks and says, "No, this one does not have one, this one does not have one, and this one and this one. We need more." Mr. Raj asks, "How many more do we need?" "Four . . . uh . . . no, maybe six. Let me count, one, two, three, four, five, six." Mr. Raj notices that she counted one of the plates twice and says to Amy, "Let's count again, slowly." He points to the plates that have no cups next to them and counts them one at a time with Amy, "One, two, three, four, five." Amy repeats, "Five." "Yes, we need five more cups," Mr. Raj answered. Mr. Raj helps Amy get five more cups and asks Amy, "Can you make sure we have one cup next to every plate?"

TEACHABLE MOMENT

▶ Helping to set the table provided an opportunity to practice one-to-one correspondence (e.g., one plate, one cup) and to use purposeful counting (e.g., to find out how many more cups are needed). The teacher first let the child figure out the answer. When the child counted incorrectly, the teacher invited the child to count again and counted with her while pointing to each plate to facilitate correct counting.

Support preschool children's ability to apply the counting procedure. Counting the number of objects in a set means the child has to coordinate several distinct skills, reciting the number-word sequence while simultaneously keeping one-to-one correspondence between the objects being counted and the number words assigned to the objects. Preschool children may also tag or point to objects one at a time to keep track of those objects that have been counted and those to be counted. See "Sample Developmental Sequence of Counting" on page 242. Initially, preschool children are not skillful in applying the counting procedure precisely, but experiences with counting objects help them develop their counting skills. Those experiences may be spontaneous and informal and happen with teachers and with other children. Teachers can use the following strategies to gradually build preschool children's counting skills.

- **Provide lots of objects to count.** Provide preschool children with collections of small items to count such as, unit blocks, seashells, small figures, kernels of corn, or different sets of flannel pieces. Start with objects that are uniform in size, shape, and color so that children can focus on number without the distraction of other perceptual attributes. As children get more practice, they are ready to move to more abstract counting.

- **Start with small sets of objects.** Young children are more successful at counting small sets of objects. Provide children with small sets of objects (e.g., two or three), and gradually increase the number of objects that the children count.

- **Start with objects arranged linearly.** Young children are more successful applying one-to-one correspondence to linear sets of objects. When objects are arranged in a line, the beginning and end of the set are clearly marked, and children have an easier time keeping track of which objects were already counted and which objects are yet to be counted.

- **Model counting.** Point to, touch, or move each object aside as it is counted. Pointing to or touching each object as it is counted facilitates the one-to-one correspondence between the number words and the tagged objects during the counting process. Moving each object aside is also a helpful strategy for keeping track of which objects were already counted and which objects are yet to be counted.

- **Encourage children to self-correct their counts.** If children count incorrectly (e.g., skip a number or double count an object), invite them to count again: "Let's count again. More slowly, one . . ." and give them the opportunity to correct themselves.

Consider adaptations for children with special needs. Children with special needs may not move through the stages of counting as quickly as other children. Children with certain language impairments or hearing impairments have difficulty learning the sequence of number words and may show difficulty in developing counting skills.[7, 8] They would benefit from additional opportunities to count with adults and other children (e.g., with counting songs, finger plays, and games). Children with special needs would also benefit from combining words with actions to support counting. Marching or clapping while counting adds a kinesthetic dimension. Teachers could also support children with special needs by breaking the learning down into smaller steps, giving children small, manageable tasks (e.g., begin with counting a small number of objects with adults' help while counting). Children with physical disabilities may need to demonstrate mathematical knowledge in various ways. They do not necessarily need to engage in motor behavior and should be encouraged to use any means of expression and engagement available. Children with motor impairments may need assistance from an adult or peer to manipulate objects in order to count. Alternately, a child might demonstrate knowledge in these areas without directly manipulating objects. For example, a child might count verbally while a peer touches the objects. Children with visual impairments might be offered materials for counting that are easily distinguishable by touch. Their engagement is also facilitated by using containers or trays of materials that clearly define their workspace. (See Appendix D.)

Make number-related games, books, and other materials accessible to preschool children. Board games with a spinner, a die or dice, and other games such as dominos, number blocks, and cards and puzzles with numbers provide an engaging way to promote children's understanding of number and quantity. Children's books about numbers and counting can be used to introduce counting and basic addition and subtraction concepts. The teacher should include number-related books in the home languages of the children in the classroom.

Books can be presented along with felt pieces or finger puppets to illustrate math content with action. Children benefit when teachers use props and gestures to act out, model, and demonstrate mathematical concepts.

Plan group activities focused on counting. Use large- and small-group activities to help children practice counting and use counting in meaningful contexts. Counting songs, finger plays, and children's books with numerical content provide a playful context for practicing counting and developing mathematical concepts. Preschool children enjoy counting as a group, especially when they are able to predict what number comes next as they count up or down the number list (e.g., *Ten Little Monkeys, This Old Man, Five Green and Speckled Frogs, Five Little Ducks, Un Elefante se Balanceaba, Chocolate, Los Numeros, Sé Contar del Uno al Diez*).

Mathematical Reasoning in Action: Singing and Counting

VIGNETTE

*There was **one** little bird in a little tree*
He was all alone, and he didn't want to be
So he flew far away, over the sea
and brought back a friend to live in the tree.

*Now there are **two** little birds, one little tree . . .*
(The song repeats as the number of birds increases by one)

A flannel board with felt pieces and small objects were used to act out the content of the song or story and to help children better understand the mathematical concepts. To illustrate the song above, the teacher first put one bird on the flannel board and then added a felt bird to the board each time the song repeated. The teacher paused and invited children to count. "How many birds do we have in the tree? Let's count together." The teacher also invited a child to lead the counting.

PLANNING LEARNING OPPORTUNITIES

Rhymes, finger plays, and songs with number-related content are common for practicing counting and introducing numerical concepts. Some children with special needs find it especially difficult to memorize the sequence of number words or understand the meaning of numbers. When number songs are introduced along with sets of items on the flannel board or magnet board, children have repeating opportunities to say and memorize the sequence of number words and to connect number words with quantity. Counting songs highlight the "number-after" relationship for the number word sequence and illustrate which of two adjacent numbers is a larger quantity (e.g., that four is more than three). Children enjoy counting together, especially when they are able to predict what number comes next as they count up or down the number list.

Beyond Counting: Recognizing and naming written numerals

The standard written numerals in our society are Arabic **numerals,** 1, 2, 3, and so on. Children see numerals all around the house, on the phone, the remote control, the clock, and in number puzzles, games, and counting books. They typically learn to recognize the symbols 1 through 9 sometime between the age of two and five with little difficulty.[9] The understanding of what numerals represent develops over time. Ongoing informal experiences with environmental print expose children to the link between number symbols (e.g., 1, 2, 3) and the different meanings. The numeral 5 next to five apples, for example, communicates the quantity of apples (a cardinal meaning). The numeral 5 in number labels on houses (e.g., the numeral 5 in the house address 15430), on a bus, and car license plate has a noncardinal meaning. To enhance the connection between numerals and the quantity they represent, the number symbols in the preschool environment should be accompanied by some representation for quantity whenever possible (e.g., 5 means that five children can be sitting around this table). Through everyday exposure to numbers and the use of numbers in meaningful situations, preschool children learn to identify number symbols (numerals) and to recognize the link between written numerals (1, 2, 3), numeral names (one, two, three) and numeral meanings.[10]

Integrate numerals into different areas of the classroom. Numbers are used everywhere around us. Teachers can incorporate numerals throughout the classroom in a variety of meaningful contexts: in the dramatic play area, the art area, the science area, the library area, and the sand and water area. Many items can be incorporated into different areas of the classroom, including items such as a calendar, a clock, a phone, a scale, a calculator, date stamps, address and phone books, rulers, measuring tapes, labels, and advertisements with numerals. In addition to exposing children to written numerals, such real-life items will familiarize children with everyday uses of numbers. Teachers may also include in the classroom different learning materials with numerals such as a number line, number blocks, magnetic numbers, and number stamps and cards. Consultation with specialists may be helpful to find materials that can easily be used by children with physical disabilities or other special needs.

Discuss numerals in print in a meaningful context. Refer to numerals in the environment as part of the daily activities: in books with numbers, the calendar, on labels or on measuring cups while cooking, or on the measuring tape when measuring height. Teachers can also encourage children to refer to number symbols in the environment through a search for numerals in the class (e.g., I Spy game). Ongoing experiences with environmental print will reinforce the link between the number symbols, their names, and their meanings.

Expose preschool children to quantities represented in different forms. Preschool children gain a better sense of numbers as they come across different representations of number in their environment. For example, "three," can be represented with three objects, three fingers, a pictograph, a number symbol (3), tally marks (III), or a pattern of dots (● ● ●). The teacher can expose

children to different representations of quantity through the use of finger play, tallying and graphing activities, games with dice or spinners, number cards, and dominos.

Promote use of the subitizing skill

Subitizing is the ability to quickly determine the number of items in a set, or in a pattern of dots, without counting. When children are presented with very small sets, they can tell "how many" without counting the objects in the set. Teachers should be aware of children's capacity to quantify small sets quickly. When children are asked "how many" with respect to small sets of objects, they may use subitizing and call out the answer and not necessarily count the objects one by one to find out how many. Teachers can provide children with opportunities to apply subitizing in everyday situations by asking children for the number of objects in a small set; referring to the number of objects in small sets (e.g., "There are *three* chairs in that corner," We have *two* orange slices in this bowl"); conversing with children; or when pointing to pictures in children's books.

2.0 Understanding Number Relationships and Operations

Preschool children develop the conceptual basis for understanding number relationships and operations. When comparing two small sets, they can recognize whether the sets are equal or not. They can also recognize the ordering relation of two sets that are unequal and identify which set has more or less. Experiences with number-change transformations such as "adding to" and "taking away" provide the conceptual foundation for solving simple arithmetic problems. Young children understand that addition increases the number of items in a set, and subtraction decreases the number of items in a set. They use counting strategies to solve simple addition and subtraction problems.

Young children also develop a basic understanding of **part–whole relationships,** as they recognize that parts can be combined to make a whole, and a whole quantity can be broken down into two or more parts. Experiences with part–whole relationships and the decomposition of numbers into smaller groups (e.g., decomposing "six" into "four" and "two") support the understanding of number relationships and operations and from the conceptual basis for future understanding and solving of missing-addend problems (__ + 3 = 5), and multidigit addition and subtraction problems (e.g., 11 + 2 = __). Preschool children can be informally introduced to number relationships and operations through everyday interactions, language and literacy activities, and games.

Research Highlight

Research indicates that the ability to reason about numbers starts as early as infancy.[11] Five-month-olds show sensitivity to the effects of addition or subtraction of items on a small collection of objects. Toddlers viewing three balls put into a container and then one being removed know to search for a smaller number of balls, and many search for exactly two balls.[12]

By the time children are in preschool, prior to having any formal lesson in arithmetic, they use a variety of strategies to solve simple addition and subtraction problems.[13] They may use manipulatives or fingers to represent the numbers in the problem and count out loud to find out the answer. As they get older, they rely less and less on finger counting. To solve an addition problem such as 4 + 2 presented with concrete objects (e.g., color crayons), the child may count all objects "one, two, three, four" and then continue with the second set of objects "five, six" and find out there are a total of six. At a later stage, the child may **"count on"** from the second set of objects. Knowing the number of objects in the first set (e.g., "four"), the child starts with "four" and continues to count "five, six" to find out the total number of objects, rather than starting to count from "one" with the second set of objects.

Mathematical Reasoning in Action: Playing with Balls

VIGNETTE

While outdoors, a small group of children were playing with balls, throwing them into a net basket that was on the ground. Mr. Phan was standing by, watching the children taking turns throwing balls into the basket. When all six balls were inside the basket, he took them out one at a time. "One, two, three, four, five, six," he counted while handing the balls back to the children, and they again threw the balls into the basket. Julia, one of the children in the group, was standing by the basket watching the balls go in. When all balls were in the basket, she helped Mr. Phan take out the balls and hand them back to the children. Julia started to keep track of the number of balls that went into the basket. "One," she shouted after the first ball went in, "two" after the second ball was in, and so on. When five balls were in the basket, Julia said to Mr. Phan, "One more, and then we take all the balls out again." Mr. Phan asked Julia, "How many balls would we have altogether after the last ball goes in?" Julia answered, "five, six . . . six balls!"

TEACHABLE MOMENT

Outdoor play provides numerous opportunities for counting and reasoning with numbers. Children often count while swinging back and forth, while passing a ball from one child to another, or when climbing up the steps to go on the slide. Teachers may use these opportunities to count with children and think about numbers while playing. Children, particularly English learners, need a variety of meaningful and exciting counting and arithmetic experiences, in which they can combine counting with actions and model a problem with concrete objects. In this example, Mr. Phan made children aware of the total number of balls they were shooting to the basket. It created a goal for children: all six balls in the basket before the children continued to the next round of throwing. Julia, in particular, enjoyed watching the balls adding up in the basket. She became aware of the number of balls already in the basket and those yet to be thrown by children. Julia and other children in the group have learned through play about counting, quantity (the meaning of six), part–whole relationships, and addition.

Mathematical Reasoning in Action: How Many Boys?
How Many Girls?

VIGNETTE

The teacher comments to Jennifer, "Let's find out how many children are here today. Jennifer, would you please help me count the girls?" Counting the girls, Jennifer says, "One, two, three, four, five, six." Then she announces six. The teacher responds, "We have six girls. Now let's count the boys. Brian, would you please help me find out how many boys are here today?" Brian counts, "One, two, three, four, five . . . five," and holds up five fingers. The teacher says, "We have six girls and five boys. Do we have more boys or girls?" Most children call out, "Girls." One child said, "Boys." Another child replies, "No, it's girls because six is more than five." The teacher holds up six fingers and counts, "One, two, three, four, five, and one more is six. We have five boys and six girls. We have more girls than boys. Can you help me find out how many children we have altogether?" The teacher counts together with the children, pointing to every child while they are counted: "One, two, three, four, five, six, seven, eight, nine, ten, eleven. How many?" The children call out, "Eleven." The teacher says, "We usually have twelve children, but today we have only eleven. Can you help me figure out how many children are not here today?"

**PLANNING
LEARNING
OPPORTUNITIES**

A daily routine activity, such as checking attendance during morning circle time, serves as the context for introducing and practicing several mathematical concepts and skills, illustrating part–whole relationships (e.g., six girls and five boys, eleven altogether), comparing quantities by counting, doing arithmetic, and practicing counting skills. The teacher asks children probing questions and encourages them to find the answers. The teacher combined the verbal or gestured responses (e.g., five, six, eleven) with the visual representation (e.g., fingers) to assist those children who need more than one modality for learning.

The following interactions and strategies promote preschool children's understanding of number relationships and operations:

Promote the use of comparison terms (more, same as, fewer, or less) through everyday interactions. Everyday situations provide many opportunities to explore number relationships. Encourage preschool children to use comparison terms such as *more*, *fewer*, or *same as*, when comparing numbers in the everyday environment. "We have more boys than girls," "Both of you have the same number of stickers." "This table has fewer oranges." The word *fewer* is used to describe a smaller number. The word *less* should be used to describe a smaller amount or degree: "This bottle has less water," "There is less play dough on this table," "There are fewer crayons in this box." Use comparison terms in everyday situations to help children learn the meaning of such words.

Use everyday interactions and routines to illustrate and discuss addition and subtraction transformations. At a very young age children understand that "adding to" results in more, and "taking away" results in less. Building on children's natural understanding of these concepts, teachers can introduce children to simple addition and subtraction problems through everyday routines. "You have three cars. Can you give Andrea one? How many cars do you have now?" "You have three stickers. If I give you two more, how many stickers would you have altogether?" See the "Research Highlight" on page 251.

Mathematical Reasoning in Action: More Crackers

VIGNETTE

During snack time, Veronica asked: "Can I have two more crackers?" The teacher replied, "Yes, and I see you already have two crackers. When I give you two more, how many crackers will you have altogether?"

TEACHABLE MOMENT

In this situation, during snack time the child asks for more crackers and the teacher recognizes the opportunity to reinforce the mathematical concept of addition. The teacher presents the child with an "adding-to" arithmetic problem (2 + 2 = __) and uses concrete objects (e.g., crackers) to solve the problem.

Introduce preschool children to the concepts of addition and subtraction through literature, songs, and games. Stories, songs, and games provide a playful way to introduce "adding-to" and "taking-away" operations, and part–whole relationships. Experiences with concrete sets of objects, in particular, can illustrate for children addition and subtraction concepts and enable children to solve simple addition and subtraction problems by counting objects. For example, when telling the flannel board story *Rooster's Off to See the World*, the teacher says, "One rooster met two cats," and she places one flannel rooster next to two cats and asks the children, "How many animals do we have altogether?" The story continues, "The rooster and the cats met three frogs." The teacher places three flannel frogs, "One, two, three," next to the rooster and cats and asks, "How many do we have now?" The flannel board story provides the context for introducing the "adding-to" concept. For ideas on

adapting books for children with physical disabilities, please refer to the Literacy section on pages 106 and 107.

Make estimations. Encourage preschool children to estimate: "How many balls do you think are in this jar?" "How many seeds are inside the apple?" "How many steps are outside the door?" When possible, ask children to count and check their estimate. Children enjoy this process very much. Invite children to estimate in a group setting and record their estimates. It illustrates to them that different children have different estimates. Making an estimate and then counting "to find out" is a powerful and effective way to facilitate children's understanding of number and quantity.

Use graphing with children. Encourage preschool children to collect data, tally totals, and graph the results. Children enjoy taking an active part in this process. Invite children to collect and record numerical information (e.g., the number of children who have pets, the number of people in each child's family). Create a chart or graph, using real objects, to represent numerical information collected by children. Discuss with children the information presented in the graph. Graphs lead naturally to making comparisons: "Which group has more?" Which group has fewer?" "Can you tell without counting?" "How many more are in this group?"

Bringing It All Together

Bagel Shop

While singing the "Bagel Shop" song, children count to solve an arithmetic problem. One of the children plays the role of the Baker. The rest of the children take turns buying bagels at the bagel shop and help the Baker find out, "How many bagels are left in the bagel shop?" It begins with the teacher placing bagels on an upright flannel board, and the children count to determine how many bagels are on the board. Next, the class sings the following number song, and the teacher invites one of the children to buy bagels.

"Five little bagels in the bagel shop
Sprinkled poppy seeds on the very top
Along came (child's name) with two pennies to pay
He bought two bagels and walked away."

The child buying bagels gives the Baker two pennies, and the Baker takes away two bagels from the board and gives them to the child. The remaining bagels are visible, and children are asked to predict how many bagels are left in the bagel shop. Each time the song repeats, children first predict the answer to a problem (e.g., five "take away" two), and then check their prediction by counting. The value obtained from checking their prediction then serves as the start for the next round (e.g., "Three little bagels in the bagel shop . . ."), and the singing and selling procedure repeats. At the beginning of the year, the teacher may start with a small number of bagels (e.g., five or six) and subtract only one bagel at a time. Over time, the teacher may alter the problems' difficulty level by gradually increasing the number of bagels (e.g., from seven to fifteen) and varying the number of bagels being removed (plus or minus one, two, or three).

For example, the teacher of older preschoolers placed seven bagels on the board. The children called out, "I think there are seven"; "No, eight"; "Seven, I counted"; "I counted, too; it's six." The teacher invited one of the children to count the bagels. She arranged the bagels in a row and pointed to them one at a time, as the child was counting to help keep one-to-one correspondence between the number words and the bagels being tagged. The child counted, "One, two, three, four, five, six, seven," and the class agreed that there were seven bagels. Next the class sang the song, and one of the children bought two bagels. The children were asked "How many bagels are left in the bagel shop?" Most children said five, but some said six. The teacher said, "Some of you think we have six bagels, and many of you think there are five bagels. How can we find out?" She invited one of the children "to count and find out." (Based on an example described in a research journal.[14])

During the Bagel Shop activity, children are counting and doing arithmetic in the context of a real-life setting. The subtraction problems are presented with concrete objects (e.g., taking away bagels), and counting serves a purpose. Children count to check the prediction and solve an arithmetic problem. It enhances the meaning of counting and facilitates children's problem-solving and arithmetic skills. A group-learning experience in which children take turns counting and reasoning is also an opportunity for the teachers to observe and learn about individual children's understanding of number. A context that represents a real-life setting, in particular, makes mathematics more engaging and fun, as children experience different roles in buying and selling bagels. Think of other real-life settings you can bring into the classroom or arrange outside to provide the children with a meaningful context for counting and doing arithmetic (e.g., a grocery store, shoe store, a train with a conductor collecting tickets from passengers).

Engaging Families

The following ideas may help families to develop their children's number sense:

✓ **Communicate to parents the broader meaning of number sense.** Teachers may need to explain to parents how they can support children's development of number sense. Often what parents know about mathematics education is based on their own school experiences and how they were taught.[15] Their view of mathematics at this age is often restricted to children being able to count to high numbers and to recite basic arithmetic facts. Some may ask for pencil-and-paper activities with numbers for their children long before children are ready. Teachers need to communicate to parents the broader aspects of developing number sense; for example, using counting in real-life situations, comparing numbers and discussing which is more or less, making estimations (e.g., How many grapes are in this bowl?), and solving simple addition and subtraction problems. The teacher should explain to parents that such meaningful experiences lay the foundation for a basic understanding of mathematical concepts for later learning of more advanced ones. She might share with parents how children are engaged in counting and reasoning with numbers in the preschool environment. Parents may try to apply similar ways to engage children with numbers at home.

✓ **Remind parents that daily use of numbers can become learning experiences for children.** Numbers are everywhere: in the house, on the way to school, in the grocery store, and in sport games and outdoor activities. Parents can point children to numbers and talk with them about what numbers are used for as they go about their everyday experiences. They can encourage children to count and to solve problems related to number. For example, children can count coins for purchases at the store, count the number of plates and cups when helping to set the table, count the number of crackers in the bowl, and divide them equally to two groups in order to share with a friend. Parents can talk with children about mathematical ideas. "You have five pennies, and we need seven. How many more pennies do we need?" "How do you know you both have the same number of crackers?" "How many seeds do you think are inside this apple? Now I cut it open. Let's find out." Parents should ask questions of their children rather than just telling them the answer.

✔ **Provide number-related games and books.** The teacher can also encourage parents to choose books from the local library that involve numbers and to play with children number-related games such as cards, dominos, puzzles, or board games. Parents can also use common games to engage children in counting, addition, and subtraction. For example, while playing mini-bowling at home, children can count and find out how many pins they knocked down and how many are still standing, with each turn.

Questions for Reflection

1. What have you included, or could you include, in your environment to support the development of children's counting and understanding of number?

2. Think about your group's everyday activities and routines. In what ways can you develop children's counting skills in the context of everyday routines?

3. How do you engage children in comparing numbers and use terms such as more, fewer, or same as?

4. Think about the children in your group. How do you learn about the counting and reasoning skills of individual children in your group? How do you support individual children in developing number sense? How would you modify the Bagel Shop activity to make it work for children with varying abilities?

5. What real-life settings can you set up in your preschool environment to provide a context for counting and doing arithmetic?

Algebra and Functions
(Classification and Patterning)

One may wonder how **algebra** is related to young children, as it may bring up the thought of traditional high school algebra. Obviously, preschool is not the time to teach traditional algebra, but this is the period when foundational algebraic concepts evolve and gradually develop. Children observe the environment and learn to recognize similarities and differences. They learn to sort, group, and classify objects. They learn to recognize ordering relations, such as large to small, and to identify patterns. They develop the ability to make predictions, form generalizations, and derive rules. Experiences with classification and patterning during the preschool years allows for the development and practice of algebraic thinking and reasoning—skills essential in learning mathematics and science.

Teachers have a key role in promoting preschool children's classification and patterning skills. They can:

- draw children's attention to patterns in the environment;
- set up patterning and classification experiences;
- discuss with children their sorts and patterns; and
- encourage children to come up with their own patterns or ways of classifying objects.

Teachers' interactions with children, as they classify or work with patterns, not only facilitate the children's math skills and introduce them to math vocabulary, but also provide a vehicle for language development. "How are these the same?" "Here you have all the red triangles and here all the yellow ones." "Look at the colors. Can you see a pattern?"

"This is a big pile of round leaves." "It seems like you separated the rocks into two groups." "How are they different?" (e.g., smooth and bumpy). Interactions of this kind provide children with the descriptive words they need to describe their ideas and attach meaning to their actions. The interaction is especially relevant for children who are English learners because such interactions allow them to infer the meaning of words used by the teacher or peers as they classify objects or describe a pattern and expand their vocabulary in English. Children are introduced to math concepts as well as to new vocabulary in meaningful and engaging contexts as they **sort, classify,** and make **patterns.** The next chapter describes some strategies teachers can apply to promote the classification and patterning skills of all children, including those with disabilities or special needs.

1.0   Classification

Young children naturally engage in classification activities as they separate and group things with similar **attributes** (e.g., same color, size, shape) or belong to the same **class** or category (e.g., dogs, chairs, airplanes). The process of forming a class based on similar attributes starts at infancy, as children continual form classes based on their ability to recognize "sameness" of members in a group. For example, a child may first refer to any swimming animal as "fish," but over time they see sea animals that are not fish. The notion of "fish" in the child's mind is revised, and new classes such as "whales" and "dolphins" are created. Classification involves giving descriptive labels to the feature(s) used in sorting. It facilitates the child's acquisition of concepts and language and allows children to explore their environment and organize information in an efficient way.[16]

Mathematical Reasoning in Action: Collecting Leaves on a Nature Walk

VIGNETTE

As part of a curriculum unit on the seasons, the children went for a nature walk and collected various types of leaves. During the walk and later in the classroom, the children explored the leaves and were encouraged to describe different attributes of the leaves such as shape (pointy, round, long, needle), size (small, tiny, wide, big), color (red, green, yellow, orange, brown) and texture (smooth, soft, hard, wet, dry, rough). Children were then asked by the teacher to sort the leaves: "Put leaves that belong together in groups."

The teacher asks Enrique, "Why did you put these leaves together and those leaves together?" Enrique responds, "They are same." The teacher asks, "How are these the same?" Enrique points and says in Spanish, "Café aquí, amarillo aquí, y hojas rojas." ("Brown here, yellow, here, and red leaves here."). The teacher points to each group of leaves and says in English, "Great! Brown, yellow, and red leaves. What other ways can we sort the leaves? How about putting all the big leaves here and all the small ones there?" The teacher models for the child, sorting leaves by size. "Where do you think this leaf would go?"

PLANNING LEARNING OPPORTUNITIES

 As part of children's process of exploring different attributes of the leaves, the teacher invited children to engage in a **sorting** activity. Enrique, a child who is learning English, is encouraged to explain his sorting, as are other children in the group. The teacher used this experience to introduce him to new vocabulary in a context that was meaningful for him and that allowed him to determine the meaning of the English words. For more information about strategies to support children who are English learners, see Chapter 5.

The following interactions and strategies support children's classification skills:

Organize the classroom into different categorized storage areas to facilitate classification. The basic organization of the preschool environment illustrates for children how different objects in the world belong together. Blocks of different sizes and shapes are stacked on the block shelves, books are organized in the library area, and dolls of different kinds are in the dramatic play area. Items of the same category can be sorted into subcategories. The wood blocks can be arranged by shape and size. Toys such as cars, airplanes, and trucks can be stored in separate boxes. Animal figures (e.g., farm animals, ocean animals, wild animals) or art supplies (e.g., crayons, pencils, markers) can be kept in separate containers. The music instruments can be organized by instrument families: percussion, string, and brass instruments. Organizing and labeling the classroom environment so that objects and materials that belong together are stored together facilitates children's classification skills through everyday interactions.

Include materials and objects for sorting in the environment. In addition to using the natural environment as an opportunity for many sorting and classifying activities, teachers may want to provide certain materials to sort and classify or place in a pattern: rocks, shells, seeds, leaves, buttons, beads, wheels, plastic counters of different shapes, fruits, and cubes. Teachers may want to rotate items related to the current topic of interest in the classroom. For classification, it is important to provide items that belong to the same group yet vary by one or more identifiable attributes (e.g., color, shape, size, function, texture, or visual patterns). Tools may be provided to help sort and classify, such as trays, containers, egg cartons, or cups.

Identify opportunities for sorting and classifying in everyday routines. Sorting and classifying is a natural part of the daily routine in preschool. Clean-up and other times, such as when recycling materials, setting the tables for snack or lunch, and choosing activities to explore, are natural opportunities for children to sort and classify. An organized classroom environment turns clean-up time into a sorting experience. Putting away the blocks, toys, materials, tools, and instruments requires children to think about the attributes of the items or their function and to store items together that "belong together" based on different criteria. Pictorial labels enable all children to sort toys and restore materials to their proper place. Teachers may give children support and encouragement and model for children where things go, "The rectangle blocks all go together on this shelf," the teacher gestured toward the shelf while talking. "All the crayons go together in one box, and all the pencils in another box," the teacher pointed to the box while talking. "Here is the basket for the farm animals, and here is the basket for the wild animals," says the teacher as he puts one animal in each basket. Modeling with action is particularly helpful for children who are English learners or children with hearing impairments.

An environment that is organized with areas neatly labeled facilitates sorting and makes clean-up time a learning experience. In addition to clean-up time, everyday routines provide other natural opportunities to sort and classify. Setting the table for snack and lunch may present valuable sorting experiences. As preschool children help set the table, they may set out only the small bowls, not the big ones; separate the forks from the spoons; or sort the snack foods. For example, the teacher may put slices of green apples in one bowl and slices of red apples in another bowl. Recycling is yet another unique opportunity, as children sort their trash into labeled bins for plastic, paper, glass, and aluminum cans.

Recognize sorting in play. During child-initiated play when children choose their own activities, they may sort and group objects to help organize their play activities. They may sort out the triangle blocks and the long rectangle blocks when building a castle, sort the red and yellow beads to create a necklace, sort

the firefighters or other figures in pretend play, and so on.

Engage preschool children in conversations about their sorting and classifying. Teachers have a key role in making the sorting and grouping experiences meaningful and rich with language for *all* children. Interactions with children will help them express verbally or by some other way, such as sign language, their criteria for sorting and will provide them an opportunity to explain their reasoning. Observe children, and note where children are developmentally and what vocabulary they are using.

– **Ask questions.** Ask children to explain and describe their sorting and classifying. "It seems that you have two groups of animals. Why did you put these animals together and those animals together?" "Tell me how you sorted these rocks." "What name could you give this group?"

– **Help children label the groups and verbalize their criteria for sorting.** Use simple sentences or phrases that provide the children with the descriptive words they need to expand their descriptive language: "You have the whales on this side and the dolphins on the other side." "This is a big pile of triangles." "Which ones are the wild animals?" "Here are the red cars, and there are the cars that are not red."

– **Encourage children to come up with their own criteria for sorting.** As children engage in sorting and classifying, teachers can encourage them to come up with their own criteria for sorting: "Can you sort these into groups that belong together?" "Can you sort these another way? How would you do it?"

Plan opportunities for preschool children to sort and classify. In addition to spontaneous opportunities to sort and classify objects in the environment and during ongoing routines, teachers may want to plan specific sorting and classifying activities.

– **Plan for children at different levels.** Simple, basic sorting activities are a good start. Choose appealing objects as well as those that are easy for young children to grasp and manipulate. A variety of small objects are offered on a tray, and children sort the objects into their corresponding containers labeled with a picture or a sample object. Begin with objects (e.g., blocks or crayons) that vary by only one attribute (e.g., crayons differing only in color). They make it easier to sort and classify. Continue with objects such as buttons, beads,

or dried beans of various colors, sizes, and shapes. Providing sorting activities at different levels allows teachers to meet the needs of all children, including children with disabilities and special needs. Giving children manageable tasks builds their confidence and allows them to experience successes. If the group includes young children or children with cognitive delays, think carefully about the size of the objects as some children may still be exploring items by putting them in their mouths.

– **Integrate sorting into children's current topic of interest and study.** Any collection of objects can be sorted by some criteria. Sorting activities, therefore, can be an integral part of children's exploration and study of any topic: pumpkins, apples, leaves, animals, tools, vegetables, and so on. Use classroom materials and experiences that reflect children's natural environment and culture and relate to children's interests. As described on page 260 in "Mathematics Reasoning in Action: Collecting Leaves on a Nature Walk," when children sort objects that they currently study and explore, sorting becomes more interesting and meaningful.

2.0 Patterning

Patterning, like classification, involves the child's natural tendency to organize information in the environment. It requires the child to observe discrete elements, recognize similarities and differences, and make generalizations. From a young age, children see patterns around them: on toys, clothing or quilts, and in nature. Their daily routine creates a pattern, and they listen to songs that follow patterns (e.g., "The wheels on the bus go . . . The people on the bus go . . ."). By preschool age, although children may recognize patterns in the environment, they may not always draw them with symbols or create their own patterns. For instance, they may clap or jump in a pattern (e.g., clap-clap-hop-hop), or use beads to create a red-blue-red-blue pattern. Young children appreciate the predictability that comes with patterns. They enjoy being able to predict what comes next, and they notice immediately if someone breaks a pattern (e.g., "But we always have snack first and then go outside").

Research Highlight

Compared with classification skills, relatively little is known about the development of young children's patterning skills. The Berkeley Math Readiness Project[19] examined the informal patterning knowledge of low-income and middle-income children and the effect of curricular intervention on their patterning skills. The study revealed some key findings that can help teachers in planning ways to effectively support the patterning skills of all children.

- **Identifying the core unit of a pattern is a challenge for all children.** The majority of prekindergarten children attending preschool, regardless of socioeconomic background, experienced difficulty with identifying the core unit of a pattern at the beginning of the preschool year.

- **Pattern extension is a later development than pattern duplication.** Both middle-income and low-income groups were significantly better on pattern duplication (e.g., using blocks to make a pattern that "looks just like this") than on pattern extension (e.g., presented with two repetitions of the pattern, children were asked to finish making the pattern).

- **Positive effect of curricular activity on patterning knowledge.** Both middle-income and low-income groups exhibited significant progress in their ability to duplicate a pattern correctly after participating in a patterning curriculum activity. Low-income children had more difficulty duplicating a simple pattern correctly than did middle-income children.

A **pattern** is a regularly repeated arrangement of things such as numbers, objects, events, or shapes. Young children may begin with a simple pattern (e.g., red-yellow, red-yellow, or circle-circle-square-square), keeping the number of elements in the repeating unit constant (e.g., *one* red item, *one* yellow item). More complex patterns may vary the number of each element (e.g., red-yellow-yellow, red-yellow-yellow; *one* red element, *two* yellow elements) or include more than two items in the repeating unit (e.g., a pattern with three elements: red-yellow-blue, red-yellow-blue).[17] Preschool children readily identify and duplicate patterns in their environment, but extending or creating patterns may require more guidance from adults.[18] The following strategies provide suggestions as to how teachers can help children develop their abilities to identify, describe, replicate, extend, and create patterns using various modalities throughout the day.

Mathematical Reasoning in Action: Making Bracelets

VIGNETTE

A small group of children were making bracelets by stringing different color beads together. The teacher commented, "You can choose any design you want for your bracelet. Ana created a pattern that looks like yellow, purple, yellow, purple." A few minutes later the teacher pointed to a bracelet that was created earlier but left on the table and said, "Look at this pattern: green, green, red; green, green, red. What do you think comes next?" The children became more engaged with patterns. One of the girls was trying to replicate her friend's pattern; others wanted to create their own patterns.

PLANNING LEARNING OPPORTUNITIES

The teacher planned an activity in which she deliberately introduced the concept of patterns. The small-group setup allows her to support children individually. She encouraged children to extend a pattern (e.g., "What comes next?") and supported them in the process of replicating and creating patterns.

To facilitate patterning skills of all children, including those with special needs, the teacher might at first limit the colors available to keep patterns simple and then gradually increase the range of colors. In this example, the teacher demonstrated for the children the concept of pattern and described the pattern created.

Mathematical Reasoning in Action: A Hunt for Patterns in the Outdoors

---

VIGNETTE

During outdoor play, the teacher invited a group of children to join her in a search for patterns. The teacher approached children with excitement: "Remember how we looked at a picture of a caterpillar in the book, and we saw a pattern? black, yellow, white—black, yellow, white. If we look really carefully around us, we may discover many different patterns. We may find patterns in leaves, in the trunks of trees, in flowers, even in creatures such as bees or butterflies. Look at this leaf, for example. What do you see happening over and over?" Maya looked at it closely and said, "It has the lines, the lines on it again and again." "These lines are called veins," the teacher explained and showed the veins in the leaf to everyone in the group. The veins create a pattern. Can you find veins in other leaves around us? Let's go hunt for more patterns and see what we find."

**PLANNING
LEARNING
OPPORTUNITIES**

 The teacher used the outdoor learning environment to discover patterns with children. Children learned that patterns are around them and can be found in the natural environment. The teacher has mentioned a previous experience they have had with patterns to grab children's attention and remind them what patterns are about.

The following interactions and strategies support the development of patterning skills:

Point out patterns in the environment.
Daily routines bring natural opportunities to discover patterns with children. Circle time, transition time, mealtime, and free time all become opportunities to spontaneously discover and talk about patterns. Patterns are part of the physical environment: in toys, books, on the carpet, walls or fences, on clothing and accessories. "Look at the carpet. Can you see a pattern?" Children may explore the bark on a tree, the veins in leaves, the colors in a rainbow, or the patterns in bees, zebras, butterflies, caterpillars, or snakes. Specific items in the classroom environment can present children with patterns in meaningful contexts. A calendar, for example, can illustrate for children the pattern of the days in a week or months in a year. The class schedule can illustrate for children how certain things repeat every week on the same days (e.g., every Monday Brenda's grandmother comes to preschool to read books with the children, and every Wednesday Ms. Santos comes to play the piano). Older preschool children enjoy playing a pattern hunt to see who can identify the largest number of patterns in the classroom.

Engage preschool children in conversations about patterns. Conversations with children will help them identify and analyze the discrete elements in a pattern and will facilitate their ability to recreate and extend patterns.

– **Say the patterns aloud as a group to build the rhythm of repetition:** "Red, green, yellow, red, green, yellow, red, green . . ."

– **Ask questions.** Promote children's thinking about patterns: "What would come next?" "What happens over and over again?" "Do you see a pattern?" "Is this a pattern? Why?"

– **Help children describe patterns and use descriptive words:** "First green, then red and then yellow, again and again." "Two squares, one triangle, two squares, one triangle . . ." "Tell me about the order of these colors."

Mathematical Reasoning in Action: Building a Fence with a Pattern

VIGNETTE

While playing with blocks, Joseph was sorting out the long and short rectangles: "I am making a fence."

The teacher noticed and said, "Long rectangle, short rectangle, long rectangle, short rectangle," touching the blocks while talking. "Joseph, look at your fence. You have a pattern. What is happening over and over again?" After Joseph completed the fence, the teacher suggested, "Do you want me to get you paper and a pencil so you can draw your pattern to save in the pattern book?"

TEACHABLE MOMENT

Observing Joseph playing with blocks, the teacher has noticed a pattern created by Joseph and brought it to his attention. The teacher described the pattern aloud, asked a leading question (e.g., "What is happening over and over?"), and used the term *pattern*. The teacher also offered Joseph the opportunity to draw his pattern. The teacher has created a "pattern book" with photos and drawn pictures of found and created patterns. Children look up patterns, find previous patterns, and compare them to new patterns.

Plan for children at different levels. Start by having children identify and duplicate patterns. Extending or creating patterns may be more difficult for children. You may choose to begin with simple patterns. For example, introduce children to patterns with two elements in the repeating unit (e.g., red-blue, red-blue or apple-apple-pear-pear, apple-apple-pear-pear). Have the same number of each element in the repeating unit (e.g., *one* red item, *one* blue item or *two* apples and *two* pears). At a more advanced level, you may introduce patterns with more than two items in the repeating unit (e.g., a pattern with three elements: apple-pear-orange, apple-pear-orange), and to patterns with varying number of each element (e.g., red-blue-blue, red-blue-blue; *one* red followed by *two* blues). See the Research Highlight on page 264.

Play with patterns in various formats.
Patterns can be presented in different formats: through movement, sound, language, objects, or pictures. Expressing patterns through different modalities (kinesthetic, tactile, auditory, and visual) provides different learning modes and facilitates preschool children's understanding of patterns. Variety also helps ensure that pattern experiences are accessible to all children, including those with disabilities or special needs. There are numerous opportunities for children to *duplicate, extend,* and *create* patterns through art, music, movement, literacy, and science.

– **Patterns with objects and pictorial designs.** One common way to create patterns is with concrete objects such as blocks, counters, beads, interlocking cubes, shapes, or other small objects. Objects that can be identified by touch provide tactile input for children as they duplicate, extend, and create patterns. For example, children can use plastic beads of different colors and shapes to make a bracelet with repeating patterns, or they use a variety of toppings to decorate a celery stick with a pattern. Different artistic expressions (e.g., sponge painting) may lend themselves to the expression of patterns such as when a design is repeated over and over. Children can create a desired pattern of flowers and then plant flowers in the garden duplicating this pattern. Children can also duplicate patterns they observe in the natural environment. For example, they can observe a caterpillar and record its pattern of colors.

– **Patterns through movement.**
Children can experience patterns in a physical way. Teachers may invite preschool children to create patterns physically through marching, standing, sitting, jumping, or clapping (jump-jump-clap-clap, jump-jump-clap-clap or stand-clap-sit, stand-clap-sit). Often these are duplicated while singing a song (e.g., "If You're Happy and You Know It, Clap Your Hands," or "Hokey Pokey"), or through games. For example, in playing Simon Says, children are invited to duplicate and create different patterns (e.g., Simon says, clap, clap, stomp"; "Simon says, clap, clap, touch your knee").

– **Patterns with sounds.** Preschool children can create patterns with different sounds by using rhythm instruments such as shakers or sticks. For example, they can vary the volume of sound to create a pattern (loud-loud-soft, loud-loud-soft) or create a pattern with different sounds (bell ring-shake-shake, bell ring-shake-shake).

– **Patterns through rhymes and stories.** Many nursery rhyme songs and stories have repetitive structures, phrases, or rhymes that form patterns (e.g., "The Wheels on the Bus," "Old MacDonald Had a Farm"). Many children's stories include repeating patterns. Children can easily grasp the repetitive structure and carry it to the next verses in the story. They especially have fun predicting what comes next once the pattern is identified. For example, the text in the book *Brown Bear, Brown Bear What Do You See?*, by B. Martin Jr. and Eric Carle, has a predictable pattern.

Bringing It All Together

Sorting, Counting, Graphing and Comparing Apples

During circle time, the teacher shared with the children different varieties of apples: Red Delicious, Granny Smith, Golden Delicious, and Fuji. Children discussed the features of the varieties of apples. The teacher asked the children in the classroom to bring their favorite apple from home for the next day. All the apples brought from home were put in a basket, and the children were given time to play with the apples in one of the activity areas. The basket of apples immediately sparked mathematical reasoning and problem solving by the children. The children sorted the apples first by color.

The teacher observed the children and posed questions or made comments along the way. "So here you put the green apples and here the red apples, but what about these apples? Can you think about another way to sort the apples?" The children sorted apples by variety, by color, and even by taste (sweet versus sour). Children were curious and enthusiastic. "How many apples are in the basket? How many green apples? How many red?" The teacher asked, "What is the class's favorite kind of apple?" How do you think we could find out?" After the children sorted the apples by variety, the teacher asked, "Which group has the most apples?" and the children counted the apples in each group.

During circle time, the teacher discussed the findings with the children. Together with the children, the teacher graphed the data, one column for each group of apples, using unit blocks. Then the children were encouraged to compare the columns and discuss, "Which is the class's favorite and least favorite kind of apple?" "Do more children like red apples or green apples?"

The teacher capitalized on children's natural mathematical skills and interest in the topic. Bringing their favorite apple from home made children even more engaged and enthusiastic. The basket of apples sparked children's interest, and the teacher developed it progressively into a mathematically rich experience. The teacher gave children time to explore the apples, commented on children's categories, and posed thought-provoking questions. The experience with apples illustrates the integration of math, science, and language learning and how several mathematical skills and concepts such as sorting, counting, comparing, collecting data, and graphing can come together.

(Note: If the program policy does not allow bringing food from home, or if some families are unable to provide an apple for their child to bring to school, a basket of apples could be provided by the school for this activity.)

Engaging Families

The following ideas may help families to develop children's classification skills:

✔ **Explain to parents about classification and patterning.** Teachers may need to explain to parents what classification and patterning are about and how they contribute to children's understanding of mathematics. Parents who are informed of these developing skills are more likely to engage children in classification and patterning experiences in their everyday routines.

✓ **Create classification experiences outside the preschool environment.**
The teacher can give parents some ideas about classification and patterning activities that children can experience outside the classroom. Just as the preschool environment illustrates for children how different objects in the world belong together, so does the organization of items at home, at the grocery store, or other places (e.g., vegetables and fruits are sorted and presented by kind; all cereal boxes are placed on the same shelf and so forth). Children learn how different things belong together by observing their environment.

Children have many opportunities at home to sort through objects and to look for similarities and differences among them. At a very young age, they may play with sorting toys, for example, sorting circles, squares and other shapes and inserting them in the matching opening, square in the square opening and so on.

As they grow older, parents can engage children in different sorting activities around the house. Children can sort clothes by color or type (e.g., colored shirts together, white socks and towels), sort shoes or socks and find pairs that belong together, or unload groceries and sort into different piles (e.g., boxes on the counter and cans on the table).

✓ **Create patterning experiences outside the preschool environment.**
Children also enjoy identifying things that repeat in their environment. Parents may draw children's attention to patterns in designs and pictures, in furniture, wallpapers or rugs in the house, or in songs and in children's books. For example, they may ask children to find and describe patterns in their clothing ("My shirt has a pattern. It is yellow, blue, yellow, blue"), or in picture books or magazines. They may also sing songs with children or read books with repeated rhyming phrases, emphasize the repeating phrase, and let children predict what comes next (e.g., "One, Two, Buckle My Shoe," "Head, shoulders, knees, and toes"). Such books and songs reinforce patterns through words, sound, and movement, and are playful ways for children to practice language and mathematics skills.

Questions for Reflection

1. How do you, or could you, organize your classroom environment to facilitate classification skills?

2. How could you integrate sorting and patterning experiences into children's current topic of study?

3. What sorting or patterning activities would you, or do you, offer children who are just beginning to grasp these concepts?

4. How do you engage children in exploring and describing patterns?

5. How do you, or could you, use classification and patterning experiences to develop children's language and introduce them to new vocabulary?

Measurement

Young children develop an intuitive notion of measurement through natural everyday experiences. They explore and discover properties such as length, height, volume, and weight as they look for a longer block, measure who is taller, pour sand from a small bucket to a larger one, or try to pick up a heavy box and ask for help. They make comparisons to see which is longer, taller, heavier, larger, or smaller. Teachers should build on preschool children's emerging concepts of measurement and provide experiences that facilitate the development and learning of these concepts. This practice does not suggest teaching young children how to measure in inches or pounds using measuring tools. It is about exploring and describing the height, weight, or size of objects, comparing and ordering objects by different attributes, using comparison vocabulary, and measuring with standard and nonstandard units. Exploring and reflecting on comparison and measurement sets preschool children on a path for developing a formal understanding of measurement later in school.

1.0 Compare, Order, and Measure Objects

The Measurement strand encompasses three main measurement concepts:

- **Comparing:** Children develop an understanding of attributes (weight, size, volume) by looking, touching, and directly comparing objects. They can determine which of two objects is longer by placing two objects side by side, or which of two objects is heavier by picking them up. Learning the vocabulary to describe objects (e.g., heavy, big, short) and to compare them by different attributes (e.g., "This is heavier," "Mine is bigger") is fundamental for acquiring the concepts of measurement. Older preschool children can start to compare objects, indirectly, using a third object (e.g., use a paper strip to represent the length of one object and then lay the strip against the other object).

- **Ordering:** As children explore and compare objects, they can also identify ordering relationships. For example, they can arrange three or more objects by size from smallest to largest. This requires children to observe and distinguish slight variations of the attribute and order the objects in a progressive sequence (e.g., small bear, medium bear, large bear).

- **Measuring:** Older preschool children begin measuring the length of objects, often by using nonstandard units (e.g., a block). For example, to measure length with a nonstandard unit such as a block, children position many same-size blocks along the object they measure, from end to end, without leaving a space between the blocks, and count the number of blocks. They may find out, for example, that the table is seven blocks long. Such experiences develop children's understanding of the nature of units.

Research Highlight

A research-based instructional approach suggests that teachers of young children follow a developmental sequence in helping children develop concepts and skills of length measurement.[20] First, informal activities establish the attribute of length. Children should be given a variety of experiences directly comparing the size of objects to determine equality or inequality of length and develop concepts such as "longer" or "shorter." Only then are young children ready to learn to measure and connect number to length. Research emphasizes the importance of solving real measurement problems in which children explore principles of measurement such as identifying a unit for measure and placing that unit end to end alongside the object without leaving space between successive units (referred to as *unit iteration*).

The traditional approach holds the view that children measure length with rulers only after a long experience with nonstandard units and manipulation of standard units. Recent research suggests that children as young as six years old are capable of and benefit from using rulers.[21] Children typically learn to measure with rulers in early primary grades. However, exposure to ruler and measuring tape is appropriate throughout the preschool years.

Mathematical Reasoning in Action: Playing at the Water Table

VIGNETTE

Playing at the water table outdoors, Sara was filling up different-size containers with water. The teacher, Ms. Frances, noticed that Sara had filled up a cup with water and poured the water into a bigger container over and over. Ms. Frances commented, "It looks like you are using the cup to fill up this pitcher with water. How many more cups do you think it would take to fill it up?" Sara looked at the pitcher and said, "I don't know, maybe three, no . . . five." Ms. Frances suggested, "Let's find out together how many cups of water it will take to fill up this pitcher all the way to the top." Together they filled up the cup and poured the water into the pitcher, one cup at a time, while counting, "One, two, three, and four." Sara said, pleased with herself, "It took four more cups. I said five; I was almost right."

TEACHABLE MOMENT

▶ By pouring water or sand from one container into the other, children learn about the **volume** or **capacity** of different containers. While observing Sara and other children at the water table, the teacher has recognized the opportunity to make it a learning experience of estimation and measurement. The teacher illustrated for the child that measurement involves the total number of the repeated equal-size unit (e.g., one cup).

Children benefit from repeated measurement activities and the use of measurement vocabulary. The following interactions and strategies provide suggestions as to how teachers can help preschool children, including children, with disabilities or special needs, build measurement concepts and skills.

Provide opportunities to promote measurement concepts in the environment. The indoor and outdoor learning environments have plenty of things that can be measured. Children even compare themselves to each other and to other objects: "This plant is taller than me." Objects in different sizes, such as buckets, shovels, balls, blocks, brushes, or cups, present more tangible opportunities to compare and order objects by size.

Unit blocks, for example, are especially good for measurement explorations. An environment rich with measuring opportunities should also include standard measurement tools in different interest areas, although measurement using standard units is not the primary focus in preschool. By providing an environment with measuring tools, a teacher encourages children to become familiar with them and to explore their function. Rulers and tape measures may be part of the block area, although they can be used for different purposes throughout the day. Height charts can be used to measure and track growth over time. Measuring cups, spoons, and scoops can be used in the sandbox and for any cooking activity, real or pretend. Tools to measure weight, such as a balance scale, a produce scale, or a bathroom scale, can be part of the dramatic play area. A thermometer can tell children the temperature outside or inside. Preschool children are not expected to know how to read and use these tools, but with teacher guidance they learn that specialized tools measure different attributes. The teacher can gradually increase the number of measurement tools in the environment. Not all tools should be introduced at once, and children should be given time to explore tools, learn about their function, and apply that knowledge in their play. In addition, materials for measurements in nonstandard ways may be included, such as ribbon, yarn, paper clips, same-size block units, yardsticks, or unit blocks. See the "Research Highlight" on page 273.

Observe preschool children's measurement concepts in everyday play and routines. Children placed two trains next to each other to see which is longer. The teacher commented, "How do you know which train is longer?" Another child filled up a bucket of sand. The bucket became too heavy, and the child could not pick it up. She poured out some of the sand and tried again. Preschool children learn about measurement concepts through everyday play. Such interactions with objects teach children about length, capacity, weight, and other measurable attributes. They constantly make comparisons: "My train is longer," "I have a bigger shoe," "Let's see who is taller." While observing children at play, teachers can listen to the words they use in English and in their home language to describe and compare objects, learn about their level of measurement concepts, and find out more about their interests. This valuable information will help teachers design learning opportunities that are developmentally appropriate, meaningful, engaging, and accessible to all children in the group.

Mathematical Reasoning in Action: Which Is Taller?

VIGNETTE

In the block area, a group of children built a block tower. Cathy says to the teacher, "Look how big it is. It is reaching me up to here."

The teacher says, "You built a tall tower. Which do you think is taller, the table or the tower?"

Cathy replies, "The tower."

The teacher asks, "Why do you think the tower is taller?"

Cathy responds, "Because look, the table only reaches me up to here," pointing to her waist, "and the tower is up to here," pointing to her chest.

TEACHABLE MOMENT

 The teacher is asking questions to direct Cathy's attention to the height of the objects. Cathy is interested in finding out "which is taller" and came up with a way of answering this question. She is using herself as a reference point to determine which is taller: the block tower or the table.

Facilitate and reinforce measurement concepts in everyday play and routines. Everyday interactions provide teachers with opportunities to help preschool children identify and compare attributes of length, area, weight, and volume.

- **Build preschool children's descriptive and comparison vocabulary.** Describing and comparing attributes not only attunes children to the idea of measurement, but it also expands children's vocabulary in a natural and functional way. Point to the objects as you describe and compare them. Children who are learning English, in particular, need to hear measurement-related vocabulary used in context in order to comprehend the meaning. Model the use of comparison vocabulary when talking with children. "This is a very *tall* tree. Which tree do you think is *taller?*" "Your lunch box is very *heavy* today. It is *heavier* than mine." "Look at the *long* train you built. Let's see whose train is *longer.*" "This is a *big* box. I think we a need a *bigger* box." For more information about strategies to support children who are English learners, see Chapter 5.

- **Ask questions.** Teachers' questions direct children's attention to measurable properties of objects, facilitate the child's thinking about measurement concepts, and model the use of measurement vocabulary. "Which ribbon is longer?" "Which beanstalk is taller?" "Which is heavier, the foam block or the wood block?" "Which container holds more?" Questions should be short and simple for children who are learning English and children who are just beginning to learn those concepts. The teacher should ask meaningful questions that reflect a desire to really understand the child's thinking and not overwhelm him with lots of questions. Use questions sparingly and purposely and allow children time to think and respond.

- **Challenge preschool children to use measurement to solve problems.** As teachers observe children at play, teachers pose questions to enrich children's experiences. "How far can you jump?" "How can we find out how big this rocket ship is?" Children enjoy exploring and finding the answers to such questions. Teachers can help children figure out ways to measure, using standard or nonstandard units. For instance, the teacher may suggest that the children measure the distance of their jump with same-size blocks or model for children how to use a tape measure to measure the length of a slide or the circumference of a watermelon. See the "Research Highlight" on page 273.

In addition to preschool children's natural measurement experiences through everyday play, teachers can provide rich and meaningful measurement experiences in small or large groups to target different measurement concepts.

Provide opportunities to compare and order objects. Comparison lays the foundation for understanding measurement. Offer children opportunities to compare objects based on size, weight, or capacity. For example, children can explore a pair of pumpkins and determine which one is larger. A balance scale may be used to compare the weight of different objects. Talk with children about why the scale is moving up or down. "Which object is lighter?" "Which object is heavier?" After comparing two items, children can compare three or more items and put them in order. For instance, with three pumpkins of different sizes, children can place them in order from largest to smallest and from smallest to largest. Teachers can engage children in ordering, using a variety of objects in the preschool environment, such as sticks, buckets, balls, nesting cups, or blocks. Children can arrange sticks from shortest to longest or the buckets in the sandbox from "holds the most" to "holds the least."

Use literature to illustrate measurement concepts. Read storybooks such as *Goldilocks and the Three Bears* to children that emphasize measurement concepts. Teachers can have children act out the stories and use different size objects to create the setup (e.g., large, medium, and small bowls, beds, and chairs). This allows teachers to illustrate the concept of size and use comparison vocabulary in a meaningful context: "Which bowl is largest?" "Can you put these three bears in order from smallest to largest?"

Provide small-group activities using standard and nonstandard measurement. Plan activities that show the child the need for measurement and use concrete objects to illustrate the measurement process. Preschool children enjoy finding answers to measurement questions, especially if the activity expands what they already know and is related to what is familiar to them. For some activities, teachers can illustrate the use of nonstandard measurements for children such as multiple copies of objects of the same size (e.g., wood blocks, unit blocks). For other activities, teachers can model for children the use of standard tools in real-life situations. Children who are English learners may already know a concept but need the English words or measurement-related vocabulary to describe it. Describe in words, using gestures and concrete objects, the measurement question and the process of measuring. For more information about strategies to support children who are English learners, see Chapter 5.

Some common activities that involve measurement include planting and cooking. In planting, for example, children can use same-size sticks to keep equal distances between plants (e.g., "How far apart should the plants be?"). They can use a three-inch string to find out if each hole is deep enough and track and compare the growth of plants over time. Children may keep a daily log of the plant's growth. While cooking, teachers may invite children to help measure by using measuring cups and spoons. "Now we need one cup of flour. Can somebody help me measure?" "I need half a teaspoon of cinnamon." The children can help the teacher identify the appropriate measuring tool, and the teacher can use it to demonstrate for the children how to measure exact amounts.

Children can also use measurement in exploring the body. For example, the teacher can create with children a cutout of their foot. Children estimate the length of their foot, and then the teacher shows them how they can measure the exact length using a measuring tape. Children may be able to record what they have measured. The teacher can also invite children to compare their height by creating a bar graph. He may discuss with children, "How tall are you?" "Who is

the tallest?" "Who is the shortest?" If the class includes a child who does not yet walk, teachers can encourage children to measure height while the person lies down. This technique works well for tall teachers too.

Encourage preschool children to estimate measurements. A measurement experience could start with estimation before doing the actual measuring, "How many scoops of sand do you think we need to fill this green cup?" "About how many blocks will cover the distance from here to the table?" Encourage children who are English learners to express themselves in their home language. Estimation focuses children on the attribute being measured, helps develop familiarity with standard units, and motivates children to measure and find out how close they came to their estimates.

Encourage preschool children to record and document what they have measured. Recording their measurements allows children to convey information about the process and the outcome of their measurement, using drawings, numbers, and words. Teachers can transcribe for children their observations and explanations. Children with special needs and other disabilities may use alternate methods of communication, if needed. For example, some children may use sign language, pictures, or a computer. Keeping records of their measurements allows children to compare their measurements to others or to their own measurements over a period of time (e.g., tracking growth).

Bringing It All Together

Tracking the Growth of Sunflowers

As part of exploring and learning the concept of growth, the children have planted sunflower seeds in the garden. A long stick was attached to each plant, and the teacher asked that every week the children mark on the stick the height of the sunflower. Tracking the growth of sunflowers has generated comparison and measurement experiences. For example, one week the teacher pointed to one of the sunflowers and explained to the children, "Last week when we measured this sunflower, it was up to here. It was seven inches long. This week it is up to here. How many more inches do you think it grew in the past week? What is your estimate?"

Children were encouraged to make estimates and then were invited to measure the growth of this sunflower. "How can we measure how much it has grown since last time?" Children had different ideas. Some children said, "You need a ruler." Others said, "With this" and pointed to a measuring tape. Over time, children were also comparing the sunflowers one to another. On one occasion, the teacher helped a small group of children compare the height of two flowers by using a string to represent the height of one flower and then laying the string against the second flower.

Children enjoyed tracking the sunflowers' growth and finding out, "Which sunflower is taller?" and "Which is taller?"—the child or the sunflower.

Tracking the growth of sunflowers generated opportunities for children to compare, estimate, and measure length. Measurement was a natural part of this experience, and it illustrated for the children its application in everyday life. The teacher facilitated and reinforced measurement concepts by asking questions, encouraging children to make estimates, challenging children to use measurement to answer questions, and supporting children's efforts in measurement.

Engaging Families

The following ideas may help families to develop children's measurement experiences:

✔ **Communicate to parents the importance of talking with children about measurement.** Explain to parents how early measuring experiences set the foundation for developing a formal understanding of measurement later in school. Early measuring experiences with parents or other family members will expose children to measurement terms and comparison vocabulary in the child's home language. Parents can invite children to compare the length, height, area, or weight of different objects. For example, they can play with children a game in which children have to find objects around home that are "longer than," "heavier than," or "taller than" a particular object. Teachers can invite parents and other community members to the classroom to take part in cooking, gardening, building, or other activities involving measuring.

✔ **Encourage parents to involve children in everyday measurement experiences.** Measurement is a practical math skill used in many different aspects of everyday life. Cooking, sewing, gardening, grocery shopping, a visit to the doctor or to the post office—all involve measurement. Encourage parents to include children in everyday measuring experiences and to talk to them about what they are measuring. Parents may need to be reminded of the many opportunities they have throughout the day to talk with children about measurement and to demonstrate for children the use of different measurement tools; for example, a scale to measure weight, a measuring tape or a ruler to measure length, and a thermometer to measure temperature. Explain to parents that young children may become familiar with these tools but are not expected to know how to read and use these tools without adults' guidance. Also communicate to parents that preschool children can measure length by using nonstandard units. Some examples of measurement experiences children had in class using nonstandard units coould be shared so that parents join children in measuring the length of different objects at home, using the child's own unit of measurement (e.g., "The table is six lunch boxes long").

Questions for Reflection

1. What other preschool experiences can you think of that invite children to practice measurement naturally?

2. What could be added to the physical environment to promote children's learning of measurement concepts and skills?

3. Think about the group's daily routine. In what situations could you model the use of comparison vocabulary (e.g., heavier, smaller, longer, shorter) when talking with children? How would you support English learners in learning and using comparison vocabulary?

4. How could you integrate measuring experiences into your group's current topic of study? What measuring experiences would be ones that are relevant to the culture, interests, or life experiences of the children in your group?

5. How could parents be part of measurement activities in your classroom (e.g., in cooking, building, woodworking, gardening)?

Geometry

eometry is the study of shapes and spatial relationships. Children enter preschool with a strong intuitive knowledge about shapes, spatial location, and transformations. They learn about geometry as they move in space and interact with objects in their environment. From infancy they begin to form shape concepts as they explore their environment, observe shapes, and play with different objects. Before they can name and define shapes, very young children are able to match and classify objects based on shape. During the preschool years, children develop a growing understanding of shape and spatial relationships. They learn the names of shapes and start to recognize the attributes of two- and three-dimensional shapes. They also develop an understanding of objects in relation to space, learning to describe an object's location (e.g., on top, under), direction (e.g., from, up, down) and distance (e.g., near, far).[22, 23]

Teachers have a vital role in expanding children's thinking about shapes and space. They should ask questions and provide materials that encourage children to explore, describe, and compare shapes and positions in space. The use of questions and access to materials is particularly helpful for children who are English learners to gain an understanding of geometry concepts while developing second-language skills. The following strategies will guide teachers in actively supporting preschool children's development of geometry concepts and spatial sense.

1.0   Shapes

Learning about shapes goes beyond merely knowing the names of common shapes. It involves the exploration, investigation, and discussion of shapes and structures in the classroom.[24] Experiences with two- and three- dimensional shapes allow children to learn to notice individual attributes and characteristics of shapes and to identify similarities and differences among them. Rich experiences with shape lay the foundation for more formal geometry in later years. Teachers should help children develop a deeper understanding of shapes by encouraging them to explore shapes and their attributes and providing opportunities for children to represent, build, perceive, and compare shapes.[25]

Mathematical Reasoning in Action: Discovering Shapes with Blocks

VIGNETTE

Mr. Gerry notices Amelia building wall of blocks and moves closer to observe. Amelia says to Mr. Gerry, "I need one."

Mr. Gerry responds, "Do you need another square block?"

Amelia responds, "Yes, but no more."

Mr. Gerry says, "I have an idea for you. We can use this triangle block and this triangle block to make a square." He hands Amelia two triangle blocks. "Put them facing each other just like this," he says, demonstrating for Amelia.

Amelia tries to put together the two triangles to make a square and says, "I don't know how."

Mr. Gerry responds, "Yes, you turn around this triangle and put it by the other triangle. Now look at these two triangles facing each other. What does it look like?" "A square!"

Amelia says, surprised and giggling, "I need it here."

Mr. Gerry says, "Now you finished building the wall."

TEACHABLE MOMENT

 Amelia has recently joined this preschool group. She is learning English. Mr. Gerry noticed that Amelia was looking for another square block, and the teacher used the opportunity to interact with the child. The teacher has introduced Amelia to the names of shapes (e.g., square, triangle) and has illustrated for her how a geometric shape can be composed from other shapes.

The following interactions and strategies promote understanding of shape concepts:

Refer to shapes and encourage the use of shape names in everyday interactions. Preschool children learn the correct names of shapes by hearing others call objects by their geometric names. Children first identify simple two-dimensional shapes such as circle and square. Over time, they learn to identify and describe a greater variety of shapes (triangle, rectangle, hexagon, trapezoid). Children play with three-dimensional shapes (e.g., building blocks) and, while in preschool, they may also begin naming and describing some three-dimensional shapes (e.g., sphere, cube).

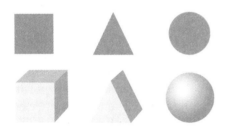

The teacher should use the correct shape names during everyday interactions and routines. Describe what you see and point to or touch objects when saying their shape names. Oral descriptions are particularly important for preschool children who are English learners. Help children understand mathematical terms by using extensive modeling, accompany words with gestures (e.g., pointing or tracing shapes in the air), point to objects, act out terms, and use short, clear sentences. For more information about strategies to support children who are English learners, see Chapter 5.

- During play, the teacher observed the children's construction with blocks and commented, "I see you used the rectangle blocks to make a wall."

"Look, you put a small triangle on top of a small square," the teacher pointed to the objects while saying the shape names. "You built a little house."

- At breakfast, the teacher asked, "What shape is the pancake?" Later, at snack time, the teacher announced, "Today, we are having crackers that are circles and crackers that are rectangles."

- When reading a storybook, the teacher commented, "Look at this snowman. What shapes can you see?"

- When playing with blocks, the teacher asked, "What shape is the block you have on top of the long rectangle block?"

Engage preschool children in conversations about shapes. Preschool children recognize geometric shapes by their overall physical appearance, but they do not yet think about the attributes or properties of shapes. For example, children may recognize a square because it looks like a square, but not think of it as a figure that has four equal sides and four right angles. Teachers can draw children's attention to the attributes of different shapes by discussing with them the parts and attributes of shapes and by encouraging them to build and represent shapes in many different ways.

- **Encourage preschool children to observe and compare shapes:** "Can you find another rectangle around the room?" "How are they similar?" "Here is a square and here is a triangle. How are they different?"

- **Talk about shapes and discuss their attributes:** "Let's find out how many straight sides are in a rectangle." The teacher counts while pointing to a rectangle, "One, two, three, four. How many straight sides do we have in a triangle? Can you help me find out?" Oral descriptions are particularly helpful for children with vision disabilities as well as those with visual-spatial challenges.

A child's world is filled with shapes in different sizes and positions, but observing shapes in the environment is not enough to build a full understanding of shape. Preschool children need to explore, manipulate and represent two- and three-dimensional shapes in a variety of ways. Hands-on experiences offer the best learning opportunities for all children, including those with special needs. The following experiences will expose children to the attributes and properties of different shapes.

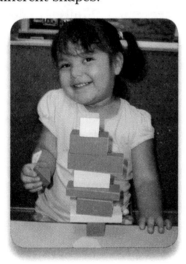

Provide materials that encourage preschool children to explore and manipulate shapes in space. It is crucial that the classroom environment include materials that encourage children to manipulate and represent shapes in a variety of ways. Children with disabilities and other special needs, in particular, need lots of hands-on sensory experiences with three-dimensional shapes and real-life objects in a variety of shapes and textures. The preschool environment should have a variety of blocks of different shapes,

colors, sizes, and thickness. In addition to blocks, shapes may be provided in a variety of forms in all areas of the classroom: interlocking plastic shapes, shape containers for sand and water play, sand molds, shape sponges, cookie cutters, stickers, magnets, shape templates, geoboards, and beads in different shapes.

Include books, games, and other learning materials with shape-related themes in the preschool environment. Share with preschool children books about shapes (e.g., *The Shape of Things, The Village of Round and Square Houses*). As teachers read aloud, point to pictures and discuss with children the names and attributes of shapes. Books can also show children objects from different perspectives and give meaning to spatially related words (e.g., *under, in, on*). Another playful way to introduce shapes is through shape-related games such as shape lotto, shape bingo, and puzzles. Some preschools may choose to incorporate a software-based mathematical curriculum. There is computer software that allows children to perform action on shapes such as flipping, sliding, and turning shapes in different angles. Software of this kind engages children in a variety of shape-related activities (e.g., solving a shape puzzle, creating a composition of shapes) on the computer.

Provide preschool children with playful opportunities to explore and represent shapes in a variety of ways. To develop their concepts of shape, young children need to handle, explore, manipulate, and create shapes in a variety of ways. Hands-on experiences offer the best learning opportunities for all children, including those with special needs. The following experiences will attune children to the attributes and properties of different shapes.

- **Play with blocks.** Preschool children learn about shapes by touching, moving, putting together, and taking apart. Block play provides endless opportunities to learn about shapes. When playing with blocks, children perceive three-dimensional shapes from different angles and discover relationships between shapes. Children can see how a circle fits between arches, two right triangles form a rectangle, and two squares form a rectangle. Children with motor impairments may need assistance from an adult or peer to manipulate objects in order to explore two- and three- dimensional shapes. A child might also use adaptive materials (i.e., manipulatives that are easy to grasp). Children with visual impairments need materials that are easily distinguishable by touch. Their engagement is also facilitated by using containers or trays of materials that clearly define their workspace.

- **Match, sort, and classify shapes.** Provide children with a collection of shapes varying in size and color. Ask children to put all the same kind of shapes together. Discuss with children why a shape belongs to a group.

- **Create and represent shapes.** Help preschool children represent shapes in a variety of ways. For example, children can create two-dimensional shapes from small items such as beads, sticks, or strings or with play dough, clay, flexible straws, or pipe cleaners. They can also form shapes with their bodies. You may invite children to pair with a friend and use their legs or fingers to create circles, triangles, squares, and diamonds. Children also enjoy drawing, tracing, and copying shapes. Preschool children draw shapes, especially when drawing a picture of a house, a person, or a tree. Teachers may offer children solid cutouts to trace shapes or encourage them to trace a shape in the air using their fingers. Tracing helps children to focus on critical attributes of each shape.

- **Compose and decompose shapes from other shapes.** Provide children with different shapes (e.g., squares, triangles, trapezoids, and rhombus) and let them use these shapes to form other shapes. For example, they can use two same-size right triangles to form a rectangle or to form another triangle.

Present preschool children with many different examples of a type of shape. Children have mental images of shapes—visual prototypes created by the culture—through books, toys, games, and other materials. Triangles are usually equilateral (i.e., having all the sides equal) and isosceles (i.e., having at least two sides equal) and have horizontal bases. Rectangles are usually horizontal and elongated. These are prototypical.

Children should be exposed to many different examples of a shape. Examples of triangles and rectangles should include a variety of shapes, including long, thin, and wide, varying in orientation and size.[26] Draw children's attention to atypical shapes and encourage them to describe why some nonstandard examples belong to a category (e.g., "This is also a triangle, but it is thinner"; "This is a long rectangle, and this is a short rectangle").

2.0   Positions in Space

When young children crawl through a tunnel, climb up a ladder, go under a table, move forward in a wheelchair, or swing up and down, they develop a sense of spatial relationships. As they move their bodies in space, they learn position, direction, and distance relationships between their bodies and other objects and between different objects in space. Preschool children need to learn many words to be able to describe and name positions and directions in space (e.g., *in and out, top* and *bottom, over* and *under, up* and *down, forward* and *backward,* and *around* and *through*). Teachers can help children develop spatial vocabulary, especially children who are English learners, by using and demonstrating the meaning of spatial words during daily activities.

Mathematical Reasoning in Action: Moving Through an Obstacle Course

VIGNETTE

It was a rainy day, and the children could not go outside. The teacher had set up an indoor obstacle course for the children. She demonstrated how to use the course, talking as she moved. "It starts here. I crawl under this table. Next, I jump over this pillow. Then I crawl through this tunnel. Next, I hop across the rug, and finally I walk in between the chairs."

PLANNING LEARNING OPPORTUNITIES

 Children learn spatial orientation through physical activity. Setting up an obstacle course provided the teacher with the opportunity to introduce and demonstrate the meaning of spatial orientation skills and vocabulary. As children went through the course on their own, the teacher described their actions, using spatial orientation terms (e.g., "Stay low as you crawl under the table; remember, you have to hop across the rug").

The following interactions and strategies can help children develop skills related to spatial relationships:

Provide materials and equipment to promote spatial sense. Young children develop their spatial sense through movement and interactions with objects in the environment. Outdoor equipment designed for large-muscle activity fosters children's spatial sense. Climbing up the monkey bars, going up and down a slide or on a swing, and driving a bike or a scooter around the play yard all help children develop their sense of position, direction, and distance. Preschool children also explore space by building a three-dimensional complex construction or a maze by using large boxes, blocks, geometric shapes, cardboard, even chairs and tables. They enjoy getting in, out, over, or under their construction. In movement, teachers use hoops, beanbags, or balls to introduce positions in space in playful ways (e.g., throw the ball up, jump in and out of the hoop, or put the beanbag under the arm). Children with motor disabilities and visual impairments need supported opportunities to experience spatial relationships in order to develop their spatial sense. Specialists working with individual children have specific ideas of how to support and promote the learning of this important concept.

Support preschool children's spatial sense in everyday interactions. As children experience concepts such as far, on, under, and over, they should learn vocabulary words to describe these spatial relationships. English learners may know the concepts and the corresponding vocabulary in their home language, but they need scaffolding to learn spatial vocabulary in English. Teachers may want to use simple concepts and vocabulary first (e.g., *in, on, under, up, down),* and then introduce more complex concepts and vocabulary (e.g., *in front, behind, beside, between).* For more information about strategies to support children who are English learners, see Chapter 5. Children with speech and language disabilities may need many opportunities to practice this vocabulary as they join with their peers in play.

- **Use spatial words and point out spatial relationships.** Point out spatial relationships naturally during play. Teachers may give directions, ask questions, or simply make comments (e.g., "Can you please put all the markers in the box?" "I see you put the beanbag on your head." "Let's see who can jump over the pond").

- **Expand preschool children's words.** Encourage children to use spatial words. When children try to describe position, direction, or distance, teachers expand on their ideas and demonstrate for them the use of spatial words in context. For example, if the child refers to his construction and says, "Look, I put the big block here like this and it doesn't fall." You may demonstrate for him the use of spatial words, "Oh, I see you put the big rectangle block on top of many small blocks."

Provide preschool children with planned experiences to promote the understanding of spatial sense. Plan small- or large-group activities to enhance children's understanding of spatial concepts and introduce spatial vocabulary words.

- **Songs and games.** Sing songs and play games that direct children to move their bodies in space. For example, "Simon says, put your hands on top of your knees, jump up and down, hold the beanbag behind your back . . ."

- **Literature.** Read aloud stories that use position words (e.g., *above, below, up, down).* Point to pictures and illustrate for children spatial positions with actions. After the reading of a book, children can act out the story and use position words to describe the characters' actions.

- **Construction.** Provide children with opportunities to organize materials in space in three dimensions using construction toys (e.g., interlocking cubes) or scrap materials. Teachers can also build with the children an obstacle course or an outdoor maze. Children experience themselves in space by going through, over, around, and in and out of different things.

Bringing It All Together

Building a Castle

The teacher had noticed that several children in her group had shown a strong interest in castles. They built castles in the block area, in the sandbox, and even looked for castles in fairy tale books when visiting the library. The teacher suggested that the group build a big castle outside. They started by gathering the materials. The children brought from home different-size boxes and figures or characters to be included in the castle. The teacher also offered big cylinders, cones, building blocks, construction boards, and other materials. The children made different suggestions: "Put all the big boxes here and the small ones on top of them." "I put it above this for the roof." "We can use these for the tower."

The teacher described their ideas using names of shape and spatial terms. "So you want to put the small square blocks on top of the big rectangle blocks." "Are you suggesting using the cylinders to build the tower?" The children enjoyed building the structure, using different shapes and materials, and were proud of it.

During circle time, the teacher invited children to describe the castle and how it was built. "Look at the castle you built. Can you tell me what it looks like?" Children were encouraged to use spatial words and the names of shapes in their talk. The activity evolved into a long-term project. The children kept adding more pieces to the structure and added different elements to decorate the castle.

The teacher presented a topic of interest to the children in the group. The castle project exemplifies how children can learn about geometry concepts by physically touching, moving, and putting together objects of different shapes. In the process of building the castle, children were encouraged to use the names of shapes and the words to describe spatial relationships (e.g., *above, below*). The teacher has made it a rich learning experience by offering children objects in a variety of shapes, observing children in their work, describing children's ideas in words, asking questions, and inviting children to observe and describe the castle in their own words. The project not only facilitated increasing the children's knowledge of shape and spatial concepts, it also promoted collaboration work and creativity.

Engaging Families

The following ideas may help families to develop children's awareness of geometric shapes:

✔ **Encourage parents to refer to shapes in the environment when talking with children.** Parents and other family members can support children's development of geometry concepts through everyday interactions with children. Teachers should encourage parents to refer to shapes in the environment when talking with children, "Look at your pancake. It's a circle. We can use this rectangle pan to bake this cake." When parents and other family members talk with children about shapes, they illustrate the concept of shape and

▲

introduce children to the names of different shapes in their home language. Parents can also help children learn names of shapes by playing games. For example, play I Spy and have children look around the house and identify as many items of a certain shape. When driving, or on the bus, parents can use traffic signs as an opportunity to identify and describe shapes. "Look at this yellow sign. What shape is it?" "The stop sign is red. It is the shape of an octagon. It has eight sides. Let's see if you can find another stop sign." In addition to identifying and naming shapes, children should explore and describe shapes. The teacher should communicate to parents that children learn best about geometry concepts through hands-on experiences. Holding and manipulating objects of different shapes, building with blocks, drawing and tracing shapes, creating shapes with play dough, or doing a

puzzle all help children learn about the characteristics of different shapes.

✔ **Encourage parents to use spatial words in everyday interactions with children.** Parents use spatial words to describe position and direction in space in everyday interactions and play with children ("I am right *behind* you," The book is *on* the chair," "Put the shoes *under* the bed"). Parents should be aware of children's opportunities to experience and describe themselves in space using words such as *above, under, up, down, in* and *out*. By listening to parents and other family members using these words, children will have a better understanding of spatial concepts and will learn spatial vocabulary in their home language. Children will start identifying themselves in space by using spatial words ("I was hiding *under* the table," "I'm going *down* the slide," "I'll climb *up* the stairs").

Questions for Reflection

1. How would you expand the castle project to include additional mathematical skills such as comparing, measuring, counting, and classifying?

2. What materials in your preschool environment engage children in exploring and manipulating shapes?

3. What songs or games involving movement in space do you sing and play with children? How could you use these opportunities to encourage children to use words describing spatial relationships?

4. How could you use hands-on construction activities (such as the Building a Castle project described above) to compare and discuss the attributes of shapes?

5. In what ways could you support and scaffold English learners' access to learning English words for shapes and spatial relationships?

Mathematical Reasoning

Mathematical reasoning is a key process in learning and developing mathematical knowledge in all areas of mathematics, including number and operations, classification, patterning, measurement, and geometry. It involves the ability to think and reason logically, to apply mathematical knowledge in different problem-solving situations, and to come up with different solutions. Mathematical reasoning is natural to most young children as they explore the environment and make sense of the world around them. As illustrated through different examples in the previous sections (see examples of "Mathematical Reasoning in Action"), young children engage in mathematical reasoning and problem solving in their play and as they go about their daily activities. "Does every child have one cup?" "Do we both have the same number of shells?" "How many children are here today?" "How much did the sunflower grow?" "What blocks can we use instead of the long rectangle block?" "Do more children like red apples or green apples?" Different situations in the

everyday environment call for spontaneous mathematical thinking. Young children are eager and enthusiastic to search for solutions and apply different strategies, especially when the context is familiar and meaningful, the question or problem is understandable and important to them, and they have some knowledge base related to the problem.[27] Effective teachers build on children's natural motivation for mathematical reasoning and problem solving. They promote children's learning of new and progressively more advanced mathematical challenges and support the development of mathematical vocabulary and language.

1.0 Promoting Mathematical Reasoning and Problem Solving

Teachers play a key role in identifying natural situations of mathematical reasoning throughout the day and turning them into teachable moments. Teachers also play a key role in initiating opportunities for children to reason mathematically. They can nurture, facilitate, and encourage preschool children's mathematical reasoning.

Mathematical Reasoning in Action: Picking up Shovels in the Sandbox

VIGNETTE

The children cleaned up the play yard before going back inside. The teacher, Ms. Denise, had noticed that not all the shovels were picked up from the sandbox. Ms. Denise asked for help saying, "We need all five shovels back in the box so our toys aren't lost. I see here only three. We need more shovels in the box. How many more shovels do we need?" The teacher had noticed that Ling Wa, one of the older preschool children in the group, was counting her fingers, trying to find out how many shovels were missing.

Ling Wa suddenly said, "Ms. Denise, we need two more."

Ms. Denise went further, asking, "Do you think we need two more shovels?" How did you figure that out?"

Ling Wa explained, "We have three. Then two more, we will have— one, two, three, four, five (Ling Wa was counting on her fingers)."

Ms. Denise said, "You are right. We need two more. Can everybody help us find two more shovels in the sandbox?"

TEACHABLE MOMENT

▶ Ms. Denise, the teacher, identified the situation of picking up the shovels as an opportunity for arithmetic thinking and reasoning. She described the situation: "We need all five shovels back . . . I see here only three" and posed a question: "How many more shovels do we need?" She challenged the children to think and solve an arithmetic problem. Even when Ling Wa came up with the right answer, Ms. Denise went further and asked "How did you figure that out?" The teacher gave Ling Wa an opportunity to explain her reasoning. Ling Wa, like many other children in this group, very much enjoyed figuring out the answer to a simple addition and subtraction problem. Recently, she had started using her fingers in solving such problems. Representing numbers in the problem with fingers or other objects (e.g., shovels) makes arithmetic reasoning more concrete and meaningful for young children.

The following interactions and strategies facilitate preschool children's mathematical reasoning:

Identify and create opportunities for mathematical reasoning. Teachers can provide children with opportunities of mathematical reasoning, whether through spontaneous questioning and reasoning with children or through carefully planned experiences. Teachers may use everyday activities to initiate moments of mathematical reasoning. For example, in the "Picking up Shovels" vignette described above, the teacher identified a clean-up situation as an opportunity to engage children in reasoning with numbers. Similarly, in the "More Cups" example (page 245), the teacher engaged the child in mathematical reasoning while setting the table for lunch. Opportunities for mathematical reasoning come up while teachers observe children closely and listen to their ideas and thoughts. Teachers capitalize on these moments to facilitate mathematical concepts and encourage children to apply and explain their reasoning. In "Who Has More Cars?" (page 243), for example, the teacher had noticed two children spontaneously counting their cars to show they have more and turned it into a teachable moment of mathematical reasoning and problem solving. Similarly, in the example of "Playing at the Water Table" (page 274), Ms. Frances observed Sara at the water table filling up a cup with water and pouring it into a bigger container. The teacher turned it into a mathematical reasoning experience of estimation and measurement, asking, "How many more cups do you think it would take to fill it up?"

The teacher may also plan in advance activities or experiences to engage children in mathematical reasoning related to particular concepts. For example, in "Tracking the Growth of Sunflowers" (page 279), the teacher planned an experience to engage children in measuring and comparing the height of sunflowers over time. Similarly, in the "Bagel Shop" activity on page 256, the teacher created a real-life setting of a bakery to engage children in counting and arithmetic reasoning.

Pose meaningful questions and challenge preschool children's thinking. One effective way to encourage preschool children to think and reason mathematically is by asking them questions that promote investigation and inquiry and challenge them to think through a problem and come up with a solution (e.g., "How do you think we can find out who has more cars?" "What is the class's favorite kind of apple? How can we find out . . .?" "Which do you think is taller, the table or the tower?" "What would happen if . . .?" "What other way could we sort the leaves?" "I wonder why . . .?"). By simply asking questions and listening to answers, teachers help children learn to reason. Give children time to answer a question or to solve a problem. Listen attentively to their ideas. Children's answers reveal what they understand and will inform teachers about how to best support their reasoning. Illustrate for children that, in many cases, there are different ways to solve a problem and more than one answer is possible.

Support preschool children in reasoning mathematically. Children may need a clue, encouragement, or the teacher's modeling of a strategy for solving a problem. In the example "Who Has More Cars?" (page 243), the teacher suggested to the children, "Let's count together." In "Tracking the Growth of Sunflowers (on page 279)," the teacher helped children compare the height of two sunflowers by using a string. Teachers should think out loud with children, make comments, and describe what the child is doing: "So here you put the green apples and here the red apples, but what about these apples?" "Long rectangle, short rectangle, long rectangle, short rectangle . . . look at your fence. You have a pattern." Encourage preschool children to express their thoughts and explain their reasoning to the teacher as well as to their peers (e.g., "How did you figure it out?" "'Look at the castle you built. Can you tell me what it looks like?"). Listening to and conversing with children helps them articulate the meaning of mathematical concepts, introduces them to mathematical language,

and gives value to knowing how to "do math." By making mathematical thinking conscious, teachers will do more of it and will develop a keener awareness of children's use of mathematical strategies and math language.

Bringing It All Together

Engaging Families

The following idea may help families to develop children's mathematical reasoning:

✔ **Encourage parents to engage children in mathematical reasoning.**
When talking about children's mathematical development, parents often think of their children's ability to count, name shapes, or say simple number facts (e.g., two plus two is four). It is important to communicate to parents what we mean by *mathematical reasoning*. It is about children being able to think mathematically and explore different ways of solving problems. To promote children's mathematical reasoning, parents should recognize mathematics in daily events and interactions and turn them into mathematical learning experiences. They can ask questions related to everyday situations: *How many more chairs do we need around the table? How can we divide these carrots equally among the four of you? Can you estimate how many spoonfuls it will take for you to finish your bowl of cereal?* Parents should encourage children to think. They may think aloud with children, listen to children's thoughts and answers, model solutions, and guide them through the thinking process.

Questions for Reflection

1. Think about a recent experience in which children in your group were engaged in mathematical thinking and reasoning.
   - What strategies have you used to engage children in mathematical reasoning?
   - What do you think children liked most about this experience? What did you like most about this experience?
   - What you would have added or changed in that experience?

2. Do you have children in your group who, like Ling Wa, enjoy figuring out the answers to simple addition and subtraction problems? How did you or would you find out? What would you do to support children's growth in mathematics?

3. What experiences related to your group's current focus or topic of interest would you offer children to engage them in mathematical reasoning?

4. How would you challenge different children in your group to reason mathematically according to their individual developmental level? How could you make a mathematical reasoning activity progressively more challenging?

Concluding Thoughts

Young children have a natural interest, curiosity, and competence to explore and construct mathematical concepts. Mathematics is a way of thinking and organizing the world around us. It is a natural part of day-to-day activities and events. Mathematics in preschool is learned through children's play and exploration as in the blocks area or the sandbox, through everyday routines such as setting the table and cleaning up, and through participation in teacher-initiated activities. Some teacher-initiated activities are designed with a focus on math, and others may focus on art, movement, literacy, or science but present opportunities for math learning. When teachers recognize the potential for exposure to math in different situations, they can turn everyday occurrences into exciting and effective mathematics-learning experiences. Children are excited to explore the size or volume of objects, to discover and create patterns, to manipulate and build with shapes, to sort and classify objects, and to try to figure out "how many." Teachers get to experience with children the day-to-day excitement of learning and discovering math. This process is joyful for the children and for the teacher, who guides and challenges them in building mathematical concepts, skills, and language.

Map of the Foundations

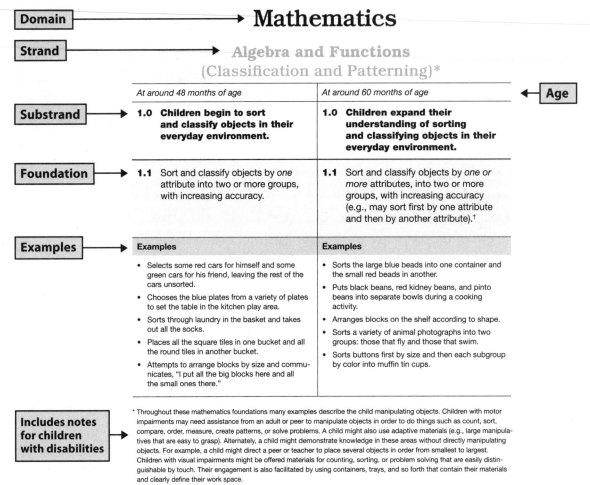

| Domain | → | **Mathematics** |

| Strand | → | **Algebra and Functions (Classification and Patterning)*** |

	At around 48 months of age	At around 60 months of age	← Age
Substrand →	**1.0 Children begin to sort and classify objects in their everyday environment.**	**1.0 Children expand their understanding of sorting and classifying objects in their everyday environment.**	
Foundation →	**1.1** Sort and classify objects by *one* attribute into two or more groups, with increasing accuracy.	**1.1** Sort and classify objects by *one or more* attributes, into two or more groups, with increasing accuracy (e.g., may sort first by one attribute and then by another attribute).†	
Examples →	**Examples**	**Examples**	
	• Selects some red cars for himself and some green cars for his friend, leaving the rest of the cars unsorted.	• Sorts the large blue beads into one container and the small red beads in another.	
	• Chooses the blue plates from a variety of plates to set the table in the kitchen play area.	• Puts black beans, red kidney beans, and pinto beans into separate bowls during a cooking activity.	
	• Sorts through laundry in the basket and takes out all the socks.	• Arranges blocks on the shelf according to shape.	
	• Places all the square tiles in one bucket and all the round tiles in another bucket.	• Sorts a variety of animal photographs into two groups: those that fly and those that swim.	
	• Attempts to arrange blocks by size and communicates, "I put all the big blocks here and all the small ones there."	• Sorts buttons first by size and then each subgroup by color into muffin tin cups.	

Includes notes for children with disabilities →

* Throughout these mathematics foundations many examples describe the child manipulating objects. Children with motor impairments may need assistance from an adult or peer to manipulate objects in order to do things such as count, sort, compare, order, measure, create patterns, or solve problems. A child might also use adaptive materials (e.g., large manipulatives that are easy to grasp). Alternately, a child might demonstrate knowledge in these areas without directly manipulating objects. For example, a child might direct a peer or teacher to place several objects in order from smallest to largest. Children with visual impairments might be offered materials for counting, sorting, or problem solving that are easily distinguishable by touch. Their engagement is also facilitated by using containers, trays, and so forth that contain their materials and clearly define their work space.

† Attributes include, but are not limited to, size, shape, or color.

Teacher Resources

Charlesworth, R. 2005. *Experiences in Math for Young Children* (Fifth edition). Clifton Park, NY: Thompson Delmar Learning.

Copley, J.V. 2000. "Appendix B: Making Math Meaningful through Children's Books," in *The Young Child and Mathematics*. Washington, DC: National Association for the Education of Young Children (NAEYC).

Early Childhood: Where Learning Begins Mathematics. The site includes mathematical activities for parents and their two- to five-year-old children and online information for parents from the U.S. Department of Education. http://www.ed.gov/pubs/EarlyMath

Early Childhood: Where Learning Begins – Mathematics. 1999. U.S. Department of Education. The site features book titles http://www.ed.gov/pubs/EarlyMath/appendix.html

Early Childhood Mathematics: Promoting Good Beginnings. The National Association for the Education of Young Children (NAEYC) and the National Council of Teachers of Mathematics (NCTM) present a joint statement. http://www.naeyc.org/about/positions/mathematics.asp

50 Multicultural Books Every Child Should Know. Madison: Cooperative Children's Book Center, School of Education, University of Wisconsin-Madison, http://www.education.wisc.edu/ccbc/books/detailListBooks.asp?idBookLists=42

Investigations in Number, Data, and Space is a mathematics curriculum for kindergarten up to grade five that includes a library with a series of papers by D. H. Clements on teaching mathematics to young children. http://investigations.terc.edu/library/bookpapers/your_childs_geometric.cfm

Issues related to math and literacy in *Young Children*, a journal of the National Association for the Education of Young Children (NAEYC). http://journal.naeyc.org/search/search.asp?printResults=1&page=1&sesID=1234477375896

Launching Into Literacy and Math, Madison Metropolitan School District, *Picture Books That Nurture Mathematical Thinking: Ages 3-5* and *Math Concepts in Spanish/Bilingual Books for Infants, Toddlers, and Preschoolers*. http://www.madison.k12.wi.us/tnl/lilm/additional_resources/good_books_preschool.html

Math Perspectives Teacher Development Center provides mathematics educators of preschool children to sixth graders with tools, strategies, and assessments that will ensure that all students are successful in the study of mathematics and can use mathematics to solve problems and think and reason mathematically. http://www.mathperspectives.com

Mathematics in the Early Years. 1999. Edited by J.V. Copley. Reston, VA: National Council of Teachers of Mathematics (NCTM).

National Council of Teachers of Mathematics (NCTM). http://www.nctm.org

Principles and Standards for School Mathematics. The new math standards released by NCTM in 2000 include standards for preschool to grade two. http://standards.nctm.org

Reading Is Fundamental. *100 of the Decade's Best Multicultural Read-Alouds, Pre-kindergarten through Grade 8*, selected and annotated by J. Freeman. http://www.rif.org/educators/books/100_best_multicultural.mspx

Selected Book Pairs for Linking Math and Literacy by P. Whitin and D. J. Whitin. National Association for the Education of Young Children (NAEYC). http://journal.naeyc.org/btj/200503/06whitin.pdf

Smith, S. S. 2006. *Early Childhood Mathematics* (Third edition). Boston, MA: Pearson Education, Inc.

Teaching Children Mathematics. The journal "offers activities, lesson ideas, teaching strategies, and problems through in-depth articles, departments, and features." "Early Childhood Corner" is a regular section of the journal. It features articles related to the teaching and learning of young children. http://my.nctm.org/eresources/journal_home.asp?journal_id=4

References

Alexander, P. A., C. S. White, and M. Daugherty. 1997. Analogical reasoning and early mathematics learning, in *Mathematical reasoning: Analogies, metaphors, and images.* Edited by L. D. English. Mahwah, NJ: Lawrence Erlbaum Associates.

Baroody, A. J., and J. L. M. Wilkins. 1999. The development of informal counting, number, and arithmetic skills and concepts, in *Mathematics in the early years.* Edited by J. V. Copley. Reston, VA: National Council of Teachers of Mathematics (NCTM).

Clements, D. H. 1999. Geometric and spatial thinking in young children, in *Mathematics in the early years.* Edited by J. V. Copley. Reston, VA: National Council of Teachers of Mathematics (NCTM).

Clements, D. H. 2004. Geometric and spatial thinking in early childhood education, in *Engaging young children in mathematics: Standards for early childhood mathematics education.* Edited by D. H. Clements, J. Samara, and A. M. Dibiase. Mahwah, NJ: Lawrence Erlbaum Associates.

Clements, D. H., and M. Stephan. 2004. Measurement in pre-K to grade 2 mathematics, in *Engaging young children in mathematics: Standards for early childhood mathematics education.* Edited by D. H. Clements, J. Samara, and A. M. Dibiase. Mahwah, NJ: Lawrence Erlbaum Associates.

Donlan, C. 1998. Number without language? Studies of children with specific language impairments, in *The Development of Mathematical Skills.* Edited by C. Donlan. East Sussex, UK: Psychology Press Ltd.

Engaging young children in mathematics: Findings of the 2000 national conference on standards for preschool and kindergarten mathematics education. 2004. Edited by D. H. Clements, J. Sarama, and A. M. DiBiase. Mahwah, NJ: Lawrence Erlbaum Associates.

Fuson, K. C. 1988. *Children's counting and concepts of number.* New York: Springer-Verlag.

Gelman, R., and R. Baillargeon. 1983. A review of some Piagetian concepts, in *Handbook of child psychology,* vol. 3. Edited by J. H. Flavell and E. M. Markman. New York: Wiley.

Gelman, R., and C. R. Gallistel. 1978. *The child's understanding of number.* Cambridge, MA: Harvard University Press.

Ginsburg, H. P.; J. S. Lee; and J. S. Boyd. 2008. Mathematics education for young children: What it is and how to promote it. *Social Policy Report* 22, no. 1.

Klein, A., and P. Starkey. 2004. Fostering preschool children's mathematical knowledge: Findings from the Berkeley math readiness project, in *Engaging young children in mathematics: Standards for early childhood mathematics education.* Edited by D. H. Clements, J. Samara, and A. M. Dibiase. Mahwah, NJ: Lawrence Erlbaum Associates.

Levine, S. C., N. C. Jordan, and J. Huttenlocher. February 1992. Development of calculation abilities in young children, *Journal of Experimental Child Psychology* 53, no. 1, 72–103.

National Association for the Education of Young Children (NAEYC) and National Council of Teachers of Mathematics (NCTM). 2002. *Early childhood mathematics: Promoting good beginnings.* Washington, DC: Author.

National Council of Teachers of Mathematics (NCTM). 2000. *Principles and standards for school mathematics.* Reston, VA: Author.

Nunes, T., and C. Moreno. 1998. Is hearing impairment a cause of difficulties in learning mathematics? in *The development of mathematical skills.* Edited by C. Donlan. East Sussex, UK: Psychology Press Ltd.

Smith, S. S. 2006. *Early childhood mathematics.* 3rd ed. Boston, MA: Pearson Education, Inc.

Weaver, L. R., and C. Gaines. 1999. What to do when they don't speak English: Teaching mathematics to English-language learners in the early childhood classroom, in *Mathematics in the Early Years*. Edited by J. V. Copley. Reston, VA: National Council of Teachers of Mathematics (NCTM).

Xu, F., and E. S. Spelke. 2000. Large number discrimination in 6-month-old infants, *Cognition* 74: B1–B11.

Zur, O., and R. Gelman. 2004. Young children can add and subtract by predicting and checking, *Early Childhood Research Quarterly* 19: 121–37.

Endnotes

1. National Association for the Education of Young Children (NAEYC) and National Council of Teachers of Mathematics (NCTM), *Early Childhood Mathematics: Promoting Good Beginnings* (Washington, DC: National Association for the Education of Young Children, 2002).

2. H. P. Ginsburg, J. S. Lee, and J. S. Boyd, "Mathematics Education for Young Children: What It Is and How to Promote It," *Social Policy Report* 22, no. 1 (2008).

3. National Council of Teachers of Mathematics (NCTM), *Principles and Standards for School Mathematics* (Reston, VA: Author, 2000), 74.

4. L. R. Weaver and C. Gaines, 1999, "What to Do When They Don't Speak English: Teaching Mathematics to English-Language Learners in the Early Childhood Classroom," in *Mathematics in the Early Years*. Edited by J. V. Copley (Reston, VA: National Council of Teachers of Mathematics, 1999).

5. R. Gelman and C. R. Gallistel, *The Child's Understanding of Number* (Cambridge, MA: Harvard University Press, 1978).

6. K. C. Fuson, *Children's Counting and Concepts of Number* (New York: Springer-Verlag, 1988).

7. T. Nunes and C. Moreno, "Is Hearing Impairment a Cause of Difficulties in Learning Mathematics?" in *The Development of Mathematical Skills*. Edited by C. Donlan (East Sussex, UK: Psychology Press Ltd., 1998)

8. C. Donlan, "Number Without Language? Studies of Children with Specific Language Impairments," in *The Development of Mathematical Skills*. Edited by C. Donlan (East Sussex, UK: Psychology Press Ltd., 1998).

9. A. J. Baroody and J. L. M. Wilkins, "The Development of Informal Counting, Number, and Arithmetic Skills and Concepts," in *Mathematics in the Early Years*. Edited by J. V. Copley. (Reston, VA: National Council of Teachers of Mathematics (NCTM), 1999).

10. P. Munn, "Symbolic Function in Preschoolers," in *The Development of Mathematical Skills*. Edited by C. Donlan (East Sussex, UK: Psychology Press Ltd., 1998).

11. K. Wynn, "Addition and Subtraction by Human Infants," *Nature* 358 (1992): 749–50.

12. P. Starkey, "The Early Development of Numerical Reasoning," *Cognition* 43, no. 2 (1992): 93–126.

13. R. S. Siegler, "The Perils of Averaging Data Over Strategies: An Example from Children's Addition," *Journal of Experimental Psychology: General* 116, no. 3 (1987): 250–64.

14. O. Zur and R. Gelman, "Young Children Can Add and Subtract by Predicting and Checking," *Early Childhood Research Quarterly* 19 (2004): 121–37.

15. G. D. Coates and V. Thompson, "Involving Parents of Four- and Five-Year-Olds in Their Children's Mathematics Education: The Family Math Experience," in *Mathematics in the Early Years*. Edited by J. V. Copley (Reston, VA: National Council of Teachers of Mathematics 1999).

16. R. Gelman and R. Baillargeon, "A Review of Some Piagetian Concepts," in *Handbook of Child Psychology*, Vol. 3. Edited by J. H. Flavell and E. M. Markman (New York: Wiley, 1983), 167–230.

17. S. S. Smith, 2006, *Early Childhood Mathematics* 3rd ed. (Boston, MA: Pearson Education, Inc., 2006).

18. A. Klein and P. Starkey, "Fostering Preschool Children's Mathematical Knowledge: Findings from the Berkeley Math Readiness Project," in *Engaging Young Children in Mathematics: Standards for Early Childhood Mathematics Education*. Edited by D. H. Clements, J. Samara, and A. M. Dibiase (Mahwah, NJ: Lawrence Erlbaum Associates, 2004).

19. A. Klein and P. J. Starkey. "Fostering Preschool Children's Mathematical Knowledge: Findings from the Berkeley Math Readiness Project," in *Engaging Young Children in Mathematics: Standards for Early Childhood Mathematics Education*. Edited by D. H. Clements, J. Samara, and A. M. Dibiase (Hillsdale, NJ: Lawrence Erlbaum, 2004).

20. D. H. Clements and M. Stephan, 2004, "Measurement in Pre-K to Grade 2 Mathematics," in *Engaging Young Children in Mathematics: Standards for Early Childhood Mathematics Education*. Edited by D. H. Clements, J. Samara, and A. M. Dibiase (Mahwah, NJ: Lawrence Erlbaum Associates, 2004).

21. T. Nunes, P. Light, and J. Mason, "Tools for Thought: The Measurement of Length and Area," *Learning and Instruction* 3 (1993): 39–54.

22. D. H. Clements, "Geometric and Spatial Thinking in Young Children," in *Mathematics in the Early Years*. Edited by J. V. Copley (Reston, VA: National Council of Teachers of Mathematics, 1999).

23. D. H. Clements, "Geometric and Spatial Thinking in Early Childhood Education," in *Engaging Young Children in Mathematics: Standards for Early Childhood Mathematics Education*. Edited by D. H. Clements, J. Samara, and A. M. Dibiase (Mahwah, NJ: Lawrence Erlbaum Associates, 2004).

24. National Council of Teachers of Mathematics (NCTM), *Principles and Standards for School Mathematics* (Reston, VA: Author, 2000).

25. D. H. Clements, "Geometric and Spatial Thinking in Young Children," in *Mathematics in the Early Years*. Edited by J. V. Copley (Reston, VA: National Council of Teachers of Mathematics, 1999).

26. D. H. Clements, "Geometric and Spatial Thinking in Young Children," in *Mathematics in the Early Years*. Edited by J. V. Copley (Reston, VA: National Council of Teachers of Mathematics, 1999).

27. P. A. Alexander, C. S. White, and M. Daugherty, "Analogical Reasoning and Early Mathematics Learning," in *Mathematical Reasoning: Analogies, Metaphors, and Images*. Edited by L. D. English (Mahwah, NJ: Lawrence Erlbaum Associates, 1997).

Appendix A

The California Early Learning and Development System

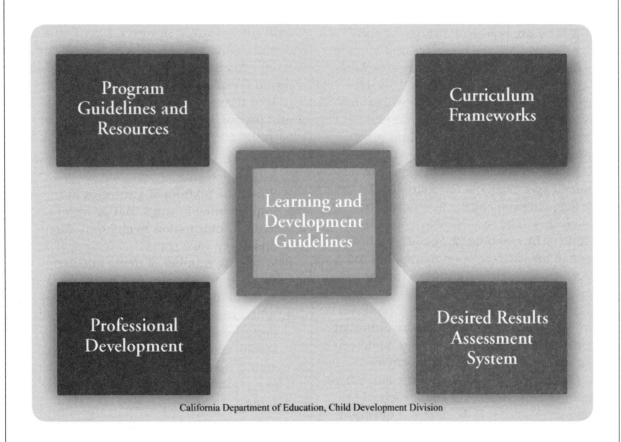

California Department of Education, Child Development Division

Appendix B

Reflections on Research: Phonological Awareness

The phonological awareness substrand in the language and literacy domain of the *California Preschool Learning Foundations, Volume I*, focuses on four levels of sound *complexity* (words, syllables, onsets and rimes, and phonemes) and three kinds of sound-unit *manipulation* (blending, segmenting, and deleting). Although segmenting is not named specifically in foundation **2.1** or **2.2**, children engage in segmenting when they take two-syllable words apart orally or by clapping (**2.1**) and as a first step in all onset deletion manipulations (**2.2**). Completely absent from the list of manipulations in the *California Preschool Learning Foundations Volume 1*, however, are (1) *detecting* and *producing* words that begin with the same sound and (2) detecting and producing words that rhyme.

During the preparation of the language and literacy chapter for the *Preschool Curriculum Framework, Volume 1*, a question arose as to whether it was necessary to restrict the suggested strategies only to those matching exactly the manipulations stipulated in the foundations. Eliminating beginning-sound and rhyme detection and beginning-sound and rhyme production was thought to restrict unnecessarily the contexts in which teachers could support children in becoming more aware of onset and rime units of sound. It would be unwise to suggest the use of detection and production strategies, in addition to the strategies suggested by the foundations, if doing so were inconsistent with the research. However, based on a comprehensive review, the writers of the language and literacy chapter for the *California Preschool Curriculum Framework* judged that the use of sound-detection and production strategies is consistent with the research:

1. When the additional strategies are used as supplements.
2. When the additional strategies are implemented in ways that provide explicit information to children about onset and rime units.
3. When the number of items in detection activities are limited to only two or three items.
4. When words used in beginning sound-detection activities have a single consonant onset rather than a beginning sound that is part of a consonant blend (e.g., *back* or *ball* rather than *black* or *brag).*

This statement includes a discussion of the research base that led to limiting sound-unit manipulations in the *California Preschool Learning Foundations, Volume I*, to blending and deleting. An understanding of this research base helps to ensure that the supplemental strategies are viewed as such—additions to and not replacements for the strategies that relate directly to the *California Preschool Learning Foundations, Volume I*. A discussion of the research base also helps to ensure that teachers' use of the supplemental detection and production strategies is closer to the approaches suggested in the *Preschool Curriculum Framework, Volume 1,* than to approaches teachers might have used in the past. Before the discussion of this research, a brief overview is provided of the sound units and manipulations that are found in phonological awareness activities.

Overview of Sound Units and Manipulations

Three main levels of *sound-unit* complexity are commonly recognized: syllables, onsets and rimes, and phonemes. Words are also sometimes included as a distinct unit of sound. For example, some phonological awareness activities at the word level require children to segment sentences into their individual words by clapping.[1, 2] Other activities involve the manipulation of words that make up compound words (e.g., blending *sun* and *shine* to make *sunshine;* deleting *sun* from *sunshine* to leave just the word *shine).* The two words in most compound words typically have just one syllable. Thus, these word-level activities involve the manipulation of syllable-size units of sound. In contrast, other syllable-level phonological activities involve the manipulation of only parts of words (e.g., children blend the two syllables, *ba* and *be,* to create the word *baby).* Word-level sound units are the easiest of all for children to manipulate. Syllables are easier to manipulate than are onset and rime units, and onset and rime units are easier to manipulate than are phonemes.

In addition to levels of sound-unit complexity, there are commonly recognized levels of sound-unit *manipulation—* levels of what children are asked to do with sound units. These manipulations include blending (synthesizing); detecting (matching); segmenting and deleting (analyzing); and producing (involves segmenting, deleting, and substituting). Blending is easier than segmenting, and segmenting is easier than deleting. Production is harder than any of these, and so may be the difficulty level of detection such as when more than two or three items are included in a detection activity.

Problems in Measuring Onset–Rime Sensitivity with Rhyme Production

In some research studies, virtually all three-year-olds performed "at floor" (i.e., could not do the tasks at all) on rhyme detection and production, and many four-year-olds also did relatively poorly.[3, 4, 5, 6, 7, 8] Moreover, in a meta-analysis conducted to determine whether phonological sensitivity at the onset–rime and phoneme levels are distinctly different kinds of phonological sensitivity or just different ways to probe the same basic skill in children of different ages, Anthony and Lonigan encountered problems when they included data from rhyme-production tasks in their analyses.[9]

The Anthony and Lonigan meta-analysis was based on four studies, each of which provided data from at least two measures of both rhyme and phoneme sensitivity. Anthony and Lonigan discovered that data from rhyme-production measures produced different results in the models they tested than did other measures of rhyme sensitivity. The problem stemmed from "floor effects" on the rhyme-production measures. In other words, many children demonstrated little or no phonological awareness (performed at floor) on the rhyme-production tasks, but they performed better on other measures of onset–rime sensitivity. When rhyme-production data were excluded from the analyses, leaving only data from rhyme-similarity and -oddity tasks (i.e., detection tasks), or onset–rime blending, Anthony and Lonigan found a better fit to a model that answered their question.

Why are rhyming-word and beginning-sound production tasks hard for young children? First, they require a fairly good vocabulary. Second, they depend on a relatively high level of cognitive skill. For example, rhyme *production* requires children to search their memories for words that might rhyme with a target word they are given. The child must hold the target word in mind and focus on its rime unit while retrieving words from memory. To focus on the rime unit, the child must segment the target word's onset from its rime. The child also must segment each word retrieved into its onset and rime parts and then compare the retrieved word's rime unit to the target word's rime unit. In a rhyme-similarity *detection* task, the tester pronounces the target word and then the tester reads three or four items, only one of which rhymes with the target word. In a rhyme-oddity *detection* task, the tester pronounces three or four words and the child must tell which word does *not* rhyme with the others. These detection tasks would be especially challenging for children who have a small vocabulary because, without familiarity with the words in a task, it is hard to remember them. If the words are not remembered, their sound structures cannot be compared.

In summary, if a child does not have an adequate vocabulary or a sufficient cognitive skill, the child cannot demonstrate whatever onset–rime sensitivity he or she might actually have in phonological awareness activities that involve detection-and-production manipulations.

It is no wonder that three-year-olds cannot perform these mental gymnastics at all or that many four-year-olds find them a formidable challenge unless the number of items in a detection task is reduced to only two or three from the typical four.[10, 11]

Implications for Instruction

The challenges inherent in rhyme- and beginning-sound detection and production tasks have implications not only for assessment but also for instruction. Suppose a teacher asks, "Can you think of words that rhyme with *boat*?" Suppose further that one child in the small group says *coat,* and the teacher says, "Yes, you are right: *Boat* and *coat* rhyme." Further suppose that another child says *goat,* and the teacher says: "Yes, *goat* also rhymes with *boat.*" The other four children in the small group do not seem to know how to play this game (i.e., they do not offer ideas). One may (and should) ask whether there is any instructional benefit to the children who cannot think of words to rhyme with *boat.* A similar pattern of response occurs when the teacher asks children to think of more words that begin with the same sound as the target word provided. A few children respond; the others do not.

What is the likelihood that the non-responding children understood *why* the teacher said that *coat* and *goat* were correct rhyming word matches for the target word, *boat?* What is the likelihood that they *will learn how* to make correct, rhyming word matches from listening to a few other children produce ideas and to the teacher who says "only these are good matches"? The likelihood is probably low if this is the only support they receive in learning to become aware of onset–rime sound units. The same would be true of a beginning-sound production exercise. Children who are not responding would probably gain little understanding or skill by listening to the teacher's lesson.

To *benefit* from listening as a rhyme- or beginning-sound production activity proceeds, a child must be able to segment the onset and rime units in both the target and the child-produced words, compare the words' rime or onset portions, and conclude that they are the same. If the child cannot yet engage in this kind of sound analysis, which is probably a fairly safe assumption when a child does not participate, unless personality or other individual characteristics can clearly account for the child's behavior, it is doubtful that listening to what transpires during a rhyme-production activity, *conducted in the way just described*, will help the child build sound-analysis skill.

The same process is required for a child to understand a rhyme-oddity or -similarity detection task.[12] Perhaps, over time, after having listened to multiple examples of target words and words that match with them (i.e., rhyme with or begin with the same sound), a child will begin to figure out what is going on. That is, a child might, through the power of insight, figure out which parts in the matching words in each task are the ones that sound the same. Good instruction, however, should reduce the need for individual children to depend on their insight to learn what teachers can teach them more easily and in a shorter period of time. Relying on the child's insight to produce the learning of interest also assumes that a child who does not yet understand *will continue to attend closely* to a task for a long period of time (i.e., across weeks and even months) even though the child does not understand what is going on. This is asking a lot—perhaps too much—from young children.

Thus, using many strategies that focus primarily on blending, segmenting, and deleting manipulations with onset–rime units rather than using many strategies that focus primarily on detection and production makes good sense and is consistent with the research.

A question can be asked, though, about whether a teacher's onset–rime options must be restricted only to strategies that use blending, segmenting, and deletion. To answer this question, several other questions must be considered:

1. What might be the likely effect of children's experiences in the blending, segmenting, and deletion of onset and rime units on children's ability to engage in detection and production tasks?
2. Must levels of task complexity used in instruction be limited to those typically used in research studies or for individual child assessments that are used in program evaluation?
3. Does the possibility for teacher scaffolding in instructional strategies matter in determining whether detection or production strategies are of benefit to children's learning? (Scaffolding should not be provided in an assessment situation, because the idea is to find out what the child knows or can do. Scaffolding may and should be provided in instruction, because the idea in that context is to support the child in figuring out and learning what to do.)

Children's Skill in Detection and Production

Strategies that involve preschoolers in blending, segmenting, and deleting onset and rime units should help them acquire some of the very skills that are needed to understand beginning-sound and rhyming-word detection and production activities. The load on processing skills of the kind that were described in the earlier discussion of sound detection and production tasks is reduced when any part of the processing becomes more automatic. Thus, as children become more skilled at segmenting onset and rime units of words, through strategies that focus directly on teaching children to notice and manipulate these units, the processing demands of the detection and production tasks (in which onset and rime segmentation is required) should also become a bit easier.

Preschool programs also provide strong support to help children develop vocabulary. In time, perhaps by early in the spring of the preschool year (for four-year-olds), increases in children's vocabularies should also be at least approaching the level needed to engage in rhyming-word and beginning-sound detection and production. An increase in vocabulary not only provides more words in memory from which a child can draw, but also shifts the child's focus in the task. If a child must spend less time on retrieving words from memory, the child can spend more time on making the necessary comparisons between the sound units in the words.

As stated in Chapter 1, a curriculum framework provides general principles and strategies for planning and implementing curriculum. The framework is written to apply to a variety of curricula. In contrast, a specific curriculum often defines a sequence of strategies for teachers to follow. To support children's developing phonological awareness, it is useful for teachers to plan a sequence of instructional activities within their specific curriculum. Although the development of phonological awareness skills

in children occurs in an overlapping manner rather than in stages (i.e., a child acquires beginning awareness of smaller linguistic units before having mastered awareness and manipulations of larger linguistic units), the sequencing of instructional tasks still needs to take into account the level of cognitive processing (i.e., the kind of manipulation) required. Segmenting a sound unit from the beginning of a word (e.g., a word in a compound word, a syllable in a word, or a single consonant onset from the rime of a syllable) is harder than blending two words, two syllables, or onset and rime units. Deletion is harder than segmenting, assuming the size of the sound unit remains constant. Production tasks are typically the most difficult manipulation. For example, one approach to rhyming-word production involves the maintenance of the rime unit while segmenting, deleting, and then replacing the onset. That is, a child first creates a word by segmenting and then deleting the onset in the target word and then adding a new onset. The child then compares the word created with items in the child's vocabulary to see whether it is a word. If the child realizes that sound play games do not require real words, the child does not search the vocabulary store to see whether a real word has been created. Nevertheless, sound segmentation and deletion are required before the child adds a new onset each time to the stable rime unit. A child without those skills is not likely to participate in either rhyming-word production activities or beginning-sound production activities. It is essential for teachers to understand when to schedule the higher-level activities during the preschool year and how to scaffold the tasks when first using them.

Detection manipulations (i.e., matching) of rhyming words and beginning sounds can also be quite difficult for preschoolers if too many items are used in activities. For example, it is relatively easy for children to detect whether the two words provided in a task rhyme or do not rhyme or begin with the same sound or not. On the other hand, if preschoolers are given a rhyme-detection task with a target word and three additional words, only one of which rhymes with the target or begins with the same sound, they often flounder.[13, 14]

Instructional Options for Reducing Task Difficulty

In most research studies of detection of rhyme or beginning sound, tasks presented to children have included four items. For example, in rhyme-similarity detection tasks, there is a target word and three words to compare with it, with only one of these matching. In rhyme oddity tasks, four items are presented, with one of the four "the odd one out" (i.e., not rhyming with the others). These tasks are much easier when three items are used instead of four. In fact, in one study,[15] researchers reduced the number of items from four to three. This change made the task suitable for the four-year-olds in the study. Five-year-olds in the study continued to get four items. Interestingly, the average scores of the four-year olds on this task were a bit higher than the average scores for the five-year-olds in the study, even on task items that focused on middle and ending sounds, not just on beginning sounds. What a difference a little simplification in a task makes when it reduces the memory and processing demands! Of course, teachers can reduce the number of items even more in an instructional context, such as by providing judgment tasks that have

only two items (e.g., "Do bat and cat rhyme?"). In one successful intervention study with four-year-olds, two-item judgment tasks were used for rhyme-detection tasks.[16]

Scaffolding in Instruction, Not in Assessment

It is instructive to return to the classroom example considered earlier in which the teacher asked, "Can you think of words that rhyme with *boat?*" One child in the small group answered *coat,* and the teacher said, "Yes, you are right: *Boat* and *coat* rhyme." Then, another child said *goat,* and the teacher said, "Yes, *goat* also rhymes with *boat.*" The other four children in the small group did not offer ideas.

The teacher in the example did not offer any scaffolding. Scaffolding involves the performance of some task elements by the teacher when a child is just beginning to learn how to do something. Over time, as the child is able to do more parts of the task independently, the teacher removes some of the scaffolding, and then all.

The examples in the detection and production strategies that have been added to the curriculum framework have the teacher isolating the beginning sound (i.e., the onset) or the rime unit that is shared across words (e.g., when looking at an alphabet book and identifying the names of pictures on a page [page 141] or when talking about some of the words in a song [pages 134–135], such as "Down by the Bay"), or the teacher uses a combination of strategies (e.g., the teacher asks for the children's *judgments* about two spoken words the teacher offers). For example, the teacher does not say, "That's right; *care* sounds like *bear* and *hair,"* and leave it at that. Instead, the teacher is very explicit (e.g., *"Care.* Yes, the last part of *care* is /air/, just like the last parts of *b-ear* and *h-air."* [pages 134–135]).

In some examples, the teacher provides onset and rime segments for the children to blend that will produce a rhyming word for a new verse in a song, and the teacher also segments into onset and rime units any whole words from a song that children have recalled (e.g., the one that rhymes with another word in the song the teacher has stated). In those cases, the teacher is embedding blended and segmented manipulations in a rhyming-word context while not relying on the children to produce rhyming words by themselves. In the rare case of a child producing a rhyming word, the teacher does not simply accept it but makes explicit why it "works" by using a demonstration in which the word's rime unit is separated from its onset and compared to other words that have the same rime unit (page 135).

Rationale for Rhyme- and Beginning-Sound Production Strategies

It is fun and empowering to notice the rhyming words in a song or a poem, and it is even more fun to play with this kind of language and *create* it. By using traditional rhyme activities as opportunities to embed detection and production opportunities, teachers give children opportunities to "run with it" by producing words that rhyme with others or that begin with the same sound. Admittedly, the ultimate goal of phonological awareness activities is to help children develop the skills they will need in learning to read and spell. It seems a

shame, though, not to provide an intermediate-level activity to which children might apply their budding phonological skill. The practice of engaging children in beginning rhyme-word production activities *without scaffolding,* such as has been typical in traditional rhyme activities in preschool classrooms, assumes that the children already possess basic sound-unit manipulation skills (i.e., blending, segmenting, and deletion skills described in language and literacy foundations 2.1 and 2.2). In fact, many four-year-old children in a typical classroom may be unable to manipulate sound units within words independently (without adult assistance) for much of the preschool year. However, if traditional rhyme activities are carefully scaffolded for *most of the preschool year* and if those activities supplement a major focus on the use of other sound-unit manipulations (i.e., blending, segmenting, and deleting), such experiences surely would promote many children's independent engagement in more traditional rhyme activities (without scaffolding) later in the preschool year.

Preschoolers also typically engage in singing songs and saying poems that contain rhyming words and words that begin with the same sound (i.e., songs and poems with alliteration). Focusing more intentionally on rhyming words and words that begin with the same sound by using words found in a familiar poem or song is potentially useful in nudging children toward applying the skills that they develop from more isolated blending and segmenting instructional activities to these other, more naturalistic contexts. Moreover, children tend to become more alert to the language used in songs and poems, if these contexts are used to provide some of the phonological awareness instruction for the class. Greater alertness to words in the songs that children sing and to the poems that children say might, in turn, contribute to the development of children's sound awareness.

If, on the other hand, teachers do nothing intentionally to link contexts that provide explicit instruction in phonological awareness with contexts in which children hear language with the relevant sound units actually used, children might gain less from singing songs and saying poems than they otherwise could. Although wise teachers do not rely too much or even primarily on children's own insights to produce some kinds of learning, they also "stack the deck" to nudge children into thinking about their experiences, including the language in the songs they sing or poems they say, for they know that learning to think is important and that children need various kinds of opportunities in which to engage in thinking.

Using children's names in a beginning-sound strategy, for example, in transition activities, might help children to learn more about their names and to use their names as a model for learning more about words in general. Of course, blending, segmenting, and deletion tasks can be used with children's names in transitions and also in other instructional contexts. Using beginning-sound detection with children's names ("If your name starts with /s/, you may go wash your hands") *simply adds to* the teacher's repertoire. Saying the children's names with another sound substituted for their first sounds, as might be done after singing "Willoughby-Wallaby-Woo," also adds to the teacher's repertoire. The more ideas a teacher has for using children's names, the more likely children will learn about the sounds and letters in their names and to link the two.

Summary

The addition of detection and production strategy contexts to the phonological awareness strategies that align exactly with the phonological awareness foundations has been done in ways that are consistent with the foundations. The additional strategies are supplemental to other strategies, and their instructional design differs from the design of detection and production activities commonly used by preschool teachers in the past.

Processes of teacher change must also be taken into account in curriculum frameworks whereas they need not be with the learning foundations. The information in Volume I of both the *California Preschool Learning Foundations* and the *California Preschool Curriculum Framework* is likely somewhat new to many preschool teachers. When asked to change teaching practices, teachers need to know in what ways, if any, their past practices relate to newly recommended practices. By including some strategies in the chapter that are similar to teachers' past practices but *altering them in ways that are more aligned* with current research, teachers can better understand how past and current strategies are similar and also different. In this way, teachers can be helped to adopt new strategies even while retaining, with adaptations, some of the strategies they have used in the past. This makes the change process more comfortable and thus more likely to occur, which is not an inconsequential consideration at a time when so much is being asked of preschool teachers.

Endnotes

1. I. Lundberg, J. Frost, and O. Peterson, "Effects of an Extensive Program for Stimulating Phonological Awareness in Preschool Children," *Reading Research Quarterly* 23, no. 3 (1988): 263–84.

2. M. J. Adams and others, *Phonemic Awareness in Young Children* (Baltimore: Brookes, 1998).

3. M. MacLean, P. Bryant, and L. Bradley, "Rhymes, Nursery Rhymes, and Reading in Early Childhood," *Merrill-Palmer Quarterly* 33 (1987): 255–82.

4. C. Chaney, "Language Development, Metalinguistic Skills, and Print Awareness in 3-Year-Old Children," *Applied Psycholinguistics* 13 (1992): 485–514.

5. V. Muter, C. Hulme, and M. Snowling, *Phonological Abilities Test.* London: Psychological Corporation, 1997.

6. V. Muter and others, "Segmentation, Not Rhyming, Predicts Early Progress in Learning to Read," *Experimental Child Psychology* 65 (1997): 370–98.

7. T. A. Roberts, "Effects of Alphabet-Letter Instruction on Young Children's Word Recognition," *Journal of Educational Psychology,* 95, no. 1 (2003): 41–51.

8. J. L. Anthony and C. J. Lonigan, "The Nature of Phonological Awareness: Converging Evidence from Four Studies of Preschool and Early Grade School Children," *Journal of Educational Psychology* 96 (2004): 43–55.

9. J. L. Anthony and C. J. Lonigan, "The Nature of Phonological Awareness: Converging Evidence from Four Studies of Preschool and Early Grade School Children," *Journal of Educational Psychology* 96 (2004): 43–55.

10. L. Bradley and P. Bryant, *Rhyme and Reason in Reading and Spelling* (Ann Arbor, MI: University of Michigan Press, 1985).

11. B. M. Phillips, J. Clancy-Menchetti, and C. J. Lonigan, "Successful Phonological Awareness Instruction with Preschool Children," *Topics in Early Childhood Special Education* 28, no. 1 (1985): 3–17.

12. H. A. Yopp, "The Validity and Reliability of Phonemic Awareness Tests," *Reading Research Quarterly* 23, no. 2 (1988): 159–77.

13. L. Bradley and P. E. Bryant, *Rhyme and Reason in Reading and Spelling* (Ann Arbor, MI: University of Michigan Press, 1985).

14. L. M. Justice and others, "Emergent Literacy Intervention for Vulnerable Preschoolers: Relative Effects of Two Approaches," *American Journal of Speech-Language Pathology* 12 (2003): 320–32.

15. L. Bradley and P. Bryant, *Rhyme and Reason in Reading and Spelling* (Ann Arbor, MI: University of Michigan Press, 1985).

16. L. M. Justice and others, "Emergent Literacy Intervention for Vulnerable Preschoolers: Relative Effects of Two Approaches," *American Journal of Speech-Language Pathology* 12 (2003): 320–32.

Appendix C

Reflections on Research: Alphabetics and Word/Print Recognition

The Alphabetics and Word/Print Recognition substrand specifies that children at around 60 months of age are able to recognize their own name and other common words in print (**3.1**), to match more than half of upper-case and lowercase letter names to the printed forms (**3.2**), and to begin to recognize that letters have sounds (**3.3**). Three examples of child behavior for foundation **3.3** are provided in the *California Preschool Learning Foundations:*

- The child makes the correct sound for the first letter in his name.
- The child says the correct letter sound while pointing to the letter in a book.
- The child indicates the correct picture when presented with four pictures—dog barking, car horn honking, letter k, and letter n—and when asked, "Which of these make these sounds: bow-wow, honk, k (letter sound), n (letter sound)?"

The foundations do not describe what children are expected to *understand* when they "begin to recognize letter sounds." That is, they do not distinguish between children who know some letter-sound associations (i.e., can say the sounds "that letters have"), but lack any realization that these sounds are heard in spoken words, and children who know some letter-sound associations and also realize that these sounds are heard in spoken words. Given the absence of information, a reader could reasonably make any number of assumptions.

Assumption 1: Preschoolers are expected to be able to bring the three areas of skill together, on their own, to develop the understanding.

Assumption 2: In the preschool years, developing phonological awareness, letter name knowledge, and knowledge of some specific associations between letters and isolated sounds (i.e., "The letter *B* makes the /*b*/ sound"), in isolation, is enough.

Assumption 3: Children need to be helped to understand the relationships between letters in printed words and sounds in spoken words, knowing that only preliminary levels of this understanding will be developed in preschool. Fuller understanding will come during kindergarten, not during preschool.

ASSUMPTION 1

Children Can Put the Pieces Together If They Have a Good Grasp of the Pieces

Some kindergarten and preschool children might indeed put these pieces together by themselves. Other kindergarten and preschool children, however, and perhaps most, do not seem to arrive at this insight by themselves. A surer approach to supporting children in understanding the relationship between letters in printed words and sounds in spoken words requires the intentional use of strategies that link letters directly to their sounds in the context of spoken words.

Research demonstrating the benefit of explicitly linking letters to sounds in words to children's later reading or spelling of words has been conducted at the kindergarten level, not the preschool level.[1, 2, 3, 4] It would be safe to assume that preschoolers have less power of insight—less ability to put things together on their own—than kindergarten children have. It is also probably safe to assume that kindergarten children typically have higher levels of skill than preschoolers in each of the separate knowledge and skill areas—letter name knowledge, phonological awareness, and letter-sound associations. In fact, in most but not all of the relevant intervention studies,[5] letters were linked to sounds in words only after children had been engaged in games and other exercises through which they developed phonological awareness, letter names, and letter-sound associations at a fairly high level. It is doubtful that children would typically reach similarly high levels in each of these areas during the preschool years.

The question, then, is whether preschool teachers should do anything at all to help children begin to develop the preliminary understanding that letters in printed words are related to and represent sounds in spoken words. Or should teachers leave this learning entirely for the kindergarten year or to insight, should a preschool child use it. Another question is whether all of the individual knowledge and skill areas—alphabet letter knowledge, phonological awareness, and some letter-sound associations—must be at a high level of development

before it is appropriate to provide heavily scaffolded support to preschoolers in linking letters to sounds in spoken words.

The preschool curriculum framework suggests a few strategies, at the preschool level, for linking letters to sounds in spoken words. The assumption is that teachers might do this most appropriately and productively in situations involving individual children who have a high level of individual literacy skill development in the three areas described above. A few other strategies, however, involve appropriately scaffolded situations that include other children in the class who may not be at the same high level of literacy skill development. The purpose of this discussion is to provide a rationale for including those strategies with appropriate support.

ASSUMPTION 2

Appropriate Expectations and Strategies for Preschoolers

There are some contexts in a preschool setting where a teacher can make a decision about whether to link letters in printed words to sounds in spoken words. For example, a child mentions to the teacher that both his name and a classmate's begin with the same letter. The teacher might say, "Yes, you are right about that," and stop at that. Or, the teacher might say: "Yes, your name and Brian's both start with the letter B, because **B**rian and **B**randon both start with the /b/ sound." Similarly, when sharing an alphabet book with children, a preschool teacher might name only the alphabet letter that is featured on a page, identifying and discussing with children the items pictured on the page (e.g., broccoli, banana, and beet on the B page). Or, after doing these things, a teacher might say, "All of these things—**b**roccoli, **b**anana, **b**eet—begin with the /*b*/ sound. When we write the /*b*/ sound, we use the letter B. That's why all of these foods are on the B page of our book." A teacher also has some choices when a child making a birthday card at the writing center says, "How do you make *Mommy?* I need it for my card." A teacher might answer simply by dictating the letters needed or by writing the word for the child to copy. Or, the teacher might go beyond simply dictating or writing out the letters to explain why some of the letters are selected. For example, to start, the teacher might say, "*Mommy* starts with the /*m*/ sound—**M**ommy—and we use the letter M to write that sound." The teacher might dictate the rest of the letters without linking any to a sound in the word *Mommy* or might dictate all but the final *y*, and then link the last sound in the word to this final letter.

In all of these instances, the teacher adds the information about the relationship between letters in printed words and sounds in spoken words as an explanation. The first explanation is about *why* different words begin with the same letter (e.g., Brian and Brandon). The second explanation is first about *how* the pictured items on a page of an alphabet book all go together—have the same first sound—and then *why* they are grouped with a specific alphabet letter—it is the one used to write this sound. The third instance is about *why* the teacher is dictating *this* specific letter and not some other letter as the first and last letters needed to write *Mommy*.

ASSUMPTION 3

Preschool Teachers Offer Explanations; Preschoolers Begin to Understand

In each instance described for linking letters to sounds in words, the teacher has a general habit of explaining the world to preschool children. Situations calling out for an explanation arise frequently in the preschool setting. For example, a child asks why lids must be put on the paint cups at the end of each day. The teacher explains: "We put lids on our paint cups because the paints would dry out if we left the cups open. The water in the paint would evaporate into the air. Would you like to put a little paint in a small cup and leave it uncovered overnight to see what happens?" Or, a child on the playground notices his shadow and announces it. The teacher comments and explains: "Yes, I see your shadow, and I see that the sun is up above and behind you. I'm going to stand over here and have you turn around to face me. Do you see your shadow in front of you now? Where is it?" "Yes, it's behind you now. Your body is blocking the sunlight from reaching the ground, and that's what makes a shadow." Or, a child playing with a magnet and some paper clips inside a closed, plastic jar, says, "Look! Look! It works from out here." The teacher comments and explains: "Yes, I see that your magnet is attracting the paper clips that you put inside the plastic bottle even though it's not touching them. Magnets have a force that goes through things. Do you feel the force pulling on the paper clips?"

Of course, a wise teacher knows that a preschool child would not understand fully the explanations provided in a single instance or even after two or three or even ten. The wise teacher also knows that a preschool child would likely not provide a very good explanation, if any at all, to someone else, if asked for one. Even after multiple experiences in the physical contexts described, all of which allow the child "to see" what happens, teachers would not expect a child to have full understanding. An important question, though, is whether the child might develop *any* understanding from such explanations and whether these preliminary, incomplete, and vague notions might serve as important first steps in the long journey toward her full development. Another question, apart from any particular understanding that a child might develop from adult explanations, even at preliminary levels, is whether there might be a general benefit to children from adult explanations. For example, might this kind of adult behavior convey a general idea to the child that things function, as the child finds them, *for a reason?* Might knowing this affect the child's later learning of specifics?

Definitive answers to these questions are not easy to find, although a wide variety of research suggests that providing explanations to children is beneficial, assuming of course that they are calibrated to a child's level of understanding. For example, in one study[6] of mothers' language to 20- and 30-month-old children, the researchers suggest that some of a mother's comments, for example, about animals, might serve to guide children to global understandings, such as the fact that some things that do not look very much alike on the surface often have something in common. In quite a different study, this time with five-year-olds, researchers found that higher levels of support (i.e., semantic and physical explanations) provided by parents for the rare words they used were associated with higher levels of vocabulary development.[7] Other researchers have found that parental use of science process talk (i.e., "discussions of the how's and whys of what was happening"), in conjunction with their child's magnet play, was more strongly related to kindergarten literacy measures than were other kinds of parental talk that did not include explanations (i.e., process-level talk).[8]

Additional examples could be cited, but these are sufficient to make the basic point: It appears that explanations provided about a range of things in the young child's physical and social worlds are reasonably beneficial to young children's learning, not harmful. It is also fairly obvious that adults often do not (and should not) expect immediate and specific results from these explanations. Giving explanations is simply a way that some adults interact with children, a way that, if responsive to the child's interests and level of understanding, appears to be beneficial.

Rationale for Including Strategies That Link Printed Words to Spoken Words

Although young children may only partially understand teachers' explanations, it seemed unwise to avoid addressing in the *California Preschool Curriculum Framework, Volume 1,* how letters in printed words are related to sounds in spoken words. Rather, strategies that offer explanations of the links between printed words and spoken words were included to show how preschool teachers can foster a beginning understanding without expecting immediate and specific results.

The majority of the strategies in the Alphabetics and Word/Print Recognition substrand focus on supporting children in learning to recognize and name alphabet letters and to recognize their names and other common words. Many different strategies, spanning a wide range of contexts, are provided for these two foundations (**3.1** and **3.2**). In addition to these strategies, however, relatively few strategies are provided in the preschool curriculum framework to support foundation **3.3,** in ways that might lead a child to begin to "recognize that letters have sounds" and also to develop a preliminary understanding of what we mean when we say that "letters have sounds."

The strategies for supporting foundation **3.3** are embedded in broad contexts, such as in the reading of an alphabet book (page 141), in helping children transition from one activity to the next (pages 141–142), or in situations in which children are writing (pages 161–162). In many instances, the description or the discussion of the strategy makes clear that the teacher's decision to explain the relationship between letters and sounds in words is prompted by a child's behavior and, further, that the explanation itself is adapted to the child's level of understanding.

There is always a risk, of course, that a teacher might misunderstand the intent of including these strategies and assume, incorrectly, that the expectation is for all children to leave preschool with some understanding of that "letters have sounds." The intent, however, was not to suggest that any understanding is expected to accompany children's displays of behavior indicating that they have "begun to recognize that letters have sounds." It seems perfectly reasonable to assume that children *will* develop this understanding in kindergarten or that they *should.* On the other hand, it also seems reasonable to assume that some children between the ages of 48 and 60 months can be supported in gaining some preliminary understanding of how letters are related to sounds in spoken words. It also seems reasonable to suggest to teachers, who are inclined to explain the world to preschool children, that they can extend this inclination to the world of print if they use appropriate strategies. Doing so might be of benefit to children's learning, and there is not a good reason to believe that the strategies suggested will do any harm.

Endnotes

1. E. W. Ball and B. A. Blachman, "Does Phoneme Awareness Training in Kindergarten Make a Difference in Early Word Recognition and Developmental Spelling?" *Reading Research Quarterly* 26, no. 1 (1991): 49–66.

2. L. Bradley and P. Bryant, *Rhyme and Reason in Reading and Spelling* (Ann Arbor, MI: University of Michigan Press, 1985).

3. L. C. Ehri and L. S. Wilce, "Does Learning to Spell Help Beginners to Learn Words?" *Reading Research Quarterly* 22, no. 1 (1987): 47–65.

4. S. A. Craig, "The Effects of an Adapted Interactive Writing Intervention on Kindergarten Children's Phonological Awareness, Spelling, and Early Reading Development: A Contextualized Approach to Instruction," *Journal of Educational Psychology* 98, no. 4 (2006): 714–31.

5. S. A. Craig, "The Effects of an Adapted Interactive Writing Intervention on Kindergarten Children's Phonological Awareness, Spelling, and Early Reading Development: A Contextualized Approach to Instruction," *Journal of Educational Psychology* 98, no. 4 (2006): 714–31.

6. S. A. Gelman and others, "Beyond Labeling: The Role of Maternal Input in the Acquisition of Richly Structured Categories," *Monographs of the Society for Research in Child Development*, Serial No. 253, 63, no. 1, 1998.

7. Z. O. Weizman and C. E. Snow, "Lexical Input as Related to Children's Vocabulary Acquisition: Effects of Sophisticated Exposure and Support for Meaning," *Developmental Psychology* 37, no. 2 (2001): 265–79.

8. P. O. Tabors, K. A. Roach, and S. Catherine, "Home Language and Literacy Environment," in *Building Literacy with Language.* Edited by D. K. Dickinson and P. O. Tabors, 111–38 (Baltimore: Brookes, 2001).

Appendix D

Resources for Teachers of Children with Disabilities or Other Special Needs

Allen, E. K., and G. E. Cowdery. 2008. *The Exceptional Child, Inclusion in Early Childhood Education* (Sixth edition). Florence, KY: Cengage Learning.

Filled with the history and research regarding the legal aspects, disabilities, and issues that are relevant to educating children with special needs, this publication addresses the approach and tools needed to provide an optimal setting for both the children and their families. Many checklists and forms are included for use within the classroom to aid educators in developing a developmentally appropriate environment. This book is useful to educators and parents/caregivers alike. http://www.delmarlearning.com/browse_product_detail.aspx?catid=31258&isbn=1418074012&cat1ID=EA&cat2ID=EA08

California Map to Inclusive Child Care

The California Map to Inclusive Child Care Project Web site, operating under the Center for Child and Family Studies at WestEd and funded by the California Department of Education's Child Development Division with a portion of the federal Child Care Development Fund Quality Improvement Allocation, includes many resources and Web links to support children with special needs. It is a comprehensive Web site devoted to inclusion and disabilities. http://www.cainclusivechildcare.org/map

Cook, R. E., M. D. Klein, and A. Tessier. 2007. *Adapting Early Childhood Curricula for Children with Special Needs* (Seventh edition). Upper Saddle River, NJ: Merrill.

The book takes a practical, "activity-based" approach that is theoretically sound and

current. It also provides ample detail related to specific intervention strategies that enhance teachers' effective use of embedded learning opportunities within daily curriculum activities and routines. Its relatively jargon-free, "readable" approach is built on evidence-based practices and is appropriate for a wide range of readers. The illustrations of techniques and strategies make it a sustainable resource long after students leave their formal education. It has always encouraged a family-centered, inclusive approach to working with young children with special needs and their families. http://www.pearsonhighered.com/educator/academic/product/0,3110,0131723812,00.html

Deiner, P. L. 2010. *Inclusive Early Childhood Education: Development, Resources, and Practice* (Fifth edition). Florence, KY: Cengage Learning.

This comprehensive special education resource book is designed to help educators navigate the early years of teaching. The text includes a coverage of disabilities as extensive as many Introduction to Special Education courses. However, it is more than a reference book. It also offers guidelines, vignettes, and hands-on program planning to prepare educators to integrate children with learning disabilities into regular classroom instruction. http://www.cengage.com/cengage/instructor.do?product_isbn=9781428320864&codeid=2F7A&disciplinenumber=29&courseid=EA08&sortby=copy&type=all_radio&codeFlag=true&maintab=About_the_Book&subtab=Overview

Early Childhood Inclusion: Focus on Change. 2001. Edited by M. J. Guralnick. Baltimore, MD: Brookes Publishing Company.

From leading experts in the field comes this important book that comprehensively evaluates early childhood inclusion over the past 25 years. Based on their research and extensive experience, the contributors examine the benefits and drawbacks of inclusion, leading influences on inclusion, and issues that face children in different environments with different developmental challenges. This timely information shows professionals, instructors, and students in early intervention and early childhood education where inclusion is today and what they need to do to move forward. The final chapter presents a national agenda for change—a framework of ideas for meeting challenges and achieving an agreed-upon set of principles and practices—in order to create optimal educational environments for all children. http://www.brookespublishing.com/store/books/guralnick-4919/index.htm

Gould, P., and J. Sullivan. 2005. *The Inclusive Early Childhood Classroom: Easy Ways to Adapt Learning Centers for All.* Upper Saddle River, NJ: Merrill.

This resource manual on how to adapt regular curriculum activities for children with special needs offers concrete suggestions that are easy to implement, giving teachers the tools to turn their classrooms into effective learning environments for all students. The goal of the authors is to help children with special needs gain the opportunity to learn new skills and concepts. Teachers, therapists, and parents learn simple modifications to help children focus on the activities, materials, and social interactions of the classroom. The modifications suggested in this book are also useful and interesting to children without special needs. This comprehensive, practical text is built on solid theory and evidence-based practices from both the fields of special education and early childhood education. http://www.pearsonhighered.com/educator/academic/product/0,3110,0131705326,00.html

Inclusion Works! Creating Child Care Programs That Promote Belonging for Children with Special Needs. 2009. Sacramento: California Department of Education.

The purpose of this publication is to provide guidance on proven strategies that promote belonging and inclusion for all children. Building on research and the experience of years of effective implementation, this handbook contains stories and examples, as well as background information and resources that support strategies for successful inclusion. By providing the benefit of high-quality care and education to all of California's children, educators will contribute to closing the achievement gap between students with disabilities and students without disabilities.

Klein, D. M., R. E. Cook, and A. M. Richardson-Gibbs. 2001 *Strategies for Including Children with Special Needs in Early Childhood Settings* (First edition). Florence, KY: Wadsworth.

This practical, hands-on text is required reading for early childhood professionals who work with children with special needs. It includes information on the most common disabilities, including cerebral palsy, Down syndrome, autism, visual impairment, and behavior disorders, as well as strategies and activities to facilitate children's participation in all components of the daily routine. It also shows how to adapt common early childhood activities for children of varying abilities to maximize their success. It uses clear and simple language to help early childhood education professionals successfully teach children with special needs. http://www.cengage.com/cengage/instructor.do?product_isbn=9780827383524&codeid=2F7A&disciplinenumber=29&courseid=EA08&sortby=copy&type=all_radio&codeFlag=false&maintab=About_the_Book&subtab=Overview

Kristal, J. 2005. *The Temperament Perspective: Working with Children's Behavioral Styles.* Baltimore, MD: Paul H. Brookes Publishing Co.

Once the basics of temperament are understood, that knowledge can be used to address children's challenging behavior and improve classroom interactions. This book is a practical guide to understanding children's individual temperaments. Guidelines on when to seek outside help are included, as well as age-specific temperament questionnaires and further readings. Based on the author's research and clinical work with more than 600 families and children at Kaiser Permanente's Temperament Program and her private practice, this book has the practical guidance needed to transform knowledge of temperament into positive interactions and better outcomes. http://www.brookespublishing.com/store/books/kristal-7918/index.htm

Mental Health in Early Intervention: Achieving Unity in Principles and Practice. 2006. Edited by G. M. Foley and J. D. Hochman. Baltimore, MD: Brookes Publishing Company.

Too often, infant mental health and early intervention are dealt with separately rather than together. Integration of these two fields is the goal of this comprehensive publication. It fully prepares readers to integrate two interdependent fields and improve practices in both. http://www.brookespublishing.com/store/books/foley-7381/index.htm

Milbourne, S., and P. Campbell. 2007. *CARA's Kit: Creating Adaptations for Routines and Activities.* Missoula, MT: The Division for Early Childhood.

This kit provides guidance for how to make adaptations for daily activities and routines so that children ages three to six can successfully participate in classroom curriculum. The teacher version contains a booklet about adaptations and a CD-ROM. http://www.dec-sped.org/index.aspx/Store/Additional_Resources

O'Brien, M. 1997. *Inclusive Child Care for Infants and Toddlers: Meeting Individual and Special Needs.* Baltimore, MD: Brookes Publishing Company.

This educational book gives child care providers helpful advice on handling daily care tasks, teaching responsively, meeting individual needs, developing rapport with parents, understanding toddlers' behavior, working with individualized family service plans, and maintaining high standards of care. Suggested play activities and intervention approaches help promote healthy development in all children. Ready-to-use quality check forms, parent report forms, and feeding/play schedules target areas in which infants and toddlers need the most help. http://www.brookespublishing.com/store/books/obrien-2967/index.htm

Sandall, S. R., and others. 2005. *DEC Recommended Practices: A Comprehensive Guide for Practical Application.* Missoula, MT: The Division for Early Childhood.

This guide contains all the helpful information found in the original recommended practices of the Division for Early Childhood, plus real-life examples and practical tips for implementation. It includes strategies for program assessment and improvement, useful checklists for parents and administrators, and an annotated list of relevant resources. http://www.dec-sped.org/index.aspx/Store/Recommended_Practices

Sandall, S. R., and I. S. Schwartz. 2008. *Building Blocks for Teaching Preschoolers with Special Needs* (Second edition). Baltimore, MD: Brookes Publishing Company.

Updated for today's educators—especially those new to inclusion—the second edition of this bestselling guide is the lifeline preschool teachers need to fully include in classrooms children with disabilities. Easy to use with any existing curriculum, including Creative Curriculum and High-Scope, Building Blocks gives educators practical, research-based inclusion strategies that promote progress in critical areas such as behavior, emergent literacy, and peer relationships. New material reflects the six years of changes in early education since the first edition. Classroom assessments, planning work sheets, and child evaluation forms are included on a CD-ROM. Through vignettes of four young children from diverse backgrounds, teachers learn examples of successful interventions. http://brookespublishing.com/store/books/sandall-69674/index.htm

Social and Emotional Health in Early Childhood: Building Bridges Between Services and Systems. 2007. Edited by D. F. Perry, R. K. Kaufmann, and J. Knitzer. Baltimore, MD: Brookes Publishing Company.

Social-emotional health is one of the most critical factors in a child's development and school readiness—a factor that depends on weaving effective mental health services into other systems and programs that support young children. Professionals will discover how to improve young children's outcomes by building sturdy bridges between mental health and medical, educational, and social services.

Brief, vivid stories throughout the book illustrate how mental health services help children and families at risk. Two extended real-life case studies give readers an inside look at effective early childhood mental health systems, including structure, financing, and outcomes evaluation. http://www.brookespublishing.com/store/books/perry-67823/index.htm

Social Competence of Young Children: Risk, Disability, and Intervention. 2007. Edited by W. H. Brown, S. L. Odom, and S. R. McConnell. Baltimore, MD: Brookes Publishing Company.

Increasing positive peer interaction can reduce future social competence problems, but how can children with developmental difficulties cultivate the social relationships they need? The most current research-based assessment and intervention strategies are detailed, along with well-matched and effective peer interaction

interventions—classroom, naturalistic, or explicit—to suit children's specific needs. http://www.brookespublishing.com/store/books/brown-69230/index.htm

Widerstrom, A. H. 2004. *Achieving Learning Goals Through Play* (Second edition). Baltimore, MD: Brookes Publishing Company.

Play is more than just fun; it is a powerful teaching tool that helps young children learn. This guide provides ready-to-use strategies for weaving individual learning goals into play throughout the school day. It was created for use with children ages two to five who have special needs—but is equally effective for typically developing children.

There is information on how play activities can help children develop cognitive, communication, motor, social, and preliteracy skills. The appendixes offer guidelines for developmentally appropriate practice, resources for including children with disabilities, and reproducible planning matrixes. http://brookespublishing.com/store/books/widerstrom-6989/index.htm

Winter, S. M. 2006. *Inclusive Early Childhood Education: A Collaborative Approach.* Upper Saddle River, NJ: Merrill.

This practical methods text has useful applications and many teaching strategies woven throughout. The book provides current information on theory and practice for inclusive education in early childhood settings. Practical information is provided about how to collaborate and communicate with families and other professionals. The interdisciplinary approach emphasizes inclusive education in early childhood contexts where cultural and linguistic diversity of children is rapidly increasing. Teachers must be culturally competent and responsive as well as sensitive to children's abilities and strengths. http://www.pearsonhighered.com/educator/academic/product/0,3110,0130423351,00.html

Glossary

Introduction

assessment. The process for obtaining information about individual children from natural observations, anecdotal records, interviews, portfolios, projects, and other sources, for the purpose of understanding the child's development and planning for curriculum intended to enhance learning and development.

culturally appropriate. Educational practice that takes into account the social and cultural contexts in which children live; culturally appropriate curriculum is attuned and responsive to family and community values, identity, language, and other culture-related factors.

interest areas. A distinct, well-stocked area divided from other parts of the classroom that focuses on a specific aspect of children's play and inquiry and that invites children to engage in self-initiated play in the company of other children.

large groups. A teacher-led gathering of a relatively large number of children, between 15 and 20 (Schickedanz 2008), with the intent of either engaging the children in discussion with one child speaking at a time and the others listening or of engaging the children in an activity in which every child participates at the same time, such as singing.

scaffolding. A process by which adults or capable peers provide supportive structures to help children learn and play. Scaffolding is helpful when children are faced with a challenge that they can solve with a simple hint, question, or prompt.

self-talk. Narrating or describing one's actions out loud when teaching or caring for a child or group of children.

small groups. A teacher-facilitated conversation or activity among a small number of children, ranging from two to ten (Schickedanz 2008). The purpose is to support children's exchange of ideas and thoughts around a topic or activity of mutual interest. The small size of the group ensures that each child's ideas and feelings are communicated and heard and enables the teacher to listen for, to observe, and to document children's ideas or emerging skills and concepts.

teacher. An adult with education and care responsibilities in an early childhood setting. Teachers include adults who interact directly with young children in preschool programs and family child care home settings. In family child care, teachers may be referred to as *caregivers.*

temperament. Traits such as activity level, intensity of emotional responses, sensitivity to stimulation, and dominant mood that contribute to an individual child's style of behaving.

Social-Emotional Development

aesthetics. The visual impression made by the colors, textures, furnishings, and other physical elements of the environment

Language and Literacy

alliteration. A series of words that begin with the same sound (e.g., soap, sun, soup, and sand).

alphabetic principle. The understanding that alphabet letters in printed words stand for sounds in spoken words.

assistive technology. Physical means of support for language that is provided to any person with visual, auditory, or motor impairments.

auditory. Perceived by hearing.

aural processing skill. The ability to understand and think about auditory input (i.e., input perceived by hearing).

blending. The process of putting linguistic units together to form a word. The sizes of the units blended vary from words (e.g., *sun–flower = sunflower),* to syllables (e.g., *ba–by = baby),* to onsets and rimes (e.g., *s-un = sun*), to phonemes (e.g., *c-a-t = cat*).

braille. A system of tactile symbols use to represent speech.

category. A group of things that have some underlying features in common (e.g., dogs, cats, and humans are all mammals because their babies are born alive, their mothers produce milk for their young, they have hair covering their bodies).

category words. Words that are not the names of individual items but of groups to which individual items belong (e.g., fruit, furniture, mammals, deciduous trees, vehicles).

decoding. The ability to convert written symbols (i.e., alphabet letters) into their spoken equivalents to produce the words the print represents. Decoding skill requires letter name knowledge, phoneme awareness, the alphabetic principle (i.e., knowing that letters represent sounds in spoken words), and knowledge of some specific letter-sound associations.

definitional vocabulary skill. The ability to explain verbally what a word means.

delete. The act of omitting a linguistic unit of a word (e.g., *catnip* without /cat/ is *nip*; *baby* without /ba/ is /be/; *cat* without /k/ is -*at*).

dictation. Oral or signed presentation of a message to someone else who writes it down.

dramatic play area. An interest area that might be called the housekeeping area, dress-up area, or kitchen area. Children engage in pretend play in the dramatic play area, often assuming roles and creating scenarios that are based on their experiences at home and in their communities.

emergent literacy. The behaviors used by young children to engage in reading and writing before they can read and write conventionally. Examples of emergent literacy behaviors include scribble writing, turning book pages pretending to read, creating pretend words, and inventing spellings, the pretend reading of directions on a soup container, and the retelling of a familiar story using the illustrations to describe the story events.

explicit instruction. Instruction in which processes are demonstrated and stated. Instruction that does not leave understanding to the learner's own reasoning or insight.

friendly explanations of words. Verbal explanations for words that are easy for young children to grasp because the words are already in the child's vocabulary. Friendly explanations work better than dictionary definitions because dictionary definitions often include words that young children do not know.

grammar. Rules for putting words together to form sentences.

hard-wired. Brain structure that is inherent in an organism's essential makeup.

inferential thinking. Reaching a conclusion through a process in which information from a variety of sources is brought together through reasoning, as when one infers that it is cold outside because there is snow on the ground and it is winter.

information books. Nonfiction books.

letter-like designs. Combinations of lines that result in forms that resembles alphabet letters but are not actual letters of the alphabet.

modeling. Showing how to do or say something by doing it or saying it. For example, repeating what a child has said but adding missing elements models for the child how the full sentence sounds. Using a cookbook shows how books offer needed information.

morphology. The elemental units of meaning (e.g., talk**ing**, talk**ed**, talk**s;** finger, finger**s**).

narrative. A story. Narratives have specific elements (settings, characters, a problem, a plot) that are combined in characteristic ways.

onset. A linguistic term for the part of a syllable that comes before its vowel. The onset in the word *big* is /b/ (b-ig). In the word *bring,* the onset is /b//r/ (br-ing).

oral vocabulary. The words a person understands and uses when listening and speaking.

overgeneralizations. The extension of morphemes (elemental units of meaning) beyond the words to which they actually apply (e.g., teach**ed**, runn**ed**; foot**s**; mouse**s**). Children's overgeneralizations indicate they are finding patterns in what they hear.

phonemes. The smallest units of sound in words (e.g., /k/-/a/-/t/ in *cat*).

phonemic awareness. The ability to notice and manipulate the individual sounds (phonemes) in spoken words.

phonological awareness. A sensitivity to the sounds in spoken language and skill in manipulating these sounds. Different levels of phonological awareness involve different linguistic units that vary in size (e.g., words, syllables, onsets and rimes, and phonemes). Tasks used to develop and assess phonological awareness differ in cognitive demands (e.g., blending sounds is easier than deleting sounds).

pragmatics. How language is used in context (e.g., the different talking style used with best friends versus acquaintances).

predictable textbooks. Books with features that make them easy for children to remember them. Features used to make books predictable include the use of refrains, stable sentence frames into which a new word can be inserted, rhyme and alliteration, and a close match between illustration and words in a book's text.

pretend words. Strings of letters that children put together when they write without any regard for selecting letters based on their sound values. Pretend words look like words but are not real words.

print convention. Customary ways of arranging print on a page (e.g., left to right and top to bottom; space between words; use of punctuation marks).

rhyme. Words or syllables that have identical rime units (e.g., c*up* and p*up*; l*og* and f*og*).

rime. A linguistic term that refers to the portion of a syllable that starts with its vowel. In the word *big*, the rime unit is /ig/. In the word bring, the rime unit is /ing/.

scribble writing. Marks that children intend to serve as writing that lack features of alphabet letters.

semantics. The meaning of words and sentences.

sign language. The language of the hands that some deaf people use. It has all the properties of other natural languages (including grammar) and allows the expression of the same range of ideas.

story stem. A phrase that starts a story, such as "Once upon a time . . ." or that teachers can ask children to complete by adding to it.

story retelling. Using one's own words to recount a familiar story, as when children describe what is happening on the pages of a book they have heard many times.

syllables. The major units that make up words (e.g., *ba-by, ther-mom-e-ter*). Syllables always have a rime unit, sometimes with just a vowel (e.g., *i*). They need not have an onset unit (e.g., *it, ice, oc-u-lar*).

syntax. Synonym of grammar, how words are put together to form phrases and sentences.

word play. Taking words out of their ordinary communicative context and calling attention to them by manipulating their elements in a lighthearted manner. Making a game of rhyming words such as hair, bear, and pear is an example of word play as is playing with the sounds in children's names.

English-Language Development

code switching. A normal part of second-language acquisition in which the child combines English with the home language.

English learners. Children whose first language is not English, including children learning English for the first time in the preschool setting as well as children who have developed various levels of English proficiency.

home language (L1). The language used primarily by the child's family in the home environment. Some children may have more than one home language (e.g., when one parent speaks Chinese and the other speaks English).

language acquisition. The mostly subconscious process of learning to understand and use a language, including the basics of phonology, syntax or grammar, semantics (meaning), and pragmatics (communication rules and skills). This process depends on children experiencing language in their social environment. Language acquisition may differ for children with certain kinds of disabilities.

read-alouds. An adult's reading of a book to a child or group of children. A read-aloud includes back-and-forth talking about the story. If a book has a patterned (predictable) text, children enjoy "reading" along with the adult after the book has been read a few times.

Mathematics

algebra. A mathematical system using letters and other symbols standing for numbers to express and generalize mathematical ideas.

arithmetic. Computations of addition, subtraction, multiplication, and division, using positive real numbers.

attribute. A property or characteristic of an object or a person such as size, color, weight, or shape.

capacity. The content, volume, or amount that can be contained or held within three-dimensional objects.

cardinality. The concept that the number name applied to the last object counted represents the total number of objects in the group (the quantity of objects counted).

class. Things grouped together because of a certain likeness or common traits.

classifying. The sorting, grouping, or categorizing of objects according to established criteria. Classifying involves giving descriptive labels to the feature(s) used in sorting.

count on. The strategy of adding two numbers (e.g., 3 + 2) by starting to count from the first addend (e.g., "three, four, five") rather than counting over from one (e.g., "one, two, three, four, five"), to find the total sum.

numerals. Symbols to express numbers. The standard written numerals in American society are Arabic numerals 1, 2, 3, and so on.

one-to-one correspondence. One and only one number word is used for each object in the array of objects being counted.

operations. Processes involving a change or transformation in quantity such as the operations of addition and subtraction.

part–whole relationships. A whole number represented by smaller subsets that, when combined, equal the number (e.g., the number 5 can be described as 2 + 3; 1 + 4; 2 + 2 +1, and so forth).

pattern. A regularly repeated arrangement of things such as numbers, objects, events, or shapes.

real-life setting. The creation of a set-up in the preschool environment taken from everyday, real-life activities that includes pretend materials and props to facilitate children acting out different roles (e.g., a bakery, a bank, a grocery store).

scaffolding. A process by which adults or capable peers provide supportive structures to help children learn and play. Scaffolding is helpful when children are faced with a challenge that they can solve with a simple hint, question, or prompt.

sorting. The act of separating things having common features into sets or groups.

subitizing. The ability to quickly and accurately determine the quantity of objects in a small group (of up to five objects) without actually counting the objects.

volume. The amount of space within three-dimensional objects.

References

Schickedanz, J. A. 2008. *Increasing the power of instruction: Integration of language, literacy, and math across the preschool day.* Washington, DC: National Association for the Education of Young Children.